QUEST FOR INCLUSION

QUEST FOR INCLUSION

JEWS AND LIBERALISM
IN MODERN AMERICA

Marc Dollinger

PRINCETON UNIVERSITY PRESS   PRINCETON AND OXFORD

Copyright © 2000 by Princeton University Press
Published by Princeton University Press, 41 William Street,
Princeton, New Jersey 08540
In the United Kingdom: Princeton University Press,
3 Market Place, Woodstock, Oxfordshire OX20 1SY
All Rights Reserved

Library of Congress Cataloging-in-Publication Data
Dollinger, Marc, 1964–
Quest for inclusion: Jews and liberalism in
modern America/Marc Dollinger.
p. cm.
Includes bibliographical references and index.
ISBN 0-691-00509-5 (alk. paper)
1. Jews—United States—Politics and government.
2. Liberalism—United States—History—20th century. I. Title.
E184.36.P64 D65 2000
973'.04924—dc21   99-089426

This book has been composed in Sabon

The paper used in this publication meets the minimum requirements
of ANSI/NISO Z39.48-1992 (R1997) (*Permanence of Paper*)

www.pup.princeton.edu

Printed in the United States of America

1 3 5 7 9 10 8 6 4 2

For Marci

Contents

Acknowledgments	ix
List of Abbreviations	xiii
"Die Velt, Yene Velt . . .": An Introduction	3
Chapter 1. "What Do We Owe to Peter Stuyvesant?" The New Deal in the Jewish Community	19
Chapter 2. Fighting Hitler: Cultural Pluralism and American Jewish Life, 1933–1941	41
Chapter 3. "The Hope of Democracy and Peace": American Jews and the Campaign for Intergroup Dialogue, 1933–1941	61
Chapter 4. "Unless That War Be Won, All Else Is Lost": American Jews and the Home Front	77
Chapter 5. Planning the Postwar Peace: The United Nations, Zionism, and American Jewish Liberalism	107
Chapter 6. The Struggle for Civil Liberties: The Cold War, Anti-Communism, and Jewish Liberal Reform	129
Chapter 7. "Hamans and Torquemadas": Southern and Northern Jewish Responses to the Civil Rights Movement, 1945–1965	164
Chapter 8. A Different Kind of Freedom Ride: American Jews and the Struggle for Racial Equality, 1964–1975	191
"Just Another Foreigner": An Epilogue	214
Notes	229
Index	289

Acknowledgments

THIS BOOK began as a study of Jewish philanthropy in the United States but soon developed into a larger analysis of modern American Jewish liberalism. It was, to paraphrase my graduate advisor at UCLA, Regina Morantz-Sanchez, a journey of self-discovery. From the earliest stages of this project, I enjoyed the good fortune of a supportive community of scholars, teachers, mentors, and friends. They helped keep my footing on a subject many described as "slippery," and I would like to offer them my thanks. Steven Zipperstein suggested an exploration of Jewish liberalism and helped me understand the European origins of American Jewry. George Sanchez placed the American Jewish experience in the larger context of ethnic history and never let me forget that history is about how ordinary people reacted in extraordinary circumstances. Jeffrey Prager introduced me to the world of normative theory and the sociology of affirmative action. Regina Morantz-Sanchez guided this project from its beginning. She taught me the art of critical thinking, helped me find meaning in sources that appeared to have little, and inspired me to become a much better writer.

Within the larger community of American Jewish historians, Jonathan Sarna of Brandeis University read several versions of this manuscript and has been a constant source of support. His invitation to address a national conference on American Jewish history in 1992 launched my academic career and created many new opportunities in the field. I first met Stephen Whitfield, also of Brandeis, as my wife's favorite undergraduate professor. Since then, he has become a colleague and friend. His critique of an early manuscript focused much of my revision and helped me avoid many common pitfalls. Murray Friedman, mid-Atlantic states director of the American Jewish Committee and director of Temple University's Feinstein Center for American Jewish history, has been a constant source of intellectual and moral support. He challenged me to consider the importance of Jewish conservatism in America and never shied from engaging difficult and controversial issues. Gerald Henig of the California State University, Hayward, encouraged me to pursue graduate studies in American Jewish history and offered invaluable advice on finishing a doctoral program.

I would like to offer a public "thank you" to a few of my best teachers: Betty Lawrence, Richard Hadley, Robert Ingraham, Jim Kinney, the late Al Costas, Gene Irschick, and Jim Kettner. Gretchen Anderson, the dean of social sciences at Pasadena City College, created many exciting opportunities for me. She understood my desire to engage in research and has become both an educational mentor and personal friend. When Milton Brown introduced himself as my new officemate at Pasadena, I had no sense that he would become such an important and influential figure in my development. Milton opened my eyes and my heart to a different way of understanding U.S. history. His perspective on race and ethnicity challenged many of my assumptions, and forced me to confront many of liberalism's hidden messages.

Grants from the Bernard and Audre Rapoport Fellowship at the American Jewish Archives, the Starkoff Fellowship at the American Jewish Archives, and the Jewish Historical Society of New York Doctoral Dissertation Fellowship from the American Jewish Historical Society helped fund this research. UCLA's Charles Young Chancellor's Dissertation Year Fellowship provided the resources necessary to complete the first draft of this manuscript, while a post-doctoral fellowship at Bryn Mawr College granted by the Andrew W. Mellon Foundation afforded me a year of focused revision. My research findings were presented at conferences sponsored by the American Historical Association, American Jewish Historical Association, Southern Jewish Historical Association, Louisiana State University, and the University of Memphis. Rabbi Allen Krause permitted me access to field notes he gathered as part of his 1967 rabbinic thesis on southern Reform rabbis and the civil rights movement. I would also like to thank Abraham Peck, Kevin Profitt, and the staff of the American Jewish Archives in Cincinnati, and Michael Feldberg, the late Nathan Kaganoff, Gina Hsai, and the staff of the American Jewish Historical Society Archives in Waltham, Massachusetts, for their research assistance.

Earlier versions of three chapters have appeared in Jeffrey S. Gurock and Marc Lee Raphael, eds., *An Inventory of Promises* (Carlson Publishing, 1996); Berkley Kalin and Mark Bauman, eds., *The Quiet Voices: Southern Rabbis and Black Civil Rights, From the Late Nineteenth Century to the Modern Era* (University of Alabama Press, 1997); and William Pederson and Thomas P. Wolfe, eds., *F.D.R. and the Shaping of Congress and Electoral Politics* (M. E. Sharpe, forthcoming). I thank the editors for allowing their reprint here.

I would also like to thank the anonymous readers for Princeton University Press for their comments and ideas. Brigitta van Rheinberg, the press's history editor, has supported this project from the very start and recommended important changes for making the book more readable and timely. Molan Chun Goldstein and Alison Zaintz ably guided the manuscript through the production process. Eric D. Schramm offered excellent suggestions in his role as copyeditor; I greatly appreciate the effort and insights he brought to the manuscript.

My greatest debt and warmest praise goes to Bruce J. Schulman, now of Boston University. Bruce nurtured this project from its beginning as a two-quarter research seminar at UCLA in 1987 to its final publication revision some twelve years later. In the intervening years, he personified the highest ideals of an academic mentor. Bruce welcomed scores of graduate students into his office and into his life. He arranged special readings courses, designed ambitious academic schedules for us to follow, and coached us on everything from our qualifying exams to delivering our first university lecture. His passion for undergraduate teaching brought overflow crowds to UCLA's largest hall and inspired the slogan, "It's not education unless it involves the fire marshal."

Bruce has read countless versions of this manuscript. His ability to see the forest through my trees sharpened my prose and strengthened my arguments. Bruce's hand has guided me through the rigor of graduate coursework, the solitude of primary research, and the joys and frustrations of revision. Through the entire process, he offered reassuring praise alongside constructive comments. Bruce models the sort of academic excellence, teaching artistry, and humanitarianism I aspire to each day.

It is impossible to give one's parents enough thanks and praise. My mother and father, Lenore and Malin Dollinger, supported my intellectual pursuits with great love, respect, and admiration. They raised me in a family culture that valued education and treasured the highest ideals of liberal social action. The publication of this book is a small "thank you" for the guidance they have shown.

This book is dedicated to my wife, Marci. An elementary school educator by training, she has become my greatest teacher and friend. When we first met, she pulled from her purse a copy of Robert Fulghum's poem, "Everything I Ever Needed to Know, I Learned in Kindergarten." "Wisdom was not at the top of the graduate-school mountain, but there in the sand pile at Sunday school. . . . Share everything; play fair; don't hit people." Those words, so typical of Marci's approach to life, helped me keep perspective and get through many frustrating days of writing and revision.

List of Abbreviations

AACI	Anglo-American Committee of Inquiry
ACJ	American Council for Judaism
ADL	Anti-Defamation League
AJA	American Jewish Archives
AJC	American Jewish Committee
AJCongress	American Jewish Congress
AJHS	American Jewish Historical Society
APC	American Palestine Committee
CCAR	Central Conference of American Rabbis
CJFWF	Council of Jewish Federations and Welfare Funds
CLSA	Commission on Law and Social Action
CNSFP	Committee on National Security and Fair Play
CORE	Congress of Racial Equality
DP	displaced persons
FEPC	Fair Employment Practices Commission
FERA	Federal Emergency Relief Act
GJC	General Jewish Council
HIAS	Hebrew Immigrant Aid Society
HUC-JIR	Hebrew Union College–Jewish Institute of Religion
JCC	Jewish Community Center
JCRC	Jewish Community Relations Council
JDC	Joint Distribution Committee
JLC	Jewish Labor Committee
JTS	Jewish Theological Seminary
NCJSS	National Conference of Jewish Social Service
NCJW	National Council of Jewish Women
NCRAC	National Community Relations Advisory Council
NJCRAC	National Jewish Community Relations Advisory Council
NRS	National Refugee Service
SCA	Synagogue Council of America
SNCC	Student Non-Violent Coordinating Committee
UAHC	Union of American Hebrew Congregations
UNSCOP	United Nations Special Commission on Palestine
WJC	World Jewish Congress
ZOA	Zionist Organization of America

QUEST FOR INCLUSION

"Die Velt, Yene Velt . . .":
An Introduction

JONAH J. GOLDSTEIN, a judge connected with New York's Tammany Democratic machine, once observed that American Jews lived in three *velten* (worlds): *die velt* (this world), *yene velt* (the world to come), and Roosevelt. Goldstein's muse captured an American Jewish political mood that lasted well beyond FDR's presidency. Between Roosevelt's first election in 1932 and the most recent presidential contest, American Jews have voted Democratic more than any other white ethnic group. They have worked their way to the top of American political, economic, and cultural life and established their community as the best-known defenders of the nation's downtrodden and oppressed.[1]

In 1932, the election that launched the modern liberal state, Franklin D. Roosevelt won an astonishing 82 percent of the American Jewish vote. By 1944, Jewish support for the New Deal architect peaked at an astronomical 90 percent. When the nation turned to the right in the postwar years, American Jews remained firm. They warned about the evils of unrestrained anti-Communism and delivered unprecedented political, financial, and physical support for African-American civil rights workers in the 1950s and 1960s. Even when many working-class white ethnics abandoned liberalism for the allure of neoconservatism in the late 1960s, Jews held fast to their Democratic roots and searched for ways to preserve their liberal ideals in the new political climate.[2]

As a religious minority often persecuted by Old World government authorities, Jews looked favorably upon the U.S. government's promise of civil protection. They fashioned many of the twentieth century's most important social welfare programs and proved instrumental in the transformation of modern American liberalism. Jews stood at the crossroads of twentieth-century American political change and helped direct the nation toward a vision of democracy rooted in tolerance, pluralism, and the rule of law.

The American Jewish community's fascination for liberalism contradicts widely held assumptions about American political culture. Jews, as writer Milton Himmelfarb quipped, lived like Episcopalians but voted like Puerto Ricans. Between 1932 and 1975, Jews rocketed to the top of American social life. Jewish-owned businesses flourished and the grandchildren of impoverished eastern European Jewish immigrants matriculated at the nation's leading universities, while the evil specter of anti-Semitism all but disappeared as a meaningful force in American life. According to classical models of acculturation, immigrants should identify with liberalism during their early years but move to the right as they climb the social ladder. For America's Jewish minority, liberalism remained a continuing strategy of choice. It offered a vision of pluralist democracy that demanded social and political inclusion and, for the first time, opened the corridors of federal power to American Jews.[3]

Quest for Inclusion chronicles the history of American Jewish liberalism between 1933 and 1975 and asks how such a small ethnic and religious minority grew to such importance in American political life. It examines the organized Jewish community's responses to major public policy questions and addresses some of the most important questions in the history of the modern liberal state. This study covers Jewish communal reactions to the New Deal, 1930s foreign policy developments, American wartime policy abroad and at home, the Cold War liberal anti-Communist consensus, and the civil rights movement, and concludes with an investigation of how some Jews left the liberal camp and became neoconservatives. Its purpose is threefold: to document the impressive contributions of Jewish liberals to American political culture, to define the limits of American Jewish liberalism, and to reconcile the apparent contradiction between Jewish liberal strength and its serious failures.

I argue that Jewish political influence grew from the community's intense desire to secure the most elusive prize in all its history: social, economic, and political inclusion in the larger non-Jewish society. In each historical epoch and across a wide geographic expanse, American Jews waged some of the most impressive liberal reform campaigns in American political history. At times risking their own personal safety to pursue policies contrary to the prevailing national mood, American Jews pressed for reforms designed to create a more tolerant, pluralistic, and egalitarian nation. For Jews intent on rising above the limited means of their immigrant parents and grandparents, liberalism proved the most viable and meaningful electoral philosophy.

Yet at historical moments when Jewish social mobility clashed with a liberal political orientation, American Jews dissented from the dominant left-leaning trend. Faced with a choice between liberal politics and their own acculturation, Jews almost always chose the latter. The politics of acculturation, the process by which Jews advocated liberal political change in order to ease their adaptation to American life, cut like a double-edged sword. While it strengthened American Jews, giving them the drive to champion unpopular causes and establish themselves as the guardians of liberal America, the politics of acculturation also erected strict barriers to Jewish liberal success.

The story of American Jewish liberalism helps untangle some of the most vexing social questions facing a democratic nation. Since the Civil Rights Act of 1964 and the Voting Rights Act of 1965 guaranteed legal equality for African Americans, the nation has divided over the advisability of affirmative action and quota programs intent on compensating for historic discrimination and breaking the "culture of poverty." The rise in ethnic consciousness, sparked by the social protest movements of the late 1960s, inspired many Americans to question whether democracy can thrive in a political culture defined by racial separatism. Faculty, administrators, and students at leading universities question the merit of a traditional western civilization–based curriculum, while debates over multiculturalism fill the editorial pages of leading newspapers. Many Americans express fears that their nation has become too "Balkanized."[4]

In the world of American politics, Jewish leaders represented the most influential liberal political constituency in America. Despite their small numbers, American Jews helped direct the most important social welfare innovations of the New Deal, offered a powerful response to American isolationism, and demonstrated the strengths and weaknesses of social reform during war. Jewish support for the creation of a United Nations organization thrust the community into the international spotlight and established Jews as champions of liberal internationalism. In the postwar era, Jewish leaders capitalized on Cold War anti-Communism to advocate a version of pluralist democracy consistent with American and Jewish ideals. By the late 1960s, continued American Jewish affinity for Democratic politics undergirded Lyndon Johnson's Great Society, inspired white liberal support for affirmative action, and sparked creative solutions to the problem of racial segregation in the urban North.

But Jewish exceptionalism does not account for the whole story. Jewish liberalism also illustrates the social roots of American political culture. By tracing the nexus between ethnic acculturation and political conviction, this study accounts for the Jewish community's many adaptations to American life and asserts that a new understanding of its political strategies must be sensitive to the dynamic nature of the American ethnic experience. Predominantly an immigrant group in only its second generation, Jews used liberal politics to power their move from the margin to the mainstream of American life. They emerged as a model ethnic minority and credited the Democratic party for much of their political and social success. Jewish leaders forged powerful intergroup alliances in a dramatic bid to demonstrate the strength of pluralist democracy and bridge the social chasms that alienated so many underrepresented Americans.

Within the Jewish communal world, this study asks one of the most important questions in modern Jewish history. Could the United States achieve what the European nations did not—civil equality for its Jewish residents? For American Jews, the failed promises of the European Enlightenment held little currency. Most American Jews rejected Zionism and considered the United States their homeland. They would have agreed with Louis Hartz's thesis that the classical liberal tradition in America signaled a dramatic shift from European ways. Constitutional protection of religious freedom combined with an activist liberal government guaranteed American Jews a level of social equality unparalleled in most of Jewish history. Among Jewish leaders, the question of American exceptionalism played out in the powerful debate between accommodationist Jews, who believed that civil equality was best achieved through social adaptation, and isolationist Jews, who struggled for a pluralist democratic vision rooted in their right to express cultural difference.

Realizing the Jewish community's goal of inclusion necessitated a complex, ever-changing, and sometimes self-contradictory strategy. Class issues, national origin, and regionalism moderated Jewish political views. The religious differences between the Reform, Conservative, and Orthodox branches often spilled over into the political arena. The exigencies of both World War II and the Cold War ended many American Jewish liberal reforms and pressed the community into a consensus political mindset. When liberalism itself faced redefinition in the 1960s, Jews often split over what direction to take. Some Jewish leaders backed affirmative action programs while others considered them anathema to Jewish liberal values.

These exceptions to Jewish liberal commitment underscore the importance of studying political persuasion through the lens of ethnic acculturation. They challenge the popular belief that equates Judaism with liberalism and question whether that political philosophy was necessarily in the Jewish community's self-interest. In most cases, Jews who rejected liberalism justified their stance with language similar to their political opponents: both sought inclusion in their larger communities. For this reason, any study of American Jewish political culture, or the political culture of other ethnic or religious minorities, must examine the effect of local conditions on national issues. American Jewish politics cannot be viewed as absolute: liberalism was not always the answer.

The politics of acculturation turn on the question of social inclusion, not liberal conviction. It accounts for the community's many adaptations to American life, for its seemingly self-contradictory liberal history, and asserts that a new understanding of the Jewish community's political goals and strategies must be sensitive to the dynamic nature of its own American experience. American Jews chose the liberal path most often because that political persuasion offered the best hope of turning a painful European Jewish past into a successful American future.

Surprisingly, few historians have examined the relationship between Jewish liberalism and the major public policy questions of the last sixty years. Most of the important work on the subject was published over thirty years ago and no monograph exists to cover the period between 1933, when American Jews entered the national political mainstream, and 1975, when the rise of ethnic consciousness pushed the Jewish community to the periphery of American liberal politics. This book fills that void by casting a wide net over forty years of American political life and the Jewish community's integral part in shaping it.[5]

Historians of the American Jewish experience have traditionally credited Jewish religious beliefs with primary responsibility for shaping the community's social reform posture. Moses Rischin, Irving Howe, Lawrence Fuchs, and Henry Feingold, the main proponents of this interpretation, cite prophetic Judaism, the centrality of *tzedakah* (charity) and *gemilut hasidim* (acts of loving-kindness), as well as the Jewish people's historic sympathy for the oppressed, in their analyses of Jewish social reform. While this interpretation does explain the attitudes of the immigrant generation, it fails to account for the development of a second, third, and fourth generation American Jewish politics. Within twenty years, native-born American Jews (as well as many of their immigrant parents) abandoned socialism and Communism in favor of liberal political reform. They understood that leftism belonged to the immigrant Jewish experience, and if they were to integrate into the American mainstream, their politics would have to move to the center. The religion school falters as well in its assertion that traditional Jewish values informed left-leaning politics. No correlation exists between a Jew's level of religious observance and his or her support for liberal social reform. In the 1984 election, for example, the most traditional American Jews voted for the most conservative political candidates.[6]

Locating the roots of Jewish political culture proves even more difficult given the changing definition of American liberalism. What Franklin Roosevelt meant by liberal in 1933 bears little resemblance to what Lyndon Johnson thought about it in 1964, while both concepts differ from eighteenth- and nineteenth-century conceptions of classical liberalism. In essence, this study chronicles the ever-changing meaning of "liberalism" and illustrates both the differences and similarities between Jewish liberalism and other varieties of the same political persuasion.[7]

American Jews traced their liberal beliefs back to the vast social and economic changes that swept across western and central Europe in the eighteenth century. In medieval times, Jews suffered under state-sponsored segregation. Forced to live within the narrow confines of ghettos,

European Jews faced severe restrictions of their social mobility. With innovations in the worlds of politics, economics, and science, the foundations of that feudal system crumbled. John Locke's social contract promised citizens the right to elect their own leaders. Adam Smith's "invisible hand" unleashed the power of free market capitalism. Experiments conducted by scientists such as Isaac Newton undermined the power of the Church and its established social order. The Enlightenment, as it came to be known, promised an end to centuries of state-sponsored persecution and generated hope for eventual Jewish civil equality. The Jewish communities of Europe welcomed the calls for emancipation: classical liberalism and Jewish equality seemed to walk hand in hand.[8]

In the United States, Thomas Jefferson invoked natural rights theory in the Declaration of Independence and the framers of the Constitution guaranteed freedom of religious expression in the Bill of Rights. While incidents of anti-Semitism did occur, American Jews in the early national period enjoyed a level of civil equality rarely equaled in western Jewish history. German-Jewish arrivals in the mid-nineteenth century built grand synagogues as a testament to their economic strength and religious freedom. The liberal promise of limited government encouraged the new American Jews who enjoyed the right to practice Judaism free from the coercive influence of the state. German-American Jewish leaders responded to their religious freedom by assuming an accommodationist political stance and pressing for the quick integration of Jews into the American mainstream. Theirs was a classical liberal orientation committed to the proliferation of universal rights and resistant to models of cultural pluralism that distinguished Jews as anything more than a religious minority.[9]

When eastern European Jewish immigrants arrived in the United States during the late nineteenth century, they encountered a classical laissez-faire view of liberalism. Government, these liberals believed, should stay clear of individuals who remained free to express their political, economic, and social will as they saw fit. They viewed government action as an unnatural artifice standing in the way of God's will. Federal efforts to limit work weeks, guarantee a minimum wage, or back the demands of organized labor loomed as grave threats to the American liberal tradition of freedom.

Yet not all American Jews offered unqualified support for nineteenth-century American liberalism. In a scenario that would repeat throughout the twentieth century, Jewish leaders modified or even abandoned liberalism when it conflicted with their communal interests. While classical liberalism bolstered the civic status of German-American Jews in the eighteenth and early nineteenth centuries, its social Darwinist orientation in the late nineteenth and early twentieth centuries set it on a collision course with eastern European American Jews. The laissez-faire approach to government, while consistent with Enlightenment ideals, proved inappropriate in an emerging industrial economy. eastern European Jewish immigrants found little relief from the oppressive working conditions in American factories and crowded tenements of New York's Lower East Side. Without a radical reinterpretation of liberal ideology, they would remain on the margins of American life. Their communal representatives wanted a liberalism committed to federal intervention and the right of ethnic expression. They launched aggressive political campaigns and dismissed their more senior co-religionists as optimistic and naive inheritors of the classical liberal tradition.[10]

American Jews celebrated the policies of President Theodore Roosevelt, who rose to the nation's highest office after the assassination of William McKinley in 1901. Roosevelt rejected the federal government's laissez-faire approach to American social and economic life and demanded that Washington intervene. He and other progressives believed that only the federal government possessed enough power to countervail the sinister influences of monopolistic business. Under Roosevelt's Square Deal programs, Americans for the first time enjoyed an activist federal government that defined liberalism in positive terms. With TR's support, Congress passed laws to make the nation's food safe, protect children from unfair labor practices, and even preserve our nation's natural resources.[11]

The course of modern American liberalism took a dramatic turn during the Great Depression of the 1930s. President Herbert Hoover, dubbed "the great engineer" for his progressive-like approach to government, failed to reverse the economic downturn following the 1929 stock market crash. Despite his approval of agencies such as the Reconstruction Finance Corporation, which sought to restore the nation's economic health by pouring federal dollars into ailing businesses, Hoover underestimated the severity of the Great Depression, alienated many Americans after mishandling several high-profile public protests, and refused to mobilize the federal government in an all-out economic offensive.

In the 1932 election, the nation rejected Hoover's voluntarism and embraced Franklin D. Roosevelt's New Deal. In his reform plan, FDR pressed for the greatest expansion of the federal government in U.S. history. The Democratic president translated national concern over the economic depression and disillusionment with the limited response of Herbert Hoover into a broad-based coalition of Americans committed to activist public policies. While Theodore Roosevelt helped lead a movement dedicated to middle-class Christian-based social reform, FDR opted for the strict imperative of economic recovery: New Dealers focused on the mechanics of reducing unemployment, shoring up the banking system, and instilling consumer confidence. Roosevelt believed in experimental government. His pragmatic approach to public policy opened government to a new breed of creative thinkers intent on finding innovative solutions to the nation's economic ills.

During World War II, liberals submerged their New Deal reform program in order to focus on Allied victory. Political unity proved paramount as American social reformers went into hiding. Executive Order 9066 interned over 67,000 U.S. citizens of Japanese descent. While gains were made by some African Americans and women during the war, they are properly seen as unintended consequences of mobilization, not a deliberate attempt by war politicians to advance liberal causes. As long as U.S. troops fought the Axis powers, Americans, liberal and conservative alike, relegated social issues to the back-burner.

In the postwar period, liberals emerged as powerful opponents of the Soviet state and embraced the anti-Communist mentality dominating the American political landscape. They allied themselves with big business and cheered economist John Maynard Keynes's contention that governmental manipulation of fiscal policy could eliminate the risk of another depression and create sustained economic growth. Capitalism, unlike Communism, would provide a higher standard of living for all, easing tensions between competing economic classes and reducing social tensions. Increased competition with the Soviet Union also highlighted domestic injustices, as white liberal America took its first serious look at the question of racial inequality. Embarrassed by segregationist policies, civil rights liberals fought for a society that lived up to the democratic promises typical of their anti-Communist rhetoric. They joined African-American activists in a successful bid to challenge the racial status quo and eliminated hundreds of local, county, and state Jim Crow statutes.[12]

Once the Civil Rights Act of 1964 and the Voting Rights Act of 1965 realized African-Americans' civil rights goal of legal equality, American liberalism turned inward, encouraging Jews as well as other ethnic groups to focus their social reform efforts on their own communities. The traditional liberal reliance on legal guarantees of individual rights gave way to group-centered programs aimed at achieving *de facto* rather than *de jure* equality. Lyndon Johnson's Great Society, a failed attempt to improve on FDR's New Deal by waging a "war on poverty," demanded that American liberals acknowledge the powerful role race plays in American society. Affirmative action programs, originated by President John F. Kennedy, alienated one-time liberals who expressed their dissatisfaction with Johnson by bolting to the Republican party. The New Deal liberal alliance, which once joined business, labor, and ethnic America, splintered into a fractious collection of ethnic and racial groups intent on advancing their own agendas without regard for consensus. As Ronald Reagan, a one-time New Deal Democrat, liked to explain, "I didn't leave the Democratic party. The Democratic party left me."

The changing definition of liberalism sparked discordant reactions among American Jews. While some issues garnered near-consensus support, most issues split Jews along various communal lines. With such a wide variety of American Jewish political responses, defining a singular "American Jewish community" blurs crucial distinctions within American Jewry. At no time during the course of this study did all American Jews, nor even the major organizations representing them, concur on public policy questions. How, then, should historians define the Jewish community? Some scholars favor a social history approach, one that attempts to recover the attitudes of the "average" person by relying on nontraditional historical evidence. While this technique is useful in gleaning popular attitudes, it omits discussion of the very people who made political decisions. Other historians study Jewish leadership, focusing on how the major decisionmakers arrived at their various positions. While this perspective does tell us something about the Jewish elite, it neglects the interactive communal forces that connected the leadership with the rank and file, and it posits the false assumption that the leadership always represented the views of its constituents.

This study bridges the gap between these two historical approaches. It focuses, for the most part, on major Jewish organizations: the American Jewish Committee (AJC), the American Jewish Congress (AJCongress), the Anti-Defamation League of B'nai B'rith (ADL), the Jewish Community Relations Councils (JCRC) of various Jewish Federation Councils, the American Jewish Conference, and the Reform, Conservative, and Orthodox branches of Judaism. During the years covered in this study, these major Jewish organizations played the most important role in the creation and articulation of a Jewish-American politics. They met, discussed, and debated the major issues of the day. They drafted the legislation and campaigned in the various states and cities. When Jewish interests were at stake, these organizations took up the call for action: they presented the most powerful face to Jewish politics.

Despite this study's emphasis on Jewish leadership, it is not an organizational history. My purpose is not to chronicle the inner workings of the various Jewish organizations. Instead, it is to show how these groups responded to national political questions. Internal political squabbles within or between Jewish organizations are considered only to the extent that they illuminated the larger public policy questions of the day. There were also some subjects in this investigation that did not lend themselves to an organizational approach. Studying civil rights activities among southern Jews, for example, cannot be achieved by examining records from southern district offices of national Jewish organizations, since these organizations were, by and large, staffed by northern Jews. In the North, many Jews labored on behalf of civil rights under the auspices of non-Jewish organizations. In cases such as these, I have moved beyond organizational records to include oral history, memoirs, and records of correspondence. Throughout the study, I supplement information gleaned from organizational records with evidence from personal papers, congressional testimony, and court briefs, as well as selected secondary sources.

The present work also describes the beliefs and attitudes of the larger community. By combining organizational records from a variety of sources, I have tried to show the positions of both the leadership and its constituents. I have selected primary sources detailing the widest experiences of American Jewry: local chapter meetings in addition to national conferences, German-American Jewish organizations as well as groups controlled by eastern European American Jews, sources from first-, second-, and third-generation Americans as well as from Orthodox, Conservative, and Reform Jews, young and old, philanthropist along with wage laborer, men and women, rabbi and layperson.

Among national Jewish organizations, the American Jewish Committee emerged as the most important in the first half of the twentieth century. Organized in 1906 "to prevent the infraction of the civil and religious rights of the Jews, in any part of the world," the AJC operated as an elitist body run by the descendants of German Jews forced out of Europe by the political upheaval of the 1840s. They emigrated to the United States by the thousands and enjoyed great success in business and commerce. A small group of twenty men decided all AJC policy, while its expanded "corporate members" numbered only 327 by 1941. As members of Reform temples, German-American Jews resisted the use of Hebrew in worship, replaced the bar mitzvah with confirmation, and did not support the early Zionist movement.[13]

The AJC adopted an accommodationist approach to American life, favoring quiet negotiations and dialogue over confrontational tactics. In one famous experiment, the Galveston Project, the well-known German-American Jewish banker Jacob Schiff offered to pay the transatlantic boat fare for any eastern European Jew willing to settle in Texas. By dispersing Jews in the West, Schiff hoped to hasten a rapid integration into the American mainstream.

For eastern European Jews, America emerged as their Zion and New York City doubled as the New Jerusalem. They enjoyed a friendly relationship with government leaders who appreciated their reluctance to challenge the status quo. While eastern European–descended American Jews joined the AJC in the 1920s and eventually led the organization into an embrace of Zionism, the Jewish defense group still resisted activities that ventured beyond the traditional mandates of religious voluntarism.[14]

The American Jewish Congress, organized in 1918 "to create in the United States an all-inclusive representative Jewish body for the defense of Jewish rights," provided a powerful alternative to the German-American dominated AJC. While its founders, Stephen S. Wise and Louis Brandeis, claimed Central European ancestry, the American Jewish Congress represented the political perspective of the nation's eastern European American Jewish community. It called for a more vocal defense of European Jews, supported Jewish claims to Palestine, and sought to define American democracy in a way that accented their belief in pluralism, intergroup understanding, and tolerance. The AJCongress adopted a democratic approach to Jewish communal life. It enlisted the membership support of a host of affiliated agencies and claimed to be the Jewish community's most representative body.[15]

Constituents of the AJCongress enjoyed the support of working-class Jews and their governing body, the Jewish Labor Committee (JLC). Organized in February 1934 by leaders of the International Ladies' Garment Workers' Union, the Amalgamated Clothing Workers of America, the Workman's Circle, the Jewish Daily Forward Association, and other Jewish labor groups, the Jewish Labor Committee initiated many of the 1930s anti-Nazi campaigns. It brought attention to Jewish victims of totalitarianism and used its appeals to advance the trade union movement in Europe. The Jewish Labor Committee served throughout the decade "as the central body of organized Jewish labor in the United States and Canada in all matters pertaining to its struggle against fascism and anti-Semitism, and as the representative organ authorized to speak on behalf of Jewish labor regarding general Jewish affairs." In the postwar period, the JLC focused on relief and rehabilitation work for European Jewish refugees and on anti-discrimination education campaigns at home.[16]

B'nai B'rith, organized in 1843, enjoyed distinction as the world's oldest and largest Jewish service organization. Like the AJC, its founding members claimed German-Jewish ancestry. By 1940, though, Eastern European American Jews moved the organization away from its traditional accommodationism. While B'nai B'rith maintained an official policy of neutrality on the question of Zionism, one of its most important leaders, Henry Monsky, aligned himself with the movement to create a Jewish state. In the late 1930s, Monsky and his B'nai B'rith constituents helped fashion critical compromises between the Zionist and non-Zionist camps.[17]

Jewish federation councils round out the major secular Jewish organizations. In the late nineteenth century, communal leaders in cities across the country organized Jewish federations to coordinate duplicative and sometimes contradictory philanthropic appeals. As early as 1864, Memphis Jews placed all their social service and fund-raising agencies under a single roof, but it was not until Boston created its own umbrella organization in 1895 that the term "federation" first appeared. By the end of the Progressive era, Jewish federations dotted the American Jewish landscape. German-American Jews led the federation movement, focusing much of their attention on the Americanization of eastern European Jewish arrivals. In the 1930s, federations coordinated almost all of the Jewish community's fund-raising efforts, giving them a quasi-governmental function. Federation leaders anchored their communities' long-range planning and helped mediate conflicts between the AJC and AJCongress. Since they held the Jewish community's purse strings, their influence strengthened as fund-raising efforts grew. By the end of World War II, almost every American Jew lived in a community served by a federation. The National Community Relations Advisory Council (NCRAC), organized in 1944, sought to replicate the federation's function in the world of Jewish communal service. Comprised of constituent groups AJC, AJCongress, B'nai B'rith, and others, the NCRAC emerged in the postwar years as one of the Jewish community's most important intergroup lobbying agencies.[18]

Within the religious world of American Judaism, the Reform movement occupied the most prominent position in American liberal politics. Along with its congregational branch, the Union of American Hebrew Congregations (UAHC), its rabbinic arm, the Central Conference of American Rabbis (CCAR), and its seminary, the Hebrew Union College–Jewish Institute of Religion (HUC-JIR), Reform Jews struggled to reconcile the ethical imperatives of prophetic Judaism with their American Jewish experience. Conservative Jews, represented by their rabbinic college, the Jewish Theological Seminary (JTS), and their clergy association, the Rabbinic Assembly (RA), did not consider active participation in American politics central to their theology but still joined a variety of liberal social reform movements. In the Orthodox community, even fewer issues inspired public comment. Only Agudath Israel, representing a relatively small proportion of ultra-Orthodox Jews, entered the political fray. It opposed Zionism on religious grounds, disagreed with most of its nontraditional co-religionists on church-state issues, and offered the Jewish community's most biting critique of affirmative action.[19]

Quest for Inclusion begins with the election of Franklin D. Roosevelt in 1932. After three years of economic depression, voters rejected the Republican incumbent Herbert Hoover in favor of the Democratic standard-bearer from New York. Unemployment peaked at about 25 percent with little hope of immediate recovery. By inauguration day, the new president was faced with the worst economic depression in U.S. history. For the first time, the federal government supported an interventionist social welfare program, abandoning a century-old tradition that left relief programs to local government and private philanthropy. By 1941, when

Americans turned from domestic reform to world war, the United States boasted a social security plan, unemployment relief, large-scale public works projects, and, most importantly, a new attitude toward poverty and the proper role of the federal government.

In the Jewish community, the Great Depression halted years of financial prosperity capped by the largest synagogue building campaign in American history and set the community on a perilous new course. Liberated in the 1920s from the confines of immigrant neighborhoods such as New York's Lower East Side, these second-generation American Jews felt "at home in America." They fashioned an ethnic consciousness rooted in both Jewish tradition and the culture of middle-class urban America. They moved into the roomier suburbs of Brooklyn in New York and Boyle Heights in Los Angeles. Jewish dollars poured into local and national philanthropic organizations. But within two years of the stock market crash, the optimism of the Jewish community and the nation at large had faded. Instead of an era of hope and prosperity, American Jews faced unemployment and poverty. Once-successful Jewish fund-raising efforts stalled and relief needs soared. Jewish agencies, unable to handle the increased client load, turned to the local, state, and federal government for help.[20]

Chapter 1 investigates how early Jewish calls for a more activist federal government anticipated many New Deal reforms and positioned the Jewish community for leadership in 1930s America. Jewish social workers, like bureaucrats in city halls across the country, sought federal dollars but feared loss of control. The union between American Jews and Roosevelt's New Deal proved mutually beneficial. The administration gained the expertise of an American Jewish community committed to New Deal–style politics, while the Jewish community enjoyed unprecedented access to the corridors of power. Ultimately, Jewish social welfare policy in the 1930s offered FDR the language he would need to steer the nation away from laissez-faire determinism and toward his pragmatic solutions to the nation's economic ills.[21]

As FDR struggled to pull the nation out of economic depression, Adolf Hitler began his reign of terror in Europe. Chapter 2 focuses on Jewish efforts to transplant American liberal ideals of cultural pluralism overseas. It chronicles how some American Jews, concerned about the fate of their European co-religionists, organized an anti-German boycott, staged public demonstrations against Nazi persecutions, and ultimately entertained the possibility of creating a Jewish national home in Palestine. It details the deepening rift between America's German- and Eastern European–descended Jews, demonstrates how each community called on competing definitions of liberalism to protect itself, and sets the stage for the awesome relief and rescue challenges of the Second World War.

Hitler's persecution of Jews in Europe inspired American anti-Semites to launch their own high-profile campaigns. Jewish leaders, fearful that domestic anti-Semites threatened their co-religionists' safety, organized an impressive interfaith dialogue movement to build constructive relationships with the Christian clergy. Chapter 3 details the organized Jewish community's bid to insulate American democracy from totalitarian threats by protecting civil liberties and developing political alliances with other religious leaders.

Yet by creating a simplistic political model that placed Nazism and democracy on polar extremes, the Jewish community unwittingly laid the groundwork for its own liberal wartime failures. Chapter 4 traces the precarious path of American Jewish liberalism between 1941, when the United States entered the European conflict, and the end of the war in 1945. The Jewish community's strategy of drawing parallels between Judaism and Americanism worked well in the prewar years, and Jewish leaders hoped for continued success after the United States declared war on Germany. American Jews thus looked forward to a unified campaign both to defeat the Nazis and rescue European Jews. Much to the Jewish community's disappointment, that would not be the case. Jewish leaders managed an impressive material campaign for overseas relief but could not convince Roosevelt to make the plight of Jews a higher priority. With the State Department antagonistic to Jewish concerns and the chief executive unwilling to intervene, Jewish leaders had little choice but to acquiesce to the status quo. Theirs was an untenable moral and political dilemma: loud public protests might have swayed public opinion, but too many calls for a diversion of military strength would have invited charges of disloyalty.

Just as the need for wartime consensus softened American Jewish calls for overseas relief, it also prevented the Jewish community from objecting to the great domestic civil rights tragedy of the war: the internment of Japanese Americans. Unsubstantiated charges of treason against persons of Japanese ancestry paralyzed a democratic nation rife with anti-Asian racism. The need for national consensus and Allied victory encouraged Americans to deny constitutional protections to U.S. citizens of Japanese descent, yet civil libertarianism demanded that liberals fight Roosevelt's infamous Executive Order 9066. Jewish leaders, fearful of sedition charges, opted to focus their civil libertarian campaigns on the needs of Jewish refugees while they ignored the plight of some 67,000 fellow citizens. Would Jewish leaders deny civil protection in order to achieve the larger goal of military victory? Almost to a person, along with the vast majority of American liberals, they answered in the affirmative.

Chapter 5 addresses the Jewish community's influence on the all-important foreign policy questions that emerged from the second world war.

When Allied leaders began formulating proposals for postwar reconstruction, the Jewish community took the lead in an impressive bid to extend principles of American liberal democracy to war-torn Europe and the world. While Jewish leaders from the AJC and AJCongress still argued over activist and accommodationist political strategies, they campaigned together for a United Nations organization. American Zionists called attention to the two million Jewish refugees languishing in European displaced persons (DP) camps to pressure non-Zionists into a nationalist compromise. Without accepting the idea of a sovereign political state, leaders from organizations such as the AJC supported Jewish immigration to Palestine on humanitarian grounds. Philanthropic Zionism, as it came to be known, reinvigorated the American Zionist movement and eventually paved the way for AJC support of a Jewish national homeland.

Throughout the 1950s, Jewish liberals struggled to keep pace with the shifting political currents of the nation. Chapter 6 chronicles the Jewish community's responses to four major Cold War public-policy debates: anti-Communism, employment discrimination, immigration reform, and church-state separation. In each of these arenas, Jewish communal leaders struggled to balance their strong anti-Communist beliefs with their desire to protect civil liberties. While mainstream Jewish organizations jumped on the Cold War bandwagon, they also used ideals of American democratic superiority to power important new social reforms through Congress.

The politics of acculturation exacted its greatest toll on Jewish liberals during the modern struggle for racial equality. For a democratic society to thrive, Jewish leaders realized, it must protect the right of minorities to ethnic self-expression, not try to accommodate them into the larger culture. When African Americans launched grass-roots civil rights protests in the early 1950s, northern Jews understood African-American frustration over the failure of liberal idealism. The Jim Crow system made a mockery out of universalist ideals. Just as Jewish leaders demanded the right to address the specific anti-Semitic nature of Nazi persecution, African-American leaders launched a campaign to alert the nation to the racist origins of segregation.

Northern Jews, embittered by liberalism's failure to address issues of ethnic inequality, helped steer postwar social reform toward the greatest democratic injustice of the postwar era, racism. Angered by the legal racism of the South, they took dramatic public steps to align themselves with the civil rights cause and bring needed change to the South's racial status quo. Most southern Jews, though, fearful of economic, social, and even physical retribution, remained on the periphery of the movement. In later years, when the civil rights movement moved to the urban North and challenged that region's Jewish community to tackle an even more insidious form of extralegal racism, the community balked. An explanation of these seeming contradictions forms the argument in chapter 7.

In the mid-1960s, the very definition of liberalism changed, testing once again the strength of American Jewish liberals and forming the basis of the final chapter. When Lyndon Johnson's Great Society advocated group-based reform programs such as affirmative action, the Jewish community flinched. Establishment of rigid hiring quotas, which many Jews believed would be inevitable, was antithetical to Jewish interests. The Jewish community stood at a crossroads, wondering whether to follow the path to neoconservatism of so many other ethnic whites or embrace the new, more militant brand of liberalism. For the most part, the Jewish community chose the latter.

In 1975, the Jewish community could reflect back on its forty-year odyssey into liberal politics with mixed emotions. It took the cause of America's dispossessed as its own and succeeded in advancing a model of American democracy that valued tolerance, pluralism, merit, and civil equality. Yet the Jewish community also suffered from periodic defeats and an eventual rejection by the liberal organizations it once created and led. Its failures, though, taught Jews a valuable lesson, one that can be applied across the American political and social spectrum. Jews learned that they could no longer use their own community's rapid social mobility as the archetype for all of America to follow. Processes of acculturation acted on racial minorities in divergent ways and often created competing political goals. The Jewish community had to acknowledge those differences and formulate a new version of accommodationism sensitive to its own historical experience.

CHAPTER ONE

"What Do We Owe to Peter Stuyvesant?"
The New Deal in the Jewish Community

SOON AFTER Franklin D. Roosevelt's inauguration, Cornell University economist Isaac Rubinow posed a rhetorical question to the National Conference of Jewish Social Service: "What do we owe to Peter Stuyvesant?" Rubinow's query recalled a well-known seventeenth-century squabble between Stuyvesant, the governor of New Amsterdam, and his employer, the Dutch West Indies Company. When the colonial leader sought the expulsion of a small group of Brazilian Jewish immigrants in 1654, his European governors, intent on using the new arrivals to bolster the local economy, flinched. Their compromise, termed "the Stuyvesant Pledge," allowed the Jews to remain in exchange for a promise that the settlers would take care of their own social welfare needs. American Jews could not, they all agreed, look to the government for relief.[1]

While the Stuyvesant Pledge never actually defined Jewish nor even U.S. social welfare policy, it proved a powerful metaphor for a community struggling to maintain its traditional collectivist orientation in the midst of the nation's worst economic depression. Governor Stuyvesant's accommodation anticipated what Jews would learn in their American experience: that the social welfare system in the United States depended upon private and often times religious philanthropic institutions. While nearly three centuries separated Rubinow's speech from the "Stuyvesant Pledge," the American Jewish impulse to "take care of its own" survived well into the twentieth century. Respecting the traditional American social welfare ethic of voluntarism, the Jewish community developed a sophisticated network of private philanthropic organizations. Jewish Federation Councils emerged in most major American cities and served as the umbrella organization for a variety of social service groups, while local synagogues solicited members for their own philanthropic appeals. As late as 1914, Jacob Schiff, the famed German-American banker and leader of the American Jewish Committee, remarked that "a Jew would rather cut his hand off than apply for relief from non-Jewish sources."[2]

The New Deal proved a critical turning point in American Jewish politics. Between FDR's first inauguration in March 1933 and U.S. entry into World War II in December 1941, American Jews blazed an unmistakable liberal path. They helped forge the New Deal coalition and provided much of the glue that kept it together for three generations. Roosevelt brought crucial relief to an American Jewish community reeling from the economic depression and, for the first time in their American experience, invited Jews to help write public policy. Not only did many American Jews occupy prominent positions in the Roosevelt administration, but thousands more filled the rolls of local New Deal agencies, determined to leave an unmistakable Jewish imprint on the national landscape. For Jews whose historic political ties ran the gamut from Republican to Communist, the Democratic party of the 1930s promised input on the most important public policy questions of the day and realization of a generation-long American Jewish dream: integration into the mainstream.

Jewish calls for increased federal intervention, whether from the ranks of FDR's own administration, front-line Jewish social workers, or the millions of American Jews suffering the ill effects of the Depression, helped create the greatest government expansion in U.S. history. A religious minority in a Christian nation and an ethnic subculture within the larger society, Jewish leaders demonstrated how a massive federal relief program could extend American civic protections, insure the survival of Jewish life in the United States, and encourage a tolerant and pluralist national political culture.

American Jewish leaders helped design several of the most important New Deal programs. When Congress approved millions of dollars in relief, the Jewish community spearheaded the drive for community control, guaranteeing its clients the best possible care and defining a central feature of New Deal liberalism—the enfranchisement of local political leaders as a means to guarantee the success of Roosevelt's national reform plan. Jewish clients could be served by their own social workers and Jewish agencies enjoyed a new lease on their communal life. New Deal liberalism meant that Jews could reap the benefits of government assistance without fearing its coercive power.[3]

Jewish communal leaders took issue with New Deal programs that threatened to marginalize Jews or failed to address issues of paramount concern to their community. When FDR limited New Deal reform measures to the narrow goal of economic recovery, Jewish social workers balked. For them, the Great Depression represented more than just a business downturn; it illustrated the failure of American social policy. The New Dealer's goal of a fiscal quick fix did little to reverse a social Darwinist welfare policy that had plagued Jews and other working Americans for over fifty years. With the unemployment rate skyrocketing to 25 percent, Jewish social workers could not subscribe to the belief that the poor had created their own misfortune. Jewish communal workers, steeped in leftist politics or in traditional religious mandates to care for the poor, challenged established conceptions of American poverty that placed the primary responsibility for poverty on the individual and the main burden for recovery on private philanthropy or local government. Instead, they advanced models more in touch with the demands of modern industrial economies. Larger economic and social factors, they argued, punished hard-working Americans who could not find work. The continued integration of Jews into American life demanded that communal leaders split from their non-Jewish New Deal allies and combat the social welfare status quo.

In the short term, these efforts brought needed relief to many Jews and helped protect them from poverty, hunger, and homelessness. On a grander scale, it established American Jews as white America's leading opponents of institutional discrimination and affirmed a tenet central to modern American Jewish liberalism: protection of individuals victimized by social factors beyond their control. By shifting social responsibility away from the unoffending individual, Jewish leaders protected their co-religionists from further social marginalization and pressed for a government committed to solving systemic economic problems instead of scapegoating its innocent victims.

While the expanding welfare state bolstered the Jewish community's civic status in many ways, it also threatened to squash American Jewish cultural expression. Heads of Jewish social welfare organizations watched as government relief checks all but replaced private contributions. Jewish leaders worried that New Deal programs would challenge the legitimacy of their agencies and hasten the assimilation of their co-religionists. In a bid to preserve their distinctive ethnic identity, Jewish social workers took advantage of New Deal assistance to free Jewish funds for educational and cultural activities. At a time when New Deal programs placed all Americans under the same economic umbrella, Jews illustrated how the liberal state could promote ethnic differentiation and provide an even safer haven for minority groups.

In recent studies, historians such as Gary Gerstle and Lizabeth Cohen have argued that the overbearing economic demands of the era necessitated an abandonment of ethnic identity and the embrace of a more universal political culture. Contrary to Gerstle and Cohen, American Jews illustrated how ethnic and religious groups could redirect liberal government programs to benefit both educational and character-building programs. Whether by replenishing their nearly empty bank accounts with local and state government subsidies in the first years of economic depression or transferring their clients to federal agencies once FDR launched his New Deal, Jewish social workers took advantage of the government's newfound relief commitment to bolster Jewish character-building programs.[4]

Eastern European American Jewish leaders, already influential by the time FDR became president, accelerated their drive for greater democratization, pressed for increased funding of Jewish educational programs, and sought alliances with the religious leadership of Christian America just as they resisted greater accommodation to American life. Proper Jewish acculturation to American life, they held, demanded basic knowledge of Jewish history, religion, and culture. A decade after Congress restricted most immigration from Eastern Europe, second-generation Jews crafted a liberal definition of Americanism founded upon their optimism for inclusion in public life, their desire to maintain a distinct ethnic culture, and their vision of a democratic nation respectful of religious difference. By cheering the liberal reform programs of the New Deal, American Jews could use government money to help protect their community's long-term survival. Judaism would occupy a sacred place in American society and the liberal state would help pay for it.

THE STOCK MARKET CRASH OF 1929

When the stock market crashed on October 24, 1929, Jewish leaders, like most other Americans, expressed little fear. The American Jewish Committee, meeting just three weeks later, failed to mention the economic downturn in its proceedings. Jewish Family Welfare Agencies experienced only slight increases in expenditures and in the number of cases served. Fund-raising efforts by local Jewish Federation Councils continued unaffected throughout the 1930 campaign as relief costs among the largest Jewish agencies increased just 7 percent.[5]

By 1931, though, Jewish social welfare organizations felt the economic pinch. More Jews applied for aid than in any previous year. Jewish social workers witnessed vast increases in case loads, expenditures, and applications for service. The American Jewish Committee disclosed that "practically every local Federation in the country was compelled to reduce its budget." For the first time in its history, the Chicago Jewish Charities ended the year with a deficit. In every relief category, Jewish agencies carried a greater burden. During the dark winter of 1931–32, relief figures reached a new high. Demand for social services mounted while contributions to Jewish philanthropic appeals plummeted. The Bureau of Jewish Social Research reported a 50 percent jump in relief and a steady decline in contributions. In 1933, Jewish social workers labored under an even heavier caseload while fund-raisers collected a third fewer dollars. With the nation sinking into economic collapse, Jewish agencies sought bank loans to cover their relief commitments and demanded that the government help them fund the nation's social service programs.[6]

Figure 1. Jews on New York's Lower East Side collecting *tzedaka* (charity) during the Great Depression. (Graduate School for Jewish Social Work, Records, nd 1925–1950, I-7, box 4 of 8, folder 66, American Jewish Historical Society, Waltham, Mass.)

When Jewish leaders called for greater government relief, they incurred the wrath of many Americans intent on keeping the social welfare system private. The shift from private to public aid in the United States developed slowly and revealed profound fears about involving government in the traditional sphere of private philanthropy. "Care of the poor," one New Dealer affirmed, "has been recognized from earliest colonial days as fundamentally a function of local government." Social conservatives warned that public assistance would create a nation full of dependents. This attitude, borrowed from the English economist Malthus, "held that the poor were responsible for their own misery and destitution, that they had no 'right' to public relief." Former Progressives such as Herbert Hoover feared that government aid would undermine the spirit of rugged individualism, while southerners opposed any federal action that might encroach on state's rights.[7]

Opponents of activist government dominated American politics throughout the 1920s and into the 1930s. Critics of government relief spending insisted that success or failure in the economic world reflected an individual's moral fitness. Invoking the memory of the late nineteenth-century industrial giants who opposed government regulation, opponents of the New Deal adhered to the principle that the economic cycle rewarded those most fit for advancement and punished those lacking the appropriate human qualities. Bright, keen, and intelligent Americans would find a way to prosper. Those who were lazy and uninterested would end up impoverished. The federal government could not be held responsible for problems created by individual vices.[8]

In 1931 Senator Thomas Gore of Oklahoma wrote that "you could no more relieve the depression by legislation than you can pass a resolution to prevent disease." Fiscal conservatives remained skeptical of government involvement as well. "Opponents of federal relief," wrote Josephine Brown, an assistant to New Deal administrator Harry Hopkins, "claimed that it would seriously impair the credit of the federal government and make it impossible to balance the budget. They claimed that this would retard the restoration of normal business and serve to increase unemployment." Tinkering with the cycles of the economy, they reasoned, could only unbalance the natural rhythm of supply and demand, production and unemployment, growth and recession. Economic downturns, like physical ailments, could best be remedied by following nature's course, and government action was not natural.[9]

Most Christian religious leaders accepted the laissez-faire critique. In the nineteenth century, traditional social Darwinist ideology dominated the sermons of leading Protestant clergy, including Henry Ward Beecher, who claimed that responsibility for poverty rested with the individual. Many of the Progressive Era's most important social reformers rooted their Alger-like appeals in Protestant theology. They justified their support for Theodore Roosevelt's activist program on its middle-class Protestant focus and could not embrace the communitarian ideology espoused by many of that era's Jewish labor, political, and religious leaders. "Social conservatism, sometimes of an extreme sort," one religious historian noted, "continued to flourish in the great middle-class denominations in which liberal advocacy was most audible."[10]

The market crash did little to change their attitudes. While a few Protestant denominations backed a New Deal–style approach to government in the early 1930s, most refused to challenge the laissez-faire system. Almost all the editorial boards of leading Protestant periodicals favored the incumbent Hoover in the 1932 presidential election, while the clergy focused their efforts on maintaining Prohibition and checking the influence of Catholics after Al Smith's 1928 presidential campaign. Most Protestant church members continued to back the Republican party by supporting Alf Landon's unsuccessful 1936 bid for the presidency. In 1938, the Southern Baptist Convention declared capitalism the "best [economic system] in the world."[11]

The Catholic Church intertwined its opposition to public relief with its own impressive history as one of the nation's leading private philanthropies. It maintained a traditional approach to social welfare, stressing the saintly responsibility of Catholics to care for the poor, feed the hungry, and shelter the homeless. In Chicago, the Catholic Church convinced the local political leadership to name its welfare organizations as constituents of the state relief organization. It became a representative of the Illinois government, distributing federal and state relief. By maintaining strict control, the Chicago archdiocese ensured that needy Catholics would receive public assistance while remaining accountable to the Catholic charities, the St. Vincent de Paul Society, and their local priests. While Jews would also seek cooperative arrangements with government, they did not use their operational autonomy as a means to maintain traditional social welfare practices.[12]

In Jewish America, social workers rejected the prevailing individualist ideology and embraced a collectivist stance that acknowledged systemic inequalities. They refused to equate unemployment and its effects with moral weakness and called for government-sponsored welfare years before the New Deal pressed the issue into the national spotlight. As early as 1918, the Reform movement called for a government-sponsored unemployment insurance program as well as a pension fund for elderly Americans. In 1923, Jewish social service agencies questioned "the need, desirability, and propriety of separate Jewish agencies." During the 1920s, Jewish organizations urged municipal governments to take a more active role in the social welfare needs of their community, while Isaac M. Rubinow worked up plans for a national social security system.[13]

Delegates to the conference on Jewish Social Service objected to President Hoover's August 1931 announcement that private charity could best redress the crisis and that poverty resulted more from administrative problems plaguing local charity than from an absence of federal participation. Convinced that the human will for self-improvement outweighed the inclination toward pauperism, they attacked the laissez-faire argument that equated wealth with moral fitness and poverty with laziness. They answered the charge that government aid created a welfare-dependent nation by pointing to the novelties of a modern industrial economy: government assistance, whether in the form of relief or public works, followed as the logical extension of Jewish social welfare thinking. By admonishing, as other American liberals had since the nineteenth century, that the "worthy poor" should not be penalized for poverty caused more by external economic factors than moral transgression, Jewish social workers protected their clients from a welfare system that had historically blamed them for their own victimization, eased their acculturation to Depression-era America, and anticipated a forty-year Jewish commitment to rally behind victims of social discrimination.[14]

By distinguishing between the worthy and unworthy poor, American Jews defended government aid while they addressed the fear of overreliance on the state. The president of Cleveland's Jewish social service bureau observed that the Depression brought new clients who were "physically and mentally fit." In previous years, Jewish social service agencies assisted only those who were unable to care for themselves. With the business downturn, he discovered, a new group of needy arose who "were merely victims of a change in the economic structure affecting the entire population." Jewish social workers pointed out that most of the nation's poor did not lose their jobs due to mental or even physical defect. Maurice Karpf, dean of the Graduate School for Jewish Social Work, concluded that "even if private philanthropy were able to deal with the problem, victims of the depression who are able and willing to work but can find none through no fault of their own, should not be forced to apply to charity but should be aided by the government whose duty it is to care for its citizens." The moral fitness argument, he explained, could not be waged in an economy where otherwise productive and competent people went jobless.[15]

Benjamin Selekman, executive director of Boston's Associated Jewish Philanthropies, proposed an eight-point plan of action that called for "the development in the United States during the depression of an elaborate program of public social work, particularly in the field of relief," while Harry Lurie, the director of New York's Bureau of Jewish Social Research, acknowledged that the Jewish community was "beginning to see more clearly that the Jewish family agency actually functions in a supplementary capacity and that its future is tied up with the destinies of the entire public welfare movement." Other leaders concurred. Henry Monsky, president of Omaha's community chest and welfare fund and later national president of B'nai B'rith, recognized "that the Jewish group is an integral and inseparable part of the larger community and must adjust itself to a program of active participation in and entire cooperation with the social agencies that minister to the social needs of the community as a whole. . . . It is totally illogical, to my mind, to hold ourselves aloof as a special and segregated group and to refuse to accept or refrain from the enjoyment of the aid and assistance justly due to our group . . . from the public agencies."[16]

Jews considered themselves a distinct ethnic community, not a separate economic entity. They focused on that difference to justify support for government aid. "Victims of the depression who are able and willing to work but can find none through no fault of their own," Maurice Karpf argued, "should not be forced to apply to charity but should be aided by the government whose duty it is to care for its citizens." Solutions to basic economic problems, Jewish leaders reasoned, extended beyond the means of the private relief agency. "Jewish poverty," Isaac Rubinow claimed, did not result from "intra-group conditions" but rather was "part and parcel of the whole economic and social problem of wealth production and wealth accumulation of the country as a whole." Rubinow held that "the economic position of the American Jew today and even more so his position tomorrow is irretrievably interwoven with the economic present and future of the American people." He believed that American Jews had "penetrated American economic life, so much so that to separate them would be as difficult a process, if not as unscrambling eggs, than at least as it would be to separate the light from the dark particles in the sands in the sea."[17]

Jewish social workers portrayed themselves as modernists among a nation of laissez-faire traditionalists. While holding to liberal Democratic party values, they embraced forms of collectivism rarely seen in American politics or social welfare. By demonstrating how the Great Depression served as an economic and social leveler, drawing millions of otherwise productive individuals into the ranks of the unemployed, Jewish social welfare leaders helped redefine popular conceptions of poverty and its causes, offered a theoretical defense of government intervention, and forged a new relationship between the Jewish community and the state.

Jewish calls for greater government relief sounded first at the local level. Though often overburdened and understaffed, city agencies responded as best they could to the new demands. They relied on local tax revenue, county and state apportionments, community chests, and the private social service infrastructure. Their efforts, though, proved inadequate. As a young Milton Meltzer experienced in Worcester, Massachusetts, municipal authorities could not meet the rising demand for social services. With unemployment at 25 percent and a winter storm blowing, Meltzer recalled how in 1932 his city government hired citizens to clear the streets. While he was careful to credit his local government for all they did, Meltzer ultimately noted that "the cities, counties, and states were not prepared to meet the crisis."[18]

Plans for state-sponsored relief began in 1929 when the New York legislature, at the request of then-governor Franklin Roosevelt, authorized a commission to study the feasibility of a social security plan. Not until 1931, though, did the New York legislature approve a $20 million grant

Figure 2. A failed Jewish business on New York's Lower East Side, ca. 1933. (Graduate School for Jewish Social Work, Records, nd 1925–1950, I-7, box 4 of 8, series IV, folder 70.)

for unemployment relief. Later that year, New Jersey allocated almost $10 million for the same purpose, while in Pennsylvania, Governor Gifford Pinchot called a special session of the legislature to secure additional funds for the commonwealth's welfare, health, and labor departments. Similar scenarios played out in Wisconsin, Rhode Island, Kentucky, Oklahoma, New Hampshire, Maryland, and California. "Never before in the history of the United States," Josephine Brown reflected, "had state governments invested so heavily in relief for any purpose. These unprecedented appropriations established once and for all the responsibility of state government for relief of persons in need, not only in this unemployment emergency but in any emergency."[19]

As local and state agencies increased their commitment to relief, Jewish welfare organizations grew more dependent upon government aid for their survival. In most cities, Jewish social workers transferred their clients to the new public agencies. Often times, the local government agency would hire Jewish professionals to continue serving their co-religionists. "Between 1929 and 1932," *Jewish Social Work* reported, "new public agencies were set up in Chicago, Philadelphia, and New York, to name only three cities. In each case, primary responsibility for relief was assumed by the public agency, the Jewish agency readjusting its program to meet needs otherwise not met." Reports issued in 1931 from New York, Brooklyn, Philadelphia, Chicago, and Detroit indicated that the majority of Jewish social work cases were not handled by Jewish agencies. Another study of some fifty-two Jewish communities found "increased responsibility assumed by governmental agencies for programs of unemployment relief and emergency funds."[20]

In some cases, local and state government allowed Jewish agencies to retain operational autonomy by funneling their relief dollars through the private social welfare organizations. In St. Louis, for example, the mayor created a "citizen's committee" in October 1930 to unite the local Jewish Federation, the Catholic charities, and the Chamber of Commerce in an effort to "coordinate relief efforts in St. Louis with national and state work." According to its agreement, the citizen's committee assigned social welfare responsibility among a variety of private agencies: the American Red Cross cared for veterans and their families, the Bureau for Women served the needs of single women, the St. Vincent de Paul Society aided Catholic St. Louisans, while the Jewish Social Service Bureau reached out to Jewish families in the community. The municipality agreed, under this arrangement, to reimburse these private agencies for any additional expenditures incurred as a result of the economic downturn. The agencies themselves maintained responsibility for administrative overhead. While the St. Louis experiment proved successful, widespread claims of fiscal irresponsibility in other cities eventually led FDR to ban the privatization of federal funds in 1933.[21]

By the time Governor Roosevelt challenged President Hoover in the 1932 general election, American Jews stood poised for political change. Even though Hoover initiated federal programs such as the Reconstruction Finance Corporation to ease the nation out of economic depression, his approach proved too limited for most American Jews, who considered the presidential contest a test of competing social welfare ideologies: the laissez-faire Hoover vs. the activist Roosevelt. Though the two politicians stood together on many social welfare principles, including opposition to direct relief, the Democratic standard bearer enjoyed much more popular support than Hoover, whose callous public comments and actions damaged his popularity. Hoover stood fast in his determination to correct the economic downturn with minimal federal government involvement, while Roosevelt, riding the coattails of an unlikely alliance of labor, farming, and business interests, readied a New Deal program that would define American politics for generations.

The National Conference of Jewish Social Service (NCJSS) had already passed a resolution at its 1931 meeting calling on Congress and the president "not only to alleviate present and immediately impending suffering, but to lay the foundations for the effective prevention of similar social and economic catastrophes in the future." A few months later, it implored Congress and the president "not only to alleviate present and immediately impending suffering, but to lay the foundations for the effective prevention of similar social and economic catastrophes in the future." NCJSS president Maurice Karpf affirmed that "the needs in the present emergency are so great that they call for concerted and constructive action from the legislative and executive branches of our government," while Benjamin Selekman alerted the delegates to the probability that they, as Jewish social workers, would "have to redouble efforts and take the lead, if necessary in getting the proper kind of governmental action in alleviating distress due to unemployment."[22]

When the Hoover administration failed to turn the economic tide, Jewish social workers looked to Roosevelt and his proposed recovery program. Just as Roosevelt's election pressed the Jewish social welfare agenda into the forefront of U.S. public policy, so too it catapulted many American Jews into positions of great influence. Jewish affinity for New Deal–style legislation would inspire nothing less than complete devotion to its chief architect, and the Jews' infatuation with FDR would prove mutually beneficial. FDR gained the experience of constituents already expert in social welfare policy, recruiting Jewish labor leaders, social workers, and attorneys to work at almost every level of the federal government, while the Jewish community enjoyed access to the corridors of governmental power for the first time. Between 1933 and the U.S. entry into World War II, Jews entered the political mainstream en masse.[23]

Almost immediately, New Deal programs slowed the downward spiral and helped put the nation on the long road to recovery. Isador Lubin, the commissioner of the Bureau of Labor Statistics, reported in May 1934 that income for the average American jumped 27 percent over the previous year and unemployment rates declined. Over half the Americans who lost their jobs between 1929 and 1933 found employment between April 1933 and April 1934. Jewish philanthropies noted an upward turn in contributions. Due in large part to an aggressive public relief and works program, Jewish social service agencies reduced their relief budgets for the first time since the onset of the Depression.[24]

Jewish leaders hailed FDR's early recovery efforts. In newspapers and magazines, synagogues and community centers, American Jews welcomed the new president's reform program and sought the government's cooperation on social welfare issues. In April 1933, the *B'nai B'rith Messenger* urged "the Jews of America" to "serve as a leaven of social reconstruction." Isaac Rubinow, speaking before a national gathering of Jewish social workers, affirmed that "it was the duty of social workers to force upon the attention of a bewildered world the necessity of a broad legislative economic program." In a January 1934 address at New York City's Free Synagogue, Rabbi Stephen S. Wise, the unofficial spokesman for

American Jewry, exulted that Roosevelt "has wrought miracles within less than one year of his administration."[25]

The excitement over New Deal programs waned as Jewish leaders settled into the difficult task of managing the day-to-day operations of their social welfare organizations. In the months and years before the New Deal, American Jews could call for increased government aid at any time. With the flurry of New Deal legislation though, Jews, like so many other Americans of the time, learned the art of political compromise. They knew that President Roosevelt could use their support to help make the New Deal a success, just as they were reminded that government aid always came with strings attached.

As the Congress debated various relief bills, Jewish social workers strove to ensure that New Deal programs respected the particular needs of their clients. They feared programs out of touch with the linguistic, dietary, and cultural differences of American Jews and worried about the public agencies' inferior standard of care. Jewish social service, according to Benjamin Selekman, focused on "those activities which are so specifically Jewish that none but Jews can be expected to support them." Religious Jews required kosher food, often spoke Yiddish, and observed Jewish traditions. In Atlanta, the Jewish agency retained its caseload because it required "a good deal of service and we have assumed that our knowledge of the psychological and cultural background of our group gives us a better understanding of the problems of these clients." Only a social worker specially trained in Jewish customs, they argued, could properly care for Jewish clients.[26]

Jewish social workers invoked traditional religious ideals in their critique of public authority, stressing the importance of remembering their client's dignity and honor as they dispensed relief. While FDR and his New Deal administrators took great strides to preserve client dignity, Jewish social workers noted their occasional lapses. Some New Deal programs, they pointed out, reflected the principle that the poor were somehow responsible for their own misfortune. In order to qualify for assistance, potential recipients were required to show up at a relief station in person and pass a means test verifying their economic status. Many complained of the humiliation involved with such a process, arguing that the focus should not be placed upon them as individuals, but rather on society as a whole.[27]

Ever since Progressive Era leaders such as Theodore Roosevelt expanded the reach of the federal government, state and local authorities as well as private organizations had worried about Washington's ability to serve its constituents. Franklin Roosevelt's New Deal only intensified their concern. Josephine Brown explained that "extravagance and waste were bound to occur when spending was so far removed from local controls, and such a regime would necessarily be more subject to political interference. Local citizens knew local conditions best." Adopting a philosophy which would become a hallmark in New Deal liberalism, Brown concluded, "The nearer the administration of relief was kept to the community affected, the sooner its evils would be detected and checked." Local public agencies received government assistance without compromising their operational autonomy, while the federal government saved the time and expense of creating duplicative social service agencies.[28]

Jewish social workers took advantage of their superior record in patient care to further bolster their claim for operational autonomy. In 1930, for example, Jewish agencies provided an average relief check of $43.09 compared to an industry average of only $22.80. One Jewish social worker called upon private philanthropy "to stimulate the public agencies to an increasingly high standard of personnel and of service," while delegates at a 1933 meeting of the Southern New England Conference of the National Council of Jewish Federations and Welfare Funds concluded that the inadequacies of government relief and training constituted "good reason for the continued existence and independence of Jewish family welfare work."[29]

The same year, Jewish Family Welfare Executives "reemphasized the responsibility of the Jewish agency to improve the standards of public relief, to preserve the essential case work services for Jews and to extend the specialized services of a constructive nature not available through the public agency." And, in 1934, Benjamin Selekman warned his colleagues that "until the public childcare agency maintains social work standards as high as those of the private, the Jewish community will probably insist upon maintaining dependent and neglected children of the Jewish faith as its wards."[30]

Roosevelt responded to these concerns by supporting cooperative arrangements between the federal government and a variety of public and private social welfare organizations. New Deal agencies supplied most of the funding; local authorities provided the personnel and expertise. While FDR's fear of economic mismanagement led him to prohibit direct funding of private agencies, he encouraged local public officials to hire social workers who understood the needs of their respective clients. For Jews, that meant increased representation in the public agencies and the promise of greater sensitivity to the community's particular needs. For Roosevelt, the strategy served two important purposes: it insured rapid delivery of welfare services by utilizing established local social workers, and it solidified valued political support from government-weary community leaders. Instead of looking to Washington with disdain, local politicians threw their considerable political clout behind the chief executive. By resolving the age-old tension between federal and state authority, FDR bolstered his New Deal programs just as he strengthened the Democratic party's appeal to voters.

The Jewish community did not have to wait long to test the new waters of affirmative government. Within eight weeks of his inauguration, Roosevelt secured passage of the Federal Emergency Relief Act (FERA), which allocated an initial five hundred million dollars "to provide for cooperation by the federal government with the several states . . . in relieving the hardship and suffering caused by unemployment." The measure stipulated that private agencies surrender virtually all relief work to the local and state government, just as it gave those public agencies wide latitude in welfare administration. The president modeled FERA after one of his New York state programs, the Temporary Emergency Relief Act, and promoted its director, Harry Hopkins, to the new federal agency. Before passage of the Social Security Act prompted FDR to phase it out in December 1935, FERA committed four billion dollars to some twenty million Americans.[31]

FERA's effect on the Jewish community proved immediate and profound. As Jewish relief cases were sent to the public social service agency en masse, the economic strains on the Jewish agencies eased. By the end of 1933, the majority of dependent Jewish families received aid from public agencies. Relief expenditures for Jewish family welfare agencies dropped from $4.04 million in 1933 to $2.38 million in 1934. The number of cases administered by Jewish agencies declined to pre-Depression levels for the first time since the market crash.[32]

"The FERA ruling," according to the Bureau of Jewish Social Research, "constituted by far the most influential factor in determining the relief, intake, case-count and staff trend for the Jewish family agency in 1933." "By executive order," the bureau explained, "the Federal Relief Administration had accelerated a process which was and is changing the entire development of a family service program under Jewish auspices." The bureau found that in large cities, "the Jewish community, as represented in its organized philanthropies, is today no longer charged with the responsibility of meeting all the relief needs of its submarginal groups. That function, perhaps permanently, has been delegated to the state." By the end of 1933, the majority of dependent Jewish families in the nation's twenty largest cities headed to public agencies, while a 1936 survey of Jews in Minneapolis concluded that once "the philanthropic burden ha[d] been transferred from Jewish to general community responsibility, the long tradition of Jewish self-sufficiency ha[d] been broken."[33]

The Jewish communal embrace of the FERA marked a turning point for American Jews who cheered a sympathetic civil government willing to translate their social welfare agenda into national public policy. Frustrated in the old country by the anti-Semitic actions of czarist officials and thwarted in the United States by generations of politicians dedicated to laissez-faire economics, the organized Jewish community reveled in Roosevelt's ability to listen to ordinary Americans. New Deal programs such as FERA reaffirmed an optimistic Jewish assessment of the American political system: government and private citizens could work together.

While almost all Jewish organizations welcomed FERA and other New Deal relief money, no two agencies adjusted to the new arrangements in exactly the same way. Jewish leaders still worried about the pitfalls of public relief and labored to create cooperative arrangements that addressed those concerns. "In nearly all cities of any size," *Jewish Social Work* reported, "the Jewish agency made known to the public agency its willingness to be of service to Jewish families on public relief." In Baltimore, Birmingham, Cleveland, Pittsburgh, and St. Louis, a 1933 Bureau of Jewish Social Research reported, Jewish agencies maintained their operational autonomy because public agencies could not be found or did not dispense relief.[34]

For most Jewish clients, though, passage of the FERA hastened a transfer to the public agency. Jewish social workers feared, as the executive director of the Federation for the Support of Jewish Philanthropic Societies of New York City explained, that with "the huge sums expended by public agencies, there has grown a feeling throughout the country that the work of the private agency is insignificant, negligible, or possibly unnecessary." Those concerns proved overstated. A 1933 Bureau of Jewish Social Research study confirmed a cooperative spirit between Jewish social service organizations and government. In the years after 1933, Jewish agencies continued to service special need cases and, whenever possible, encouraged the federal government to hire Jewish social workers to serve the public agency's Jewish clientele. In the final analysis, Jewish social workers accepted the limitations of federal relief and acknowledged that the future of their social work programs depended on continued government funding. Ultimately, the New York City Federation head concluded, "Public relief will continue for a long period and . . . it will become increasingly effective with higher and better standards of administration."[35]

When appropriations from FERA expired in 1935, most Americans on relief rolls shifted to the Works Progress Administration (WPA), where they labored on public improvement projects. In St. Louis, 25,000 able-bodied Jewish residents received word that they had been transferred to WPA projects. Of those unable to work for the WPA, some returned to Jewish organizations while others alternated between Jewish and New Deal agencies. At the nadir of the Depression in 1933, thirty-nine of the largest Jewish family agencies cared for approximately 31,000 families. After implementation of FERA, that number dropped to 23,000. While local Jewish agencies assumed increased financial obligations after 1935, relief expenditures dropped below pre-Depression figures and continued to decline throughout the remainder of the decade.[36]

While Roosevelt's New Deal philosophy rested many Jewish leaders' concerns about the relationship between private and public welfare agencies, the huge influx of government relief accelerated a bitter debate that had been brewing in the American Jewish community for over thirty years. "The impact of vast social changes," Benjamin Selekman explained at a 1936 meeting of the Conference of Jewish Federations and Welfare Funds, "has give new challenge once again to the Jewish tradition of communal responsibility. For, like all people, American Jewry faces today the central problem of our times—adaptation to rapidly moving economic and social forces." Selekman called on his co-religionists to explain how they could justify and protect their community's particularist interests at a time when all Americans were realizing the universality of economic depression. He understood the irony of supporting government aid when that meant challenging the Jewish organization's raison d'être. An embrace of government action not only promised great social and political rewards, but also demanded accommodation, compromise, and communal reorganization.[37]

Selekman's concern reflected a generation-long tension between America's more traditionalist Eastern European Jewish majority and the accommodationist German-American minority. When over two million eastern European Jews immigrated to the United States between 1881 and 1924, the established German-American Jews provided critical support. They offered education, vocational opportunities, and created an organizational infrastructure for long-term social service programs. Yet when the established Jewish leadership decided to act, it did so without explicit support or representation from the community at large. The AJC operated at the will and pleasure of a small group of men committed to an accommodationist approach to American life. As the Eastern European Jews acculturated to their new surroundings, they began to voice opposition to both the style and direction of the German-American Jewish programs.

Some supported Jewish educational programs such as Talmud Torahs and Jewish supplemental schools to make sure their children received formal religious instruction. "As the later Jewish immigrants, especially those from eastern Europe attained a more secure place in the [American Jewish] community," Selekman explained, "they urged another directing impulse for Federation programs." In a strategy bound to force a confrontation with his accommodationist co-religionists, Selekman noted the Eastern European Jewish community's "strong feeling that every Jewish child should be given a Jewish education."[38]

Others opted for character-building activities designed to promote Jewish social and recreational life in the more secular Jewish Community

Centers (JCC) and Young Men's Hebrew Associations (YMHA). In 1928, when these programs comprised a mere 6 percent of Federation budgets, Dr. John Slawson, the head of the Jewish Welfare Federation in Cleveland and later the executive vice president of the American Jewish Committee, asserted that the "Jewish organization cannot rest on pure philanthropy. It must not be based on a foundation of misery and woe. We should not duplicate state and private social instruments; we should supplement to the extent that our Jewish cultural interests make it advisable for us to do so. But our reason for being must be ethnic culture, and not only the maimed, the sick and the blind. Pathology should not be relied on solely as a community integrator." Slawson tried to steer his colleagues away from relief-oriented activities and toward the development of culturally rich Jewish organizations. "The [Jewish] Federation [Council] is no longer a Federation for philanthropy," he insisted, "but becomes a Federation for Jewish ethnic group expression. The dependent is no longer exploited for purposes of emotional satisfaction, but the cultural tone, in all of its manifestations, of the Jewish group as a whole becomes the concern of Jewish organized welfare endeavor—a cooperative enterprise on the part of all American Jewry."[39]

While Jewish education and character-building advocates often clashed in their earlier funding appeals, both succeeded in redirecting Jewish communal dollars to their anti-accommodationist programs. By 1933, these American Jews, most of Eastern European descent, enjoyed enough economic strength and political power to challenge their patrician co-religionists. They crafted a communal identity that cheered ethnic distinctiveness at a time when most had left the Orthodox fold of their parents and encouraged Jewish Americans to fund their educational and character-building programs as a way to preserve Jewish traditions. The ideas they espoused reflected conflicting definitions of what it meant to be Jewish, what it meant to be an American, and how liberal programs would help define each. While the more established community sought a continuation of its middle-class integrationist policies and did not want to spend their New Deal windfall on preserving Jewish traditions, the immigrants and their children advocated a pluralistic approach to American democracy at a time of growing economic interdependence. Jewish education and character-building advocates translated New Deal liberal programs into vehicles for their own ethnic acculturation. If American Jews could participate on an equal footing with other Americans in the national political process, they reasoned, then they should have equal right to protect their distinctive ethnic culture within the limits of their own communal organizations.[40]

Jewish education advocates urged Federations to fund their local programs. Synagogues, the Jewish community's first line of defense against assimilation, suffered from massive declines in fund-raising and were forced to rely on communal funds for survival. Private Orthodox Jewish schools reeled from their own financial losses and appealed, mostly in vain, for more support. In the early months and years of the Great Depression, Jewish educational programs suffered from severe cutbacks. A study on the effects of the Depression on Jewish philanthropy revealed that by the latter half of 1930, Federations showed a "precedence of relief over all other needs." While a 1931 report to the National Conference of Jewish Social Service noted "no great changes" in Jewish child care agencies, health agencies, community centers, or national agencies, it did acknowledge budget cuts in Jewish education. The executive secretary of the United Jewish Social Agencies in Cincinnati reported in 1932 that the "Federation is under great pressure and temptation to curtail seriously its allotments to educational constituents."[41]

Jewish character-building programs suffered a similar fate. By 1932, one social worker discussing the effects of the Depression on intermediate-sized communities noted, "The swing in the direction of devoting huge sums for relief has . . . made it necessary to eliminate cultural activities, and to reduce personnel and salaries, at a time when the facilities of these character-building and morale-saving units of community life are needed most." Cincinnati's Jewish leadership reported that its work in recreational fields "is being deserted rapidly." "Any appeal for Jewish culture or other communal needs," another social worker warned, "becomes a very difficult matter from an ethical point of view. If it is to be made an appeal in competition with the needs of the hungry, and the starving, and the widows, and the orphans, if it be a question between feeding the needy and giving up communal and cultural values, we are all human enough to give precedence to the feeding of the hungry."[42]

While those supporting relief ostensibly did so out of compassion for needy Jews, proponents of education programs charged that the "false opposition of bread versus education" was merely a guise for assimilationist Jews to halt the growing influence of more isolationist and religiously traditional Jews. The Russian-born president of the National Council of Jewish Education looked beyond immediate relief needs and framed the debate in a larger context: "Jewish education finds itself between two opposing antagonisms," he explained. "On the one hand there is the group that is basically assimilationist and regards Jewish education as an attempt to impose an outmoded religion and the belief in a set of myths upon the modern generation. On the other hand," he continued, "the traditional religionists, taking their religion very much in earnest, regard Jewish education as religious education . . . designed to make the young conform to the beliefs and rituals of traditional Judaism."[43]

Albert P. Schoolman, the director of New York's Central Jewish Institute, reminded his colleagues that "no poor parents have come clamoring to Jewish schools that these be closed and that the school funds be given them for relief, that the children's Jewish education be neglected and that bread and clothing be given them instead." As far as Schoolman was concerned, "The first and most compelling challenge that is brought forth out of the very lowest depths of economic misery produced by the depression is the now familiar cry, 'in times of depression, what shall it be, bread or education?'" Schoolman thought it "significant that this apparent dilemma is being posited by those in our community who are physically satiated, but Jewishly, spiritually starved, and not by those whose body may be hungry but whose Jewish spirit has not been emaciated."[44]

Schoolman's veiled reference to German-American Jews points out the inherent contradiction in the bread-versus-education debate. Jewish leaders could not argue for increased government aid on the one hand and then criticize Jewish education for taking needed relief funds on the other. "Does the cry of bread vs. education really present mutually exclusive alternatives?" Schoolman asked. It did not. Accommodationist Jews sought to capitalize on the Depression to achieve ulterior motives: the more rapid Americanization of the traditional community. Schoolman was accurate when he concluded that "the policy of bread at the expense of education will yield no bread but will consume education."[45]

When New Deal agencies assumed financial responsibility for Jewish clients, proponents of both Jewish education and Jewish character-building programs steered the private dollars they raised to fund their respective activities. By 1935, these programs were, according to the executive director of the New York City Federation, "large and growing fields" and commanded over 60 percent of local Federation expenditures. According to Harry Lurie, the shift from relief to character building constituted "a shift of emphasis from the submerged part of the community to the community as a whole and from merely physical and economic need to cultural and spiritual satisfaction." In 1937, Jewish educators reported "marked improvements" in school classrooms, buildings, and decorations. Harry Glucksman, in his presidential address to the National Conference of Jewish Social Welfare, stressed that "our profession is now in a strategic position to enlarge its field of influence by becoming directly involved in the total pattern of Jewish group life." Another social worker noted approvingly that "the emphasis in Jewish life has changed from preoccupation with the unfortunate minority of maladjusted, the poor and helpless to an almost general concern with problems affecting Jews in all walks of life that arise from the fact that they are Jews." The American Jewish Year Book's 1936–37 *Year in Review* credited the economic recovery for revitalizing Jewish education. In Los Angeles, over half of the 1938 United Jewish Welfare Fund (UJWF) budget for local activities paid for Jewish education and cultural and social programs. In 1939, those figures jumped even more.[46]

Advocates of character-building programs also found a way to translate high Jewish unemployment into a means for greater ethnic expression. At the nadir of the Great Depression, thousands of young Jews lost their jobs and could not find new work. Jewish social workers feared that their disillusionment with the American economic system might lead them to criminal behavior. Directors of local JCCs and YMHA clubs responded with low-cost recreational programming meant to get Jewish youth off the street and into more productive activities. While the youth joined the centers and clubs for social reasons, Jewish educators celebrated their return to organized Jewish life. In 1937 alone, New York City's JCCs claimed a monthly attendance rate of almost half a million, while figures doubled between 1929 and 1937 at fifteen New York and Brooklyn area centers. While German-American Jews would continue to play a leading role in communal affairs, the growing strength of the Eastern European majority signaled an end to the German-American monopoly in organized Jewish life.[47]

The New Deal taught American Jews the wisdom of accommodation and compromise. "The most important lesson coming out of this emergency," the president of Cleveland's Jewish social service bureau concluded in an understated 1931 prediction of the decade to come, "is the fact that an unwilling Jewish community has come to realize that relief work can, under proper safeguards, be financed by public funds without detriment to the Jewish families thus served." Not only did the Jewish community learn the plausibility of government aid, it fashioned the Roosevelt reform program into a powerful advocate of American ethnic life. Jews led the call for federal government action, reflecting a faith in civil administration almost unknown in modern Jewish history. Jewish leaders spearheaded the drive for local community control of New Deal moneys. Jewish social service clients enjoyed a higher standard of care and assurances that their particular religious needs would be addressed. The Roosevelt administration enjoyed the support of ethnic Americans as well as state and municipal political leaders who shared the Jews' drive for greater fiscal and operational autonomy. And, in a consensus era when most Americans lined up behind the Democratic party and its standard-bearer, the organized Jewish community showed how a common economic problem could be fashioned into a vehicle for greater multicultural expression.[48]

The marriage between American Jews and Roosevelt's New Deal proved beneficial for both. The administration inherited the legacy and expertise of an American Jewish community committed to New Deal–style politics, while the Jewish community enjoyed unprecedented access to the corridors of power and official confirmation that they had "made it" as Americans. By the end of the New Deal, the American Jewish community moved from archaic slogans of Jewish self-sufficiency to the realization that its economic future was tied to that of the nation at large. No one would ask again about Stuyvesant. As one New York Federation leader concluded, "The ghost of Peter Stuyvesant has been permanently laid."[49]

CHAPTER TWO

Fighting Hitler: Cultural Pluralism and American Jewish Life, 1933–1941

IN A FEBRUARY 1915 *Nation* article, Horace Kallen, a German-born American Jew, offered a reinterpretation of the traditional "melting pot" model of immigrant acculturation. Instead of viewing the United States as a monolithic soup reducing a variety of ethnic backgrounds into a common stock, Kallen employed another metaphor, the symphony orchestra, in a bid to celebrate diversity. "American civilization," he wrote in reference to the millions of immigrants arriving on the eastern seaboard, "may come to mean the perfection of the cooperative harmonies of 'European civilization.' " Under Kallen's model, each minority group lent its own unique sound to a powerful and harmonious crescendo. "As in an orchestra," he explained, "every type of instrument has its specific timbre and tonality.... So in society, each ethnic group may be the natural instrument." Respect for ethnic difference would forge, in Kallen's words, "a multiplicity in a unity, an orchestration of mankind." Kallen's ideas helped establish "cultural pluralism" as the best alternative to the "melting pot" assimilation model.[1]

At the time, few Americans shared Kallen's views. Scientific racism reached its zenith in the 1920s as a series of restriction acts ended immigration from Asia and instituted strict national origins quotas against southern and eastern Europeans. Some cultural anthropologists posited pseudo-scientific theories tying intelligence to race and ethnic origin, while more and more Americans read the xenophobic works of Madison Grant and William Z. Ripley. The Ku Klux Klan reemerged and enjoyed great success in Indiana and Colorado, where it elected scores of candidates to statewide office and prevented the Democratic party from including an anti-KKK statement on its national platform. The Klan's "100% Americanism" motto translated into a rejection of both cultural pluralism, since it encouraged immigrant ethnicity, and assimilation, since it demanded the integration of non–Anglo-Saxon traits in native-born American stock. Nativists, whether in the KKK or the halls of Congress, harbored strong anti-Semitic feelings. The Anglo-Saxon nation they dreamed of creating did not include Jews.[2]

During the New Deal, American Jews of Eastern European origin looked to the liberal policies of the federal government to strengthen their community's educational programming. They found friends in Washington willing to link the economic recovery of the nation to a pluralist model of American democracy. Kallen's "symphony orchestra," embraced by a benevolent government, acted as a defense against bigotry and a powerful tool to help ensure Jewish inclusion in American life. Contrary to the optimism their German-American co-religionists held for universalist liberalism, the Eastern European Jews' old-world experience taught them the limits of the European enlightenment. For most of the more recent arrivals, liberalism not only permitted but demanded ethnic differentiation: a diverse society that was built upon the sacred principle of tolerance offered the best defense against totalitarianism. In a truly liberal society, they argued, all people would be free to express their particular traditions, and government would use its authority to protect the civil rights of minorities. Nativism threatened to undo impressive social advances achieved by second-generation American Jews, who responded by embracing liberalism and the Democratic party. As Jewish leaders learned in the New Deal, liberalism offered the promise of inclusion: while many political conservatives sought to limit American Jewish expression, most liberals backed Kallen's call for intergroup understanding.

In the 1930s, the strength of FDR and the Democratic party slowed the nativists' exclusionary campaign. Overseas, though, the social conditions for Jews proved far more severe. In 1933, Adolf Hitler began a twelve-year campaign to translate his pseudo-scientific theories of racial supremacy into reality. His Nazi government persecuted Jews, gypsies, the physically handicapped, homosexuals, and a variety of other non-Aryan peoples. What began with laws limiting Jewish mobility degenerated into plans for the mass-murder of all Jews in Europe.

American Jews responded to the Nazi threat by translating their New Deal campaign for pluralist expression to Europe. Activist Jewish leaders pressed for special recognition of the anti-Jewish nature of Hitler's discrimination, demanded that the U.S. government take action to ameliorate Jewish suffering in Europe, and proved willing to advocate public protests in defense of their cause. They hoped to offer European Jews the same civil protections enjoyed by American Jews, and they seized on German political intolerance to justify a new model of American adaptation that encouraged difference and protected Jewish interests. German-American Jews still favored a more accommodationist approach. They strove for consensus, rejected activist political strategies that distinguished Jews from other citizens, and funded programs intent on homogenizing their more traditional co-religionists. Both leaderships equated Hitler's policies with everything un-American and linked Jewish values to the spirit of unqualified Americanism. As they did on the domestic front, American Jews embraced a liberal political view that justified their opposition to Hitler while it safeguarded the interests of Jews at home.

While most American Jews and the scholars analyzing them have positioned Zangwill and Kallen at opposite ends of the liberal spectrum, their positions proved remarkably similar. Eastern European American Jews shared much more in common with their German-American co-religionists than they assumed. Those who argued for "melting pot" assimilation still took pains to distinguish themselves as Jews, and those who embraced cultural pluralism demanded a large measure of accommodation. Kallen's metaphorical symphony could not play unless all the musicians agreed on the most basic of issues: the piece to be played, the appropriate key, and the timing necessary to coordinate dozens of instruments. In similar fashion, cultural pluralism could never prove viable in American society unless its citizens agreed on their own set of basic rules: that tolerance of difference is a virtue worthy of praise, that all must respect the rule of law, and that a variety of ethnic traditions could strengthen the national character.[3]

Eastern European American Jews embraced minority rights because they accepted the basic tenets of American political culture. Even as they fought with their accommodationist co-religionists for control of organized Jewish life, the new arrivals and their children assimilated American values. The classical liberal protections of the United States Constitution limited the power of the federal government and promised American Jews that they would never face the state-sponsored anti-Semitism typical of Czarist Russia. The American tradition of private philanthropy meant that Jews could establish their own communal structure without fear of retribution from the state.

German-American Jews sought accommodation but still enjoyed the benefits of a pluralist democracy. They affiliated with religious institutions, reached out to their immigrant co-religionists, and expressed their Jewish identities because the universally accepted principle of church-state separation encouraged it. Their American Judaism respected difference just as it strove for an improbable consensus. As Alexander Dushkin, the executive director of New York's Jewish Education Committee, explained, "Perhaps both the term 'cultural pluralism' and the term 'assimilation' need radical reinterpretation." The New York Jewish leader thought that instead of having to opt for one of two opposing models of acculturation, Americans look to the center, to develop a theory "of 'cultural unity with variations'; cultural supplementation rather than cultural pluralism; unity with variations rather than assimilation or non-assimilation." While American Jews fought with one another over political strategy, their embrace of liberalism proved more a source of unity than dissension.[4]

THE RISE OF HITLER

Hitler's reign of terror in Europe forever changed the ways American Jews helped their own, reignited an internal debate over competing approaches to pluralist democracy, and forged a new definition of what it meant to be an ethnic American. While the American Jewish community faced overseas crises before, none generated the intense debate provoked by events in Germany. In 1881 and 1882, a wave of pogroms numbering into the hundreds threatened Jewish communities across Eastern Europe and garnered an immediate response from American Jewish leaders. The Bolshevik Revolution of 1917 inspired grave concern when Communist revolutionaries persecuted Russian Jews. In 1929, Arab rioting in Palestine inspired the Joint Distribution Committee (JDC) to allocate emergency relief funds. In each case, the American Jewish leadership, headed by the wealthy German-American elite, responded with little internal conflict or discord. Protection of one's co-religionists at home or abroad did not conflict with their accommodationist beliefs: Jews could be expected to defend religious freedom since it was consistent with American democratic ideals. The AJC and JDC subscribed to a late nineteenth-century model of ethnic behavior which demanded that overseas Jews receive aid from a private, volunteer, religious organization that followed traditional American social welfare precepts.[5]

The new generation of American Jewish leaders rejected the AJC's version of accommodationism. The rise of Nazism in Europe, they pointed out, elevated the debate over cultural pluralism to new and more ominous heights. Modern Germany had prided itself on its cultural sophistication. Jews fought in that nation's army during World War I and considered themselves full-blooded citizens. When Hitler began his systematic assault against German Jews, activist Jews in the United States questioned the viability of universalism. Assimilation, they argued, inevitably led to persecution. Cultural pluralism emerged as the only viable political system for ethnic minorities.

While the AJC placed the campaign to aid Europe's Jews in the same context as earlier overseas missions, AJCongress leaders staged massive public demonstrations, lobbied government officials, embraced several forms of American Zionism, and attempted to organize Jews on both a national and international basis. By the time the United States entered the war against Hitler in 1941, the AJC's approach to Jewish self-defense had failed. The old guard, which held the reigns of communal power for generations, handed over much of its influence to a younger generation of ethnic activists who demanded that Jews adopt a more public defense of their own needs. A new generation of American Jewish leaders applauded cultural difference, expanded the limits of acceptable ethnic expression, and redefined what it meant to be a patriotic American. Jews once again offered a liberal definition of "Americanism" that valued difference and understood the strengths of a multicultural approach to modern democracy.

In their struggle against Nazi aggression, Jewish leaders reprised the political strategies they employed during the New Deal. Liberalism, as defined by organizations such as the American Jewish Congress, encouraged Jewish social workers to build a strong educational infrastructure. That emphasis on cultural·pluralism translated to overseas relief work when Jewish leaders demanded that European Jews enjoy the same civic security as American Jews. Once again, Jews demonstrated how liberalism eased Jewish acculturation by encouraging ethnic differentiation. While labor historians have concluded that ethnic institutions "at best . . . served as liaisons to mainstream alternatives" and the 1930s signaled "a disintegrating ethnic culture," Jewish leaders showed how liberalism could protect ethnic minorities from discrimination, heighten ethnic consciousness, and challenge the Depression-era consensus.[6]

Yet even as the new Jewish leadership criticized the AJC for refusing to chart a more activist course, they too learned a painful lesson. While the American Jewish Congress mounted an aggressive anti-Hitler campaign, it still needed to demonstrate its accommodationist roots. It faced the difficult challenge of packaging its political program in language acceptable to the dominant culture. The very force that fueled a soft-spoken approach, a desire to secure Jewish rights without compromising the community's standing as loyal Americans, also erected strict barriers to activist Jewish leaders. Any actions deemed contrary to U.S. interests risked alienation and charges of un-Americanism. AJCongress leaders followed by adopting strategies that portrayed the Nazis as un-American and their own efforts as consistent with the best democratic ideals. While their approach helped garner needed support from Christian America, it also weakened American Jewish efforts to combat the particular anti-Jewish nature of Nazi discrimination. As much as American Jews tried to convince themselves otherwise, the interests of the Jewish minority did not always mesh with those of the larger majority.

THE ANTI-GERMAN BOYCOTT

American Jewish leaders faced their first overseas test within months of Hitler's rise to power. On April 1, 1933, the Nazi government backed a one-day boycott of Jewish businesses and within a week limited almost all civil service positions to "Aryans." Jewish physicians and lawyers faced severe restrictions on their ability to practice, and Jewish academics faced dismissal as the German government began a campaign of terror against Jews in Nazi-controlled Europe. The JDC reacted swiftly, transferring its world headquarters overseas and devoting even larger sums of money to relief. Repeating a familiar refrain, JDC leaders justified their overseas aid by appealing to the religious rights of a persecuted minority. By emphasizing protections guaranteed to all citizens by the Constitution, the JDC dodged questions of double loyalty and placed defense of European Jews squarely within the American liberal tradition of religious freedom.[7]

For most in the Jewish community, though, the JDC/AJC position translated into a dangerous defense of the status quo. Rabbi Stephen S. Wise emerged as the leading spokesperson for more activist Jews. Despite his affiliation with the Reform movement and his Central European ancestry, Wise took the lead against the old guard and offered a powerful critique of their version of liberal accommodationism. From his position as president of the American Jewish Congress, Wise demanded a tough public campaign against Hitler. In early March, the AJCongress broke with the AJC leadership and called for a March 28 protest meeting at Madison Square Garden in New York City. Two days later, rally backers journeyed to Washington to enlist President Roosevelt's support.[8]

The AJC and B'nai B'rith blasted Wise and the American Jewish Congress for what they considered a counterproductive effort. In a bid to redirect American Jewish Congress strategy along more conventional lines, they pointed to opposition by both the State Department and leaders of Germany's Jewish community. "The agitation, instead of calming," one critic believed, "continued to grow in intensity and we were told that unless some good news were forthcoming . . . , the speeches and resolutions [at the rally] might prove exceedingly embarrassing." Joseph Proskauer agreed. Born in Mobile, Alabama, in 1877 to German immigrant parents, Proskauer spent almost his entire life as a New York attorney and later as a judge. A classical Reform Jew, Proskauer took over leadership of the American Jewish Committee in 1943, guided his organization through its most turbulent time, and eventually helped secure U.S. government support for the new state of Israel. In 1933, though, he considered marches and mass meetings "unintelligent" and feared that they would have an adverse effect on German Jews.[9]

Tensions mounted when leaders of the American Jewish War Veterans decided to counter Hitler's anti-Jewish boycott with one of their own. Rejecting the accommodationism of the AJC, JDC, and B'nai B'rith, they appealed to a sympathetic Jewish polity frustrated with Hitler's anti-Semitism. In May, the American League for the Defense of Jewish Rights, created for the expressed purpose of expanding the boycott, joined the cause. The league's vice-president, Abba Hillel Silver of Cleveland, used the boycott to launch a fifteen year anti-Nazi crusade. Silver, a Reform rabbi who would become a fiery proponent of American Zionism and nemesis of the old guard German-Jewish elite, argued that Hitler "must be attacked with political weapons and the strongest political weapon, when all others fail, is the economic boycott." Within months, the Jewish Labor Committee, representing 500,000 Jewish workers in the United States, approved the boycott as well.[10]

Initially, Rabbi Wise opposed the boycott, hoping that his strategy of combining public protests with quiet negotiations would achieve the same result. Boycotts, he believed, should be "the last and not the first weapon of the Jewish people." On August 14, though, Wise and the American Jewish Congress reversed their position and, much to the delight of organizers, joined the economic boycott of Germany. The Congress Boycott Council planned protests such as the October 1934 international trade fair in New York City, which advertised that "no merchandise or products shall be exhibited which have been created, manufactured, fabricated in or imported from Germany." After two years of deteriorating overseas conditions, the non-Zionist Jewish Labor Committee's boycott committee added its support and the sponsoring organizations merged to form the Joint Boycott Council in 1936.[11]

The AJC and B'nai B'rith opposed the boycott from the outset. AJC President Morris Waldman considered the boycott "futile [and] possibly dangerous" as well as "a threat to the United States" and suggested that the AJC seek the intervention of President Roosevelt. Proskauer feared that boycott activities, like rallies and marches, would further imperil German Jews. He advocated a policy of "quiet diplomacy" and enjoyed the support of several German-Jewish leaders who feared the American action would prompt a wave of Nazi retaliation. With the United States suffering from a trade imbalance with Germany, the AJC also worried that a boycott would exacerbate the economic depression.[12]

In synagogues, some rabbis took positions even more extreme than the AJC's. "A publicly declared boycott by the Jews," a rabbi from Glencoe, Illinois, explained in December 1933, "means the excuse for the furthering of Nazi propaganda here." Twenty million German Americans lived in the United States, and fears of an anti-Jewish backlash ran high. "Blood," he stated, "is thicker than water [and] can quickly be brought to hatred of the Jew." The religious leader, in a response typical of both the AJC and B'nai B'rith, feared that a boycott would "encourage the purchase of German goods because their fatherland was attacked by Jews." He believed that Jews should only boycott "as American citizens affiliated with some movement in which all American citizens join. They cannot with safety to their own position come out as Jews in declaration of war against anyone. They are not too well loved in our own country or any other country."[13]

Boycott organizers, even as they advocated a more aggressive public posture, shared many of the AJC and B'nai B'rith's concerns. With domestic anti-Semitism on the rise, activist leaders also feared a backlash. They needed to articulate an acceptable justification for their boycott, demonstrate how it strengthened the nation, and show how it would protect the interests of Jews in both Germany and the United States.

In its infancy, the American Jewish Congress's boycott committee limited its efforts to Jewish-owned businesses in the United States. An appeal to secular America, it believed, could not be successful until the movement secured the support of its own community. When officials of the boycott committee heard of Jewish businesses violating the embargo, they issued terse letters demanding compliance.

In one such exchange, Emanuel H. Licht, a representative of the American Jewish Congress's boycott committee, received word in June 1934 that two Jews, Abraham Gottinger and Simon Gansl, hired German boats for their shipping business. Licht ordered an associate to draft a letter telling "them that they should be ashamed of themselves that it should even be necessary for the Congress to point this out to them." Later, boycott leaders answered their critics' charges by mounting a public campaign to illustrate how their action helped American businesses. If Americans refrained from purchasing German goods, the American Jewish Congress boycott committee explained in a February 1935 report, then they could be encouraged to buy domestic goods instead. Organizers encouraged the buying public to boycott only those German products that were also produced by American manufacturers.[14]

International trade agreements with Germany complicated the boycott effort as well. The U.S. government maintained economic treaties with Germany: breaking them exposed the Jewish community to charges of wrecking American economic opportunity in the midst of the nation's worst depression. To resolve the issue, the chairman of the American Jewish Congress boycott committee, Joseph Tenenbaum, asked attorney Jacob Chaitkin to determine if the U.S. government had any legal precedent for ending trade with Germany. On July 24, 1934, Chaitkin returned with news that the Jewish community could use the U.S. government's 1911 abrogation of the 1832 Russo-American treaty to call for the end of trade with Germany. Chaitkin quoted then–Secretary of State Philander C. Knox, who, on December 16, 1911, argued that humanitarian concerns could be used as a basis for ending trade with Russia. Applied to Hitler's Germany, Chaitkin believed that an appeal could be made for a German boycott for "purely humanitarian reasons" and "on grounds of commercial discrimination against Americans by the German government."[15]

The American Jewish boycott of German goods continued until the United States entered the war in 1941. While it succeeded in raising the consciousness of many Americans, it failed to translate anti-Hitler sentiment into support for cultural pluralism in the United States. Americans tended to respect the Jewish impulse for self-defense but wanted it expressed in universalist terms. Jews found they could articulate their particular ethnic and religious needs only if they couched them in language acceptable to the dominant political culture. The boycott's victories owed more to its accommodationist appeal to non-Jewish Americans than it did to ethnic activism. While organizers broke much of the AJC's communal hold, they never fully departed from the old guard's all-American liberal strategy.

THE WAR IN EUROPE

On March 13, 1938, the Nazis invaded Austria without firing a shot: the *Anschluss*. Two weeks later, they annexed their southern neighbor, bringing 190,000 Jews under Nazi occupation. Within six months, the Germans annexed the Sudetenland. By March 1939 they took the rest of Czechoslovakia and in September 1939 invaded Poland; the following year they occupied most of France. After each conquest, the local Jewish populations suffered from the anti-Jewish edicts imposed by the German regime. In a succession of laws enforceable throughout the Reich, Jews were prohibited from practicing medicine, forced to register their property with authorities, and required to add distinguishable names, such as "Israel" or "Sarah." Mass arrests, deportations, and pogroms followed. In the most notable attack, "Kristallnacht," "the Night of Broken Glass," the Nazis destroyed hundreds of synagogues, looted 7,500 Jewish shops, and killed some ninety Jews in the night of November 9–10, 1938. "At no time during recent centuries," the president of San Francisco's Federation of Jewish Charities observed, "has the status of the Jew throughout the world been so imperiled." Finally, on September 1, 1939, Hitler invaded Poland. When Great Britain and France entered the conflict two days later, World War II had begun.[16]

Hitler's totalitarian ambitions inspired a political backlash in the United States. Domestic anti-Semitism eased in the late 1930s. A Gallup poll revealed that most Americans would join in a movement to stop buying German-made goods, and the German-American Bund lost much of its membership. Montana congressman Jacob Thorkelson incurred the wrath of Jewish groups when he published anti-Semitic literature in the *Congressional Record*; he was subsequently defeated in his bid for reelection. There was, reported the AJC in 1940, an "intensification of feeling in the United States against pro-Nazi and anti-democratic manifestations," forcing anti-Semitic groups to alter their strategies.[17]

The renewed threat to European Jews pressed Jewish communal leaders into even more intensive relief work. Across the nation, Jewish organizations solicited donations for European missions. In 1931, before Hitler's seizure of power, American Jews devoted little attention and few resources to their European brethren: a group of twelve American Jewish welfare funds devoted a paltry 1.3 percent of its expenditures to overseas aid. In the mid-1930s, these same organizations were devoting half of their budgets to European aid. By 1935, the AJC failed to mention the economic depression in its "year in review," choosing instead to focus on deteriorating conditions for European Jews. As demands intensified, Jewish leaders redoubled their fund-raising for European relief. The National Refugee Service (NRS), the Jewish community's immigrant absorption agency, reported that over 15,000 individuals sought assistance during the first two weeks of the European war, while total refugee immigration to the United States more than doubled between 1938 and 1939. The JDC's share of overseas aid jumped and income for other Jewish relief organizations in Europe recorded similar gains. By 1939, Jewish welfare agencies had proliferated, spending the lion's share of their efforts (and nearly three-quarters of their funds) on overseas relief.[18]

Increased overseas aid did not temper the Jewish community's infighting. While Harry Lurie reported in 1938 that "campaigns for European relief have cut across group lines and have enlisted the widest type of participation," Jewish leaders continued to question one another's liberal strategy. The AJC, JDC, and most Reform movement organizations did not alter their earlier accommodationist approach, arguing that Congress's declaration of neutrality reaffirmed the wisdom of their universalist thinking. As they did in the debate over New Deal–inspired Jewish educational programs and the boycott of German goods, they demanded that Jewish leaders illustrate the ways their liberal social reform efforts mirrored the national political mood. A precipitous rise in domestic anti-Semitism, fueled by demagogues such as Father Charles Coughlin, punctuated their position: Jews could succeed best in a society committed to treating all its citizens the same. Attempts by activist leaders to separate Jewish political goals from those of the society at large would only invite further hostility and marginalization.[19]

One JDC leader warned, "Ethnic or religious groups have no standing as such and it is to endanger that democratic process when groups, either religious or ethnic, attempt to create power through such groupings." He disagreed with a growing number of Jews who saw no conflict between American democracy and a rigorous defense of Jewish minority interests. "It seems to me," the JDC official explained, "that Jews in America must accept the ideals of democracy as the basis of their philosophies or alterna-

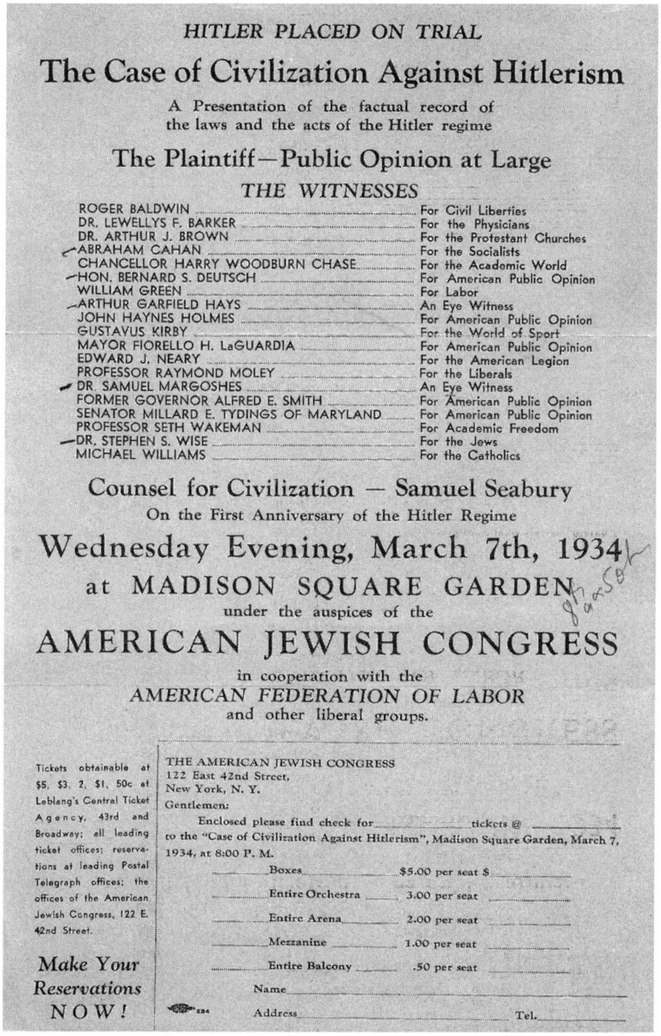

HITLER PLACED ON TRIAL

The Case of Civilization Against Hitlerism

A Presentation of the factual record of the laws and the acts of the Hitler regime

The Plaintiff—Public Opinion at Large

THE WITNESSES

ROGER BALDWIN	For Civil Liberties
DR. LEWELLYS F. BARKER	For the Physicians
DR. ARTHUR J. BROWN	For the Protestant Churches
ABRAHAM CAHAN	For the Socialists
CHANCELLOR HARRY WOODBURN CHASE	For the Academic World
HON. BERNARD S. DEUTSCH	For American Public Opinion
WILLIAM GREEN	For Labor
ARTHUR GARFIELD HAYS	An Eye Witness
JOHN HAYNES HOLMES	For American Public Opinion
GUSTAVUS KIRBY	For the World of Sport
MAYOR FIORELLO H. LaGUARDIA	For American Public Opinion
EDWARD J. NEARY	For the American Legion
PROFESSOR RAYMOND MOLEY	For the Liberals
DR. SAMUEL MARGOSHES	An Eye Witness
FORMER GOVERNOR ALFRED E. SMITH	For American Public Opinion
SENATOR MILLARD E. TYDINGS OF MARYLAND	For American Public Opinion
PROFESSOR SETH WAKEMAN	For Academic Freedom
DR. STEPHEN S. WISE	For the Jews
MICHAEL WILLIAMS	For the Catholics

Counsel for Civilization — Samuel Seabury

On the First Anniversary of the Hitler Regime

Wednesday Evening, March 7th, 1934

at MADISON SQUARE GARDEN

under the auspices of the

AMERICAN JEWISH CONGRESS

in cooperation with the

AMERICAN FEDERATION OF LABOR

and other liberal groups.

Tickets obtainable at $5, $3, 2, $1, 50c at Leblang's Central Ticket Agency, 43rd and Broadway; all leading ticket offices; reservations at leading Postal Telegraph offices; the offices of the American Jewish Congress, 122 E. 42nd Street.

Make Your Reservations NOW!

THE AMERICAN JEWISH CONGRESS
122 East 42nd Street,
New York, N. Y.
Gentlemen:

Enclosed please find check for ______ tickets @ ______ to the "Case of Civilization Against Hitlerism", Madison Square Garden, March 7, 1934, at 8:00 P. M.

______	Boxes ______	$5.00 per seat	$ ______
______	Entire Orchestra ______	3.00 per seat	______
______	Entire Arena ______	2.00 per seat	______
______	Mezzanine ______	1.00 per seat	______
______	Entire Balcony ______	.50 per seat	______

Name ______

Address ______ Tel. ______

Figure 3. The American Jewish Congress sponsors a trial against Hitler, March 7, 1934. (American Jewish Congress records, 1916–present, I-77, box 197 of 201, folder "Conference and Events," American Jewish Historical Society, Waltham, Mass.)

tively, if they do not accept it, they must not pretend that their own conceptions do not interfere with the processes of American life."[20]

He traced his definition of liberalism to the European enlightenment: "I feel that we in America are not alone the product of Jewish culture but are even more strongly the product of the gifts of liberalism to the modern world. All that we are we owe to those who, perhaps touched by a Messianic vision, saw the world as a place in which human beings had attained dignity and freedom, the fits of emancipation, political rights, and equal opportunity. The free gifts to the present from a liberal past are much more responsible for what we are than our Jewish heritage."[21]

In September 1939, a member of the JDC executive committee advised his organization to "lean over backward to avoid engaging in any relief work that might infringe the country's laws." He feared "frightfully difficult problems" if any of his relief agency's work could be construed as unlawful. "We must not and cannot let our desire to help suffering cause us to lose our moorings," he pleaded; "our rule must be 'when in doubt, ask the State Department.'" When contributors to the JDC got word of public opinion polls critical of American Jews, they advised the directors of the overseas relief aid society to stress Jewish loyalty to America and warned that an all-out campaign for European relief aid might compromise the safety of Jews at home.[22]

The Reform movement, which counted most of the AJC and JDC leadership among is members, echoed the univeralist liberal stand. A former head of the Reform movement's rabbinic authority, the Central Conference of American Rabbis, appealed to the American conscience by describing what he called the "irrepressible conflict between Americanism and Hitlerism." For him, the conflict between the two ways of life could be no better illustrated than "by comparing the object of the Nazis' mystic worship—Hitler—with the man who is enshrined in all American hearts to whom we too cling with a sort of mystic devotion as the embodiment of all that America means—Abraham Lincoln." The Reform rabbi boasted of an American tradition which recognized the Jewish community's desire to maintain its distinctive culture. He appealed to his followers to help realize a Jewish mandate for society, one centered on forging Americans "of various origins into one patriotic consciousness." If Americans of differing religions, races, and national origins could co-exist, he concluded, America could realize its mission as "the symbol and prophecy of what some day will exist all over the world."[23]

The AJC continued to stress the inherent symmetry between its Jewish overseas relief programs and American patriotic ideals. It universalized the Nazi threat in a bid to capture the support of non-Jewish America. One official declared that "the American Jew refuses and will refuse to include in his Jewish thought or conduct anything which can, by any reasonable interpretation, make his Americanism suspect. That is why I say that there is no place in American life for a separate nationalism or civilization. That is why I also say that there is room for free religious and cultural expression by all minority groups within the larger unity of American life." "What was originally taken as primarily and perhaps exclusively anti-Semitic in character," the AJC noted in its 1939–40 annual report, "was finally realized to be a threat to all forces of decency and humanity. Protestants and Catholics as well as Jews; labor and capital; in short, to all those who believe in democracy."[24]

The AJC approach earned a ringing endorsement from New York senator James Mead, who in February 1939 took to the airwaves of Washington radio station WOZ in support of Jewish overseas relief work. "It is typical Americanism," he explained, "to oppose oppression and persecution wherever it may exist." Senator Mead considered Jewish self-defense activities illustrious of both "good citizenship" and "an American virtue that rises far above racial and religious differences." He concluded that the Jewish community had followed the dictates of both religious and political conscience and that its defense of its European co-religionists amounted to nothing less than "democracy in action." Mead's beliefs lent credence to the AJC's contention that "the American public had been shocked into a full understanding of what the Nazi dictatorship means."[25]

The American Jewish Congress responded to Hitler's expansionism by stepping up its overseas political efforts. It continued to mount public campaigns, searched for ways to unite the entire organized Jewish community behind its strategy, and eventually embraced Zionism as the best long-term hope for European Jewish refugees. The American Jewish Congress, joined by sympathetic individuals from B'nai B'rith and the Reform movement, rejected the accommodationist interpretation of American liberalism. In a biting criticism of the AJC, a professor of education and history at the Jewish Theological Seminary (JTS) condemned "those who feel it is un-American to be Jewish in anything but religion." His conception of American pluralism demanded that, as he put it, "real Americanism" mean "not only a toleration of religious difference, but a toleration of ethnic and national differences as well." "Real Americanism," he concluded, "should mean an *active encouragement* of cultural diversity."[26]

Yet even as the JTS professor and others advocated direct action protests, they still based their appeals on a basic symmetry between Judaism and Americanism. Like the AJC, they argued that American citizenship demanded protection of one's co-religionists, vocal condemnation of evil in the world, and commitment to human rights. At a May 1940 conference of Jewish social workers, one communal leader expressed his belief that "in the United States, thank God, we have a right to demand and to live up to the conception of equal rights, equal responsibilities and equal citizenship. We are not a minority group. Such a doctrine is inconsistent with American principles." At the same gathering, another delegate argued that the United States "welcomes and encourages cultural supplementation, provided it is intended to enrich the character and broaden the outlook of American citizens," while the director of the refugee service committee in Los Angeles and former editor of the *Jewish Social Service Quarterly* asked his fellow Jewish social workers to keep in mind the "extremely close identification between the preservation of Judaism and Hebraism and the protection and preservation of democracy." He pointed to the U.S. Constitution as he warned his colleagues not to "forget that our government has been based upon the principles repeatedly emphasized in the Bible and in the writings of our prophets."[27]

Mordechai Kaplan, the Lithuanian-born Conservative rabbi who spent his career developing an American style of Judaism he called "Reconstructionism," suggested that Jews search out a new strategy drawing on "the best in the American tradition and promise" and rooted "in the future of unlimited democracy with which the Jewish future has come to be definitely bound up." Kaplan's desire to marry Jewish expression with American tradition stemmed from ideas he set forth in his controversial 1934 book *Judaism as a Civilization*. Kaplan's monumental work described Judaism as an evolving civilization, vulnerable to American cultural influences and dependent upon creative change for its very survival. While Kaplan faced rebuke from many of his colleagues, his idea of creating dynamic social institutions anticipated the rise of Jewish Community Centers, the *havurah* movement, and the campuslike architecture of many modern synagogues.[28]

On the question of how American Jews might justify their overseas relief program, Kaplan took issue with the AJC position. "Jews cannot serve the cause of genuine democracy better," Kaplan wrote in 1940, "than by surviving as a group and rendering their group activities creative of cultural, ethical, and spiritual values." He appealed to his friends and colleagues not to "preach the moral defeatism implied in the statement that the day of small nations is over, and that cultural minorities have no longer any place in the framework of national life. To accept this trend as inevitable," he concluded with sullen reference to the war raging in Europe, "is to resign oneself to the final destruction of democracy and the universal triumph of Nazism."[29]

Kaplan's ominous reference to Hitler illustrated the seriousness of the Nazi threat and underscored the need for a unified American Jewish response. Despite their considerable ideological differences, the leaderships of the AJC and American Jewish Congress, as well as other organizations, had set aside their disagreements in the past. At the Paris peace conference ending World War I, Louis Marshall, arguably the most visible and respected American Jewish leader of his generation, led a delegation dominated by Eastern European Americans from the American Jewish Congress. When Arabs rioted in Palestine in 1929, both the AJC and the American Jewish Congress joined in condemnation. While the anti-German boycott failed to gain support from many of the old-guard accommodationists, it still represented a concerted effort by organized American Jewry to set aside its differences in the name of defeating Hitler.[30]

THE GENERAL JEWISH COUNCIL

In June 1938, four major national Jewish organizations tried again. Zionists and anti-Zionists, German and Eastern European, secular and religious came together in Pittsburgh at the behest of local businessman Edgar J. Kaufmann to form a General Jewish Council (GJC) dedicated to launching a coordinated plan for European relief and rescue. While the council dissolved after just one year, its story offers a vivid snapshot of the conflicting ideologies, strategies, and goals of American Jewry at a critical time in its history.[31]

At the first organizing meeting, representatives of the American Jewish Committee, American Jewish Congress, B'nai B'rith, and Jewish Labor Committee worked to establish a set of goals and objectives consistent with the varying perspectives of the member bodies. The AJC, still the financial center of organized Jewish life, demanded concessions from the American Jewish Congress before it would agree to participate. AJC leaders feared that the American Jewish Congress would use the council to advance its own activist political goals in the United States and Zionist ideals in Palestine. They worried, for example, that once the council was established, the American Jewish Congress might try to ally with its international counterpart, the World Jewish Congress. The notion of a specifically Jewish political body, especially one working to promote a Jewish national homeland, antagonized the AJC. At a time when members of the AJC worked tirelessly to show the inherent compatibility between its American citizenship and Jewish religious affiliation, it feared that the American Jewish Congress and JLC would use the council for their own ideological purposes.

After some discussion, the AJC prevailed. The GJC welcomed the holdouts with hopes that the alliance would help the council emerge as a powerful national voice for American Jewry. In deference to its newest member, the GJC agreed not to "make decisions on matters that involve racial, national, religious, and economic philosophies; nor shall any decision be made that impairs the organizational autonomy of the affiliated bodies." It adopted a three-part program for European relief: the council focused its activities on the plight of Europe's Jewish community, created committees to monitor changing events and suggest courses of action, and bound the decisions of the council on all member bodies. While internal squabbles would continue between the AJC and the other organizations, creation of the GJC marked an important union between accommodationist Jews and their more activist critics.[32]

Following their initial meeting, the new GJC leadership sent a telegram to their respective memberships praising "the culmination of Pittsburgh's efforts to bring together representatives from four national Jewish organizations dealing with defense rights of Jews." They expressed their "earnest hopes and emphatic desire that meeting today will establish promptly a coordinated effort and plan for effectively meeting needs of world Jewry." Five days later, Henry Monsky, president of B'nai B'rith, sent a telegram to Kaufmann informing him that "the executive committee of the B'nai B'rith has given its approval of the plan of coordination proposed at the Pittsburgh conference on June thirteenth." The Jewish Labor Committee agreed "that during this emergency the determination of policies relating to the defense of Jewish rights in the United States and abroad, and the prosecution of all measures for the defense of Jewish rights in the United States and abroad, shall be by and through the GJC, the constituent organizations of the GJC to act, in all their defense activities, solely as agents of the GJC and under its direction and supervision." In August, Kaufmann issued a press release in New York announcing the formation of a General Jewish Council "to coordinate the activities of these organizations 'that bear specifically on the safeguarding of the equal rights of Jews.' "[33]

As its constituent groups had done prior to the council's formation, the GJC labored to equate its mission with American democratic principles. "We American Jews, as part of the American community," the council explained in one of its early statements, "find solace and satisfaction in the unanimity of American opinion voicing indignation against the oppressors and sympathy for the oppressed. . . . As part of the American people, we express our profound satisfaction at the public statements and acts of the President of the United States, speaking the mind and conscience of the entire nation." The GJC reaffirmed "comfort in the fact that the world has come to realize that Nazism has become a menace to all democracy and civilization itself."[34]

In a bid to further universalize the Hitler threat, the umbrella organization publicized Nazi threats against Protestants and Catholics: "The Jew has not been the only victim of Nazi brutality, as Cardinal Innitzer and Cardinal Faulhaber could testify from their shattered homes, and Pastor Niemoeller from his lonely cell at Oranienberg." The GJC called for assistance, "not only for Jews, but for all religious and political refugees from the Reich." It argued that German Jews should be saved, "not primarily because they are Jews but because they are human beings and as such represent a fraction of the dignity and of the potentialities of humanity itself." Stressing that it did "not wish any plan be adopted for the rescue of German Jews which would be detrimental to the interests of the United States or of any democratic nation," the GJC reminded its audience to "always remember that by saving the innocent Christian and Jewish objects of persecution we shall fortify and safeguard the very elements of modern civilization—democracy, liberty, and justice."[35]

Overseas, the GJC strengthened its commitment to relief. It streamlined its operations, relying on the expertise of established organizations. In Europe, for example, the GJC deferred to the established and experienced Joint Distribution Committee for implementation of its relief program. At home, the GJC went to work monitoring the related work of state and local legislatures. In a memo to its branches, the council asked that each affiliate "advise this office promptly whether or not the legislature of your State is in session, and if not, when it will convene and how often it convenes, that you forward to this office promptly copies of all bills introduced into the legislature of your state which, in your opinion, affect Jews or other minorities either adversely or beneficially, together with reasons for your opinion, and your advice as to whether the passage of such bills should be opposed or encouraged." It petitioned its constituents to keep apprised of legislation "which in your judgment ought to be enacted in order to safeguard the political status, the economic opportunities and the civil liberties of minorities," and it coordinated local and national protests, the largest of which was a January 1940 Madison Square Garden vigil to dramatize the persecution of Jews in Nazi Poland.[36]

When the U.S. Congress considered a variety of bills to help European refugees, the GJC followed the proceedings and briefed its constituent members on the legislative process. In each case, GJC organizations supported increased aid and justified their support on patriotic grounds. The American Jewish Congress, responding to several European overseas aid bills under debate on the House floor, petitioned "its membership to do everything possible to register with their representatives in Washington their support of these measures, which are in the tradition of the American people, and which would render assistance in a fashion which no private agency can hope to render under present day conditions." The American Jewish Committee, Jewish Labor Committee, Anti-Defamation League, and the American Jewish Congress gave their consent to the proposed laws after receiving assurances "that the relief would be administered on a non-sectarian basis and under American supervision." The NRS, concerned that European Jewish émigrés might provoke anti-Semitism, urged its field workers to encourage the rapid assimilation of the new arrivals by discouraging them from settling in heavily Jewish urban areas. "To avoid the natural tendency of the refugees to huddle together in New York, the port of entry, to associate only with émigré friends, to continue speaking and thinking in a foreign language, to dream of the past rather than build for the future, let us send the refugee out, on a carefully planned program, into the smaller cities and towns throughout the United States, where he will soon think of himself as American."[37]

THE RISE OF AMERICAN ZIONISM

In 1939, the leaderships of the American Jewish Congress, Jewish Labor Committee, and B'nai B'rith pushed the council to consider a Jewish national homeland as one option for Europe's oppressed Jews. The American Jewish Committee balked. Its historic position on Zionism had been clear: it did not support the creation of an independent national homeland for Jews in Palestine. Its German-American Jewish leadership traced its liberal roots back to the European enlightenment and Judaism's Reform movement. Emancipation, it believed, freed Jews from the provincialism of Jewish nationalism just as it welcomed their contributions as equal citizens in the larger non-Jewish society. When German Jews immigrated to the United States, they placed their new homeland at the center of world Jewish life and feared that nationalist sentiments might compromise their reputation as loyal and devoted citizens. Civil protections meant that American Jews could express their religious identities without fear of state-sponsored anti-Semitism. AJC members naturally objected when American Jewish Congress delegates offered a resolution calling for Jewish settlement in Palestine. The AJC demanded that the council remain "non-political" and committed to the limited objective of providing overseas aid, not a Jewish national homeland. Only after the American Jewish Committee threatened to leave the GJC over the Zionist issue did the other three bodies agree to capitulate.

The issue of American Zionism proved complex and divided Jews into a number of divergent and sometimes competing camps. While the AJC and Reform positions dominated American Jewish organizational life throughout the late nineteenth and early twentieth centuries, many American Jews, including several of the most important German-American leaders of the AJC, offered a defense of American Zionism. Louis Brandeis, the celebrated jurist, emerged as one of the nation's most important Zionist leaders when he argued that American citizenship permitted a Zionist orientation. He discounted the dual loyalty threat by postulating what became known as "the Brandeisian synthesis," a belief that American Jews could embrace the Zionist cause since it did not conflict with the ideals of American democracy. Brandeis, according to one of his biographers, concluded that "the Zionists were attempting to build in Palestine the type of free and democratic society that Jefferson and the Founding Fathers had envisioned for the United States." "Zionism," he wrote, "embodied the traditional Jewish and American ideals of democracy and justice."[38]

Brandeis stopped short of endorsing the style of political Zionism proposed by Theodore Herzl at the First Zionist Congress in 1897. While Herzl and other Zionist leaders around the world came to their ideological positions as a result of their pessimistic assessments of Jewish life outside of Palestine, Brandeis and most American Zionists gloried in their U.S. citizenship. American Zionists did not seek a Jewish state because they yearned to emigrate. *Aliyah*, Jewish resettlement in Palestine, never gained much strength among American Jews. Most American Zionists, looking for a safe Jewish haven in the wake of the restrictive Immigration Act of 1924, based their appeals on humanitarian grounds.

By the time the GJC met in 1938, American Zionism stood in the midst of a great transformation. Most in the AJC, B'nai B'rith, and the Reform movement still clung to the Pittsburgh Platform's rejection of Jewish nationalism. But events in Europe focused renewed attention on the need for a long-term solution for European Jews. In a debate that began with the rise of Hitler in 1933 and did not end until after the creation of the State of Israel in 1948, American Jewish leaders reached an ideological compromise. Non-Zionists would embrace the idea of a Jewish homeland, but only as a practical solution to the refugee crisis and not as part of any cultural or political movement. They never contemplated emigration from the United States and framed American Zionism in philanthropic terms. The dilution of Jewish nationalism, while infuriating to Zionist ideologues, proved a critical compromise for American Jews. By stripping Zionism of much of its nationalism, anti-accommodationist Jewish leaders succeeded in bridging the gap with the AJC, B'nai B'rith, and much of the Reform movement. The creation of an American style of philanthropic Zionism illustrated the accommodationist roots of even the most ardent Jewish nationalists.[39]

When the AJC and the Anti-Defamation League embarked on a fundraising campaign outside the jurisdiction of the GJC, the American Jewish Congress quit the council in protest, bringing an end to another short-lived attempt at American Jewish unity. The GJC's inability to reach consensus on the Zionism question illustrated a wrenching paradox in organized Jewish life: American Jews could never realize their full potential to save their European co-religionists as long as they let domestic concerns qualify their overseas efforts. Yet it was that symmetry with the larger political culture that strengthened their appeals. In the early years of the European war, the Jewish community's quandary simply diluted its overseas relief strength. Once the United States entered the conflict and later heard of Hitler's "Final Solution," it foreshadowed even more disturbing events to come. The American Jewish community could not place European Jewish lives ahead of American soldiers. Despite their best efforts, American Jews could not wage an unqualified battle for Jewish relief and rescue.

CHAPTER THREE

"The Hope of Democracy and Peace": American Jews and the Campaign for Intergroup Dialogue, 1933–1941

DURING THE 1930s, the Great Depression loomed as the greatest threat to American life, and the New Deal dominated national, state, and even local politics. American Jews, however, could not view the political landscape through such myopic lenses. They needed to keep one eye focused on the New Deal, the other keyed on events overseas, and still retain enough peripheral vision to prepare for an uncertain political future at home. For despite efforts to expose Hitler's racist attitudes as undemocratic and un-American, anti-Jewish attitudes remained strong throughout the United States. Isolationist organizations such as America First blamed Jews for Roosevelt's pro-British policies, and anti-Semitic demagogue Father Charles Coughlin broadcast his message of hate to millions of radio listeners. When the Gallup organization conducted a survey in April 1938, it discovered that more than half the American public believed the persecution of European Jewry was either partly or entirely the Jews' fault. The next month, 20 percent of the respondents said they wanted to "drive Jews out of the United States" in order to check their power, while almost one quarter sought Jewish exclusion from government.[1]

Once again, American Jews looked to liberal politics to pacify the threats against their community. In their call for interfaith dialogue, Jewish leaders demonstrated how a universalist approach to American liberal democracy legitimated religious difference. The organized Jewish community abandoned the particularist tenor of its anti-Hitler campaign in favor of an all-American appeal rooted in the optimistic belief that communication, education, and the rule of law could remedy intergroup conflict. Civil equality remained the Jews' primary goal, and any strategy that antagonized mainstream America compromised Jewish security. While representatives of the AJC and AJCongress differed in their approaches to the New Deal and the rise of Hitler in Europe, all agreed that the fight against domestic discrimination necessitated a univeralist perspective.

When the government proposed bills to limit American civil liberties, Jewish leaders brought their liberal defense of First Amendment rights to the halls of Congress. Both the AJC and AJCongress joined in a campaign to protect free speech and took the unusual step of defending the rights of Nazi sympathizers in the United States. Jewish leaders adopted this position because they believed the freedom to promote anti-Semitism helped guarantee a nation friendly to the interests of Jews. Opposition to hate literature legislation established American Jews as stalwart liberal defenders of individual rights, just as it illustrated their optimistic appraisal of American society: they perceived a far greater threat to their status as American Jews from violations of civil protections than they did from fears of domestic anti-Semitism. Liberalism offered Jews the best hope for civil equality even as it handed their detractors a powerful legal weapon. While some considered this Jewish defense strategy naive, it demonstrated the depth of Jewish optimism in the legal process, the fascination Jews held for liberal consensus, and showed in the most provocative way how citizens could fashion the government into a champion of minority rights.

American Jews invoked patriotic appeals to counter isolationist charges of Jewish war-mongering as well. As Hitler amassed the military machine he would eventually use to launch World War II, American Jews feared an anti-Semitic backlash. Caught between their desire to defeat Hitler and American neutrality, Jewish leaders offered a universalist defense of their overseas campaign. They feared that American isolationism would only encourage continued Nazi aggression. Jews maintained their faith in a liberal internationalism that valued diversity and sought to extend American-style democratic freedom overseas.

Jewish leaders highlighted the similarities between Judaism and Christianity because they wanted the nation to perceive Jews as honest, loyal, and patriotic citizens. They contrasted the restrictive rhetoric of domestic anti-Semites to the liberal ideal of equality for all peoples. Instead of demanding the right to express ethnic difference, Jewish leaders wanted to show that religious minorities were really the same. When confronted with demagogues intent on proving Jewish exceptionalism, communal leaders saw little choice but to argue for accommodationism and promote interreligious consensus. The American Jewish response to domestic anti-Semitism in the 1930s showed the malleability of Jewish liberalism: strategy proved less important than goal.[2]

THE INTERFAITH DIALOGUE MOVEMENT

Jewish leaders from across the ideological spectrum participated in an interfaith movement that celebrated the similarities between Protestants, Catholics, and Jews. While dialogues between various Jewish and Christian religious denominations had existed for years, the 1930s efforts were the first to focus on ameliorating threats associated with Nazi designs on Europe. Jewish leaders took advantage of popular antipathy toward Hitler in order to strengthen interfaith relations. On the local as well as national level, through conferences and seminars, on the pages of the nation's newspapers and on the airwaves, the communal leaders launched an all-out assault on intolerance. By 1945, 123 different national organizations worked for better intergroup relations. Jewish academics emerged as leaders in new social scientific research. Rabbis, communal workers, and other Jewish professionals reached out to their Christian counterparts, shaping important new understandings about the nature of American citizenship and helping continue their own successful acculturation to American life.[3]

By forging personal relationships with their Christian counterparts, Jewish leaders defined their political activities within a larger religious context. The nation's Christian majority would grow to understand Jewish political behavior in the same way as their own: an attempt to infuse American culture with the importance of religious voluntarism. If Christians understood the necessity of protecting minority rights, then Jews could more easily make America home. If the American people desired a free, open, and democratic nation, Jewish leaders urged, then they would have to begin by working toward tolerance and pluralism in their relations with one another. Democracy flourished in an atmosphere of openness and understanding. Fascism, on the other hand, fed on hatred and prejudice. As one Jewish leader urged, "The hope of democracy and peace lies in the ability of democracy to eradicate these prejudices and intolerances. We must come not only to respect differences, but to be proud of them, to regard them as our greatest asset, and thus to provide for the complete expression of the individual capacity and personality in the interest of the common welfare."[4]

Jewish religious organizations led the interfaith movement, invoking common Judeo-Christian bonds as a basis for discussion, communication, and union. Just as their secular co-religionists would, the various religious movements within American Judaism stressed the contribution of interfaith dialogue to American democracy. The Synagogue Council of America joined with Protestant and Catholic umbrella organizations to draft peace proposals which would serve as an "expression of the religious spirit." At its 1940 annual convention, the Reform movement's Union of American Hebrew Congregations chose "The Synagogue and the American Way" as its theme. Conference activities stressed "the vital role of the synagogue in maintaining and promoting the principles of democracy and religious freedom," and in April 1940, it initiated a national campaign for the advancement of religion and democracy.[5]

The Conservative movement's United Synagogue organization focused on the symmetry between Judaism and American democracy at its May 1940 annual convention, where it organized a "national committee for defense of the American way." Other Conservative institutions followed in kind. When the largest Conservative synagogue in Cleveland celebrated its ninetieth anniversary later that month, the keynote address focused on "the vital importance of the religious factor in democracy."[6]

The leadership assumed by the Reform and Conservative branches should not be surprising. Jewish denominations enjoyed great influence on the American religious scene. As Will Herberg would later observe, the small American Jewish minority, representing just 3 percent of the national population, enjoyed claim to a full third (and some might argue half) of American religious life. As an equal partner in the Protestant-Catholic-Jew triad, Reform and Conservative rabbis could approach their Christian colleagues with instant credibility and establish a common interfaith movement. The decision to take advantage of the United States' status as a "Judeo-Christian" nation afforded the Jewish minority legitimacy and religious power.[7]

Conservative and especially Reform Jews struggled to reconcile ancient traditions with the modern world. They wanted to join the larger non-Jewish majority and believed that their brand of Judaism could accommodate a more integrated lifestyle. Reform Jews eschewed the dietary laws of kashrut, violated the traditional laws of Sabbath observance, and relied on principles of ethical monotheism to govern their lives. Conservative Judaism, while committed to ritual observance, still searched for its own compromise between forces of stability and change. The interfaith movement accelerated each denomination's acculturation: a public alliance with other religious groups testified to their inclusion in the American mainstream.

The absence of the Orthodox movement is equally telling. The Orthodox, still a sizable minority in the 1930s, subscribed to a tradition-based lifestyle that placed a much smaller premium on outside interaction. Their American acculturation remained within the traditional Jewish world and did not demand an aggressive public posture. Interfaith understanding, while certainly important on a humanitarian level, did not carry the same political or social importance it did for Reform and Conservative Jews. The Orthodox did not make a concerted effort to join the interfaith movement because social integration did not prove as important to them as it did to less traditional Jews.[8]

Secular Jewish organizations joined the interfaith dialogue movement for the same reasons as their Reform and Conservative counterparts: it promoted ideals consistent with the acculturation of their respective constituents. For the American Jewish Committee, interfaith dialogue promised to ameliorate anti-Semitism, and it advanced strategies consistent with the German-American Jewish perspective: emphasis on dialogue rather than political action, consensus instead of conflict, and integration over isolation. The AJC, which always expressed a preference for dialogue over confrontation, lauded interfaith efforts as the most effective means of advancing Jewish priorities. The American Jewish Congress, which favored more confrontational strategies in the campaign against Nazism, understood that cultivating better communication with non-Jews mandated a softer approach. The Anti-Defamation League of B'nai B'rith thought ignorance caused intergroup hostility; they favored intergroup dialogue as an effective educational antidote.

The American Jewish Committee's annual "year in review" report on the status of national and international Jewry devoted more and more space to the new movement. In 1939, the American Jewish Committee noted a "significant expansion of goodwill activity and interfaith movements which have as their objective the preservation of democracy as a bulwark against intolerance and discrimination." It reminded its readers that if they were to win "the present struggle for justice and decency" in the world, they would have to rely upon "individual liberty, equality and civil rights, freedom of conscience, mutual respect and understanding." The AJC concluded with praise for "Christian and Jew alike, Catholic and Protestant, liberal and conservative, men and women of all races, creeds and shades of opinion" who, through their dialogue efforts, had rallied "to the common standards of religion and democracy."[9]

In 1940, the AJC reported that the Jewish community had expanded "efforts aimed at strengthening the buttresses of democracy through the promotion of wholesome attitudes towards and between various racial and religious groups in the country. Incitation to inter-group hatred," it explained in reference to the domestic anti-Semitic campaigns of the era, "had been and was being used as a means of disrupting national unity." By May of that year, the director of the Conference of Christian and Jews acknowledged that events overseas had helped unify Protestants, Catholics, and Jews in the United States. Hatred against Jews in the United States declined, he noted, due to the efforts of Christian clergy "to uproot anti-Semitism from Christian heritage. Anti-Semitism," he argued, "is an instrument in the Trojan Horse tactics used to divide a people so they may be rendered impotent in the face of attack." The following year, another prominent Protestant noted that "the last two years have been marked by a very definite increase of sympathetic interest on the part of all the three major religious groups in America in the fortunes and in the activities of the other two."[10]

The interfaith dialogue movement provided Jewish leaders with ecumenical support at a critical time. With U.S. involvement in the European war looming as a real possibility in 1941, a group of 150 clergy from the three major American religious groups formed an Interfaith Committee for Aid to the Democracies. The group urged President Roosevelt to gather delegates from democratic nations around the world in order "to set forth our common purpose to achieve a world in which free men can live." Jewish religious denominations stepped up their interfaith appeals with a prayer session at the U.S. Capitol and a renewed interest in National Brotherhood Week. In February, leaders from the Jewish, Catholic, and Protestant communities joined together to form the United Service Organization for National Defense, an agency created to provide for the religious and social needs of those serving in the armed forces. The National Conference of Christians and Jews, organized in 1928 by the Federal Council of Churches "to counter the anti-Semitic and anti-Catholic agitation of that era," sponsored seminars, goodwill pilgrimages, and roundtable discussions, and enjoyed a renaissance in the late 1930s and early 1940s.[11]

RADIO AND THE CAMPAIGN AGAINST DOMESTIC ANTI-SEMITISM

Consensus, more than ever, remained the key ingredient to successful acculturation of American Jews in the 1930s. American Jews needed their Christian friends to defend them against domestic anti-Semites. When one of the most powerful anti-Semites of the era, Father Charles Coughlin, emerged from the ranks of the Roman Catholic clergy, Jewish interfaith leaders asked for support from the Christian world. Coughlin, a priest from Detroit, earned a national reputation for Jew-baiting. In both his newspaper, *Social Justice*, and on his weekly radio show, the Catholic demagogue propagated age-old anti-Semitic canards against Jews. At his most extreme, Coughlin in a November 1938 radio address blamed Jews for Russian Communism, defended the Germans for the destruction they wreaked on Jewish businesses during *Kristallnacht*, and parroted the Nazi contention that Jews caused Germany's postwar troubles.[12]

Coughlin enjoyed tremendous popularity. By December 1938, forty-five radio stations carried his bigoted messages. Three and a half million Americans counted themselves as regular listeners while fifteen million more listened on at least one occasion. Public opinion pollsters noted that more than one third of the American public backed Coughlin's ideas, and up to 350,000 subscribed to *Social Justice*. In the northeast and midwest, home to more than 85 percent of the American Jewish community, escalating anti-Semitism combined with physical threats to unsettle the nerves of millions of American Jews.[13]

Jewish organizations took their universalist anti-discrimination campaign to the American people by harnessing the most powerful tool in American politics: radio. Pioneered as a political tool by FDR in his famous "fireside chats," Coughlin's and Roosevelt's success as radio politicians reflected the widespread influence of the new technology. A 1939 survey of over 1,000 middle-school boys in Chicago revealed that "less than one percent of them had no radios in their homes." *Fortune* magazine announced in 1938 that listening to the radio proved more popular than watching movies or reading. A survey published the following year concluded that "seventy percent of Americans relied on radio as their prime source of news, fifty-eight percent thinking that it was more accurate than the press."[14]

Jewish leaders used the new medium to spread their message of interfaith understanding and pressed radio station managers, celebrities, and political leaders to sponsor their public interest segments. These appeals projected an "all-American" image of Jews to millions of people who otherwise lacked personal relationships with Jewish people. For the first time in American Jewish politics, thousands and sometimes millions of people could be reached instantaneously. Radio offered Jewish leaders an unprecedented opportunity to highlight the symmetry between Judaism and American values.

While Lizabeth Cohen has noted that "radio, probably more than any other medium, contributed to an increasingly universal working-class experience," Jewish organizations demonstrated how the new technology could be harnessed to educate Americans on the need for intergroup understanding. Jewish leaders wanted to take advantage of the conclusions drawn by social scientists Robert and Helen Lynd in their 1935 study of Muncie, Indiana. Radio, they argued, brought "people away from localism" and afforded "them direct access to the more popular stereotypes in the national life." Aware of the immense popularity and power of the airwaves, Jewish leaders created radio departments within many of their organizations.[15]

Among the major Jewish organizations, the American Jewish Committee, American Jewish Congress, B'nai B'rith, and Jewish Labor Committee emerged as leaders in exploiting the new medium. The AJC took the most aggressive stance, favoring radio as an ideal means to advance its commitment to consensus building. It opened a radio department in 1937, employing two full-time professionals and two secretaries. The AJC used its national organization as a radio clearinghouse for communities across the country. Its experts produced and distributed radio kits comprised of scripts, records, and transcripts to stations throughout the country. As the packets arrived, local radio personnel would either play the records on the air or enlist their own people to read from AJC-prepared scripts.[16]

Program titles, designed to promote goodwill among Americans, included the "All-Americans program" for children; a mother-daughter chat about current events called "The Warren Family"; a fifteen-minute script on current religious events, "Religious News Service," for Christians and Jews; "The Bookman," a review of books; "Let Freedom Ring," for civil liberties; "Milestones of Freedom," about great liberal documents in history; and a program on democratic ideals and racial equality called "The American Way." Records included the Jewish War Veterans' production "America Answers," as well as talks by Catholic priests on why Jews were persecuted.[17]

While the American Jewish Congress lacked a specific radio department, it did broadcast special appeals as necessary. The JLC used radio to promote "the aims of the pro-democracy and pro-human rights organizations which the JLC in association with the AJC helps support and direct." The labor organization boasted that it produced foreign language radio programs in addition to its regular English schedule. The ADL produced its own show in New York City and offered its resources and expertise on Jewish affairs to interested radio stations coast to coast. It produced shows in German and Italian for broadcast on some 360 independent local radio stations and wrote speeches "emphasizing the democratic principles in American history, which is made available on recordings to several hundred radio stations throughout the country." Its dramatization of United States history, entitled "Lest We Forget," focused on the importance of "democratic principles and the fight in this country for civil and religious liberties."[18]

Jewish organizations created radio departments, forging the mass media tool they needed to protect their civic standing. While they ostensibly used the airwaves to promote a pluralist approach to American democracy, their campaign demonstrated, once again, the community's consensus orientation. American Jews demanded inclusion and were willing to accommodate their particularist ethnic agenda to larger currents in American political culture. What was good for the Jews, they argued, was good for America.

CIVIL LIBERTARIANISM AND THE NAZI THREAT

In that frame of mind, Jewish leaders should have been ecstatic in 1940 when the United States Congress, fearful that the Axis powers would encourage their compatriots to launch totalitarian political campaigns in the United States, proposed legislation to limit the proliferation of Nazi propaganda. HR 5454, better known as the Flaherty bill, promised the government increased discretionary power to limit pro-Nazi threats. The bill sought to prosecute any individual who "advises, advocates, or teaches... principles of government based upon opposition to or discrimination against individuals of any religious creed." The Flaherty bill would have outlawed association with any discriminatory organization or publication of any discriminatory literature and afforded the Justice Department power to strip citizenship rights from offending naturalized Americans.[19]

Jewish leaders could have viewed efforts to stifle German sympathizers as the ultimate affirmation of Judaism's symmetry with American values. Instead, Jewish organizations criticized them for violating the free speech protections of the U.S. Constitution. While the Flaherty bill aimed to prevent Nazi-like organizations from taking root in the United States, its ambiguous phrasing and harsh penalties alarmed the leadership of American Jewish organizations. Enforcement measures far outweighed the seriousness of the crimes, and the Jewish community feared that with such a precedent, violations of other civil liberties could easily get out of control. A nation that failed to protect extreme speech could not be trusted to defend the rights of Jews or other minorities. Jewish leaders argued that if American society were to remain open, pluralistic, and tolerant, even the rights of unpopular people and ideas deserved protection.

The General Jewish Council, created primarily to address overseas relief, objected to the Flaherty bill on the grounds that "the measure would impose the drastic penalty of cancellation of citizenship and deportation for the mere expression of political beliefs" and thought it "irrelevant that those beliefs do not call for the use of force or any unlawful means." The council considered the bill "a flagrant violation of the right of free speech" and stressed that "no matter how abhorrent are the political views condemned, the Bill of Rights guarantees freedom to advocate them as long as they do not constitute incitements to illegal action." The Jewish umbrella organization pointed out that since, according to contemporary immigration law, "deportation may be ordered for aliens—not naturalized citizens—who advocate, or belong to organizations that advocate, the overthrow of the government by force or violence," the Flaherty bill "affords no precedent for the drastic inquisition into the political views of citizens."[20]

The council offered a similar critique for Joint Resolution 228, which barred "all papers, pamphlets, magazines, periodicals, books, pictures, and writings of any kind" that were "intended to cause racial or religious hatred or bigotry or intolerance or to directly or indirectly incite to racial or religious hatred or bigotry or intolerance." The bill directed the U.S. Postal Service "not to deliver any such matter" and provided for a fine of $5,000, a one-year jail term, or both to "whoever knowingly deposited such matter in the mails."[21]

The GJC feared that "under this measure, the truth or falsity of a writing would be irrelevant." Council leaders indicated that vagueness in the bill's wording "might very possibly be held to bar from the mails writings which are true, which proceed from the most innocent motives, and which, in the public interest, men should be free to distribute." The council objected to JR 228 on the grounds that it did not consider motive when assessing the guilt of an accused individual. "The measure," the GJC argued, "would make irrelevant the motive of the person who deposited the proscribed writing in the mail. So long as he knew its contents," the council explained, "he would be subject to a severe criminal penalty, even if he were entirely free of any purpose to cause racial or religious hatred." To exemplify its point, the GJC noted that the proposed law would "make it a crime for anyone to mail a copy of Mein Kampf, regardless of his motive in doing so."[22]

Instead of these congressional efforts, the council adopted a set of legislative guidelines that aimed to protect the American public from damaging hate literature, while at the same time safeguarding the civil rights of the accused. In a four-point program, it advocated legislation which, unlike the Flaherty bill, would articulate precise definitions for unlawful acts and would set reasonable enforcement criteria. Its proposal limited the authority to institute proceedings to "only responsible public officials." The council wanted to confine prosecutions "to libels upon racial and religious groups," and in order to prevent the bill from being used as a means to squelch political opposition, it stipulated that "no liability should be imposed for the publication of any statement that is true or which is reasonably believed to be true." Finally, it sought to restructure the enforcement statutes to reflect the seriousness of the crime. "Criminal liability," the GJC concluded, "should be imposed only if the defendant acted maliciously, i.e. if he was animated by ill-will against the racial or religious group defamed."[23]

The General Jewish Council offered its own alternatives to the Flaherty bill and JR 228. These bills, reflecting dissatisfaction with the congressional attempts, included provisions that granted the defendant trial by jury, gave the Postmaster General power to prosecute groups for mailing documents that contain group libel, allowed the courts to intervene except in cases where "the court determines that the group libel complained of is true or that there is reasonable ground for believing it to be true," and defined, for the benefit of the accused, all legal terms included in the law.[24]

Council leaders pressed Congress to support bills that could achieve its anti-Hitler goals without compromising civil liberties. It found some satisfaction in HR 5757, the Gillie bill, which required "the name and address of the publisher to be printed on all publications carried in the mails or interstate commerce" and "would make it unlawful to deposit in the mail or introduce into interstate commerce any publication unless the name and address of the publisher is printed thereon." The GJC supported the bill, believing it to be "of some assistance in dealing with anti-Semitic publications that are distributed anonymously or in the name of unknown organizations." The council argued that "its value would lie principally in the fact that it would make it possible to fix responsibility for publications that might be made the basis of either civil or criminal liability" and would also be "useful in discrediting certain documents by revelation of their source."[25]

American Jews continued the fight for the protection of American civil liberties on the local level, where public fears of Nazism on American shores led many communities to adopt alien registration laws. The ordinances, which varied in wording from town to town, established limitations on the rights of both immigrants and naturalized American citizens and advocated various degrees of enforcement. The General Jewish Council, concerned once again that these community measures signaled a dangerous compromise of constitutional authority, mobilized against the threat. "Local registration," it argued, "is plainly unconstitutional" since matters regarding immigration and naturalization belonged to the federal government. When a Pennsylvania Alien Registration Law went before the U.S. Supreme Court for review, council attorneys drafted briefs detailing Jewish opposition to the state's action. The GJC enlisted the assistance of the American Civil Liberties Union and petitioned the U.S. attorney general's office to warn offending communities of their unlawful activity.[26]

Jewish efforts to challenge anti-alien laws on jurisdictional grounds faltered when the U.S. Congress passed the Alien Registration Act. At the same time, President Roosevelt transferred the Immigration and Naturalization Service from the Labor Department to the Justice Department in an attempt to expedite prosecution of illegal immigrants. While the GJC feared some provisions of the federal alien registration law, it preferred the national law to the more restrictive local measures. Given the political climate, the council also realized that opposition would prove fruitless. "Owing to the overwhelming statement of the country in favor of alien registration and the obvious grounds for that sentiment in events abroad," the GJC explained in a 1940 committee on public relations report, it "decided in May that alien registration should not be opposed, but that every effort should be made to see that the bill requiring it should contain all possible safeguards against abuse." The organization took particular care to ensure that enforcement officials understood that "failure to register is not made a ground for deportation and that there is an express provision that all registration records shall be secret and confidential." Representatives of the GJC worked with government officials, especially the Solicitor General, to monitor the Registration Act of 1940.[27]

Members of the GJC followed by producing pamphlets detailing the terms and provisions of the Registration Act and distributing them to local organizations. They also sent memoranda to their constituent organizations summarizing the status of the most important anti-alien bills and advising them what action they thought should be taken. The GJC opposed one bill that would have established detention camps on American soil for immigration law violators and another that would have provided for "the deportation of those advocating any change in the American form of government." When Senator Robert Reynolds, a Democrat from North Carolina, offered an amendment to the LaFollette Industrial Espionage Bill that "would prohibit the employment by any interstate business of aliens to the number of more than 10% of the total number of employees," the GJC objected: "This attempt to deprive aliens of employment represents the most extreme form of anti-alien bias." The council expressed concern that the measure would interfere with refugee assistance and that it would effectively ban aliens from working in businesses with fewer than ten employees.[28]

The GJC offered its strong support for only one measure, the Voorhis registration bill, introduced by California Democratic congressman Jerry Voorhis. It required the registration of just three types of organizations: "those subject to foreign control which engage in political activity; those subject to foreign control which engage in military drill or training; and those which engage in both political activity and military training." Unlike the other registration bills, the Voorhis bill offered a strict definition of what constituted unlawful behavior and stipulated that prosecutors target only those organizations that actively sought the overthrow of the government. Council members rejoiced in the bill's rapid movement through Congress, saddened only because the bill's final draft lacked a prohibition of private military organizations that the GJC advocated.[29]

While the efforts of the General Jewish Council to protect the free-speech rights of Nazi sympathizers established the civil libertarian credentials of the organized Jewish community, it did little to stem a rising tide of domestic anti-Semitism. In 1940, the American Jewish Committee reported, "Anti-Jewish groups at home attempted to take advantage of the war tension to disunite American democratic forces by appeals to racial and religious hatred." A poll in May of that year revealed that 64 percent of the American people considered the defeat of Hitler less important than peace. When the Congress considered ending the European embargo, pro-German groups rallied to prevent what would have been significant American aid to the Allied forces. In 1941, the AJC expressed concern over the influence of Nazi sympathizers on American soil: "Organized anti-Semitism in the United States lost the distinction of being confined to a small group of native pro-fascists and Bundists." The AJC concluded that by the middle of that year, "Nazi-inspired anti-Semitism had become a potent factor in the American political scene."[30]

As late as July 1942, a full seven months after American entry into the war allied the entire nation against Hitler, 44 percent of those polled still believed American Jews possessed too much power and influence. While the AJC explained that it "refrains from publicizing the activities [of anti-Semites] because of the danger of focusing too much attention on problems of anti-Semitism" and preferred to follow what it called an "attitude of dignity rather than defense," Rabbi Stephen S. Wise wondered out loud if a Hitleresque movement could someday dominate American politics. Jewish leaders learned that, contrary to sociological research conducted by their own organizations, intergroup hostility did not grow from ignorance. Neither educational campaigns nor interfaith dialogue nor even a vigorous defense of First Amendment rights addressed the deeper social tensions girding intergroup relations. While liberal political ideology promised Jews equal status with non-Jews, the anti-Semitic subculture thriving in 1930s America proved too difficult a challenge. As the Jewish community learned in its overseas campaign, sometimes a vigorous defense of Jewish interests demanded pluralist strategies: liberal universalist appeals rarely realized their goals in the midst of a hostile nation.[31]

ISOLATIONISM AND "AMERICA FIRST"

In the late 1930s, several right-wing isolationist groups, among them America First, called on the Roosevelt administration to keep American soldiers out of the European war and blamed the Jewish community for risking the lives of U.S. servicemen and women. The well-orchestrated American Jewish campaign to justify anti-German economic and political measures fell on millions of deaf ears and threatened to degenerate into charges of American Jewish conspiracy and sedition. "As the administration took rapid strides towards aligning the United States with the democracies in their fight against the Nazi menace," one AJC official explained, "it became increasingly clear that certain of the isolationists were not above making use of anti-Semitic propaganda in their determination to keep this country on the sidelines."[32]

Formed in 1940 with the support of Father Coughlin and Henry Ford, America First emerged as the most powerful isolationist group and routinely employed anti-Semitic rhetoric in its bid to keep the United States neutral. Charles Lindbergh, the famed aviator and America First's best-known spokesman, embodied all that American Jews feared in the isolationists. In a September 16, 1941, Des Moines speech, delivered just weeks after North Dakota Republican senator Gerald Nye called for a

Senate investigation into allegations that Jewish Hollywood producers used their media clout to develop pro-war films, Lindbergh charged that "the three most important groups which have been pressing this country toward war are the British, the Jewish, and the Roosevelt administration." He claimed that they "planned first to prepare the United States for foreign war under the guise of American defense; second, to involve us in the war, step by step, without our realization; third, to create a series of incidents which would force us into actual conflict."[33]

Lindbergh, like his friend Henry Ford, invoked language from one of the most infamous anti-Semitic documents in Jewish history, *The Protocols of the Elders of Zion*, a Russian forgery purporting to detail a Jewish cabal to control the world through ownership of banks and newspapers. "The greatest danger to this country from the Jews," Lindbergh explained to his Iowa audience, lies "in their large ownership and influence in our motion pictures, our press, our radio, and our government. . . . If any of these groups—the British, the Jewish, the Administration—stops agitating for war . . . , there will be little danger of our involvement." While Lindbergh was certainly correct in his assertion that American Jews, like the Roosevelt administration, favored the Allied over the Axis powers, his anti-Semitic rhetoric baited Americans into Jew-hatred. It compromised the tolerance and pluralism that Jewish leaders worked so hard to create and reduced what was a complicated and multidimensional international political situation into a classic case of Jewish scapegoating.[34]

Isaiah Minkoff of the GJC typified the reaction of the organized Jewish community when he criticized America First for taking advantage of the pervasive isolationist mentality to promote hatred and prejudice. The issue, according to Minkoff, was not the Jewish community's alleged culpability in bringing the United States to war. Instead, Minkoff pointed out how the anti-Semitic tactics of America First actually compromised the very values of democratic freedom that the isolationists sought to protect: "This kind of anti-Semitic propaganda, if permitted to develop and if not perhaps properly counteracted by American democracy, becomes an American issue and the Nazi laboratory in Berlin hopes that these seeds germinated in Germany will take root in the soil of America."[35]

Minkoff considered isolationism a threat to American democracy, "not because it divides the country on the question of peace or war, not because it divides the country on a question of bundles for Britain or help to Russia—but because it combines all of the Fascistic elements into an American movement, because it elevates the movement to a level of respectability, and, because it weaves into the isolation philosophy, the Jewish problem; and no matter how gratuitously the isolationist leaders try to solve this Jewish problem for us, they still are the spokesmen for open anti-Semitism in our country."

For Minkoff and the Jewish community, America First and its allied organizations posed as great a threat to American society as the intolerance of German totalitarianism. "If isolationism does take root and grows," Minkoff concluded, "then it is Hitler who succeeds."[36]

American Jews faced an impossible predicament. Relief for European Jews mandated support of the Allied forces. Yet despite the obvious pro-British inclinations of the Roosevelt administration, Jewish leaders could not rally behind U.S. military intervention. FDR's reluctance to take decisive action against Germany challenged the basic tenet of Jewish politics: the symmetry between American and Jewish interests. The American Jewish community had always voiced its support of FDR, and so when the administration adopted an official policy of neutrality in September 1939, Jewish leaders had little choice but to back the president. While many Jews thought that U.S. intervention loomed as inevitable, they offered nothing except unqualified support for Roosevelt's foreign policy.

Rabbi Wise, who considered "peace through appeasement and surrender to Hitler . . . deeper and fouler than Hell," refused to support American intervention. "My sympathy for England and France," he wrote, "will not move me to action in favor of war." The GJC backed both the president and Congress in their efforts to keep the United States out of war. While it acknowledged that Nazi anti-Semitism made Jewish impartiality in the European conflict impossible, the council still believed that it voiced "the hope of the overwhelming majority of American Jews that our government will succeed in remaining at peace with all nations." The following month, the Jewish labor organization, Workman's Circle, urged America to stay out of war as well. "We must do so not only for our own sake," it explained, "not only because we do not wish to spill the blood of American youth, not only because we are aware of the ultimate fatuity of war, but also, and perhaps even more so, because at least in one great and powerful land the lamps of civilization must not be extinguished." In June 1940, the AJC reported that the Synagogue Council of America had "declared its support of President Roosevelt" while the Reform movement's CCAR "endorsed the national defense policy and acclaimed the determination of the President to keep the nation at peace."[37]

In 1940, Roosevelt inched the nation closer to war by instituting the nation's first peacetime draft and offering economic aid to Britain through the Lend-Lease Act. The presidential edicts smoothed the political waters for Jewish leaders who could now frame their interventionist desires in more favorable terms. In April 1941, the UAHC pledged its "wholehearted support to the government of the United States in defense of our nation and of our American institutions." Two months later, the Jewish

War Veterans reaffirmed its faith "in the fundamental principles of human freedom and human dignity as expressed in the declaration of independence, the Constitution of the United States, and its bill of rights," and declared "as an organization and as individuals that we gladly place our persons and our possessions at the call of the government and the President of the United States in the defense of American democracy." In July, the Workman's Circle split from the Socialist party and offered its support of FDR and the war effort. "We shall all rejoice," it declared, "if America will succeed in keeping out of the bloody struggle. Should America be drawn into war, we pledge our loyalty to the government of America, we pledge ourselves to defend the freedom of America and the freedom of the world with our blood and with our life."[38]

Just eight months after the National Conference of Jewish Social Welfare meeting, Jewish concerns about the isolationists would be rendered moot, following the Japanese attack of Pearl Harbor on December 7, 1941. The next day, President Roosevelt traveled to Capitol Hill and received Congress's near-unanimous declaration of war against the Axis powers. Germany reciprocated with its own declaration of war against the United States two days later. As a result, Americans of all religions and races joined in a common battle to liberate Europe, where Jews faced a horrific future. The order authorizing the mass murder of European Jews had already been in place for nine months, and by the summer of 1941 the implementation of Hitler's "Final Solution" had begun. As Japanese planes swooped down on Pearl Harbor, the first Nazi death camp, Chemno, was already in operation.[39]

For Jewish Americans, U.S. entry into the war eased many apprehensions they had about involving themselves in the rescue of European Jews. "American Jews," the AJC reported with a solemn premonition of events to come, "are realizing that they have been spared for a sacred task—to preserve Judaism and its cultural, social, and moral values, to ransom Jewish captives as much as this can be done, to alleviate the sufferings of their brethren and to prepare themselves against the coming of the day when the way will be open for them to succor and rehabilitate the survivors of the unspeakable disaster which has temporarily prostrated them." In 1941, neither the American Jewish community nor the Allied nations knew how accurate the AJC prediction would be.[40]

CHAPTER FOUR

"Unless That War Be Won, All Else Is Lost": American Jews and the Home Front

IN THE 1945 Academy Award–winning film "The House I Live In," Frank Sinatra happens upon a group of children chasing a Jewish boy. When the popular singer asks them why they are bullying the boy, one of the offenders answers, "We don't like him"; another explains, "We don't like his religion." Sinatra, calm and poised, admonishes the gang: "Religion made no difference except maybe to a Nazi or somebody as stupid." He tells them of his immigrant roots and reminds them that America was built on tolerance and diversity. In battle, Sinatra continues, one's religion never matters, and he cites the cooperative efforts of a particular Presbyterian pilot and his Jewish bombardier to illustrate the point. The preservation of democracy, the famous crooner implies, demands that Americans understand one another.

"The House I Live In" captured the Jewish community's hope for social inclusion after Pearl Harbor. With a common enemy, Jewish leaders believed all Americans could join together in a unified campaign to defeat the Nazis. The United States' declaration of war weakened domestic anti-Semites who had used American neutrality as the focus of their bigoted campaigns. *Look* magazine wrote that Hitler had discredited anti-Semitism; meanwhile the U.S. Senate halted its investigations into Jewish moviemakers. Rabbi Stephen S. Wise reported an increase in Jewish employment and a decrease in on-the-job discrimination: "The acute manpower shortage helped to break down many existing barriers. . . . Unlike mountains, these racist barriers could be moved." News of Nazi persecutions inspired Americans to take an appreciative new look at their enlightened political system. By 1941, many Americans had come to embrace cultural pluralism as the best model for American democracy. After eight years of intensive interfaith dialogue work, American Jewish leaders believed that the struggles of the prewar period would ease with the new national focus.[1]

Jewish interfaith dialogue efforts enjoyed unprecedented growth. Between 1939 and 1942, the AJC awarded over $400,000 in grants to the National Council of Christians and Jews and a host of other intergroup relations organizations. "Internecine conflict," one AJC official reported, "was weakening national defense efforts by confusing issues and aiding the common enemy." After having focused its argument for intergroup understanding on principles of inclusion in the prewar years, the AJC looked forward to the possibility "for us to argue our case, not merely in the language of tolerance, but rather in terms of the one outstanding public interest of the moment, national defense." One Chicago-area rabbi proclaimed in his weekly sermon that on December 7, 1941, "the divided American people became one" as "prejudices against fellow Americans, whether Jews, Catholics, or Protestants, white or colored, were buried." The need for national unity galvanized efforts to draw Americans together. In a time of war, the nation's leaders proclaimed, prejudice and discrimination would only aid the enemy.[2]

The optimistic mood of American Jews in late 1941 should have bolstered their commitment to liberal reform. The Japanese attack on Pearl Harbor and Germany's subsequent declaration of war on the United States achieved in a matter of days what Jewish interfaith leaders had struggled eight years to achieve: a national consensus against Hitler and an appreciation for religious diversity. The interests of the American Jewish minority seemed to match the defense imperatives of the U.S. government. American patriotism, as Frank Sinatra admonished, demanded an end to Nazism. The American Jewish liberal social reform efforts of the 1930s had succeeded in achieving their goal: Jews had entered the American mainstream. In both foreign policy and domestic intergroup relations, communal leaders believed, Americans had come to embrace the Jewish call for pluralism and tolerance.

Unfortunately, Jewish leaders proved mistaken in almost all their wartime analyses. Popular opposition to Hitler did little to stave off domestic anti-Semitism, which took a turn for the worse during the war years. When pollsters asked Americans in 1940 if they heard any criticism or talk against Jews in the last six months, almost half responded in the affirmative. In 1942, that number inched higher and topped out at 64 percent by 1946. In 1945, more than half of those polled believed that American Jews possessed too much power, a steep climb from prewar levels. The war did not, as communal leaders hoped, ease the integration of Jews into the American mainstream.[3]

Liberal social reform slowed during the war years. FDR "retired" his New Deal as the nation refocused on the mobilization effort. Unfounded fears of sedition led to the internment of over 67,000 U.S. citizens of Japanese descent. The federal government exercised expanded powers to limit the civil liberties of "enemy aliens" and others it considered a military threat. Respect for cultural diversity weakened as mass media outlets trumpeted all-American ideals and discouraged cultural pluralism.[4]

While New Deal liberalism proved the political strategy of choice during the 1930s, its usefulness in protecting Jewish interests waned during the war years. American Jewish leaders could not advocate political positions at odds with the war effort, and when the nation turned away from liberal social reform, so too did the Jews. Acculturation to the World War II home front demanded unqualified support of U.S. forces, and American Jews jumped at the opportunity to show their patriotic colors. Jewish leaders trumpeted the disproportionate number of GIs recruited from the ranks of their co-religionists. Almost all the national Jewish organizations issued statements declaring their support for FDR and the war effort. In Hollywood, Jewish writers, producers, and directors turned out scores of Allied propaganda films as American Jews placed themselves squarely behind their president and their government.[5]

While leaders from the American Jewish Congress favored an activist approach in the 1930s, they needed to show that they supported the president and that their future was tied to Allied victory. On almost all policy issues the American Jewish Congress joined the AJC in its preference for accommodationism. As Rabbi Stephen S. Wise explained, "The Jewish community's first and sternest task, in common with all other citizens of our beloved country, and with all the citizens of the United Nations, is to win the anti-Fascist war. Unless that war be won," he concluded, "all else is lost." U.S. entry into the war forced Jewish leaders to juggle an impossible array of competing interests and priorities. They could not be expected to divorce their communal agenda from larger currents in American politics: no American ethnic minority lived in such a civic vacuum.[6]

The American Jewish leadership's concern for maintaining the consensus silenced the organized community during one of the most serious violations of civil liberties in U.S. history: the internment of Japanese Americans. Jewish organizations, committed in the 1930s to principles of tolerance and inclusion, failed to protest Executive Order 9066. Jewish leaders, who had labored for nearly a decade to guarantee their own civic equality, nevertheless felt they could not go on record opposed to actions the government deemed critical to national security. A community that boasted of its "willingness to stand up and speak out against bigotry" failed to see the deeper racism hiding beneath the action against Japanese Americans. Jewish leaders who would fight to reclassify German Jewish "enemy aliens" refused to include Japanese American "enemy aliens" in their civil libertarian appeals.[7]

The Jewish communal silence proved typical of almost every liberal constituency during World War II. Widespread fears of a "fifth column" threat cast a dark shadow over internment opponents. If the dominant wartime political culture defined Americans of Japanese descent as potential saboteurs, then neither Jews nor any other ethnic group could lobby for them. Jewish leaders would have been foolish to defend Japanese Americans in the weeks and months following Pearl Harbor. Anti-Japanese sentiment ran so deep that opponents of internment risked charges of treason.

The politics of acculturation once again guided the American Jewish response. Given the organized community's earlier efforts to preserve the civil liberties of Nazi-sympathizers, Jewish leaders should have understood that their own principled commitment to the rule of law demanded a repudiation of internment. Instead, Jews feared that a liberal defense would be interpreted as abetting the enemy. Had Jewish liberalism gained its strength from idealism, tradition, or even the community's long history of persecution, Jewish leaders would have responded to the wartime emergency by protesting the military's action. Security concerns, more than liberal principle, dictated the Jewish community's reform agenda.

Overseas, the deteriorating condition of European Jewry demanded that American Jewish leaders take more decisive action, even when that meant exceeding the limits of acceptable ethnic group expression. Yet the wartime consensus erected imposing barriers between American Jewish welfare agencies and the victims of Nazi oppression. Despite their optimistic hope that the war would bolster their efforts, Jewish leaders learned that American entry often complicated their overseas relief and rescue programs. Jewish organizations could not launch unrestricted campaigns to rescue their European co-religionists from Hitler's death camps because the self-defense interests of the Jewish community did not always match the military needs of the Allied governments. Jewish leaders had little choice but to channel their anti-Hitler campaign through the State Department; anything less opened Jews to charges that their ethnic interests outweighed the need for victory. Liberal appeals for cultural pluralism, tolerance, and minority rights, while effective during the 1930s, threatened to marginalize wartime Jews as more self-interested than patriotic. The best way to save European Jews, many argued, would be to rest any particularist campaigns and join in the national effort to defeat Hitler.[8]

The American Jewish Committee, the Reform movement, and several other non-Zionist groups embraced the wartime consensus with a passion. Their fears, once again, centered on concerns about dual loyalty. For the AJC, the United States remained the center of Jewish life and it fought for overseas relief programs emphasizing the universal rights of Jews. The AJC opposed campaigns that stressed Jewish exceptionalism for fear that they might compromise the continuing integration of American Jews in the United States. As the president of the AJC's executive committee explained, "There is one stark fact that in the concentration of our own problems we must at no moment forget. Our country is at war. That is the paramount fact which must shape all our actions and against which must be measured the validity of any position we take. It imposes upon us the highest duty of taking only such action as will contribute to the well-being of our country." The AJC framed its overseas relief campaigns in all-American terms, notified the State Department in advance of any major policy changes, and refused to endorse the concept of a Jewish national home in Palestine.[9]

The American Jewish Congress and its Zionist allies adopted the most active posture during the war. In a move that alienated their non-Zionist colleagues, they eventually abandoned their earlier preference for overseas material aid in favor of a cultural pluralist political strategy that focused attention on a large-scale, permanent solution: the creation of a Jewish state in Palestine. Goodwill alone, typified by the AJC's earlier interfaith dialogue campaigns, would not save European Jews. Sovereignty, they hoped, would. The AJCongress acknowledged the unique legal status of European Jews and insisted that the Allied powers guarantee their protection, reversing a long-standing informal policy that forbade Jews from lobbying as an autonomous political group. Led by the Reform rabbis Abba Hillel Silver and Stephen Wise, American Zionists believed that their Christian compatriots would understand the gravity of the European situation and support a Jewish state as the most viable long-term remedy for Jewish refugees from Nazi-ravaged Europe.[10]

By war's end, the national Jewish organizations reached an ideological compromise that addressed non-Zionists' dual loyalty fears, Zionist demands for a Jewish state, and the political imperatives of home-front America. Advocates of a national home in Palestine agreed to soften their ideological stand and base their appeals on the humanitarian needs of Jewish refugees. Non-Zionist leaders, while careful to distance themselves from any nationalist sentiment, backed Jewish independence on grounds that it was the only viable plan for settling Jewish war refugees. While the rapprochement bolstered the Zionist position, it signaled a decisive victory for the liberal accommodationism of the non-Zionists. The demands of American Jewish acculturation shaped the political face of American Zionism more than the particularist needs of European and Palestinian Jewry.[11]

World War II taught Jewish leaders that their interests were not always served by liberal politics. The Jewish communal abandonment of their prewar social reform appeals once again points to the political importance of the acculturation process. The continued safety of American Jews demanded that they join the consensus, and Jewish leaders obliged. They moderated their views on almost every political issue, including those of greatest concern to their community. While American Jews enjoyed civic rewards from liberal campaigns in the 1930s, the wartime political culture proved less benevolent.

AMERICAN JEWISH REACTION TO PEARL HARBOR

In the days and weeks following the Japanese attack on Pearl Harbor, the Jewish community offered unqualified support for President Roosevelt and the Allies. Internal debates over accommodationism and cultural pluralism all but disappeared as American Jews leaped at the opportunity to demonstrate their love of the United States and their disdain for Germany. In its 1942 year-end review, the AJC reported, "Synagogal and rabbinical bodies immediately apprised the President of the United States of their unstinted support and of their confidence in ultimate victory." Jewish fund-raising organizations launched new appeals, working on behalf of the Red Cross, the USO, and other wartime philanthropies. Young American Jews answered the call to arms by volunteering as civil defense workers or heading to their local enlistment centers. By 1945, an estimated 500,000 Jews, or roughly 9 percent of U.S. uniformed personnel, had joined either the Army, Navy, Coast Guard, or Marines. Synagogues offered leaves of absence to their rabbis so they could enlist in the armed forces chaplaincy corps, while Hebrew Union College, the Reform movement's seminary, provided an accelerated study program for students wishing to join the war effort. By 1945, half of America's rabbis claimed World War II veteran status.[12]

Jewish organizations from across the religious and ideological spectrum cast their votes in unanimous support of FDR's war declaration. The Synagogue Council of America offered its prayers for "a speedy victory of the principles of international right and justice for which our country is at war" and encouraged its member congregations to introduce prayers of peace at their worship services. The ultra-Orthodox Agudath Israel notified President Roosevelt that it stood under his "leadership in this decisive hour for our country as for the entire democratic world. We are certain that with the help of the almighty, the crisis will lead to victory over the dark powers enlisted by our enemies." The National Council of Jewish Social Welfare approved a resolution pledging the generous use of its "resources as individuals and our services as professional social workers as our contribution towards the victory of the United Nations under the leadership of our President and commander in chief, Franklin D. Roosevelt."[13]

Jewish fund-raisers pledged their wholehearted support of the community chest concept as the most effective means of mobilizing the nation's volunteer social service agencies for the cause of victory. Community chests, originated in the 1920s as a means to pool the many private and often competing fund-raising efforts of a particular locale, enjoyed a resurgence. While American Jews in the 1920s feared that community

Figure 4. Chaplain Herman Dicker leads Yom Kippur services on September 28, 1944, for the Fifth Division stationed in France. (A Lev 273; box 40 of 58, American Jewish Historical Society, Waltham, Mass.)

chests would collect more Jewish money than they would dispense to Jewish organizations, wartime Jews offered no such critique. The demands of mobilization inspired Jewish leaders to revise their political outlook. As Louis Kraft of New York's Jewish Welfare Board affirmed, "Jews may be counted upon to do their full part in war chests as they do in all the war effort of the nation."[14]

While almost all Americans backed FDR's call for war, Jewish support for the war effort surpassed that of Christian religious denominations. Protestant and Catholic churches enlisted about 8,000 chaplains, encouraged lay voluntarism for the war effort, and coordinated fund-raising campaigns for a variety of service groups. Still, wartime social and political pressures took a political toll on Jewish organizations. The Nazi persecution of European Jews pressed American Jews into an interventionist mindset long before the mainstream Christian churches engaged the question. Once the United States entered the conflict, Jewish leaders threw their enthusiastic support to the president in hopes of both defeating Hitler and refuting the isolationist claim that Jews had dragged the nation into an unnecessary war.

The politics of acculturation weighed on Jewish organizations much more than on their Christian counterparts. American Jewish leaders linked their support for the war effort to protecting their co-religionists abroad, fighting anti-Semitism at home, and insuring civil protection for their constituents. These endeavors politicized Jewish organizations and infused their rhetoric with powerful civic dimensions. Jewish communal politics incorporated ethnic, religious, and even nationalist elements. Jewish leaders carried the burden of social inclusion on their shoulders while churches did not serve that function for Christian America. Protestant and Catholic denominations, steeped in the traditional voluntarism of American religious life, responded to the war declaration from more limited theological and philanthropic perspectives. While they did offer material aid through their constituent social service groups, some Christian organizations faced internal dissent from pacifists opposed to war on any grounds. Others supported wars only when they could achieve a higher moral good. While the defeat of Hitler offered a powerful justification for intervention, churches faced opposition from those who remembered the U.S. government's refusal to enter the League of Nations, viewed by Christian religious reformers as a necessary step to end international conflict, after World War I. Under those pressures, it was not surprising that, as Sydney Ahlstrom concluded, "even with the provocations which Hitler provided . . . , the churches did not repeat the unrestrained capitulation to the war spirit which had left them disgraced after 1918."[15]

ENEMY ALIENS AND CIVIL LIBERTIES

Once the United States declared war on Japan, Germany, and Italy, President Roosevelt faced a serious national security question: how should nationals of the Axis powers residing in the United States be controlled? The commander-in-chief understood that without proper safeguards, the nation faced certain threat of espionage and "fifth column" activity. Within weeks of American entry into the war, the president issued new immigration guidelines declaring Axis nationals to be "enemy aliens" and requiring these foreign citizens to obtain and carry certificates of identification.[16]

The most immediate problem facing the Jewish community concerned the status of Jewish emigrants from Nazi Germany. Legally, these oppressed refugees could not be distinguished from other German nationals residing in the United States who might be considered a threat to national security. "With this nation's entry into war," the executive director of the National Jewish Refugee Service explained, "our Government issued regulations governing enemy aliens which, by an ironic turn of fate, were fully applicable to a majority of America's pro-democratic refugees." The government's policy affected about 130,000 of the 200,000 European Jewish refugees residing in the United States. Even though Jewish refugees "were persons who had fled Nazism and Fascism, and were obviously loyal to this country and to democracy," he explained, "they came within the technical classification of 'enemy alien.' " The Jewish immigration expert lamented the fact that "practically all of them were no longer considered nationals by the countries from which they fled; their former citizenship had been cut off and they were actually 'stateless.' Nevertheless, restrictions were imposed by this country on their freedom of movement, their right to live in certain areas which might be designated as necessary to defense and to possess many war-useful articles."[17]

Jewish leaders successfully lobbied the government to modify its "enemy alien" classifications. San Francisco's Committee for Service To Émigrés, a part of the city's Federation of Jewish Charities, petitioned Congress "to afford fair treatment to all concerned" in testimony before Congressman John H. Tolan's Select Committee Investigating National Defense Migration. The committee submitted a report that outlined the history of anti-Semitism in Hitler's Germany, highlighting the obvious estrangement of German Jews from their native land. It affirmed the value of the German Jewish émigrés to the U.S. economy and reminded subcommittee members that "practically no refugee who came to the United States since 1933 has become a public charge." The San Francisco Jewish group closed by affirming "the eagerness with which the refugees have sought to become integrated into American life" and suggesting "after due hearing and investigation, those who are recognized as being beyond suspicion, should be removed from the enemy alien classification."[18]

Protection of German refugees reaffirmed the community's commitment to democracy as it promoted the continued acculturation of the American Jewish minority into the wartime mainstream. As a representative of the Jewish Club of 1933 implored, Jews "were the first martyrs and the first victims" in the conflict between democracy and Nazism. Speaking on behalf of the anti-Nazi Jewish refugees in Los Angeles, he wanted to avoid repetition of a dangerous precedent already established in France and embrace instead an "enemy alien" plan typical of the one instituted in England: "France made the terrible mistake of having detracted her attention from the fight against fifth columnists by fighting senselessly the loyal democratic anti-Nazi refugees in their midst." England, on the other hand, bolstered her war efforts by "setting up tribunals for the refugees, who exempted the genuine refugees from restrictions and stamped in their registration certificates 'refugee from Nazi oppression.' " In subsequent hearings, others presented evidence of specific Jewish refugees who faced unwarranted persecution because of their German birth.[19]

The Roosevelt administration agreed that the victims of Nazi aggression were not meant to be included in the president's directive. In a 1942 report, the Immigration and Naturalization Service recommended that immigration officers exercise flexibility as they enforced the new edict. "Natives, citizens, and denizens of hostile nations," it reported, "are as a group more likely to be dangerous to the United States than are other persons." But, the board pointed out in reference to the Jewish refugees, "a person who has been deprived of his citizenship and of his property by Germany, and who faces punishment and perhaps death if he returns to Germany, will not in all probability be friendly to the Nazi regime, even though he may be technically classified as an enemy alien."[20]

The argument in favor of special classification for German Jewish nationals provoked almost no opposition in Washington. Government officials correctly viewed European refugees from Nazism as allies. The American Jewish campaign against enemy-alien laws coincided with the larger aims of the war. The community's actions did not compromise nor conflict with consensus ideals. Americans should unite in the spirit of fairness and grant an exception. Almost as soon as the Roosevelt administration realized its oversight, it introduced appropriate legal measures to distinguish Jews from the rest of the German enemy alien population.

THE INTERNMENT OF JAPANESE AMERICANS

Japanese Americans in the western United States did not enjoy the same protection. Despite assurances from organizations such as the Japanese American Citizens League that it would provide its "fullest cooperation" to the war effort, the military developed contingency plans to relocate Japanese and Japanese Americans to the interior of the American West. Politicians from both the executive and legislative branches (and later the Supreme Court) backed the military's proposal.[21]

In both public and private, Jewish leaders either supported the government's decision or remained silent. Werner Rosenberg, writing in the AJC's *Contemporary Jewish Record*, avoided any mention of the internment and focused instead on a discussion highlighting the differences between German Jewish and Japanese enemy aliens living in the United States. Unlike German Jewish refugees, Rosenberg explained, Japanese enemy aliens "present a special problem which must be considered on its own merits and handled under a different procedure." Like most in the Jewish community, Rosenberg glossed over the action taken against Japanese Americans, preferring to focus instead on the needs of German Jewish refugees.[22]

In Los Angeles, Rabbi Morton A. Bauman of Temple Israel of Hollywood, Rabbi Edgar F. Magnin, the powerful leader of the city's largest synagogue, Wilshire Boulevard Temple, and Mrs. Isaac Pelton, president of the Council of Jewish Women, signed their names to a statement issued by the Los Angeles County Committee for Church and Community Cooperation, a body created by the Board of Supervisors to promote interfaith understanding. The committee statement gave almost unqualified support for internment of Japanese and Japanese Americans and reflected the depth of anti-Japanese prejudices on the west coast. Illustrating attitudes typical of most wartime Californians, the committee seconded claims that Japanese and Japanese Americans posed a "fifth column" threat to U.S. security.[23]

"In case of a Japanese attack," the committee explained, "most Americans believe that some enemy aliens, and even some claiming citizenship, would attempt to aid the invaders. Whether the potential saboteurs form a small or large percentage of the enemy alien population and their children, seems to us not the main issue." The committee made no distinction between Japanese citizens residing in the United States and U.S. citizens of Japanese descent: "There seem to be a few authenticated instances where citizen-Japanese, while proclaiming their loyalty to the United States, have been carrying on disloyal activities." "Any evacuation proposed," committee members convinced themselves, "is not prompted by race hatred, prejudice, or selfish business interests, but is contemplated only for military protection."[24]

Often times when political issues generate volatile public responses, reformers opt for quiet diplomacy. Private discussions can sometimes provide a powerful impetus for social change: they can inspire adversaries to meet without fear of public scrutiny and offer a safe haven for complex negotiations. While several southern Jewish leaders would use just such a defense in a subsequent era, nearly all Jewish leaders avoided any behind-the-scenes lobbying. The national board meeting minutes and weekly newsletters of both the AJC and the AJCongress offered no evidence of private or public discussions on the internment question. Wartime Jewish leaders connected their support of internment to their own acculturation. In the decade previous, Jewish interests demanded a principled defense of individual rights. In 1942, social integration required that Jews accept the Army orders to evacuate "without making any objection, and without further debate." The need for national unity subverted dissent and if American Jews coveted their civic reputation, they had no choice but to urge Japanese Americans "to act obediently and cheerfully" in their own incarceration. For wartime Jewish leaders, the continued viability of American Judaism demanded consent. "Those who claim

American citizenship," they admonished, "should be among the first to demonstrate to their new communities their sincerity and loyalty."[25]

In Portland, Oregon, ground zero for many Japanese-American internees, Jewish leaders refused to engage the injustice unfolding in front of them. About 4,000 Japanese Americans resided in Portland, and within months of the attack on Pearl Harbor they were subject to a curfew and eventually interned at Manzanar. Portland's newspaper, the *Oregonian*, published about ten articles a week on Japanese Americans between December 1941 and March 1942, including at least thirty-three front-page stories. Between March 22 and April 4, editors ran no fewer than forty-three different articles. During the same period, the local Jewish paper, the *Scribe*, offered no coverage of internment. Portland Jewry's fear of social marginalization proved more powerful than their commitment to liberal ideals: a visitor to Portland reading only the *Scribe* would have no knowledge of the injustices unfolding there.[26]

When word reached Portland about the government's intention to classify German Jewish refugees as "enemy aliens," editors at the *Scribe* followed the lead of national Jewish leaders and offered immediate press attention. One journalist explained that "German refugees have by the very fact of their flight established themselves as enemies of Hitler" and should benefit from a government inquiry "with a view to clearing them of the stigma of enemy alien." The Portland Jewish community, like those around the country, could support the rights of German Jews since the enemy alien law victimized the very people it should have protected. Exemptions for German Jewish refugees did not threaten U.S. security and in many cases actually helped the Allied cause. The Japanese, on the other hand, could not be compared to German Jews.[27]

National Jewish organizations followed in the spirit of their Los Angeles and Portland co-religionists. While the AJC in January 1943 called on "our brethren of all creeds" to join "in the continued fight against those who through bigotry and prejudice endeavor in any way to imperil the rights of any group of American citizens and thus to divide our country and undermine the foundations of American liberty," nowhere in its review of the years 1942, 1943, 1944, and 1945 was any mention made of the internment. The AJC's public relations committee, charged with responsibility for maintaining links with other American minority groups, failed to acknowledge the plight of Japanese Americans in its wartime annual reports. The December 26, 1941, Los Angeles–based B'nai B'rith *Messenger* did carry a one-line news summary of New York congressman Samuel Dickstein's efforts to give the Justice Department power "to cancel the citizenship of naturalized American citizens who might be considered friendly to a foreign power," but neither the *Messenger* nor B'nai B'rith's *National Jewish Monthly* offered editorial comment on the west coast situation. Wartime ADL chief counsel Arnold Forster maintained that his organization opposed internment though it published no official position at the time. Other ADL evidence contradicts Forster's claim. In March 1941, the National Council of Jewish Women offered a resolution proclaiming that "the wholesale evacuation of the Japanese without regard to their citizenship creates a 'second class citizenship' which disregards Article 14 of the Constitution of the United States of America." Yet National Council of Jewish Women president Blanche Goldman rejected it, refusing to counter actions deemed "absolutely necessary for the safety of our war effort."[28]

The only serious opposition to internment originated in San Francisco's Jewish community. Acculturated to a city boasting the mainland's largest Japanese-American population, Jewish leaders in the Bay Area understood the government's edict from a different perspective. They witnessed the wholesale relocation and understood, perhaps better than many in Washington, that Japanese Americans remained loyal to the Allied cause. Their American experience demanded a political posture different from Jews in the rest of the nation. While theirs would remain a minority view, the San Francisco Jewish leadership's opposition to the internment program reaffirms the importance of local factors in ethnic political development.

In testimony before Congressman Tolan's House subcommittee, Rabbi Irving F. Reichert, as a member of the Committee on National Security and Fair Play (CNSFP), urged government officials "to keep the infringement of the civil rights of citizens to the lowest possible minimum, and to base it on military necessity—not on race or any other consideration." While the CNSFP, composed of San Francisco political, business, educational, and religious leaders, did approve of detaining any Japanese or Japanese Americans proven to pose a threat to national security, it rejected wholesale internment.[29]

The CNSFP proposed a plan to keep loyal Japanese Americans in their own communities and reminded Congress that "the proposed evacuation of the entire group of Nisei, but of no other group of citizens, apparently on the basis of race, is already embittering some of them and making them turn a ready ear to Communist and other subversive ideas. It is also causing acute distress," it explained, "to many white citizens like ourselves who are concerned over every violation of the democratic principles for which we are fighting." The CNSFP statement criticized as well the double standard created by government officials who did not propose internment of Germans or Italians. "Since the Nisei are full-fledged American citizens by virtue of birth and upbringing in this country," it urged, "certainly they should be given not less consideration than German and Italian aliens, sympathetic as they are with those among them who are thoroughly loyal to democratic ideals."[30]

The Jewish community's responses to internment of Japanese Americans mirrored those of the larger society. Almost no liberal voices in the United States protested the mass evacuation, and almost all those that did hailed from the San Francisco area. American citizenship demanded support of the administration on this issue, and it was liberals in the White House who engineered and approved of implementation plans for Executive Order 9066. Men such as Earl Warren, Walter Lippmann, Henry L. Stimson, Abe Fortas, Milton Eisenhower, Hugo Black, and John J. McCloy all backed the civil rights travesty. Despite subsequent regrets about their participation, Attorney General Francis Biddle (later a judge at the Nuremberg trials) and Tom Clark (then the coordinator of Alien Enemy Control and later attorney general in the Truman administration and Supreme Court justice) emerged as central figures in the internment process.[31]

The Supreme Court, empowered with the ultimate authority to protect the constitutional rights of U.S. citizens, upheld the legal basis of internment in the Hirabayashi, Yasui, Korematsu, and Endo cases. Despite intense deliberations over both the larger constitutional issues and the specifics of each case, the Court failed to stop what Justice Frank Murphy, in his *Korematsu* dissent, called "one of the most sweeping and complete deprivations of constitutional rights in the history of this nation in the absence of martial law." Although a 1983 Supreme Court appeal did reverse the criminal convictions, the Court refused to intervene during the whole of the war. The last Japanese Americans were not able to return to their homes until 1946, a year after Japan offered its unconditional surrender to the United States.[32]

Support for interment reached the left as well. The radical Japanese-American newspaper *Doho* urged its readers not to protest evacuation: "This is no time to holler that our civil liberties and constitutional rights are being denied us." *People's World*, the west coast's Communist daily newspaper, considered the internment of Japanese "unfortunate, but vital" and argued that General John L. De Witt, the officer in charge of the internment, had created "a sensible program."[33]

Even the American Civil Liberties Union wavered in its opposition to internment. The national office of the ACLU backed the government's actions, much to the dismay of the local branch in San Francisco. "All they wanted was that we should concern ourselves with the manner in which the evacuation was carried out," Ernest Besig, then the executive director of the San Francisco office, explained. "They felt that hearing boards should be established to determine which persons should be removed and which should be allowed to remain." When the leadership conducted a mail-in survey of their constituents, it learned that it lacked decisive support even in its own backyard: the tally revealed nearly an even split between supporters and opponents of internment.[34]

Norman Thomas, a co-founder of the ACLU and six-time Socialist candidate for president, blasted the national leadership for what he called "dereliction of duty." "What is perhaps as ominous as the evacuation of the Japanese," Thomas argued, "is the general acceptance of this procedure by those who are proud to call themselves liberal." In the July 29, 1942, issue of *Christian Century*, Thomas lamented that "in an experience of nearly three decades I have never found it harder to arouse the American public on any important issue than on this."[35]

In a society where almost everyone agreed with Japanese internment, Jewish opposition would make no sense. Dissent would have proven both ineffective, since Jewish protests could not have reversed the policy, and self-damaging, since it would only manage to cast the American Jewish community in the most unfavorable light. Under the intense pressures of the wartime consensus, Jewish leaders retreated. In an ironic twist, both Japanese Americans and American Jews eventually experienced the sting of consensus politics. For Americans of Japanese descent, the forced migration to relocation camps throughout the West demonstrated the authoritarian potential of consensus. For Jews who trusted FDR to save their European brethren, the wartime consensus proved equally harmful. Jewish American leaders struggled to navigate a course that respected the commander-in-chief's military strategy while offering Jewish victims of Nazism the support they needed. Like Japanese Americans, they could not protest U.S. war policy, even when that meant compromising the safety of their co-religionists abroad.

EUROPEAN RELIEF AND THE ZIONIST CAUSE

America's entry into the war coincided with tragic reports from the European theater. Most Jews under Nazi control faced imprisonment in ghettos by November 1941, and in the summer of 1942 American Jewish leaders fielded unconfirmed reports of mass murders in Nazi-occupied Europe. In August 1942, disturbing news reached the director of the Geneva office of the World Jewish Congress (WJC), Dr. Gerhart Reigner: Hitler had designed a plan to gas all Jews under Nazi control. The WJC leader tried to get his findings forwarded to Rabbi Wise via the American legation in Switzerland, but officials at the State Department in Washington withheld the vital information. Only through Reigner's British diplomatic connections did the American rabbi learn of the impending genocide. Wise took the news back to the State Department, which asked the AJCongress leader not to publicize the report until it had confirmed its accuracy. Three months later, on November 24, 1942, Wise received U.S. government confirmation: Hitler's "Final Solution" had begun.[36]

As word of Hitler's intentions reached American Jewish leaders, the Zionist and non-Zionist factions in American Jewry struggled in vain to project a united front. Disagreements between the AJC and the AJCongress, simmering for almost two generations, exploded as leaders of both communities fought over the wisdom of a Jewish national home in Palestine. In ferocious debates that would last until after the State of Israel was created in 1948, Jewish leaders revealed, in dramatic fashion, how conflicting visions of American life informed different definitions of American Judaism and Jewish nationhood. For non-Zionists, Americanism demanded a repudiation of Jewish nationalism. Liberal universalism proved their most viable political philosophy. For supporters of a Jewish state, cultural pluralism reigned. Citing arguments first articulated in the Progressive era, Zionist leaders held that the long-term survival of American Judaism depended on its ability to advance particularist goals. The wartime split between American Zionists and non-Zionists demonstrated the importance of the acculturation process in American Jewish political culture: Jewish leaders needed to build their Zionist campaigns on platforms sensitive to the political needs of the dominant culture. Unfortunately, those limitations also diluted Jewish political strength and established impenetrable boundaries for Jewish activists intent on doing everything they could to save European Jews.

Despite the strong correlation between national origin and political persuasion, the development of American Zionism defied categorization. While most Zionists descended from Eastern European stock, several of the movement's most important spokespeople, including Stephen Wise, claimed Central European ancestry. Reform leaders such as Abba Hillel Silver advocated political Zionism, while many of his rabbinic colleagues rejected such a strident form of Jewish nationalism. Though AJC president Joseph Proskauer remained non-Zionist throughout his life, he lobbied President Truman to accept the United Nations partition plan of Palestine; most in his organization were willing to support the development of the yishuv, Palestine's budding Jewish government, if it offered hope to European Jews. When David Ben-Gurion asked for AJC support of his Palestinian program in 1942, the committee agreed, asking only that Ben-Gurion and his Jewish Agency end their relationship with the WJC (an organization that threatened AJC principles by uniting the world's Jews into a single political body). Even the AJC's most famous leader, Louis Marshall, embraced a cultural form of Zionism in the 1920s, and his friends helped fund the Hebrew University of Jerusalem as an affirmation of Palestine's centrality in Jewish life.[37]

Despite their differences, Jewish leaders from both communities searched for ways to cooperate with one another in defense of their overseas co-religionists. Their first wartime opportunity arose in January 1943 when Henry Monsky, president of the non-Zionist B'nai B'rith from 1938 to 1947, called on various local, regional, and national American Jewish organizations to forge a single unified body empowered to act on behalf of overseas Jews. "American Jewry, which will be required in large measure to assume the responsibility of representing the interests of our people at the Victory Peace Conference," Monsky wrote in a January 6 letter, "must be ready to voice the judgment of American Jews along with that of the other Jewish communities of the free countries with respect to the post-war status of Jews and the upbuilding of a Jewish Palestine."[38]

The B'nai B'rith leader hoped that the pluralist and inclusive nature of his international Jewish organization could bridge the gap between the Zionist and non-Zionist camps in American Jewish life. Few Jewish organizations, Monsky believed, could successfully appeal to such a broad range of opinion. The dire conditions in Europe demanded a mediator between the two sides, and Monsky performed that role beautifully. While a Zionist himself, Monsky boasted of a B'nai B'rith organization peopled by Jews of almost every political, religious, and ideological persuasion. By asking Jewish leaders to honor the liberal imperatives of tolerance and dialogue within their own communal structure, Monsky hoped to minimize the infighting and project a more powerful voice to the non-Jewish world.[39]

Monsky launched his plans by inviting representatives of thirty-four major American Jewish organizations to a January 23 planning meeting at Pittsburgh's Hotel William Penn. The sole item on the agenda, Monsky explained, would be a proposal to organize an American Jewish assembly "to bring together the representatives of major national Jewish membership organizations, in order that they may consider what steps should be taken to bring about some agreement on the part of the American Jewish Community." Seventy-eight delegates from thirty-two organizations attended the organizing meeting. Much to Monsky's disappointment, both the American Jewish Committee and the leftist Jewish Labor Committee failed to show.

Representatives of the Jewish Labor Committee blamed their absence on logistical problems and joined the assembly in time for its first conference. For the American Jewish Committee, involvement in the national body involved more complicated issues. The creation of a national Jewish political body threatened American Jewry's civic status and, it believed, hindered American attempts to aid European Jews. The AJC's understanding of American Judaism demanded that one's citizenship responsibilities, such as voting, remain independent of one's religious affiliation.

If mainstream America questioned Jewish loyalty, then they would also doubt the efficacy of American Jewish calls for overseas relief.[40]

The Zionist camp seized on the AJC absence and pressed for the creation of a powerful democratic body. If it could secure wide-reaching political power based on equal representation, then it could break the traditional AJC oligarchy and turn American Jewry toward more activist positions. When delegates first met in Pittsburgh, they pressed for just such a group. "In anticipation of the problems that would face the Jewish people in the post-war period in Europe and Palestine," meeting organizers wrote following the planning sessions, "American Jewish citizens of every shade of opinion and affiliation felt the need of organizing a representative body to unite upon a common program of action."[41]

Organizers announced the creation of an American Jewish Assembly, a "body of American Jews democratically organized to plan the immediate rescue of European Jewry, to take action upon post-war Jewish problems in Europe, and to implement the rights of the Jewish people to Palestine." Until the assembly could be formed, Monsky and his colleagues organized the Emergency Committee for European Jewish Affairs to coordinate their response.[42]

The AJC, as might be expected, balked at the prospect of joining the assembly. It first objected to the organization's very name. The word "assembly," it feared, implied "a separate political enclave . . . through which sections of America's population would rule themselves, deal with the national government, or negotiate with other governments in the interest of their group." The AJC argued that by voicing the political demands of foreigners, Jewish or not, assembly delegates treaded in murky legal waters. It held firm in its belief that American citizens respect the law of the land, especially during a time of war. Pluralist liberal ideals did not serve AJC leaders who feared that the proposed assembly would threaten the civic safety of American Jewry.[43]

The AJC also objected to the assembly's nationalist orientation, and in a 1943 "Statement of Views" it sought a compromise that could satisfy its aversion to political Zionism while still safeguarding European Jews. On some issues, the statement moved the AJC closer to the Zionist camp. It backed unrestricted overseas immigration and resettlement and demanded equal rights for European Jews. The statement offered words of praise for the yishuv and included Palestine as one of many options for postwar European Jews. Joseph Proskauer, the president of the American Jewish Committee between 1943 and 1949 and principal author of the paper, alarmed the anti-Zionist wing of the AJC when he invited Zionist leader Chaim Weizmann to offer input on the document and later gave his assurances that the AJC would not let the statement interfere with Weizmann's Palestine campaign.

In other parts, the AJC appeared to retreat from some of its earlier positions. While it had once supported the British government's Balfour Declaration, which promised Jews the right to create a national homeland in Palestine, it did not mention the edict in the Statement of Views. Instead, it advocated an international trusteeship over the British mandate. The AJC statement steered clear of expressing Jewish exceptionalism, nor did it demand a Jewish homeland: "We urge upon the United Nations and upon those who shall frame the terms of the peace the relief from the havoc and ruin inflicted by Axis barbarism on millions of unoffending human beings, especially Jews." The AJC's decision to focus on "human beings" first and list "Jews" second reflected Proskauer's universalist orientation. American Jews did possess the right to protect their co-religionists, but that campaign must focus on human rights, not Jewish particularism.[44]

Proskauer fashioned a document he hoped would reconcile the disagreements between American Zionists and non-Zionists. Proskauer, an anti-Zionist, refused to impose his own ideology on his organization. The new AJC policy represented a dramatic shift from Proskauer's personal belief that the creation of a Jewish commonwealth in Palestine would be a "Jewish catastrophe" and his contention that nationalist calls only threatened to undo the basic symmetry between American citizenship and Jewish religious principles. "I am satisfied that from every point of view of safety for Jews in America," the AJC head warned, "there has got to be an open, vocal dissent from nationalism and political Zionism: and if the American Jewish Committee doesn't make itself the mouthpiece of this public position, some other organization will have to." Proskauer's admonition reaffirmed his belief that the pluralist models of liberalism supported by the Zionists damaged the reputations and social standing of American Jews.[45]

Proskauer faced criticism on all fronts. American Zionists outside the AJC feared that an international trusteeship would strip Jews of control over Palestinian immigration. Anti-Zionists within the AJC thought that their leaders went too far in praising the yishuv and advocating nationalism as a remedy for Jewish refugees. Zionist members of the AJC, such as Louis Levinthal, president of the Zionist Organization of America (ZOA), thought that the statement represented an abandonment of the group's earlier support for the Balfour Declaration. When Levinthal proposed that the AJC amend the statement to guarantee Jewish control of immigration under the proposed trusteeship, he was rebuffed by Proskauer and others. The AJC president succeeded in straddling the Zionist, non-Zionist, and anti-Zionist constituencies in his organization. In the end, the statement did not offend anyone enough to warrant disapproval, nor did it contain provisions to make it powerful. It did offer a rapprochement between the

Zionists and non-Zionists and served, despite the objections of the Zionist leadership, as the unofficial starting point for subsequent negotiations.[46]

In its continuing efforts to bridge the gap between itself and American Zionist leaders, the AJC offered a compromise proposal to dilute the strength of the original assembly and bring it more in line with its non-Zionist position. AJC leaders sought a conference that could survey the attitudes of each constituent organization to "find what areas of agreement exist that ought constitute a common ground for united action." They stipulated that "such a conference would not make any claim to speak on behalf of the totality of American Jewry," nor would it "attempt to bind or coerce its own minorities or in any way challenge their right to express their point of view or to take any action they deem fit or proper." "Its objective," the AJC admonished, "shall be to secure the largest possible measure of agreement." The AJC wanted the conference to be voluntary and each constituent group to possess "complete freedom of action . . . irrespective of the vote of the Conference."[47]

Proskauer defended the AJC's call for greater autonomy by affirming that his organization yielded "to no one in our devotion to the cause of Judaism and to the protection of the rights of Jews throughout the world. We have demonstrated a deep and abiding concern for the welfare of Palestine and its full and proper development." Proskauer pointed out that his organization had already "asked for the abrogation at once of the White Paper, and have requested that the gates of Palestine be immediately opened for the freest entry of the victims of Nazi tyranny."[48]

When the American Jewish Assembly's executive committee met with the AJC to negotiate a compromise, it reassured the patrician group that the umbrella organization's name "did not imply political connotations" and protested the AJC's request to give constituent organizations "complete freedom of action." "Such 'freedom of action,' " executive committee officials argued, "would be contrary to the very purpose of the proposed 'assembly' which was to bring about a program of united action."[49]

After detailed discussions, the executive committee of the American Jewish Assembly, fearful that an AJC exodus would diminish the new group's claim to represent all American Jewry, capitulated on both points. It decided to change the name of the proposed organization from the "American Jewish Assembly" to the "American Jewish Conference" and it agreed to honor "the right of any participating organization to dissent from, and so dissenting, not to be bound by, the conclusions of the Assembly, or Conference." For Proskauer, the agreement signaled an important breakthrough in American Jewish life: "The impulse of self-preservation and of the preservation of our American ideals requires that we use here every effort to avoid schism and to achieve cooperation. For here, as always, the enemy would rejoice in a program of divide and conquer." Proskauer's universalist model of American liberalism triumphed. The Jewish community, in Proskauer's estimation, could ease its fears of social ostracization. On March 13, the AJC joined the Emergency Committee for European Jewish Affairs (then renamed the Joint Emergency Committee for European Jewish Affairs) and a month later, on April 18, 1943, the American Jewish Conference was born.[50]

THE FIRST AMERICAN JEWISH CONFERENCE

The First American Jewish Conference convened on August 29, 1943, at New York's Waldorf-Astoria Hotel, with Monsky and American Jewish Congress president Stephen S. Wise presiding as co-chairs. Over a million American Jews voted to elect the 501 delegates attending the conference. Three-quarters of the seats were assigned to various Jewish communities around the country, according to size. The remaining delegates represented sixty-four different Jewish organizations. At the conference, delegates organized themselves into seven voting blocs according to their various political and religious perspectives. Delegates from the American Jewish Congress, B'nai B'rith, and the Jewish Labor Committee represented their own organizations while conference attendees from the Reform, Conservative, and Orthodox movements created their own umbrella coalitions. The Zionist organizations split between general Zionists and labor Zionists, and a final group of unaffiliated delegates remained independent.[51]

From the very beginning, debate at the First American Jewish Conference reaffirmed the growing strength of the more militant, Zionist, Eastern European, American Jewish majority. In his address at the first plenary session, Henry Monsky, the conference organizer, rejected the American Jewish community's traditional reliance on the established German-American Jews and appealed for wide-scale action based on equal representation, aggressive defense of Jewish rights, and an end to the assimilationist mindset of an earlier era. The Jewish leader linked the safety of his co-religionists with the activist liberal ideals of cultural pluralism. "One of the essential virtues of this Conference," he proclaimed, "is that it comprises leadership democratically chosen from the ranks of American Israel. It is the antithesis of the one prevalent practice of representation by 'shtadlonim' "—a veiled reference to the aristocratic style of leadership typical of the American Jewish Committee. Monsky added: "The spirit of democracy and the development and appreciation of democratic processes have changed the whole concept of Jewish leadership. Leaders must be responsible for the yearnings, the aspirations and the hopes of those for whom they presume to speak."[52]

Abba Hillel Silver, the controversial Zionist, spiritual leader of Cleveland's largest synagogue, and co-chair with Stephen S. Wise of the American Zionist Emergency Council, pressed the question of a Jewish national home in an impromptu address: "We cannot truly rescue the Jews of Europe unless we have free immigration into Palestine. . . . We cannot have free immigration into Palestine unless our political rights are recognized there. Our political rights cannot be recognized unless our historic connection with the country is acknowledged and our right to rebuild our national home is reaffirmed." Silver considered the establishment of Jewish political rights "inseparable links in the chain" and warned that "the whole chain breaks if one of the links is missing."[53]

Wise's and Silver's prominence in American Zionist circles capped a generation-long shift for many Reform leaders. Universalist liberalism, once the guiding principle of Reform, gave way as an impressive group of second-generation American Jews including Wise, Judah Magnes, Barnett Brickner, and Silver argued that a pluralist political orientation would better safeguard American Jewish interests. At its 1920 convention, the CCAR went on record in favor of the Balfour Declaration and opposed to a fifteen-year prison sentence leveled against Vladimir (Zeev) Jabotinsky, the chief of Jerusalem's *Haganah* (Jewish army), for defending local Jews during an April 1920 Arab riot. Jabotinsky, who would later reject the minimalist strategies of Weizmann and form his own Revisionist movement, endured several months of incarceration before British high commissioner Herbert Samuel offered him amnesty. In 1923, the CCAR backed Jewish settlement in Palestine. Rabbi Felix Levy, an ardent Zionist, earned election as president of the CCAR in 1935 and two years later, the Reform movement rebuffed its nineteenth-century anti-Zionist Pittsburgh Platform with the "Guiding Principles of Reform Judaism." The Columbus Platform, as it came to be known, represented "a bold attempt to rejoin ethnic Jewishness and Judaism, which earlier Reform thinkers had done much to separate." While the Columbus Platform passed only after a number of non-Zionists departed from the conference, its reference to Judaism as "the soul of which Israel is the body" signaled a dramatic departure from classical Reform ideology. Six years after Rabbi Levy's election as CCAR president, James Heller, another Zionist, assumed the mantle of rabbinic leadership and in 1942, CCAR members passed a resolution affirming the right of Jewish Palestinians to arm themselves.[54]

Silver's fiery passion for political Zionism catapulted him to the leadership of the First American Jewish Conference and helped reshape the course of American Zionist politics. While Stephen S. Wise led the American Zionist movement in the years before the conference, Silver soon emerged as the leading national spokesman for the cause. Under Wise's direction, American Zionism developed as a compromise between advocates of political Zionism and accommodationists favoring a philanthropic form of Jewish nationalism. The New York rabbi, an ardent Democrat and personal friend of FDR, mediated between his fierce commitment to European Jewry and his loyalty to a president he considered a genuine friend of the Jews. Silver, on the other hand, maintained strong ties to the Republican party, befriended Senator Robert Taft, a fellow Ohioan, and did not share Wise's confidence in the president or his administration. He led a movement to make political Zionism the official position of organized Jewry, and his strategic disagreements with Wise made for a contentious relationship. For Wise, FDR remained a true friend of the Jewish people, while Silver countered that protection of Jewish interests did not mandate support for the liberal Democratic president.[55]

The split between Silver and Wise intensified just three days before the American Jewish Conference convened. Zionist leaders arranged for a meeting to discuss the fate of the American Emergency Committee for Zionist Affairs, established in 1939 under the chairmanship of Wise to coordinate the efforts of some twenty-four separate Zionist entities. In early 1943, the umbrella group splintered when four of its members resisted the centralizing efforts of its director, Emanuel Neumann. By June, Zionist leaders resolved to reconstitute the organization as the American Zionist Emergency Council. With the support of Chaim Weizmann, Silver was deemed the "most suitable" leader for the new group. Under pressure, Silver's supporters agreed to a compromise naming Wise, along with Silver, council co-chairs.[56]

The AZEC quickly emerged as the most important and effective organization in American Jewish political life. It did not suffer from the same fractiousness that ruined its predecessor. Jewish leaders understood the severity of their overseas mission and labored to keep their alliance together. For the first time since Hitler rose to power, Zionist groups took advantage of their ideological differences. Each constituent group lobbied its own segment of American society. Religious Zionists reached out to the Orthodox Jewish community while labor Zionists appealed to the AFL and the CIO. In 1943 and 1944, AZEC mobilized at the local and national levels, forged alliances with Christian groups, other Jews, and organized labor, and called on Congress and the president to support their Zionist resolutions.[57]

At the American Jewish Conference, both Wise and Silver faced opposition from the AJC. "It is with profound regret that, for the American Jewish Committee, and my two fellow delegates from that organization," Proskauer explained, "I must register dissent from the resolutions [on Palestine] which have been introduced and which I have no doubt will receive the vote of this conference." Proskauer pressed delegates to delay any action on the Palestine question. "Quite apart from the validity or invalidity of these proposals," he explained, "we believe at this time, when the gravest and most delicate military and world-wide political questions are involved, the present issuance of these proposals contained in the resolutions is unwise because it may carry with it embarrassment to the governments of the United Nations, and is calculated to jeopardize the status of Jews and even prejudice the fullest development of the Jewish settlement in Palestine itself."[58]

Proskauer's position may have been rooted in earlier State Department objections to the conference. When government officials heard that American Jewish leaders intended on advancing a Zionist agenda at the First American Jewish Conference, they sought a postponement. The AJC, hoping that the policymakers would not take offense at an American Jewish call to alter Allied strategy, advanced Washington's concerns to the floor of the conference. "At this time," Proskauer admonished, "it is our duty to concentrate on victory for the United Nations." The AJC feared that public debate on the Palestine issue would "divide the peoples of the United Nations and create added difficulties. And it is for that reason that we endeavored, without success, in the Palestine committee, to secure the passage of a resolution deferring action on this matter until some subsequent session of this Conference."[59]

Proskauer and the AJC hoped to deflect attention away from the Zionism question by pressing Jews to remain in Europe after the war. One AJC representative, Joseph Hyman, took issue with the Zionist's claim that Palestine served as the only viable long-term home for European refugees and mobilized his colleagues to fight what he called the "clever manipulation" of the opposing camp. The JDC concurred, holding to the premise that Jews could enjoy recognition as citizens in "their" countries. The administrative secretary of the JDC, Evelyn Morissey, agreed, affirming in April 1943 that it was the policy of her organization "to help Jewish populations in the countries in which they reside and to adjust them to the conditions in their own countries." Only after German Jews endured deportation did the JDC alter its policy.[60]

Jewish settlement in Palestine evolved into a basic feature of the American Jewish Conference's platform. Only the UAHC, out of respect for non-Zionist Jews within the Reform movement, joined the AJC in its refusal to endorse the emerging consensus. When the conference plenary approved the resolutions supporting the creation of a Jewish commonwealth in Palestine, the AJC left the Jewish body in protest. But unlike the AJC, the UAHC opted to abstain from voting rather than casting a negative vote or leaving the conference altogether.[61]

One anti-Zionist organization, the American Council for Judaism (ACJ), provoked debate on the Palestine question, even though none of its representatives attended the conference. The ACJ, organized by a small group of Reform rabbis in a June 1942 protest of the CCAR's emerging Zionist affiliations, pushed for a clear delineation between humanitarianism and Zionism. They understood the need to open Palestine to Jewish immigration but rejected any proposal to create a national state. ACJ executive director Rabbi Elmer Berger explained that in America, "we feel a Jew should be an American first and a Jew afterward—just as another is an American first and a Protestant afterward." The liberal models of cultural pluralism espoused by American Zionists evoked powerful dual loyalty fears among the ACJ membership. Even the more benign universalism of non-Zionist groups conflicted with the anti-Zionists' narrow conception of American ethnic expression. For Berger and the ACJ, the acculturative demands of American Jewry mandated a political philosophy at odds with even the slightest embrace of Jewish nationalism.[62]

The ACJ infuriated conference delegates when it published a broadside denouncing Zionism in the August 31, 1943, *New York Times*. James G. Heller, the Zionist head of the CCAR at the time of the ACJ's creation, condemned the organization and by more than a three-to-one vote, the Reform rabbinic group called for the ACJ to disband. The spiritual leaders considered the American Council for Judaism "a disruptive force" that "at a tragic time in Jewish history" had "chosen to attack and to attempt to destroy the greatest hope of the Jewish people" and had "drawn an unreal and misleading distinction between faith and people." Authorities from American Judaism's other major rabbinical bodies echoed the CCAR's convictions. Rabbi Robert Gordis, vice-president of the Conservative movement's Rabbinical Assembly, Rabbi Joseph H. Lookstein of the Religious National Orthodox Bloc, Mizrachi, and an unnamed officer of Rabbinical Council of America all argued against the anti-Zionist ideology of the ACJ.[63]

Despite their opposition to the ACJ and the AJC, Zionist delegates to the conference emulated much of their accommodationist brethren's rhetoric. The political demands of wartime America constrained Jewish leaders, regardless of their ideological orientation. Not even the most dedicated Zionists could campaign for a national homeland if non-Jewish Americans considered it antithetical to U.S. interests. Throughout the various committees dealing with the issue of Palestine, the Zionist leadership agreed on the need to fashion their political statements in language acceptable to mainstream American political culture. They reminded the nation that American Jews remained the only "spokesmen for the silenced Jewish communities of Europe," and called "for the loyal and faithful fulfillment of the covenant entered into between the nations of the world and the Jewish people." They promised to "integrate Jewish Palestine within the new democratic world structure" and pledged "scrupulous regard for and preservation of the religious, linguistic, and cultural rights of the Arab population in Palestine, and to the civil and religious equality of all its inhabitants before the law." They cast the Jewish state in the democratic shadow of the United States, portrayed the Nazis as anti-American bigots, and affirmed the right of a religious minority to protect itself.[64]

The American Jewish Conference affirmed its loyalty to the United States and to democracy in a statement drafted at its initial 1943 meeting: "We Jews, citizens of the United States dwelling in security in this our beloved land, which because of its democratic institutions and just laws 'gives to bigotry no sanction and persecution no assistance' and dedicated in undivided loyalty to the noble spirit of our country, are gathered here as an American Jewish Conference, a democratically elected body representative of American Jewry to cope with the tragic problems of our fellow Jews all over the world." It skirted the difficult dual-loyalty question by justifying its support for a Jewish state on the humanitarian needs of its European brethren rather than any dissatisfaction with American Jewish life. Delegates sought common political ground with other American ethnic minorities. By illustrating how American Jews benefited from the rewards of U.S. citizenship, delegates hoped to affirm both their love of America and the appropriateness of their overseas campaigns.[65]

Zionist leaders bolstered their civic standing by enlisting the support of Christian religious leaders. These interfaith appeals stressed the common prophetic tradition shared by Jews and Christians, reaffirmed the Jewish origins of Christianity, and illustrated the intimate relationship between Jewish politics and processes of ethnic acculturation. By wooing sympathetic Christians, Zionist leaders hoped to demonstrate the symmetry between Americanism and Jewish nationalism and derail their critics inside and outside the Jewish community. Supreme Court Justice Louis Brandeis, a leading American Zionist, himself urged Zionist leaders to use Christian supporters as a tool to convince Jewish "doubters" that the campaign for a Jewish homeland did not conflict with American values. In April 1941, hundreds of prominent Christians, including sixty-eight U.S. senators and two hundred congressmen, re-created the American Palestine Committee, which had dissolved nine years earlier. The APC sponsored a host of public relations events meant to educate Americans on the need for a Jewish homeland. Its notable members included New York Democratic senator Robert Wagner, who served as the new APC chief; AFL president William Green and CIO head Philip Murray; and Christian intellectuals Monsignor John A. Ryan and Dr. Henry A. Atkinson.[66]

While Orthodox Jews remained on the periphery of most liberal political appeals, they emerged as one of the Jewish community's most vocal supporters of interfaith outreach. Zionism occupied a sacred place in traditional Jewish life: many Orthodox Jews linked the arrival of the messiah with their return to Zion. Though earlier reform campaigns did little to influence their communal priorities, efforts to win Zionist support from Christian leaders promised to enrich their tradition-based American Jewish experience. The acculturative needs of the Orthodox community, in this case an opportunity to help build a Jewish homeland in Palestine, inspired its leaders to adopt a universalist approach to American politics. Rabbi Wolf Gold of the Religious National Orthodox Bloc, for example, believed that a theological justification for Zionism would solidify support from Christian America. He petitioned the conference to add a religious interpretation of Zionism before presenting its Palestine resolutions to President Roosevelt: "Religious America will understand Jewish aspirations to Palestine, better than any other community in the world," adding that the "pilgrim Fathers built their society on the religious foundations of the Bible" and pointing to the Liberty Bell, inscribed with a phrase from Leviticus, "Proclaim liberty throughout the land and unto all the inhabitants thereof."[67]

Jews, Rabbi Gold boasted, possessed the highest degree of patriotism as defined by the greatest American patriot of the era, President Franklin Roosevelt. Gold noted that the commander-in-chief, whom he referred to as "the great humanitarian and lover of liberty and democracy," believed that "the war was being fought for the freedom of man created in the image of God, as conceived in the Book of Genesis." He pointed out that Vice President Henry Wallace called on the Jewish Bible in his "marvelous philosophical address" justifying U.S. involvement in the European conflict. "Thus," the rabbi concluded, "the Bible permeates the thinking and sentiments of the American people and their great spokesmen."[68]

In his resolution on Zionism, Rabbi Gold opted for wording that built on the common ground joining traditional Judaism with American democracy: "We, the people of the Bible, we, the people who gave America the inspiration for liberty, we, the people of the Tanach [the Hebrew acronym for the Jewish Bible], come to you in the name of the Tanach to demand our rights to build Eretz Israel as a Jewish commonwealth." Gold believed "that it is impossible for the world to be free without the Jewish people regaining their freedom and independence," and pointed to the talmudic statement that "if liberty will exist in the Land of Israel and there will be a free, independent Jewish nation in Eretz Israel, liberty will be possible in the rest of the world."[69]

Despite the theological differences between Orthodox and Reform Judaism, the two movements shared a common belief in the acculturative value of interfaith Zionist appeals. In a resolution passed at its 1943 biennial convention and presented to the American Jewish Conference for its approval, the UAHC argued that "because we are Jews, the ideals of America have always been and must always be near and dear to us." The

Reform group prayed "that the United States, together with all the United Nations, may soon achieve all-comprehending victory everywhere upon earth" and "that out of the thunders and the ruins of war, a new world may arise, in the spirit of America, and that hatred and fierce cruelty may be succeeded by a long era of brotherhood, of international cooperation and security, and of that peace which is the work of righteousness." It pledged "loyalty to America" and proclaimed "that the very purpose of this Conference is to strive to apply and carry into effect those lofty tenets of our religious and ethical heritage, which are the common possession of America and of the Jew."[70]

The American Jewish Conference's committee on resolutions drafted its own version of the UAHC tract. In "Faith in the United States and in the Cause of the United Nations," delegates detailed the many reasons for their love of America and its democratic principles. The committee noted its co-religionists' impressive commitment to the American armed forces. "Our brothers and sons, our husbands and fathers," it proclaimed, "are giving themselves all over the world upon the field of battle on the side of the allies." The committee affirmed its "gratitude to the United States for the many decades of its open-hearted hospitality to the oppressed and persecuted, for the friendliness with which we and our brethren have been received, and for the institutions of liberty and justice upon which these United States were founded and upon which they rest unshakably." It drew links between American democracy and Jewish tradition. "Because we are Jews," the conference representatives wrote, "the ideals of America have always been and must always be near and dear to us. The passionate cry for justice and brotherhood that issued from the lips of the Hebrew prophets, the search after a government in which these principles should be forever incorporated, the age-long, passionate devotion to righteousness for the individual and in the complex of society; all these are ours, and all these are at the very heart of the American tradition."[71]

Despite the organized Jewish community's overriding preference for accommodationism, some Jewish leaders resisted the pressures of consensus and braved outright condemnation of the U.S. government. In these pronouncements, activist Jews stepped into terrain fraught with civic danger. Caught between their support of the war effort and their desire to bring needed attention to the plight of European Jews, they risked political alienation in order to advance the cause of their overseas brethren. The politics of acculturation demanded that they acquiesce to the war aims of the U.S. government, but their willingness to articulate a public rebuke of Allied leaders demonstrated an overriding commitment to the survival of Jewish life in Europe and Palestine.

Israel Goldstein, president of the Synagogue Council of America, co-chair of the American Jewish Conference, and a leading Zionist voice in the United States, criticized the apathy of government policymakers who offered only token assistance to European Jews. "The reluctance on the part of the leaders of the democracies to employ special measures to save the remnants of a people uniquely marked for extermination," he decried, "cannot be permitted to pass unchallenged even if it means that we must criticize our friends in high places." He maintained that "as citizens of a free democratic country," Jews had "the right and duty to offer constructive criticism to our leaders."[72]

Goldstein rejected the argument of Jews who opposed "special action for the rescue of European Jewry because they [did] not wish to give pretext to the enemies within democracy who claim that this war is being fought to save the Jews." The Zionist leader wanted nothing less than the creation of a Jewish state in Palestine, both as a haven for European refugees and as a future guarantee of Jewish security in the world. While Goldstein acknowledged that American Jews "should be the last to make unreasonable requests of our government," he affirmed their right to demand U.S. action on behalf of their European co-religionists. Goldstein took a commonsense approach to Jewish communal life. He was less concerned with philosophical concerns about dual loyalty and more impassioned by the pressing everyday needs of Europe's Jews. American Jews deserved the right to petition their government, he believed, "because the largest Jewish community in the world is domiciled here" and "because Jews are loyal citizens here and are pouring out their substance and their blood to bring victory to the Stars and Stripes."[73]

While Judge Morris Rothenberg of the World Zionist Organization (WZO) reminded his co-religionists that they were "in the midst of a war" and "must be very careful that we do not do anything which might embarrass our Government," he cautioned against delaying advice on postwar reconstruction, especially with regard to Jewish settlement in Palestine. "There is every likelihood that if we postpone the demands of the Jewish people to a later date," he explained, "we may be confronted with a situation in which the major decisions upon the question of Palestine will have been made." The WZO leader pleaded with the delegates to take strong and immediate action to ameliorate conditions for Jews in Europe. "Will it not be a very serious responsibility that we will have to bear before the bar of Jewish history," he warned, "that when we were called upon to give expression to the will of the Jewish people, and especially to speak in behalf of silenced Jewry, we kept quiet because someone told us that someone else had said that it is not a good thing for us to speak at this time."[74]

At the conclusion of the conference, delegates passed a stinging indictment of U.S. and Allied inaction. They deplored "the failure of the democracies to take sustained and vigorous action to halt the tide of slaughter and to save what may yet be saved," and lamented the fact little had been done in the eight months since the Allied powers officially condemned the European genocide. While the democratic governments tarried, delegates concluded, "Additional tens of thousands of Jews have been hurried to unnatural death."[75]

Despite the pleas of Goldstein and others, the First American Jewish Conference failed to unite American Jews on the question of Zionism. Instead, it demonstrated the structural limits of American Jewish nationalism. For American Jews, the politics of acculturation demanded that they tailor their Zionist ideology to the requirements of American life. Only by defining Zionism as a patriotic American movement or by appealing to humanitarianism could Jewish leaders garner broad-based support. While traditional Zionist thinking forced its subscribers to owe primary allegiance to a Jewish government, Jews in the United States found a way to call themselves "Zionists" without threatening their American civic status. That philosophical reformulation generated remarkable similarities between American Jews who considered themselves "Zionist" and those who preferred the term "non-Zionist." The few critics willing to step outside the bounds of acceptable American wartime political behavior demonstrated that the Americanized form of Jewish nationalism could not address the urgent needs of European Jewry. As news accounts of the unfolding Holocaust detailed, the vision of those antagonists proved both accurate and ominous.

CHAPTER FIVE

Planning the Postwar Peace: The United Nations, Zionism, and American Jewish Liberalism

As the Second World War drew to a close, American Jewish leaders reassessed the effectiveness of their overseas campaign. News reports from the European theater undermined Jewish communal confidence in accommodationist rescue efforts and inspired a broad-based challenge to the American Jewish old guard. In January 1943, more than 10,000 Dutch Jews were deported to the Auschwitz concentration camp. On February 5, Nazi forces murdered 1,000 Jews in Bialystok and forced another 10,000 to Treblinka and Auschwitz. The following month, the Germans set up Jewish labor and internment camps in Bulgaria and Yugoslavia and removed over 40,000 Jews from Salonika, Greece. While some Jews offered resistance to the Nazi authorities, including a group of 2,000 who attacked their SS guards after being transported from Wlodawa, almost all faced certain death, including the Wlodawa rebels who were killed by machine gun and grenade fire. As the months passed, Hitler continued his calculated plans for the deportation, concentration, and destruction of European Jewry.[1]

Focusing American attention on the plight of European Jews proved a difficult task. During the last two years of the war, Jewish leaders struggled with a public unwilling to give credence to the horrific reports emanating from Europe. Inflated claims of German brutality during World War I helped moderate reaction to the latest news. Accounts of Nazi atrocities filtering to the West included such seemingly ghastly claims that many Americans refused to believe them. A November 1944 Gallup Poll, the first conducted after Americans learned of the "Final Solution," showed that almost one-quarter of the American people did not believe that the Germans had mass-murdered people in concentration camps. When those who answered in the affirmative were asked how many had died, their responses revealed a gross underestimation of Nazi brutality. Only 4 percent of the respondents correctly guessed that the number of people killed exceeded six million (in fact, the figure was closer to eleven million).[2]

While earlier consensus-oriented appeals linked Jews and Christians in the interfaith dialogue movement, safeguarded constitutional protections through civil libertarian campaigns, and trumpeted American Jews as loyal patriots during World War II, they proved an unworthy protector of European Jewish interests in the early postwar years. The liberal strategy that sought to protect Jewish interests by linking them to universalist ideals crumbled under the weight of the Nazi genocide. Only programs that safeguarded the particularist needs of a Jewish minority, Jewish leaders realized, offered hope for long-term communal survival in Europe and Palestine. For most American Jews, a pluralist approach to American democracy supplanted wartime accommodationism. In their bid to create both a United Nations organization and a Jewish state in Palestine, Jewish leaders articulated a vision of liberal internationalism reminiscent of their 1930s overseas campaign.

Yet Jewish leaders from the Zionist and non-Zionist camps still disagreed on which liberal strategy would offer the greatest protection to world Jewry. The AJC and some of its backers in B'nai B'rith and the Reform movement feared that bold action would compromise their continued acculturation into American life. They still believed that Jewish interests were best served by laws that protected the rights of all. Whether in their refusal to go along with proposals to grant Jewish displaced persons (DPs) special status in Europe or their campaign for an international human rights declaration, Jewish communal moderates held fast to their traditional embrace of universal idealism. They shied away from public confrontation with government officials and refused to participate in cooperative ventures with their more activist American brethren.

Zionist leaders called on pluralist ideals to justify their confrontational tactics. Still reeling from details of Nazi atrocities, they demanded special acknowledgment of the crimes against European Jews and sought restitution based on ethnic affiliation. They charged that the AJC's preference for quiet dialogue translated into political acquiescence and reaffirmed what activist Jewish leaders had known since 1942: that European Jews could only enjoy civil protection in a nation governed by Jews. Between 1944 and 1947, they countered AJC strategy, galvanized the Jewish community behind the idea of a Jewish state, pressed Allied leaders, and lobbied for partition of the British mandate in Palestine. Zionist leaders, led by Rabbis Abba Hillel Silver and Stephen S. Wise, could not imagine a postwar plan blind to the particular anti-Semitic nature of Hitler's "Final Solution." They ran out of patience for their non-Zionist co-religionists and organized protests meant to garner attention from both the American public and the Roosevelt administration. The politics of acculturation, which encouraged Jews to accommodate to dominant political trends during World War II, pressed American Zionists toward postwar ethnic distinctiveness.[3]

The rapprochement between the two camps did not emerge quickly or easily. Each group maintained its own strategic preferences and continued to fight for control over Jewish communal policy. While the non-Zionists managed to dilute Jewish calls for political independence into philanthropic requests for humanitarian aid, they never regained the influence or respect they once held. American Zionist organizations, pushed to the periphery of communal life just a decade earlier, emerged as the leading voice of American Jewry in the postwar years. Jewish acculturation to postwar America demanded that ethnic minorities enjoy the specific right to lobby for their own group's welfare. The postwar reconstruction taught American Jews the limits of classical liberalism.

THE SECOND AND THIRD AMERICAN JEWISH CONFERENCES

At the second and third sessions of the American Jewish Conference, Jewish activists renewed their calls for a national homeland and labored to secure special legal protections for European Jews after the war. Buoyed by widespread anti-Nazi attitudes, Zionist leaders played to a much more receptive American audience. After U.S. entry into the European war, Jewish leaders could count on widespread American opposition to Hitler. In the Zionists' minds, the ideals of American democracy demanded that they press for the creation of a Jewish state in Palestine. Borrowing a page from Louis Brandeis, postwar American Zionists agreed with the jurist's contention that "the highest Jewish ideals are essentially American in a very important particular. It is Democracy that Zionism represents. It is Social Justice which Zionism represents, and every bit of that is the American ideal of the twentieth century."[4]

The AJC, disappointed in the Zionist resolutions adopted at the first session of the American Jewish Conference, boycotted both the second and third meetings and launched a year-long verbal campaign to discredit the American Zionists and blame them for the dissolution of American Jewry. "After the [Zionist] steamroller was finished," Joseph Proskauer reflected in a 1962 interview, "we adjourned and I began to turn my attention to the question of how I was going to destroy what I regarded as a nefarious Jewish movement." Reconciliation attempts failed when leaders of the AJC and the American Jewish Congress could not come to terms on the difficult question of Palestine. The AJC charged that militant American Zionists had needlessly split what could have been a united American Jewish community. Since calls for a Jewish national homeland still conflicted with the ideological perspective of most German-American Jews and many in the Reform movement, AJC leaders thought it appropriate to set aside the divisive question of Jewish nationalism in order to secure much-needed consensus on the practical relief and rescue needs of European Jews.[5]

The American Zionists, led by Wise and Silver, objected to the non-Zionist boycott of the American Jewish Conference and blamed it for breaking up the Jewish union. Silver, who headed the Second American Jewish Conference's Commission on Palestine, argued that the "slogan of 'Jewish unity' which was used fifteen months ago in a desperate effort to defeat your Palestine Resolution, and which was used throughout these last fifteen months to discredit the composition, the authority and the purposes of the American Jewish Conference—this slogan of Jewish unity is one of the most misleading and disruptive ones in American Jewish life." The universalist liberalism typical of the AJC "unity" campaign, in his estimation, harmed Jewish interests. Assertions of ethnic difference bolstered Jewish overseas campaigns and helped protect ethnic self-expression in the United States.[6]

In a counterargument to the AJC's Americanist claims, the Cleveland rabbi called on popular wartime democratic ideals to defend his Zionist position and portray the AJC camp as un-American. "Every organization seeking to maintain a privileged position, every organization unwilling to submit to the judgment of the majority, and every one who out of assimilationist tendencies wishes to hold down American Jewish life to minimal program," he said in reference to the elite Jewish self-defense body, "has sheltered himself behind this slogan of unity." His vision of America demanded democracy in Jewish communal life just as it required freedom and liberty for Europe's oppressed Jews. No one, Silver believed, could achieve consensus in a community of five million. "Only dictatorship," he explained in a chilling parallel to Hitler and Mussolini, "can achieve such a specious unity of action, never of thought, and certainly not for any long time."[7]

Instead of striving for cultural homogenization, Silver sought a nation committed to protecting distinctive expression. His goal for the American Jewish Conference centered on creating an atmosphere "in which all points of view can find their legitimate expression and by means of which the majority can properly receive its authority to speak and act for the entire community." Silver acknowledged the rights of the AJC minority to be heard but refused to grant them the "right to sabotage and disrupt efforts at organization in the hope of keeping the majority from exercising its rightful authority." He knew that the Zionists enjoyed an overwhelming majority at the conference and he exploited his strength as much as he possibly could. Silver and the rest of the American Zionists in attendance looked forward to an opposition-free campaign to bolster their own position in organized Jewish life, reinforce the Zionist base at the conference, and continue their efforts for a more vocal political program.[8]

At its first meeting in 1943, the American Jewish Conference devoted scant attention to postwar issues. Overwhelmed by the immediacies of the war effort, it articulated only the broad contours of what would later become a detailed plan for European and Jewish reconstruction. Delegates to the inaugural American Jewish Conference issued statements calling for the prosecution of war criminals, the "immediate constitution of the allied Commission on War Crimes in London," recognition of the "right of temporary asylum for every surviving Jewish man, woman and child who can escape from the Hitlerite fury into the territories of the United Nations," as well as funding of Jewish relief and self-defense agencies.[9]

At the 1944 conference, though, delegates devoted virtually all their debate to questions involving the postwar reconstruction. They set their sights high, embracing an overly optimistic vision for the future of European Jews forwarded by Rabbi Maurice N. Eisendrath, head of the Reform movement's Union of American Hebrew Congregations and co-chair of the Commission on Post-war. The postwar commission, he affirmed, "is conceived in the spirit of traditional Jewish optimism and is dedicated to the proposition that Yisrael Chai, that Israel lives and shall continue to live not alone in America, in Eretz Israel, and in other lands of freedom, but Israel shall live again even in those areas debased and debauched by the diabolic intruders who have driven our brethren from territories that have been their homes for more than a thousand years." Eisendrath's ideal of settling Jewish refugees in the United States, Poland, and Germany as well as Palestine reflected the Reform movement's humanitarian approach to Zionism and universalist liberal perspective. Jewish immigration to Palestine, according to the Reform movement leader, paralleled resettlement efforts throughout the world and should not be viewed as an ideological commitment to political Zionism.[10]

Even this tempered approach proved almost impossible to achieve. The United States government all but refused to admit Jewish refugees and even if European Jews desired to live in Germany or other Axis nations, they would need specific legal protection from their former oppressors. Eisendrath's task loomed even more difficult given that the postwar committee agenda also included debate on a plan for punishing war criminals, strategies for securing the rehabilitation and reconstruction of postwar Europe, a program to guarantee Jewish political rights, and a proposal for an international bill of rights. The question of immigration to Palestine involved such complex issues that it required debate in its own separate conference committee.[11]

The postwar committee debate centered on a crucial issue dividing American Jews: whether to support programs that offered distinct legal protection for the European Jewish minority or back human rights measures that sought to aid Jews on universalist grounds. Delegates focused discussion around a January 1944 AJC proposal for an international bill of rights. "An international bill of human rights must be promulgated," Proskauer stated, to guarantee "the fundamental rights of life, liberty, and the pursuit of happiness." The AJC plan called for their bill to "be made part of the constitutions of all the members of the United Nations Organization." It demanded that "the peace treaties with all former enemy states should obligate such states to include the Bill of Rights in their constitutions" and that "each member nation should confer upon its courts the power, and impose upon them the duty, to pass judgment on complaints of violations of the Bill of Rights." The AJC also wanted a UN Commission on Human Rights to "be authorized to intervene before national courts in matters relating to violations of the bill of rights" and asked that the commission "be empowered, through the appropriate channels, to call upon the General Assembly or the Security Council to intervene in any case of violation of the Bill of Rights."[12]

While delegates to the second American Jewish Conference session agreed with the overarching principles of equality contained in the AJC proposal, they objected to its insistence that Jews receive no specific mention. Protection of individual rights did not satisfy a more aggressive conference delegation intent on providing special protections for Europe's Jewish population. It was an "inescapable fact," Eisendrath explained in a dramatic break from his Reform brethren in the AJC, "that in seeking to establish the inalienable rights common to all men, we cannot ignore the Jew, qua Jew, nor dissolve an entire people out of existence by ignoring its presence, in our anxiety to secure for all men an International Bill of Rights." Eisendrath reasoned that since "the Nazis have sought to destroy the Jews not merely as individuals, but as a people," it was "not enough to seek rights for man in the abstract." "The test of a democracy," the Reform leader believed, "is to be found in its attitude not only to the individual but to the group."[13]

The commission supported a proposal that acknowledged the group needs of Jews. It passed a resolution calling "for an international bill of rights and for the outlawing of anti-Semitism, with the necessary machinery to implement these demands." In a departure from the AJC, it emphasized the necessity of guaranteeing "the inalienable rights of all religious, ethnic, and cultural groups to maintain and foster their respective group identities on the basis of equality." The commission called for "abrogation of all anti-Jewish measures, for recognition of the right of displaced persons to return to their former places of de facto residence, indemnification for property losses, and for detention and punishment of all persons who committed crimes against international law and humanity." When the commission debated the question of punishing Nazi war criminals, Eisendrath again demanded specific acknowledgment of the injustices waged against the Jewish population. "The demand of the post-war commission," he explained, is "not vengeance, but justice meted out to every despicable criminal who has brought destruction and death upon the Jew—not merely as individuals but as a people."[14]

Conference leaders continued by demanding material relief and political power for their European brethren. "The economic position of the Jews will be regulated primarily by the extent to which their property will be restored," Dr. Nahum Goldmann, leading Zionist, one-time chairman of the World Jewish Congress executive board, and head of the Jewish Agency in New York, said. "It would be naive to believe that the restoration of democratic governments in liberated areas will automatically solve this problem." With Jewish property losses estimated at between six and ten billion dollars, Jewish leaders pleaded with the Allies to take care of the Jews' special needs. They requested funds for vocational training, religious institutions, and welfare programs and demanded free Jewish emigration to Palestine. Delegates concluded their appeal by asking for Jewish representation on all postwar relief, rehabilitation, and resettlement agencies.[15]

Eisendrath took the postwar commission's reconstruction plan to Allied and U.S. government leaders. He reminded them of "the many pronouncements and promises that have been made by the leaders of the United Nations" and insisted "that these promises be kept in order that those who are tempted to mimic the Nazis in their attacks against the Jews shall be deterred by the sure knowledge that there is a moral law respected by the nations of the world which metes out full punishment for this specific crime." In a letter to Secretary of State Cordell Hull, the Commission on Post-War demanded that in Allied-occupied Europe, "all discriminatory laws and measures enacted against the Jewish population . . . be abrogated and the constitutional and treaty rights the Jews of those areas possessed after World War I . . . be restored." It called for the restoration of citizenship "to persons displaced from their former countries, unless they themselves refuse such restoration. The right of communal, religious, and cultural organization shall be restored and the governing authorities shall facilitate the re-establishment of Jewish community organizations." Edwin C. Wilson, director of the government's Office of

Special Political Affairs, responded with a letter informing Eisendrath "that the statement prepared by the commission on post-war of your conference will receive careful and sympathetic consideration."[16]

CREATION OF THE UNITED NATIONS

After its exit from the American Jewish Conference, the AJC turned its attention to an international effort to revive the failed League of Nations. For American Jews in both ideological camps, the creation of the United Nations stood as the single most important liberal development of the immediate postwar period. While many Jewish relief and recovery plans suffered when the Cold War eclipsed anti-Nazism as the major issue in world politics, Jewish efforts on behalf of the international organization forged a new consensus among American Jews and placed the community in the vanguard of postwar liberal internationalism.

The United Nations offered American Jews an ideal political compromise: the AJC valued the UN for its commitment to universal rights, while American Zionists waged their most important Jewish nationalist campaign there after Great Britain relinquished its mandate of Palestine to the new body. As the unofficial representatives of European Jewry, American Jewish leaders looked to the proposed United Nations as a vehicle to guarantee future protection for their co-religionists around the world. At a critical turning point in world history, the United Nations offered American Jews a rare opportunity to bolster their own domestic standing as a Jewish minority, just as they translated the most-cherished American democratic ideals on a global scale. The United States remained a promised land for the Jews, whose communal leaders hoped that a United Nations fashioned in the American image would help other nations, including Palestine, achieve the same sort of tolerance, understanding, and freedom enjoyed by most U.S. citizens.

The AJC launched its UN campaign as soon as James T. Shotwell, a Columbia University historian selected by the government to help create a new international body, established a Commission to Study the Organization of Peace. Addressing the Shotwell committee on January 30, 1944, Proskauer proposed that the commission include the AJC's "international bill of rights" in its postwar plan and that the UN incorporate it into its charter as well. Proskauer used the commission meetings, held in advance of a formal organizing conference in San Francisco in the spring of 1945, to rally support around his plan to protect ethnic minorities by securing universal human rights affirmations and extending American-style protections to postwar Europe and the world. The AJC president's lobbying paid off. By December 15, Proskauer had secured the approval of some 1,326 Americans, including President Roosevelt.[17]

When FDR asked Proskauer and AJC executive committee chairman Jacob Blaustein to attend the San Francisco convention as consultants to the U.S. delegation, they readily agreed. Before they left for California, Roosevelt laid out to them their mission: "Work to get these human rights provisions into the Charter so that unspeakable crimes, like those by the Nazis, will never again be countenanced by world society." After seven years of struggle to get their voices heard in Washington, they now faced the daunting task of formulating a Jewish plan for postwar peace. "For the first time in the course of the Hitler war against the Jews," Louis Lipsky boasted of the Jewish representatives to the San Francisco meeting, "we were able to create a united front of the largest combination of Jewish communities ever assembled since the days of the Versailles Treaty."[18]

While they were ultimately disappointed with the conference's relative indifference to the plight of Jewish refugees, they enjoyed several important victories, chief among them the American Jewish Committee's international bill of rights proposal. In an impassioned appeal to Secretary of State Edward R. Stettinius, Jr., on the floor of the conference, Proskauer warned the State Department head that if he did not back the bill, "you will have lost the support of American public opinion." Proskauer and Blaustein proposed that a UN Commission on Human Rights "declare a public or organized incitement against religious, ethnic, or racial groups to be contrary to the principles and interests of world democracy and a danger to the peace and security of the world." They demanded that the UN serve as a forum for human rights debate and that it guarantee the enforcement of human rights laws.[19]

The AJC chief fought an uphill battle in his campaign for passage of human rights guarantees. While he tried to emulate American ideals in his human rights proposals, Proskauer ironically faced his greatest opposition from the United States and Britain, not to mention an expected rejection by the Soviet Union. The United States, sensitive to the continued government-sanctioned racial discrimination in the Jim Crow South, was not interested in inviting international (and especially Soviet) scrutiny. The British still maintained colonial control throughout the world and feared that the AJC proposal would encourage more movements for national liberation. The Soviet Union feared that its brutal Stalinist purges and widespread policy of repressing dissent would leave it vulnerable to criticism. According to Proskauer, the Soviets were "very suspicious of any proposal which might eventually lead to interference with internal Soviet Affairs."[20]

Delegates to the UN conference ultimately agreed on a compromise proposal that guaranteed the principle of human equality, yet remained vague enough to appease the victorious nations. The relevant articles in the UN charter advanced only the broadest pledges and, as was indicative of the UN as a whole, offered no enforcement clause. The preamble to the UN charter affirmed an ill-defined faith in "fundamental human rights, in the dignity and worth of the human person, in the equal rights of men and women and of nations large and small." Article 55, section c, for example, stipulated that the UN promote "universal respect for, and observance of, human rights and fundamental freedoms for all without distinction as to race, sex, language, or religion," while Article 1, section three reinforced the need for "fundamental freedoms for all without distinction as to race, sex, language, or religion." Article 13, section 1b, impressed the UN General Assembly with "responsibility for implementing and guaranteeing the human rights provisions of the charter." In terms of aiding European Jewish survivors of the war, the broad-based human rights articles offered no specific protection.[21]

Wherever possible, AJC representatives forwarded consensus-oriented plans that hailed the virtues of tolerance and sought to safeguard ethnic minorities with American-style universal protections. The AJC employed legal guarantees basic to the U.S. Constitution as it drafted its model postwar peace plan. From the Bill of Rights, the AJC culled guarantees of "freedom from arbitrary arrest and search, full freedom of religion, speech, press, association, and assembly." From the Thirteenth, Fourteenth, and Fifteenth Amendments, it demanded "full equality of legal status, administrative treatment, and economic opportunity, without discrimination because of religion, race, or color," as well as "the right without discrimination on the basis of race, creed, or color, of and to citizenship, including naturalization" and the "freedom of elections and secrecy of ballot." From the principle of a separate church and state, it petitioned for "the right of ethnic, religious, or linguistic groups to maintain their own cultural and religious institutions, and to use their own languages." It sought judicial protection by guaranteeing "the right of any individual . . . to appeal."[22]

The AJC lobbied against the theft of Jewish property and also worked on important immigration and resettlement issues. During the war, Nazi authorities seized millions of dollars worth of Jewish belongings, and the AJC asked the San Francisco conference for a special "trusteeship of indemnification" to handle the complicated legal process of returning Jewish assets to their rightful owners. It called on the Allied powers in occupied Germany to continue "identifying and registering all assets which were subjected to any form of confiscation, whether by expropriation, forced alienation or otherwise, and act as trustees for all such assets." It closed by petitioning the German government to return illegally obtained Jewish property. In cases where the original owners either perished in the

Holocaust or could not be found, the AJC asked that their property "be assigned to the local Jewish communities for the reconstruction of religious, welfare, educational and cultural institutions, and for the relief and economic rehabilitation of Jewish victims of Nazi persecution."[23]

On the issue of Jewish refugee resettlement, the AJC responded to thousands of Jewish refugees who did not want to return to their native lands. In an unusual reversal of their moderate political tactics, the AJC directed its universalist rhetoric against U.S. immigration policy, postwar treatment of Jews in Europe, and in favor of an ideologically acceptable brand of Zionism that encouraged Jews to migrate on humanitarian grounds.

"The end of the war," the AJC explained, "has revealed that a large number of persons cannot or do not wish to return to the countries from which they were uprooted as victims of religious persecution, racial laws and war conditions." To protect the rights of these Jews, the AJC issued a broadside demanding that no displaced person be "compelled to return to the country from which he was displaced." If any war refugee wished to emigrate from one nation to another, the AJC insisted that such movement not be inhibited by the race, creed, or ethnic origin of the individual. "Displaced persons," it argued, "should be allowed, if they so desire, to continue to live in the country in which they reside, or, in which they have found a temporary haven of refuge."[24]

The AJC requested that the UN form a Commission on Migration to "work for the adoption and ratification of an international migration convention based on the principle of non-discrimination." In the interim, it asked that immigration laws "be liberalized by all countries for individuals and groups who have suffered particular hardships during the war, and who continue to labor under unusual disabilities." It petitioned the postwar authorities to "encourage family reunion and rehabilitation" by creating "special migration facilities" for "orphans, children separated from their families, and other close relatives, who have become separated in the course of mass upheaval and war." To ease the refugee crisis, the AJC favored "increasing the social, economic, and psychological retentive capacity of countries of emigration and the absorptive capacity of countries of immigration."[25]

The AJC's universalist strategy still faltered when Jewish interests conflicted with larger political concerns. While the AJC enjoyed several successes in its campaign to build the UN, Jewish leaders from across the ideological spectrum agreed that their pleas had not been adequately addressed. As long as Jewish representatives posited plans that promoted popular democratic values and did not challenge the victorious allies, their ideas were warmly received. Certainly, the experiences of the AJC supported this assertion. But when Jewish leaders pressed for more aggressive action or criticized the Allies for their indifference, they made little progress.

While Jewish leaders did persuade the UN Relief and Rehabilitation Administration to allow Jewish organizations into occupied zones to help Jews, its subsequent victories were few and far between. The San Francisco conference refused to allow formal Jewish representation and, within a period of three years, scaled back its programs for European Jewish refugee relief. Louis Lipsky, the head of the third session of the American Jewish Conference, lamented the U.S. government's refusal to send more than a single delegate from the Jewish umbrella organization. With Jews "not even counted among those whose cause may properly be considered," Lipsky feared, the allied powers "might dismiss the Jewish problem altogether as not being really as urgent as they thought." "When a meeting is held of states and peoples to consider wrongs to be righted, life to be recognized, reparations to be made," he asked in rhetorical fashion, was it "too much to expect that an occasion would be found, say in San Francisco, on the day the collapse of the world aggressor was acclaimed, to hail the people that had survived, the remnant of them, or their surviving heirs, or those who spoke in their name, and to ask them to join in the celebration?"[26]

Ruth Hershman, editor of the conference proceedings, shared Lipsky's demand for Jewish representation. "Throughout the war," she lamented, "the Jewish people had been sustained by the hope that the cessation of hostilities would be followed by the emergence of a new world in which they would be granted their right to freedom, equality, and justice." She had hoped that the American Jewish Conference, an organization created for the express purpose of representing the will of the Jewish people, "would be in a position to present forcefully its demands before the peace tribunal." It was not. Lipsky's and Hershman's frustration typified Jewish communal displeasure with UN relief operations and dramatized the limitations of a Jewish reform program based on universalist political strategies.[27]

AMERICAN ZIONISM IN THE POSTWAR PERIOD

Throughout 1944, the AJC maintained its opposition to the political Zionism espoused by Lipsky and others. At its thirty-seventh annual meeting held in January, the AJC reaffirmed its call for the resettlement of European Jews in their nations of birth. The AJC president called on the natural law traditions of both the French and American revolutions to demand fair treatment of Jews wherever they may reside. An embrace of political Zionism translated in Proskauer's mind to a rejection of Enlightenment ideals. Zionists, he inferred, advocated a racist methodology since, in his view, it based one's freedom on group status rather than individual rights. The AJC head dismissed his activist co-religionists' calls for massive European Jewish emigration and demanded that international authorities supervise any incidental movement of Jews from Europe to Palestine. "What we do for America," Proskauer urged in a 1944 speech, "our brethren may do for every country in the world."[28]

Toward the end of the war, the AJC faced increasing pressure from Zionists. It feared that the growing popularity of American Zionism would marginalize the AJC and diminish its authority as a representative national Jewish organization. Despite its continued support from the non-Zionist Jewish Labor Committee, UAHC, CCAR, and B'nai B'rith, the AJC feared that Americans, Jewish and non-Jewish alike, might confuse their non-Zionism with the anti-Zionism of the ACJ and blame them for the lack of American Jewish unity. In a calculated attempt to move themselves toward the new American Jewish political center, the AJC tried and failed to solicit new members, democratize its organization, and rally against the British White Paper, which limited Jewish immigration to Palestine. Despite its national recruitment efforts, the AJC learned that it was increasingly out of touch with the political mood of American Jewry: an elite leadership core maintained its control of the organization.[29]

The organized Jewish community emerged from the war in 1945 ill-prepared to manage the European crisis, following what proved to be a tumultuous year for the Allies, for the American people, and for American Jews. President Roosevelt, who had led the nation out of the Great Depression and into World War II, died in April in Warm Springs, Georgia, where he often traveled to convalesce. American, British, and Russian units turned the tide of the war and brought the Axis powers to defeat, both in the European and Pacific theaters. And with the end of the war, greater details of Hitler's plan to murder Europe's Jews reached a shocked American public. "Little more than a year has gone by," Rabbi Eisendrath observed in February 1946, "and yet I hazard the guess that never before has so much history been packed into so brief a period of time."[30]

The Jewish population of Poland plummeted from 3.25 million in the prewar period to a scant 80,000 in 1945. Almost 800,000 Jews perished in Soviet Russia, 425,000 in Romania, 210,000 in France, and 204,000 in Hungary. A September 15, 1945, United Nations estimate placed the total number of displaced persons remaining in western Germany at 1.675 million. Of these, the smallest group, concentration camp survivors, numbered about 30,000; a larger group comprised Jews who remained in hiding during the war. The largest group of these displaced persons was composed of Polish Jews who had returned to Poland after the war, only to flee once again in the face of renewed anti-Semitism. A

February 1946 AJC report noted that "of the nearly seven million Jews of Continental Europe outside Russia, there remain, according to a survey made by the Joint Distribution Committee, only 1,688,000."[31]

For the first time since Hitler's rise to power, the Jewish community enjoyed the overwhelming support of the American people, who responded with understandable horror to news of the Nazi genocide. In an April 1945 poll that anticipated what came to be known as the "Nuremberg defense," the Gallup organization asked Americans what they thought about soldiers who claimed "that they committed crimes under orders of higher-ups in the party." Forty-two percent of the respondents answered "imprison them," 19 percent said, "kill them," and another 19 percent wanted to "try them and punish only if found guilty." Three percent thought that the Allied powers should "try to reeducate them," while only 2 percent felt no action was necessary. The following month, another Gallup poll revealed that 84 percent of the American public believed reports of Nazi atrocities, up from 76 percent in December 1944. Only 4 percent were doubtful or did not believe them.[32]

The American media projected powerful and sympathetic portraits of European Jewish suffering. *Newsweek* ran photos of the Buchenwald concentration camp after liberation, while the *New Yorker* dedicated several of its pages to covering the Nazi genocide. Edward R. Murrow chose a concentration camp as a backdrop for one of his reports, and General Dwight D. Eisenhower, then the Supreme Allied Commander, gave the journalistic reports even more credibility by ordering camp inspections. Powerful political figures lent their moral support as well. Former vice-president Henry Wallace believed "that there will never be peace in the world until justice is done to the Jew," while Eleanor Roosevelt reversed her wartime position and called for the legalization of Jewish immigration to Palestine. President Harry Truman ordered a delegation under the leadership of Earl G. Harrison to tour the displaced persons camps in Europe and report their findings to him. The delegation's August 1945 review pointed to the horrendous conditions overseas and called for the free immigration of 100,000 Jews into Palestine.[33]

Yet the American anti-Hitler consensus did not translate into popular support for Jewish refugees. While most Americans remained sympathetic, few were willing to offer public policy remedies. A December 1945 poll on immigration revealed that only 5 percent of the American public "wanted more immigration from Europe than before the war," 32 percent favored keeping immigration numbers constant, 37 percent preferred a decrease in the number of new arrivals, while 14 percent wanted it stopped completely. Rabbi Philip Bernstein, a ZOA leader and publicist for the Zionist cause, reported that with the rehabilitation of Germany assuming increased importance in world politics, displaced persons grew to be "an irritation and an obstacle" to Allied soldiers concerned with other seemingly more important issues. "Ugly incidents between them are increasing," Bernstein warned, "and bode ill for the future." Maurice Eisendrath observed that "a strange malaise and dissatisfaction and disappointment have seized hold of some of us as we begin to question whether—even though the war is over—the peace is won—whether the Four Freedoms for which supposedly we fought have been attained." While Eisendrath acknowledged the restoration of freedom of speech and worship in Hitler's former empire, he warned that "there is precious little freedom from want for the pitiful and pathetic remnant of our fellow Jews in Europe." Government policymakers, who had earlier created what historian David Wyman has called bureaucratic "paper walls" to keep out Jewish refugees, refused to open U.S. borders to more than a handful of war victims.[34]

In 1946, Judge Simon Rifkind, sent to Europe as the Jewish advisor to the U.S. Army, offered his own sullen account of conditions. Jewish concentration camp survivors, he surmised, "expected the miracle of liberation to be followed by a repentant mankind which had permitted them to suffer such barbarism. There was no such welcome." Instead, Rifkind found, "They awoke to find themselves in the chilly atmosphere of a displaced persons center with every avenue of escape to a land of freedom and dignity closed to them." Even the UN, which had taken over refugee responsibilities on July 1, 1947, from an overworked and underprepared U.S. Army, could not handle the incredible task before them. Thirty months after Allied victory, an estimated 250,000 Jews still languished in DP camps. International support for Jewish refugees ended the same year Secretary of State George C. Marshall's European recovery plan sent the first of $12.4 billion in economic relief payments to the Jews' former oppressors.[35]

The future of Jewish life, for the time being at least, rested in the United States. After Henry Monsky reported that close to six million Jews had perished in "this horrible and incomprehensible tragedy," he urged American Jews "to assume an unprecedented measure of responsibility for the preservation of the remnants of Israel in the war-devastated lands and for the establishment of an acceptable post-war status." He called the rescue of European Jews "the greatest [challenge] in all of our history as a people" and reminded his fellow American Jews that their European brothers and sisters "who remain after years of the most cruel and gruesome experiences, cry out for aid and succor."[36]

Louis Lipsky affirmed Monsky's solemnity when he reported that "a whole generation had been completely swept from the earth." Lipsky berated world indifference to the Jews' plight. "As never before," Lipsky extolled, "the Jews fought valiantly—arrayed all on one side—in every army, on every front that faced the enemy." He pointed out that "wherever there was a resistance movement, Jews in large numbers fought side by side with the underground forces." He noted "the genius of Jewish scientists, gathered from many countries, that made the atomic bomb available to speed victory over the Japanese." "And yet," Lipsky lamented, "at the end of the war, with the flags of victory flying everywhere, the only stateless and unprotected people in the world, whose remnants are being chivvied about the fields of Europe, with no claim that is recognized, with no status that is defined, with no hope that they can rely upon, are the people who have suffered most and longest during this time."[37]

American Zionist leaders, frustrated with the UN's inability to meet the needs of the DPs, stepped up their campaign for a Jewish commonwealth in Palestine. At the third session of the American Jewish Conference, boycotted again by the AJC, Zionist leaders devoted almost every moment of debate to the rescue of Jewish refugees, recognition of Jewish legal rights in Axis and Axis-controlled lands, restitution of lost property, and creation of new plans for long-term Jewish settlement. Stephen S. Wise, Abba Hillel Silver, and Nahum Goldmann pressed openly for an independent Jewish state in Palestine. They lobbied government officials, made passionate speeches whenever and wherever possible, and launched fund-raising campaigns aimed at the widest cross-section of American Jewry, regardless of previous Zionist affiliation.

Zionist hopes were buoyed in November 1945, when the U.S. and British governments called for the creation of an Anglo-American Committee of Inquiry (AACI) Regarding the Problems of European Jewry and Palestine. The council investigated various plans for refugee resettlement and examined in particular a proposal to permit the massive immigration of Jews into Palestine. Its final report, issued May 1, 1946, called for an end to the British White Paper and the issuance of 100,000 Palestine immigration visas, but it refused to endorse a national homeland for Jews. While committee members looked forward to the time when Jews and Arabs could govern Palestine together and in peace, they called for a continued British presence.[38]

American Zionists met the formation of the AACI with trepidation. Abba Hillel Silver feared that British authorities had created the commission in order to delay action on the Palestine question; he enjoyed limited support in his call for a communal boycott of the AACI. Most Zionists, led by Stephen Wise, feared that opposition might leave the diplomatic door open to a non-Zionist or anti-Zionist monopoly on the proceedings and called for American Zionist support. AJC leaders still took care to avoid an association with political Zionism. In a September 29 meeting with the chief executive, AJC leaders made clear their conviction that the government not confuse calls for humanitarianism with support for a

Figure 5. The Jewish War Veterans March on Washington, D.C., during their July 15, 1946, Great Palestine Protest. (Jewish War Veterans collection, I-32, box 2 of 5, American Jewish Historical Society, Waltham, Mass.)

sovereign Jewish state. Proskauer took Rabbi Silver to task for campaigning against the British mandatory control over Palestine. The AJC head warned Silver not to use the DP crisis to fuel political goals. Since the AJC moderated its views regarding immigration, Proskauer reasoned, the Zionist leadership should temper its call for immediate statehood.[39]

While the AJC urged the AACI to recognize Jewish claims to Palestine under the Balfour Declaration and allow unrestricted Jewish immigration into the British mandate, it justified its support in language typical of American liberal democracy, refusing to embrace the Zionist ideology of most American Jews. It sought UN support for an independent Palestine and petitioned the yishuv's new leaders to apply American-style political guarantees for the new state's minority populations. By safeguarding "the religious, political, and civil liberties and rights of all persons and all elements of the Palestine population," the AJC hoped that the new Jewish state could foster good relations between Jews and Arabs and make "possible the attainment of a democratic and independent commonwealth with equal rights for all." Despite an October 1945 Gallup poll which revealed that over 80 percent of Americans thought "a Jewish state in Palestine is a good thing for the Jews," the AJC still feared a backlash.[40]

Other Jewish leaders followed the AJC lead. Rabbi Julian Morgenstern, the anti-Zionist head of the Reform movement's seminary, Hebrew Union College, proclaimed himself a non-Zionist and assured his co-religionists that he would not campaign against a Jewish state. Representatives from B'nai B'rith, the JDC, and the United Jewish Appeal all backed Jewish immigration to Palestine, even though their organizations did not formally ally themselves with the Zionist cause. Most would have agreed with the sentiments of Adele Rosenwald-Levy, sister of ACJ anti-Zionist Lessing Rosenwald, after she heard first-hand accounts of the misery in European DP camps: "Zionism or no Zionism, ideology or no ideology—that is not my concern. But if Palestine means that they will once more be able to laugh and sing, then we must help these Jews in all possible ways." While the AJC made sure that it justified its support for Jewish settlement in Palestine on humanitarian concerns and not political ideology, it came to the conclusion that only a Jewish state could solve the refugee crisis. "The events of 1945–1947," the historian Menahem Kaufman wrote, "led the American non-Zionists to the conclusion that without Jewish sovereignty there would be no security for the refugees; with great hesitation and misgiving, they lent their support to the establishment of the Jewish state."[41]

Efforts to create a Jewish state in Palestine reached a critical turning point on April 2, 1947, when the British government made a surprise announcement: it would relinquish control of Palestine and allow the UN to decide how best to resolve the competing sovereignty claims of the Jews and Arabs. UN member nations, led by the unlikely alliance of the United States and the Soviet Union, agreed to the British request and on May 14 created the United Nations Special Commission on Palestine (UNSCOP) to decide the fate of the British mandate. Over the next several months the UNSCOP, comprised of eleven non-permanent Security Council nations, invited representatives from the interested parties to give testimony at specially arranged hearings. While Nahum Goldmann and Abba Hillel Silver took different tacts in the negotiations, Goldmann's plan for a partition of Palestine eventually won American Zionist support.[42]

Even though the AJC still insisted that it embraced the idea of a Jewish state as a humanitarian rather than an ideological solution, the debate over partition marked its generation-long reversal on the question of Zionism. Ultimately, the exigencies of war shattered the AJC's time-worn concept of American Jewish accommodationism. Few could charge American Jews with dual loyalty under such dire conditions. In the face of brutal inhumanity, any American would be expected to protest, the AJC came to realize. It offered a memorandum to the UNSCOP affirming its interest "in the preservation and development of the Jewish homeland in Palestine, and the protection of the rights of Jewish immigration and land ownership," but avoided any direct Zionist language, hoping instead that it could mediate "the solution of the problem by processes of reason and good will." Reform Jewish leaders in the CCAR maintained their official non-Zionist stance, divorced immigrant resettlement questions from issues of political sovereignty, and under the leadership of then-president Silver, pressed for open immigration. While Silver himself would have carried his message much further, he moderated his views in order to avoid alienating his non-Zionist colleagues.[43]

The following September, the commission submitted two reports to the General Assembly. The first, a minority report authored by representatives from India, Iran, and Yugoslavia, sought a single independent federal state with independent Jewish and Arab cantons. The majority view, presented by representatives from Canada, Czechoslovakia, Guatemala, the Netherlands, Peru, Sweden, and Uruguay, called for partition into a Jewish state and an Arab state, with Jerusalem remaining an international city. UNSCOP accepted the end of the British mandate and pressed for the immigration of 150,000 Jewish refugees. The commission sent the majority plan to the General Assembly with a unanimous vote of approval, and when debate ended there on November 29, 1947, the plan was adopted by a 33–13 vote. Ten nations abstained. Coincidentally, on that same day, the Third American Jewish Conference was meeting in Cleveland. Bolstered not only by the UN vote but also by public opinion polls showing that 90 percent of American Jews supported partition, Louis Lipsky led the plenary in an emotional rendition of both "The Star Spangled Banner" and "Hatikvah," the anthem of the yishuv movement.[44]

The American Zionists, while internally split over several aspects of the majority partition plan, ultimately resolved to support it as the best solution available. Silver exulted in the strategic potential of the UN vote. With the international community leading the call for partition, Silver could offer a well-timed acceptance. He labeled partition a "very heavy sacrifice" for the Jewish people and pointed out that it offered his brethren much less than Britain had promised in the Balfour Declaration, but Silver nevertheless backed the UN plan. "The proposal makes possible the immediate re-establishment of the Jewish State," he explained, "an ideal for which our people ceaselessly strove through the centuries, and because it ensures immediate and continuing Jewish immigration which, as events have demonstrated, is possible only under a Jewish State." As long as he received assurances that Jews would control immigration policy and maintain political sovereignty, Silver called for his co-religionists to adopt partition "as our contribution to the solution of a grave international problem and as evidence of our willingness to join with the community of nations in an effort to bring peace at last to the troubled land which is precious to the heart of mankind."[45]

The AJC backed partition as well, finding creative ways to justify its newfound support for Jewish statehood on universalist grounds. Some in the non-Zionist organization thought that the creation of a Jewish state might ease dual loyalty concerns by silencing the Zionists. "There is a possibility that, with the establishment of the Jewish state in Palestine," one AJC representative explained, "the Zionist movement all over the world will be dissolved. Its ultimate aim, the creating of a sovereign Jewish state, achieved, Zionism will no longer have its *raison d'être* for political activity abroad." Proskauer hoped that the Jewish state might offer American Jews yet another opportunity to export democratic pluralism. In a speech before the forty-first convention of the AJC on January 18, 1948, he called for American-style protections of "race, religion, national origin [and] social outlook." In a speech the following month, Jacob Blaustein reaffirmed his organization's philanthropic focus by reminding his co-religionists that "Palestine to us is perhaps the most important, but by no means the sole, potential center for DP settlement." The AJC sought to represent themselves as an organization committed to American ideals instead of a particular Jewish-defense body. "We subscribe to the view," staffers wrote, "that there exists no contradiction of interests between our Palestine objectives—the largest possible DP immigration to Palestine and the building of a Jewish homeland—and those of the United States, the Middle East, and the needs for safeguarding and strengthening the UN in its role of protecting the peace of the world." Continued concern over dual loyalty, though, led the AJC to oppose American Jewish enlistment in the three Palestinian Jewish military underground units, violations of the British-maintained arms embargo, and an American expeditionary force to keep the peace in Palestine.[46]

After the UN partition vote, the AJC used its government contacts to lobby support. Proskauer shuttled back and forth between Truman administration officials in Washington and various American Jewish leaders. He negotiated a careful path in his support of the Jewish state. On the one hand, he explained that "partition was now the project both of the Jewish Agency for Palestine and of the government of the United States," and he therefore "gave my whole-hearted support to the accomplishment of the plan." Yet in a bid to gain support from the non-Zionists in his organization, he qualified his enthusiasm. Rejecting the political Zionism of Silver and Wise, Proskauer supported partition only because "it had become apparent that partition was the most promising, if not the only means of throwing open the gates of Palestine." The AJC leader admitted that, in truth, he had "no position on Palestine in the sense of a fixed ideological plan. The one great overwhelming objective is to get immediate and substantial immigration into Palestine and within limits, of course, I don't care very much how I get it."[47]

Despite the overwhelming support of the American public and Truman's backing of the Jewish claims to statehood, Proskauer still feared a challenge to the Jews' reputation as loyal American citizens. On January 19, 1948, he wrote a letter to the New York *Herald Tribune*, reassuring its readers of continued Jewish loyalty to the United States: "We are told by the anti-Semite, through malice, and by some small sections of American Jewry, through confusion, that this partition has created a problem of possible inconsistency between our obligations as Americans and as Jews." In response, Proskauer stated simply, "There is no such problem." He reminded the newspaper readers that five years earlier, the AJC had published a statement affirming that "there can be no political identification of Jews outside of Palestine with whatever government may there be instituted." Proskauer assured the public that "the Jews of America suffer from no political schizophrenia. Politically we are not split personalities, and in faith and in conduct we shall continue to demonstrate what the death rolls of our army on many a battlefield have attested that we are bone of the bone and flesh of the flesh of America."[48]

Even after the State of Israel was created in May 1948 and recognized by the United States soon after, the AJC remained squeamish about the possibility of dual-loyalty conflicts. In 1949, Proskauer convinced Israeli prime minister David Ben-Gurion to promise that officials of the new Jewish state would not challenge the loyalty of American Jews, assert that American Jews were "living in exile," nor encourage large-scale immigration of American Jews to Israel. The following year, Proskauer's successor as AJC president, Jacob Blaustein, secured a letter from Ben-Gurion reiterating that "the Jews of the United States . . . owe no political allegiance to Israel." Ben-Gurion went on to reassure Blaustein and his constituents that "we, the people of Israel, have no desire and no intention to interfere in any way with the internal affairs of Jewish communities abroad. The Government and the people of Israel fully respect the right and integrity of the Jewish communities in other countries to develop their indigenous social, economic, and cultural institutions in accord with their own needs and aspirations." Ben-Gurion closed with an affirmation that he was "anxious that nothing should be said or done which could in the slightest degree undermine the sense of security and stability of American Jewry."[49]

The debate over Palestine and over Jewish representation at the San Francisco UN conference marked the end of a fifteen-year transformation for American Jewry. A community that in 1933 shunned any association with specifically Jewish political causes campaigned in 1948 for the Jewish people's right to represent itself in the international arena and for the creation of an independent state. Most Jews in postwar America, unlike their Depression-era predecessors, lobbied for explicit recognition of their community's special group interests. One who embodied this new American ethnic consciousness was Henry Monsky, the Omaha social worker who rose to head B'nai B'rith. As the third session of the American Jewish Conference drew to a close, Monsky delivered an inspiring and impassioned message. The end of World War II, he affirmed, signaled "the dawn of a new era," a time "in which the destiny of peoples shall be determined on the basis of fundamental justice." For American Jewry, the Jewish leader's words could not have been more prophetic. In the decades to follow, the Jewish community labored to realize Monsky's vision. After demonstrating the evils of intolerance and prejudice on a global scale, it turned its attention to injustices at home, intent on showing an increasingly conservative America the virtues of fighting domestic anti-Semitism, discrimination, and racial prejudice.[50]

CHAPTER SIX

The Struggle for Civil Liberties: The Cold War, Anti-Communism, and Jewish Liberal Reform

THE END OF World War II heralded an era of renewed hope in the United States. After fifteen years of depression and war, Americans looked forward to better, more secure days. The postwar economy boomed. By 1960, 75 percent of American families piled into their own automobiles, 87 percent tuned in their own televisions to their favorite programs, and 75 percent enjoyed the luxury of a washing machine. The GI Bill of Rights funded thousands of college educations, new home purchases, and small business loans. In politics, fear of Soviet Communism eclipsed anti-German and anti-Japanese sentiment. Democrats and Republicans alike eschewed extreme ideologies in favor of what Arthur Schlesinger, Jr., called "the vital center." The nation joined in a consensus that celebrated economic expansion, ridiculed Stalin and his system of government, and hailed American democracy as the quintessential model of freedom and liberty.[1]

Despite its benevolent outward appearance, the anti-Communist consensus also created a political culture ripe for abuse. In 1947, President Truman investigated the political backgrounds of more than three million federal employees. Three years later, the government ignored due process rights when it dismissed individuals it considered security risks. In Hollywood, scores of actors and actresses faced blacklisting for their supposed association with Communists. Public libraries removed liberal magazines from their shelves while schools across the country banned classic works of literature out of fear that they might turn the nation's children toward the Soviet system of government. The nation's morbid obsession with anti-Communism led to the rise of Joseph McCarthy, the junior senator from Wisconsin, who took to the television airwaves with far-flung accusations linking U.S. army personnel to Communist subversion.[2]

The Jewish community straddled both experiences. By 1960, it enjoyed many of the benefits of middle-class citizenship. The size of the Jewish working class shrunk as professional fields opened to Jews for the first time. Cold War policies such as the GI bill helped Jewish veterans enroll in college, buy homes, and open businesses. Between 1945 and 1965, one out of every three Jews left urban centers for the quiet and affluence of America's new suburbs. Within the philanthropic world, American Jews embarked on the most ambitious building campaign in their history, donating a billion dollars to construct almost a thousand new synagogues. The postwar boom inspired American Jews to follow the lead of other white middle-class Americans and join the anti-Communist consensus. "There can be no ultimate peace," one local Jewish Community Relations Council asserted, "between democracy and communism." Opposition to Communism not only placed American Jews within the larger political framework of Cold War liberalism, but it served as an important vehicle for Jewish social mobility.[3]

Jewish leaders feared that their community's historic links to leftist politics might spark an anti-Semitic backlash. Many turn-of-the-century Jewish immigrants voted for Socialist candidates in local elections and the Yiddish-language leftist newspaper, The *Jewish Daily Forward*, emerged as the largest circulation non-English daily periodical in the nation. As late as the 1930s, the American Communist party counted a disproportionate number of Jews on its rolls. Jewish leaders hoped that an embrace of anti-Communism would prove to skeptical Americans that Jews had abandoned leftism and joined the American political mainstream. Acculturation to Cold War America demanded that Jews distance themselves from those negative associations, and Jewish agencies followed the lead of most liberal secular organizations when they purged suspected Communists from their ranks. Even the American Jewish Congress, known for its activist defense of Jewish interests, joined in the anti-Communist action. Jewish leaders linked the human rights abuses of Soviet-bloc countries with anti-Semitism and racism and equated Communism with all that was harmful to American democracy. As one official of the National Community Relations Advisory Committee explained, Jews had "to demonstrate to the American people that they are not merely disassociating themselves from communists by word of mouth, but that they are strongly, violently opposed to communism because of its danger to democracy, and because of its danger to the Jew." The continued integration of Jews into the American mainstream demanded that they join the national Cold War consensus.[4]

Yet as a religious minority vulnerable to discrimination, they viewed the national landscape with more suspicion. Anti-Communism provided the political glue necessary to achieve a remarkable nationwide consensus, but its concomitant threats to civil liberties challenged constitutional protections cherished by the Jewish community. The civil libertarian approach to American liberalism that typified the Jewish community's 1930s social reform campaigns weakened when Cold War fears branded even the most benign defense of free speech rights a threat to national security. American Jews, unlike their non-Jewish neighbors, still worried about political and social marginalization. Persistent domestic anti-Semitism reminded the community that the anti-Communist consensus did not mean an end to discrimination. Jews could not adopt the complacent attitude of other white ethnic minorities: they understood the limits of American democracy. The political behavior of American Jews between 1945 and 1960 illustrated the complex and often contradictory impulses basic to Cold War liberalism.[5]

As they did during the New Deal, Jews responded by crafting liberal politics into a powerful civic ally. They co-opted arguments usually reserved for proponents of the status quo to justify their calls for greater tolerance, equity, and opportunity. Threats against American civil liberties, Jewish leaders warned, challenged the wisdom of an ambitious anti-Communist campaign. When faced with an upswing in anti-Semitic employment discrimination, Jewish leaders called on Cold War ideals to highlight how such behavior challenged American democratic superiority. Popular beliefs that a strong educational system would strengthen American democracy fueled a Jewish campaign to protect public schools from religious incursion while other Jews argued that American immigration laws embarrassed a nation purported to be the leader of the free world.

While the Jewish community managed an impressive liberal campaign at a time of overwhelming conservatism, its decision to wed its social reform program to the larger consensus diluted its political strength. By tailoring their politics to the attitudes of the mainstream, Jewish leaders created a glass ceiling beyond which they could not be effective. When Jewish liberals exploited anti-Communist sentiment to advance their employment anti-discrimination program, for example, they did not anticipate that political conservatives would one day void their efforts by using Cold War fears to limit American civil liberties. The Jewish community's emphasis on civil libertarian principles proved a marriage of convenience as well. Social inclusion remained the Jews' primary goal. In the debate over church-state separation, most Jewish organizations registered their unqualified opposition to any breach of the sacred constitutional barrier. If the government sanctioned Christianity in any way, they reasoned, the rights of the Jewish minority could be compromised. These Jewish leaders were surprised to hear that some parents, desiring to integrate their children into the non-Jewish majority, demanded that they be allowed to participate in school-sponsored religious events. Many in the Orthodox community, much less concerned with how public schools would aid in the acculturation of Jewish students, opposed their liberal co-religionists from the start. They embraced state support of private education as a means to strengthen their own Jewish day schools and the religious character of the United States.

Demographic changes within the American Jewish community extended the influence of its Eastern European–descended majority and inspired many postwar political reforms. By 1950, fewer than 10 percent of American Jews claimed Central or Western European ancestry. A younger generation of second-generation American-born Jews of Eastern European descent seized the mantle of leadership from older German-American Jews and continued its campaign for a more democratic Jewish communal structure. In 1955, sociologist Nathan Glazer observed that Eastern European American Jews had risen "more or less to the level previously achieved by the German Jews." These new Jewish leaders jumped into national public policy debates with greater enthusiasm and inspired a more activist Jewish polity.[6]

The American Jewish Congress, reconstituted during World War II to aid European Jews, adopted high-profile political strategies and earned a reputation as the Jewish community's most aggressive advocate of liberal causes. Protection of minority rights rose to the top of its communal agenda: the AJCongress believed that, in the wake of the Holocaust and amidst continued domestic anti-Semitism, the best defense of Jewish rights was an aggressive campaign to safeguard the rights of all American minorities. AJCongress leaders understood the dire consequences of intolerance and fought for a principled defense of civil liberties. They preferred legal challenges over quiet dialogue and created a Commission on Law and Social Action (CLSA) to advance their platform. While enjoying less popular support than during the war, the American Jewish Congress drew ample strength from younger, liberal, second-generation American Jews in the Northeast, Midwest, and West. Most AJCongress leaders received liberal anti-Communism with great skepticism. While they shared a basic aversion to the Soviet Union, they feared anti-Communist excesses as well. The AJCongress and its allied organizations adopted an opportunistic relationship to the postwar liberal consensus, carrying their reform mandates on its coattails as they maintained a vigil against its most offensive civil libertarian abuses.[7]

Even though many Eastern European American Jews joined the American Jewish Committee in the postwar years, the organization retained its traditional strategy of education, dialogue, and compromise. More accommodationist than the AJCongress, it shied away from political confrontation, preferring instead to underwrite studies and programs geared toward promoting interracial understanding. AJC members remained optimistic about intergroup dialogue and did not perceive great differences between Jews and the rest of the nation. Most AJC leaders expressed genuine fear of a Communist threat. They subscribed to the dominant belief that leftist political expression did not enjoy constitutional protection and rejected a principled defense of civil liberties. They hoped a quiet compromise would end the civil libertarian threat and protect the Jewish community's reputation as lovers of democracy and opponents of Soviet-style government. Just as the AJC and AJCongress split on expressions of New Deal liberalism and American Zionism, their conflicting approaches to postwar liberalism once again illustrated how Jewish leaders employed competing strategies to reach the same goal: inclusion in a pluralist democracy that would value Jewish participation and protect the rights of its minority citizens.

Mediating between the moderate AJC and the progressive AJCongress was the National Community Relations Advisory Committee (NCRAC), an umbrella organization representing scores of local and regional Jewish organizations, organized in March 1944. With constituents in local community federations of varying sizes and locales, the NCRAC prided itself as the most representative national Jewish body.[8]

THE ROSENBERG CASE AND JEWISH ANTI-COMMUNISM

Jewish leaders feared that their efforts to join the "vital center" would take a dramatic turn for the worse when two American Jews, Julius and Ethel Rosenberg, were arrested on suspicion of furnishing atomic secrets to the Soviets. Even though their own organizations' public opinion polls failed to show a strong anti-Jewish backlash, Jewish leaders worried about their community's safety. National Jewish groups weighed their actions carefully, always mindful of how their public pronouncements would be received within the larger anti-Communist society. Their responses to the Rosenberg case illustrate the classic connection between American Jewish Cold War political culture and processes of ethnic acculturation. The Rosenberg case was more about American Jewish civic security than it was about two particular defendants, the criminal justice system, or even the Cold War. It served as an important metaphor for postwar American Jewish life.

Even before the Rosenberg's arrest, the American Jewish Committee went to great lengths to insulate the Jewish community from Communist associations. It devised an education program geared toward enlightening the American public to the "inherent incompatibility of Judaism and communism" and pledged to work on "the unmasking of any new communist fronts and communist-dominated organizations which attempt to work in the Jewish community." If anti-Semites successfully linked Jews with Communists, one committee member feared, Jews might become scapegoats for a Third World War. The AJC official warned that "declarations of equal opposition to dictatorship, whether from one side or the other, are not sufficient." If Jews were "to engage effectively in the fight against this hysteria," the AJC leader extolled, "organizations must have a record and a reputation for anti-communism."[9]

By distancing themselves from the Communist conspirators, Jewish leaders could turn a potentially disastrous show trial into an affirmation of Jewish Americanism. They hoped that adept handling of the Rosenberg case would end speculation about their community's historic link to leftism and affirm the Jewish people's love of country. With a Jewish judge, Jewish defendants, Jewish defense attorneys, a Jewish prosecutor, and Jewish witnesses, the Rosenberg trial celebrated the social and political integration of postwar American Jews just as it raised serious concerns about Communist influences in American Jewish life.[10]

During the trial, Jewish leaders, fearful that public pronouncements could create a negative association between Jews and Communism, remained silent. The head of AJC's Staff Committee on Communism recommended that his organization "not admit even by implication that there is group responsibility for this crime." Heeding his advice, the AJC refrained from commenting on the case in order "to avoid any publicity which would help the communists attract attention to the case." If one of the most important American Jewish organizations separated itself from the case, AJC leaders believed, then the Rosenbergs could be portrayed as isolated saboteurs and not part of a larger group-based phenomenon. Silence proved the most powerful strategy for the AJC because it shielded Jews from unwanted attention.[11]

When two pro-Communist American Jewish newspapers, the *Morning Freiheit* and *Jewish Life*, alleged that anti-Semitism contributed to the Rosenberg's April 1951 death sentence, Jewish leaders abandoned their strategy of silence. Representatives of the Anti-Defamation League and AJC in particular distrusted the Communists, whom they accused of capitalizing on anti-Jewish sentiment. Mainstream American Jewish leaders thought the leftist press imperiled the American Jewish community by dramatizing the religion of the Rosenbergs. What the ADL and AJC wanted to portray as an isolated case of espionage became, in the words of one Jewish Rosenberg defender, "the Dreyfus case of cold-war America." While the pro-Rosenberg contingent remained quite small, it struck fear in the heart of American Jewry. The major national Jewish organizations defended the Rosenberg's convictions and rejected any connection between their religious background and their propensity for treason. Even though the fight against anti-Semitism was the organized Jewish community's most important priority, Jewish leaders worried that playing the anti-Jewish card in the Rosenberg case would cause grave damage to American Jewish interests.

Jewish leaders took particular offense at their co-religionists who supported the Rosenbergs. When a group of American Jews committed to the innocence of the Rosenbergs formed the National Committee to Secure Justice in the Rosenberg Case, the organized Jewish community responded with barely concealed wrath. The AJC launched a massive campaign to thwart its efforts, while a representative from the Jewish War Veterans denounced his brethren in a letter to the trial judge. The ADL joined the AJC in a published report accusing the National Committee of complicity in a Communist plot to curry favor with American Jews; both groups tried to convince local Jewish communities not to give the Rosenberg sympathizers a forum. The NCRAC issued a statement condemning "efforts to mislead the people of this country by unsupported charges that the religious ancestry of the defendants was a factor in the case."[12]

Imitating AJC and AJCongress political strategy, Jewish Rosenberg sympathizers tried to show how a civil libertarian defense of the accused would translate into a nation more friendly to Jews. Jewish commitment to the rule of law, they argued, demanded that the organized Jewish community reverse course on the Rosenberg case. One Rosenberg supporter even warned of a "wave of Hitler-like genocidal attacks against the Jewish people throughout the United States" if the Rosenbergs received unfair treatment. The AJC and ADL rejected that logic out of hand. It was, in their opinion, an underhanded ploy to bolster the Communist cause by capitalizing on the American Jewish desire for social inclusion.[13]

Most national Jewish organizations did not consider the leftist claims credible. Rather than representing a valid alternative interpretation of American Jewish life, the AJC, ADL, and even the AJCongress suspected Communists of using civil libertarian protections to mask their seditious intentions. Jewish leaders did not safeguard Communist dissent in the same way they fought for the right to air other unpopular opinions. They embraced Sidney Hook's famous formulation that Communism was a criminal conspiracy rather than a legitimate, if heretical political ideology. When Jewish leaders learned of radical attempts to influence Jewish organizations, they followed the example set by secular liberal organizations and purged suspected Communists. Unfortunately, in their bid to root out Communists, they sacrificed a large measure of their liberal idealism, employing many of the anti-Communist strategies they deplored in others.[14]

In a 1950 memo, anti-Communist AJC official Rabbi S. Anhil Fineberg argued that "the Jewish community has no responsibility whatsoever in reference to persons so accused [of Communism], unless there is adequate reason to believe that the accusation is false and that civil rights are being violated." In a reversal of American due process rights uncharacteristic of the AJC, he urged that "anyone refusing to say whether or not he is a communist should be regarded as one." Others in the organization took offense at Fineberg's remarks. The head of the AJC civil rights division feared that an AJC embrace of anti-Communism would compromise the organization's mission, while the Staff Civil Rights Committee offered a June 1950 opinion that "it shall be the position of the American Jewish Committee that no individual should be deprived of his civil liberties for reasons of his personal beliefs, and that individuals should be judged on the basis of specific actions and not on the basis of ideas or convictions that they may hold." Sociological studies commissioned by the AJC revealed a strong correlation between anti-Communists and anti-Semites, while the dilution of constitutional protections threatened to weaken the Jews' civic status by robbing them of their right to dissent.[15]

Despite these reservations, the AJC hardliners succeeded. The same month that the Staff Civil Rights Committee urged otherwise, the AJC Domestic Affairs Committee called for the banishment of all "demonstrably Communist-affiliated or Communist-led" groups from Jewish communal activity. The ADL followed the AJC with its own edict that "together with other community agencies, our national organization and regional office shall help to expel communist groups from organized Jewish life." Local Jewish community councils purged Communists from their ranks and when Jewish labor unions fell under Communist suspicion, a host of Jewish organizations, including the AJC, AJCongress, Hadassah, the Federation of Jewish Philanthropies of New York, and the National Council of Jewish Women, ended their relationships.[16]

The AJCongress took issue with the AJC's anti-Communism even as it participated in its own leftist purge. While the more moderate Jewish communal agencies expelled suspected Communists, AJCongress leaders worried about their community's diminishing commitment to civil liberties and civil rights. In a thinly veiled 1951 reference to the AJC, AJCongress Executive Director David Petegorsky found it "difficult to understand what useful contribution certain Jewish organizations are rendering by the continuing volume of their anti-communist literature and activities." He lamented that "the anti-communist campaign has long passed from responsible and sober concern with the communist problem to a hysterical and overly sensitive fear of its dangers." For Petegorsky, the AJC approach proved counterproductive: the continued safety and security of American Jews depended more on civil liberties protection than on unrestrained anti-Communism. As he explained, "The vital stake of Jews—together with all Americans—in preserving the principles of freedom and equality should dictate that Jewish organizations use their resources more vigorously than many are doing in defense of those principles."[17]

When word reached the AJCongress leadership in 1949 that two of its affiliates, the American Jewish Labor Council and the Jewish Peoples Fraternal Order, were suspected of Communist organizing, it severed its sponsorship. Civil liberties protections, the AJCongress inferred, extended to innocent victims of Communist smears, not to the radicals themselves. The following year, the AJCongress's National Administrative Committee announced that it would "continue to refrain from association with Communist, pro-Communist and all other groups who deceptively employ the language of freedom to promote programs which are a basic denial of human freedom." Even its president argued that "totalitarianism is as contrary to Jewish tradition as it is to American concepts. Consequently, American Jews must oppose totalitarianism in any guise, whether of the right or the left."[18]

THE McCARRAN ACT AND JEWISH LIBERALISM

Despite the AJC and AJCongress purges, the Jewish community could not embrace anti-Communism with the same vigor as other Americans. Hypernationalism reaffirmed the patriotism of Main Street Americans. But Jews remained, in many ways, out of the mainstream. Hopping on the anti-Communist bandwagon would not necessarily prove American Jewish patriotism: the Jewish community's immigrant roots connected them to radical politics, while domestic anti-Semitism limited Jewish mobility. Despite their tremendous upward drive, American Jews continued to face widespread marginalization. Jewish leaders responded to their community's plight by voicing opposition to anti-Communism earlier and with greater force than other citizens.

American Jews distinguished themselves not only from most Americans but also from other religious minorities, especially Roman Catholics, who used support for anti-Communism as a tool for their own social inclusion. For American Jews, anti-Communist excesses demanded vigilance, and when right-wing American politicians threatened civil liberties, Jewish leaders organized in opposition.[19]

Senator Patrick McCarran, a Democrat from Nevada, posed just such a threat in 1950 when he lobbied for congressional passage of the Internal Security Act (better known as the McCarran Act). The bill sought to check domestic Communist influence by curtailing the freedom of suspected traitors. It proposed creation of a subversive activities control board responsible for registering Communists and their front organizations, new rules governing unlawful conspiracy, revocation of passports of those with suspected ties to the Communist party, detention camps for possible use during times of national emergency, and new controls on espionage and sabotage. With impressive margins of 354–20 in the House and 70–7 in the Senate, Congress passed the McCarran Act and sent it to the White House. President Truman, wary of the bill's discretionary power and fearful of its possible misuse, vetoed the bill—only to be overridden by a Congress controlled by Democrats.[20]

During Congressional deliberations on the McCarran Act, the Jewish community mobilized against what it considered a flagrant violation of American civil liberties. In a point-by-point critique of the McCarran Act and its forerunners, the Mundt-Ferguson-Johnston and Nixon bills, the NCRAC focused attention on the bill's unconstitutional exercise of government power, potential for misuse, imprecise enforcement clauses, and possible utility by the very Communists it was directed to suppress. The NCRAC warned that "the civil liberties of Americans are threatened today by a trend toward accusations by innuendo, assessment of guilt by association, and disregard of the traditional concepts of due process." It objected to "any violation or weakening of the civil liberties guaranteed in the constitution—freedom of speech, press, and assembly; due process; and all the other great foundations of our democracy." While advocates of the McCarran Act exploited Communist fears, the Jewish umbrella organization responded by detailing the ways in which rabid anti-Communists themselves threatened American democratic principles: "The only important fear which we need have of communists in this country today is that they will provoke us into suicide, by piece-meal destruction of our own free institutions. Police-state tactics will not destroy Communism. We must not forget that in Czarist Russia, the first nation in which Communism triumphed, these tactics turned out to be a boomerang. By refusing to adopt police-state tactics, America will strike the heaviest possible blow against communism, and preserve its own democracy."[21]

Ambiguities in the bill, according to the NCRAC, made "criminal any act which would substantially contribute to the establishment of a foreign-controlled totalitarian dictatorship." It feared that the proposed law "might well be construed as making criminal the performance by an attorney of his duty in defending a communist client. It might even make criminal the mere advocacy of the repeal of the law itself. It would inflict serious penalties on individuals—criminal sanctions, social and economic ostracism and character assassination—merely on the ground of association with certain organizations whose nature is not itself defined with sufficient precision, and would thus inevitably restrict inquiry and thought, belief and expression."[22]

The NCRAC worried that the McCarran Act would become a weapon against legitimate liberal protest and could even rally Communists against a common enemy. "While the government must protect itself against totalitarian infiltration," it warned, "at the same time, it must not abrogate the civil liberties of any individual or group, since such obligation leads to the disintegration of democratic freedom." The NCRAC's arguments revealed an abiding belief that dissension served noble purposes. Mindful of the anti-Semitism of Hitler's Germany, the umbrella group feared that "if this proposed action is taken against communists today, a dangerous precedent is created for extending it tomorrow to progressives, socialists, or trade unionists." It argued that the McCarran Act would in fact diminish the nation's ability to fight Communism and pointed to the fact that laws against subversion already existed. The law, it concluded, would "undermine the structure of the American government and the American society which it ostensibly is meant to buttress."[23]

The American Jewish Congress echoed the NCRAC in the style and substance of its McCarran Act critique. It called Congress's override of Truman's veto "a victory for the xenophobe, a defeat for American prestige abroad, a subversion of domestic morale and a repudiation of democratic principle." It warned that "if the Communist Party can be destroyed by legislation today, other political parties can be legislated out of existence tomorrow, and the democratic right of the American people to political instruments of their own choice is at end." The American Jewish Congress held that in both its stated goals and in the mechanisms it created to implement them, the McCarran Act violated precepts of American democracy held dear by the Jewish community. The AJCongress took special exception to the bill's provision allowing an organization to be labeled "Communist" if any of its program goals matched those espoused by known Communists. "Once avowedly communist bodies have endorsed liberal or civil rights legislation," the AJCongress feared, "every other group can endorse such legislation only at its peril. . . . We cannot defend our rights by destroying them."[24]

While the American Jewish Committee opposed the McCarran Act as well, it offered the weakest critique of its content. Leaders in the AJC, committed to greater understanding between Americans of different religious groups, treaded carefully and held to their organization's traditional reliance on public dialogue and compromise. They did not want to threaten the Jewish community's new reputation as liberal anti-Communists and elected to phrase their opposition to the McCarran Act in practical rather than ideological terms. Unlike the AJCongress, which felt more comfortable asserting fears of Jewish exclusion, the AJC hoped that gentle dialogue could achieve the same result without alienating potential non-Jewish allies. By maintaining the conviction that American Jews remained as anti-Communist as other Americans, the AJC protected, in its own way, the civic status of its constituents.

The AJC noted that the McCarran Act "was passed in great haste and under unprecedented pressure" and commended Truman for his veto and for delineating "its blunders." Yet the AJC faulted the plan because it doubted McCarran's bill could be enforced, not because it articulated any principled opposition to civil liberties infringements. "The provisions requiring registry of members of the Communist Party, and of officers of communist front organizations," the AJC wrote, "would be difficult, if not impossible to enforce and might victimize non-communist groups." The AJC went as far as backing the anti-Communist activities of the FBI who had "given every indication of being adept at counter-espionage." It supported the trial of eleven Communist leaders, calling their prosecution "reassuring." Its chief criticism of the bill centered on what the AJC considered a needless diversion of "government energies from this necessary police job." "On the whole," it concluded, "despite certain blunders, the Communist house-cleaning has worked well."[25]

AJC support for the FBI's Cold War tactics typified a larger communal ambivalence toward anti-Communism. The AJC could not offer unconditional disapproval of Cold War politics because it feared that such action might compromise the Jewish community's civic status. It cherished intergroup relations and took care to avoid unpopular public comments. Between 1945 and 1955, AJC leaders tried and failed to foster consensus between militant anti-Communists and civil libertarians: they succeeded only in dramatizing the shortcomings of its accommodationist approach. As the civil libertarian threats mounted in the early 1950s, the AJC leadership traveled down an even more treacherous path. Over the objection of some in the AJC and most in the AJCongress, the AJC joined the All American Conference to Combat Communism, a right-wing umbrella organization that included several anti-Semitic groups in its ranks.[26]

When Senator Joseph McCarthy began his high profile anti-Communist attacks, the AJC remained relatively quiet. It waited until 1955, after McCarthy had been censured by the Senate and discredited in American politics, before it called for the Jewish community "to replace demagogic anti-Communism with a positive program for defending democratic values against all totalitarian tendencies." In language usually preferred by organizations such as the AJCongress, the AJC argued, "The current acceptance of anti-Communist measures which disregard the rights of individuals, the circulation of wild accusations and smears, and the tendency to label as Communists all who hold liberal or non-conformist opinions today create grave problems." In contrast, most Jewish organizations launched anti-McCarthy campaigns years earlier, when opposition to the Wisconsin senator carried with it great political risks.[27]

In 1952, for example, the National Women's League of United Synagogue called for the "abolition of the present procedures of the House Committee on un-American Activities because its sensational methods jeopardize the individual's standing in the community and his means of earning a livelihood"; in addition, the organization demanded "curbs on Senatorial immunity to check the spread of McCarthyism, in order to prevent senators from engaging in irresponsible and ruthless character assassinations of loyal Americans." The following year, the Conservative movement's Rabbinical Assembly condemned "the perversion of the investigative function by some of the Congressional Committees whose attitude toward the reputation of innocent persons is reckless and malicious" and "deplore[d] the defamation of the innocent under the cloak of immunity and favor[ed] the enactment of legislation designed to protect witnesses before Congressional Committees against slanderous attack." The Rabbinical Assembly called on "the President of the United States to assert his leadership in his party and country by repudiating in emphatic terms the tactics of Senator McCarthy and other legislators who have, by their indiscriminate accusations, done much to confuse the American people about the nature of the Communist menace, and whose behavior has discredited us in the eyes of our friends abroad."[28]

In October 1953, the NCRAC also passed resolutions condemning McCarthy's tactics and opposing "efforts to censor books and motion pictures, to prescribe mechanical and meaningless loyalty oaths, to pillory individuals and associations, and in general to curb dissent and enforce rigid molds of conformity." It rejected the "philosophy that national security requires the abandonment of our individual liberty" and reiterated its belief "that totalitarian-like measures of coercion weaken the American spirit and undermine the strength of the United States in meeting both external and internal threats to its security." The council called on the president "to appoint a Commission of National Security and Individual Liberty to consider these problems and to present recommendations on how we can best retain security and freedom."[29]

The American Jewish Congress reaffirmed its commitment "to the ideals of democracy" and opposition "to all forms of totalitarianism," noting especially "the misuse of Congressional prerogatives and the violation of fundamental American principles of fair play by Senator Joseph McCarthy." It called on "the United States Senate to fulfill its responsibility by approving the report and recommendations of the Watkins Committee to censure Senator McCarthy for the abuse of his prerogatives as a member of the United States Senate." The NCRAC issued a statement affirming the responsibility of "private agencies concerned with the preservation of traditional American principles of justice and of individual liberties to join in sponsoring an educational campaign with a view to eliminating the shameful and damaging spectacle of character-assassination and reputation smearing."[30]

Anti-Communism did not offer Jews a clear political choice. An embrace of the national consensus pulled the Jewish community through the Great Depression and World War II. In the postwar years, though, liberalism showed a face fraught with civic danger: consensus threatened to restrict political expression just as it promised Jews unparalleled mobility. As the AJCongress demonstrated in its more aggressive opposition to anti-Communism, Jews differed from the rest of liberal America. While most American ethnic groups participated in Communist purges without concern for reprisal, American Jews did not. Even though restrictive quotas and incidents of domestic anti-Semitism plummeted in the late 1950s and early 1960s, the novelty of American Jewish social integration kept them vigilant. They feared the civil libertarian threat associated with rabid anti-Communism and adopted a contrarian approach to postwar politics. AJCongress leaders maintained a healthy skepticism for anything Communist but still pressed for another patriotic imperative; protection of the American constitutional system. When mainstream America realized that Senator McCarthy had sacrificed the latter in order to attack the former, activist Jewish leaders celebrated. Their qualified embrace of the Cold War consensus proved prophetic and legitimated American Jewish concerns about anti-Communist excesses.

While leaders from the AJC and AJCongress disagreed over the seriousness of the Communist threat, they still understood that the Cold War consensus possessed tremendous strategic potential for American Jewish social mobility. Whenever communal leaders wanted to highlight the virtues of their political program, they reminded Americans of the evil Marxist state. Once again, liberalism paved the way for continued Jewish acculturation to American life. While the Cold War narrowed the bounds of acceptable political expression, it still left room for creative interpretation. Jewish leaders chose to exploit that opportunity, redefining the meaning of anti-Communism in ways that supported Jewish interests. They took advantage of anti-Soviet rhetoric to push for a fair employment practices commission, maintain a strict separation between church and state, overhaul the nation's immigration system, and press racial injustice into the national political spotlight.

Unlike their earlier social reform efforts, postwar Jewish leaders emphasized the importance of a pluralist approach to American democracy. In the 1930s, Jews sought access to American political life by pursuing accommodationist programs. Despite their impressive education campaign, New Deal–era Jewish leaders rooted their liberal appeals on the essential similarities between their constituents and other impoverished Americans. During World War II, though, American Jews learned the value of a pluralist approach to American democracy. Universal liberal ideals failed to protect European Jews from Hitler and did little to counter domestic anti-Semitism. Only a passionate embrace of political difference could guarantee the democratic rights of ethnic minorities. While New

Deal–era Jews failed to protest FDR's indifference to the racial status quo, postwar Jewish leaders led white America in the fight for black civil rights. Cold War Jews understood the limits of consensus and designed liberal programs to protect minority rights.

THE JEWISH CAMPAIGN FOR A FAIR EMPLOYMENT PRACTICES COMMISSION

In the early years of the Cold War, American Jews continued to suffer from discrimination in education, employment, and even recreation. A survey of New York businesses revealed that 15 percent asked job applicants to indicate their religion; 9 percent of New York employment agencies did the same. But outside New York, those numbers were as high as 60 and 67 percent. Seven percent of New York job applicants were refused a job by reason of religion; 15 percent of applicants outside New York suffered the same fate. A 1952 American Jewish Congress survey of New York City found "that 65 percent of white collar employment agencies were willing to receive and accept discriminatory orders, although they were aware that they constituted a violation of the law."[31]

Studies of colleges and universities across the country revealed rigid quotas for Jewish students until at least the mid-1950s. A March 1951 report by the Illinois Interracial Commission showed that "about one-seventh of the openings received by high school and college placements offices included religious restrictions and about one-twelfth had nationality specifications." That same year, the Maryland State Employment Service revealed that more than one-third of the listings received by the clerical and professional division "listed 'gentile' among the qualifications specific by the employers." A Los Angeles Department of Employment survey of job openings noted that 17 percent of the positions discriminated against Jews. When American Jews packed their belongings for a summer holiday, they knew that many resorts and hotels maintained a policy of "Gentiles Only."[32]

Discrimination reminded Jewish leaders that their constituents could not entirely disappear into the American political landscape. Strategies that may have been appropriate for other Americans would not work for a community unable to free itself from recurring anti-Semitism. American Jews shared in the optimism of the postwar era but could not translate that hope into an embrace of the status quo. Instead, Jewish leaders sought reform strategies that protected their minority rights and earned popular support through broad political appeals. They portrayed discrimination as un-American and those who perpetuated it as anti-democratic. By fashioning a new definition of American patriotism from ideals of civil equality, the Jewish community hoped to harness liberal anti-Communism for their own benefit and that of other minorities. In the employment arena, Jews focused their attention on both local and national efforts to outlaw discrimination through creation of fair employment practices commissions (FEPC).

Led by the American Jewish Congress with support from national and local organizations, the Jewish FEPC program gained strength from both Jewish communal desires for social equality and the larger anti-Communist political rhetoric of the era. Settling in their new suburban communities, American Jews looked for protection against employment discrimination as the logical and necessary next step in their continued acculturation to American life. By tying their reform plan to the larger anti-Communist mood, Jewish leaders hoped to channel the political strength of the Cold War consensus in their direction. Whether represented by the American Jewish Committee or the American Jewish Congress, labor organizations or religious denominations, American Jews joined in a broad-based appeal to the anti-Communist American mindset. Show your love of country, each of these groups articulated in its own way, by ending discrimination against Jews.

The postwar campaign for a federal anti-employment discrimination law built upon work initiated during the 1941 March on Washington movement. Just months before the United States would enter World War II, A. Philip Randolph, president of the Brotherhood of Sleeping Car Porters, threatened a march on Washington to protest continued racial discrimination in the United States. President Roosevelt, fearful of such a public display of disunity, negotiated a compromise with Randolph: the president would issue an executive order committing the federal government to fair employment practices if Randolph called off the threatened march. Executive Order 8802 forbade "discrimination in the employment of workers in defense industries or government because of race, creed, color, or national origin." While FDR did little to enforce the edict, the episode signaled a tactical shift within the African-American community and established, for the first time, the federal government's commitment to end racial discrimination.[33]

Wartime attempts to secure congressional passage of a fair employment practices act failed. Senate Bill 2084, introduced on June 23, 1944, along with a companion bill in the House, died without action at the end of the Seventy-eighth Congress. No fewer than thirteen separate bills were introduced in the Seventy-ninth Congress and not a single one gained committee support. When Harry Truman assumed the presidency, he followed Roosevelt's lead and signed Executive Order 9664, extending the life of his predecessor's anti-discrimination office. Still, the new president struggled with a recalcitrant Congress, winning a mere $250,000 appropriation for an ever-increasing fair employment practices workload. On May 30, 1946, congressional appropriations ran out and the fair employment officers closed their doors.[34]

The Jewish campaign for a permanent FEPC began in earnest when the American Jewish Congress hired Will Maslow, one-time field director for Roosevelt's wartime FEPC, to direct its lobbying efforts. Maslow's rhetoric connected Jewish interests with those of American society at-large and encouraged appeals that focused on the common ground between Jews and their fellow citizens. Jews faced severe discrimination, and Maslow's universalist appeals proved his most effective strategy. In a 1946 memo to his regional offices, Maslow proclaimed "that Jewish interests are threatened wherever persecution, discrimination, or humiliation is inflicted upon any human being because of his race, creed, color, language, or ancestry." He called "for a democratic society in which all peoples can participate freely in accordance with their fullest talents and capacities. A basic pre-requisite to a free society is the right to seek employment without discrimination because of race, color, or religion." For Maslow and the American Jewish Congress, freedom meant employment opportunity, while discrimination summoned memories of the oppressive policies of the Axis powers.[35]

On June 12, 1947, Stephen S. Wise helped Maslow's cause when he offered testimony in support of a federal FEPC bill before the Senate subcommittee on labor and public welfare. Wise echoed Maslow's universalist strategy, arguing that a democracy-loving nation could best survive when it jettisoned harmful discrimination. In his testimony, Wise explained that "during the war, we mobilized all the resources and strength of this country to defeat those who sought the destruction of democracy and who, if victorious, would have bound the peoples of the world into slavery." "Today, in peace," he continued, "we have victories no less significant to achieve. Among the most urgent is victory in the campaign against those barriers of prejudice and discrimination which still divide so many of our citizens and which violate our democratic pretensions."[36]

Evoking postwar fears of fascism and totalitarianism, Wise reminded the senators of the country's new leadership position among the democratic nations of the world: "Throughout the world, nations are looking to this country for democratic leadership. It is only natural that they should do so because we have led the world in developing the concepts and practice of liberty and freedom. But as these nations look at us closely, they see many things which disfigure and tarnish our record." Calling attention to American violations of the UN Charter, Wise held that the United States "continue[d] to deny, through discrimination and segregation, the democratic rights of many of our citizens because of their race and color." The American Jewish Congress president wanted to draw attention to what he called the "gap between our professions and our practices." Only by implementing "federal legislation such as S. 984," Wise asserted, could the government "bring our social and public practices into complete harmony with our professions of equality and democracy."[37]

During congressional testimony, Irving Engel of the American Jewish Committee expanded the universalist appeal by focusing attention on important foreign policy considerations. Like Maslow and Wise, Engel invoked broad-based political themes to advance his tactical goal: an end to anti-Semitism in the United States. He reminded the committee of the "detrimental effect which the continued existence of job discrimination in this country has upon international relations." Quoting Wendell Wilkie, Engel argued that "the equitable treatment of racial minorities in America is basic to our chance for a just and lasting peace. . . . We as Americans cannot be on one side abroad and on the other at home. We cannot expect the small nations and men of other races and colors to credit the good faith of our professed purposes and to join us in international cooperation for future peace if we continue to practice an ugly discrimination at home against our own minorities."[38]

Engel typified the strategy of most in the Jewish community when he placed FEPC reform at the heart of American democratic ideals. "Out of the right of fair employment flow many of the other rights we hold dear," he affirmed. "The man who is denied the chance to earn a decent living because of the color of his skin, the place of his birth, or the way he worships God, finds it difficult, if not impossible, to enjoy the other privileges of democracy. Not only is he unable to buy adequate food and clothing for his family; he cannot even afford the education that would teach him and his children just what their democratic privileges, rights, and duties are."[39]

Engel steered the legislators on a course that would guarantee passage of anti-discrimination legislation by focusing on Cold War competition with the Soviet Union. "Today, when the United States is once again the arsenal of democracy for the entire world," Engel told the assembly, "discrimination in employment is again a problem both moral and economic. And once again, the creation of a Federal Fair Employment Practice Committee seems to be the only logical answer." By tying FEPC to domestic anti-Communism, the American Jewish Committee forged a plan that advanced its liberal agenda just as it guaranteed its constituents status as loyal and patriotic Americans.[40]

Opposition to FEPC arose from southern Democrats and Republicans who charged that government could not legislate attitudes, and that education, not coercion, cured prejudice. While supporters countered that FEPC laws legislated against discrimination, not prejudice, and that FEPC laws allowed only "a few, reasonable limitations . . . in order to ensure greater freedom, greater equality, and greater prosperity for all," Congress refused to act. Southern Dixiecrats, fearful that federal protections would challenge the racial status quo, labeled the FEPC "a communist-inspired conspiracy designed to destroy our republican form of government." The best compromise FEPC supporters could achieve was a watered-down version that did not mandate compliance. Jewish organizations, including the NCRAC, rejected the proposed law. "Expressions of support at this time for a 'voluntary' federal bill," it held, "would seriously hamper pending campaigns for enforceable state legislation." An uncompromising Congress forced the NCRAC to conclude in 1953 that it did "not believe that such efforts should receive the high priority which was obtained in the past."[41]

Frustrated at the national level, Jewish organizations focused a second FEPC offensive on state and local governments. The Commission on Law and Social Action (CLSA), the division of the American Jewish Congress responsible for the FEPC effort, drafted model FEPC statutes for local constituent use. Its proposals, framed in all-inclusive language, drew on the popular themes of the day. One draft read: "We maintained that the campaign against anti-Semitism has to be viewed as part of the much broader struggle against racism in America. Successful prosecution of that struggle demanded that Jews join with all other groups in confronting their common problems." While the exact wording of these proposed laws varied from city to city and state to state, all concluded with the provision that "it shall be unfair employment practice for any employer, employment agency or labor organization to establish, announce or follow a policy of denying or limiting through a quota system or otherwise, employment or membership opportunities or any group because of its race, color, religion, national origin, or ancestry."[42]

New York became the first state to pass anti-discrimination legislation when Governor Thomas Dewey signed an FEPC bill into law on March 12, 1945. New Jersey, Massachusetts, and Connecticut quickly passed similar laws, while Indiana, Wisconsin, and Oregon adopted legislation that did not provide for enforcement. Attempts to secure passage in California met defeat when an opposition group, the Committee for Tolerance, opposed an FEPC measure on the grounds that forcing whites to work with blacks and Mexican Americans would only provoke greater racial hatred. In 1949, Chicago emerged as the first city to adopt FEPC legislation, with Milwaukee and Minneapolis following close behind. During the 1950s, increasing numbers of local and state governments passed fair employment statutes, despite the reluctance of Congress to address the issue. FEPC proponents would not secure an effective federal anti-discrimination law until President Lyndon Johnson signed the Civil Rights Act of 1964.[43]

THE DEBATE OVER CHURCH-STATE SEPARATION

Sometimes, postwar Jewish leaders faced resistance when processes of adaptation led Jews to embrace positions in conflict with their representative's accepted wisdom. When increasing numbers of Jewish children enrolled in predominantly Christian public schools, most leading Jewish organizations launched a legal campaign to maintain a strict separation of church and state. The nation's interest in Christian values promised renewed hope for interfaith dialogue, just as calls for prayer in public schools compromised the religious protections afforded Jewish students. The continued acculturation of American Jews to their new surroundings, they argued, depended on an educational system free of overt or even tacit mistreatment of religious minorities. Fifty years of American Jewish history taught communal leaders that a solid public school system strengthened American democracy and acted as the most effective tool for social mobility in the United States.[44]

Yet the organized Jewish community's constitutional struggle to maintain a strict division between church and state faltered when many American Jews rejected their leader's efforts. To the surprise of most national Jewish leaders, many local Jewish parents adopted an alternative interpretation of the church-state question. These middle-class Jews reveled in the glory of their consensus-era social integration and did not want to participate in political campaigns that distinguished them from their Christian neighbors. What appeared a principled defense of strict constitutional interpretation actually masked a deeper and more important priority: the successful integration of Jewish children into the social world of their new suburban communities.

For middle-class American Jews, successful acculturation to American life could best be guaranteed by demonstrating the inherent compatibility between Judaism and Christianity. Learning about Christian holidays, even allowing time for religious instruction and observance, illustrated the highest ideals of pluralism, tolerance, and understanding. American Jews would be most secure in a community that understood and accepted the religious diversity of its population. In an argument typical of many supporters of Catholic parochial schools, they argued that as long as government refrained from endorsing a particular point of view, no constitutional promise had been breached. Their confidence in the worthiness of interfaith understanding and dialogue outweighed concerns that minority religious rights might be compromised.[45]

This new minority view differed from the Jewish community's traditional position on church-state separation. In the nineteenth century, Reform Jews from Germany and central Europe cherished the legal distinction between religion and nation. They hoped that constitutional protection of religious rights would realize the post-Emancipation vision of civil equality lacking in Europe. With the rapid immigration of Jews from Eastern Europe at the turn of the twentieth century, separation of church and state gained greater importance. The new immigrants, their children and grandchildren, embraced the American educational system. With the exception of some in the Orthodox community, American Jews resisted the temptation to establish their own private schools. For most, public schools offered not only a free education, but the opportunity to become American. Students learned to speak English without a foreign accent, studied the history of their new country, and received lessons in civics. At a time when Jews searched for ways to resolve conflicts between their brand of Judaism and their vision of what it meant to be American, the clear delineation between church and state in the public schools offered the best chance for rapid and successful adaptation to American life.[46]

The issue of church-state separation touched a sensitive nerve in American Jewish life. In Europe, Jews learned that whenever the state adopted an official religion, it foreshadowed disastrous consequences for their community. The United States' constitutional guarantee of religious expression promised American Jews that their experience would be better. More than any other ethnic or even religious minority, Jews held fast to the First Amendment stipulation that Congress make no law respecting an establishment of religion. While many Catholics believed that "the maintenance of a separate school system reflecting their distinctive religious and moral values was a legitimate expression of pluralism, thoroughly in line with American principles—and in no way a threat to democratic unity," most Jews perceived religious influences as threatening.[47]

As they did in their other liberal campaigns, Jews called upon universal democratic ideals to sell their program to the nation at large. Cincinnati's Jewish Community Relations Council (JCRC), for example, affirmed "that religious liberty is an indispensable component of American democracy, and that as a nation of people who are attached to more than 250 different religious sects and denominations or else to none, we owe our survival and unity to the acceptance of the unique American concept that the relationship between man and God and his religion or his irreligion, is not, and may not be, subjected to governmental control." A past president of Los Angeles Jewish Federation argued that "not only did this division [of church and state] provide the spiritual framework for group self-expression, but it became the practical method by which America established itself with all of its uniqueness as a pluralistic rather than monolithic society."[48]

Different Jewish organizations held competing ideas about how best to integrate into Christian America. For the American Jewish Congress, it demanded the strictest sense of religious separation. AJCongress leaders

Figure 6. The Synagogue Council of America's radio committee recording a broadcast on NBC. (Synagogue Council of America records, 1935–1974, I-68, box 45 of 56, folder "Miscellaneous," American Jewish Historical Society, Waltham, Mass.) Courtesy of National Broadcasting Company, Inc. All Rights Reserved.

pointed to the divisive effects of religious incursions on Jewish students and held to the principle that all citizens enjoyed the right to a public education free of religious interference. Their approach grew in part from the American Jewish community's wartime political experience: goodwill alone did not protect Jewish interests. Consensus politics conflicted with Jewish relief and rescue efforts during the war, and continued domestic anti-Semitism in the early postwar years destroyed any chance for AJCongress accommodation. While New Deal–era Jewish leaders relied on interfaith dialogue to ease their social integration, postwar Jewish leaders could no longer count on its effectiveness.

For others, social integration entailed continuing dialogue without judicial intervention. The American Jewish Committee favored an accommodationist approach and gave greater priority to interfaith dialogue and educational programs. By teaching Christians about Jewish observance and by showing Jews the common ties they shared with Christians, the AJC believed that it could find common ground to bind all Americans without such strident constitutional appeals. Universalist liberalism, despite its earlier failures, still held out hope for them. AJC leaders and many Jewish parents considered their participation in Christian rituals a sign of their successful integration into the American mainstream. Disagreements between the AJC and AJCongress approaches reaffirmed the centrality of acculturation, rather than legal principle, in the church-state debate.

Figure 7. Rabbi Simon G. Kramer (left) introduces "Show Them the Way This Week," the Synagogue Council of America's theme for the 1952 "Religion in American Life week." (Synagogue Council of America records, 1935–1974, I-68, box 45 of 56, folder "Religion in American Life," American Jewish Historical Society, Waltham, Mass.)

Four distinct church-state issues dominated Jewish communal efforts in the early postwar period: federal aid to education, release time programs, school prayer, and joint holiday observance. When Congress considered federal funding for private and parochial schools, most Jewish leaders advanced a strict interpretation of the establishment clause of the First Amendment in an effort to protect the sanctity of public education. Yet the Orthodox dissented, lobbying instead for support of their yeshivot and talmud torahs. The continued use of release time programs, public school prayer, and the debate over joint holiday observance prompted most Jewish leaders to take their case for Jewish inclusion to the Supreme Court, where they faced opposition from members of their own community.

In 1947, Congress considered legislation to provide federal funding for private and parochial schools. While the relationship between Washington and both public and private universities strengthened throughout the postwar period, almost all in the Jewish community opposed any alliance between the national government and private religious primary and secondary schools. Jews, with the exception of some in the Orthodox community, feared that government support of private schools would create an educational system divided along religious, ethnic, and economic lines. Only public education, credited with bringing diverse Americans together in the same classroom, could create a pluralist nation receptive to its Jewish citizens. A viable public school system, Jewish leaders believed, demanded a monopoly on government support.

In testimony before the Senate subcommittee on education, Stephen S. Wise, AJCongress president, asked that "federal funds be limited exclusively for public school education." Invoking the dominant anti-Communist tone that characterized his FEPC testimony, Wise petitioned the committee to remember that education stood as "the foundation upon which true democracy rests" and warned that Americans could not "faithfully fulfill our obligations to preserve and maintain democracy without expending our energies toward the extension of educational opportunity." He pointed to studies, undertaken by various Jewish organizations, which stressed the importance of education in ameliorating racial and religious prejudice: "Anti-Semitism, as well as all other forms of racial prejudice, is the offspring of ignorance and cannot exist where ignorance does not exist."[49]

Cincinnati's JCRC also appealed to the patriotic spirit of the times when it argued that "governmental support of parochial school education is not only destructive of the constitutional prohibition against the support of religious activities, but it is also destructive of our public school system which is the very foundation of our democratic society." Religious liberty, it contended, was indispensable to American democracy. "As a nation of people attached to many different religious faiths, or to none," the council argued, "the United States owes its survival and unity to the unique American concept that the relationship between man and God is the concern and responsibility solely of the home, the synagogue, the church; that the growth of democracy in this country is due in large measure to the adherence to this principle; and that any impairment of this principle affects not only religious liberty but all freedoms."[50]

Representatives of the three major Jewish denominations opposed federal aid to private education. The Reform movement's Central Conference of American Rabbis went on record against "any legislation that seeks to provide state funds for the aid of private and parochial schools regardless of the denominational auspices under which they are conducted." The Conservative movement's Rabbinical Assembly agreed, passing its own resolution in opposition to federal support for religious schools. The only significant dissent to the dominant Jewish platform regarding church-state separation came from some segments of the Orthodox community. While the Orthodox Rabbinical Council of America formally opposed federal support for religious schools, other traditional groups dissented. In March 1961, for example, the executive vice-president of the ultra-religious Agudath Israel of America urged Congress to include funds for private schools in its aid-to-education bill. Committed to religious education and opposed to their children's interfaith integration, Agudath Israel welcomed many proposed plans for government subsidy of private schools.[51]

Those Jewish groups that opposed federal aid to private education feared that it might one day challenge the integrity of public schools. In contrast, release time programs, which permitted students to be "released" from their regular studies in order to participate in private sectarian religious study, threatened Jewish social acceptance in a more immediate and profound way. Under the terms of these programs, teachers would be permitted to lead a daily class in Christian theology. In some cases, Jewish students would be permitted to excuse themselves to the school library for the duration of the lesson. In other cases, though, teachers could demand that all students participate in the class's religious study. Both scenarios alienated Jewish students from their peers and inspired the Jewish communal leaders to petition the nation's judicial authorities for redress.[52]

In 1947, the Supreme Court considered its first constitutional test of a release time program in *Illinois v. McCollum*. Litigation in the case began following the 1944–45 school year when the Champaign County Board of Education approved a release time program providing for religious instruction classes within school grounds and during normal school hours. During the academic year in question, James Terry McCollum, a non-Jewish student who had elected not to participate in the release time program, was subjected to verbal harassment by his classmates. His parents subsequently filed suit against the school board on the grounds that the release time program violated the establishment clause of the First Amendment. McCollum lost his case first in the Circuit Court and then again on appeal in the Illinois State Supreme Court. On June 2, 1947, the United States Supreme Court agreed to hear the case.[53]

In an impressive show of solidarity, a broad coalition of Jewish organizations from across the denominational and ideological spectrum joined in signing an *amicus curiae* brief. Attorneys for the major Jewish groups used the brief as their front-line strategy to influence the high court. Through it, any concerned body could address the judiciary, even though it was not a named party in the suit. Orthodox, Conservative, and Reform Jewish organizations teamed with local, regional, and national Jewish groups to register their opposition to the Illinois Board of Education. Henry Epstein, attorney for the Synagogue Council of America (SCA) and the NCRAC, and the author of the brief, linked broad notions of American democracy to the specific issue of church-state separation: "Both political liberty and freedom of religious worship and belief," he affirmed, "can remain inviolate only when there exists no intrusion of secular authority in religious affairs or of religious authority in secular affairs."[54]

While Epstein delineated the grand constitutional and social issues tied up in the church-state debate, he made sure to comment on the more personal and painful effects release time programs exerted on Jewish students. His concern focused more on the nature of American Jewish integration than on legal principle. Release time programs illustrated, in the most human terms, why Jews needed to keep church and state separate. In his forty-two page brief, Epstein reminded the Court of "the divisiveness which inevitably results whenever sectarianism enters the public school" and pointed to "the stigmatizing effect of teaching Jewish participation in the crucifixion." He distinguished between the theoretical goals and objectives as outlined by school administrators and the reality of social ostracization experienced by his co-religionists who often were forced to sit outside the classroom, alone, as the instructor taught Protestant students inside.[55]

As supporters of release time sought new test cases to bring before the court, Jewish organizations continued to voice their concern. The Conservative movement's Rabbinical Assembly opposed the granting of release time at its 1950 convention, and the movement's National Woman's League of United Synagogue went on record opposed "to religious practices or celebrations in the public schools" and against "the use of public school premises during school hours for religious education or worship." The American Jewish Committee concurred, arguing that these programs interrupted the normal school program and caused nonparticipating students to lose valuable class time. The practice of excusing students for religious instruction, the AJC held, "threatens the independent character of the public school" and permitted the public schools to do indirectly what they could not do directly because of constitutional limits. Thinking specifically about the reaction of its own community and echoing Epstein's comments, the AJC expressed fear that overzealous teachers, insensitive to the plight of religious minorities, would embarrass their Jewish students.[56]

In 1948, the Court ruled that release time, when it occurred during school time and on school property, violated the establishment clause of the First Amendment. Justice Hugo Black, writing for the majority, repeated his conviction that the wall of separation between church and state must be kept "high and impregnable." The Jewish community's celebration, though, was short-lived. In the 1952 case of *Zorach v. Clauson*, the

Court reversed the McCollum decision when it struck down the limitation that prohibited religious instruction from school grounds. Justice William O. Douglas, in the majority opinion, wrote, "We are a religious people whose institutions presuppose a Supreme Being." He warned Americans not to read "a hostility to religion" into the Bill of Rights.[57]

Nine years after the *Zorach* case, Jewish leaders rallied once again when school officials in Hyde Park, New York, required students to recite a nondenominational prayer in class. *Engel v. Vitale*, or the New York regents case as it came to be known, began when the parents of ten students brought suit against the district, claiming that "use of this official prayer in the public schools was contrary to the beliefs, religions, or religious practices of both themselves and their children." On July 14, 1961, the New York Court of Appeals, in a 5–2 decision, affirmed the Board of Education's policy. "Belief in a Supreme Being is as essential and permanent a feature of the American governmental system," wrote Justice Charles J. Desmond, "as is freedom of worship, equality under the law and due process of law." The case was then brought on appeal to the Supreme Court.[58]

Unlike the *McCollum* case, the New York regents case did not pose as direct a threat to the religious freedom of Jewish students. While the release time programs separated children according to religion and, in many cases, subjected them to unflattering interpretations of Jewish history and religion, the regents prayer made no mention of a specifically Christian God and did not require students to identify their religion. Since nondenominational use of the word "God" already appeared on the nation's coinage and in the Pledge of Allegiance recited by most school children everyday, proponents of the prayer made a strong case that support of the regents did not constitute a violation of the establishment clause.

For the Jewish community, the regents case reached far beyond invoking the name of God. The separation of church and state stood as a symbol of tolerance and understanding. American Jews offered a principled defense of the establishment clause because they believed its strict preservation offered assurances that the rights of religious minorities would be protected. In *amici curiae* briefs, the American Jewish Congress, the American Jewish Committee, the Synagogue Council of America, and the New York Board of Rabbis registered their opposition to the regents policy. The Cincinnati JCRC affirmed the position of its national body when it petitioned the court to reaffirm its policy of making "high and impregnable" the wall of separation between church and state.[59]

On June 25, 1962, the Supreme Court overturned the lower court decision and ruled that "the action of the New York Board of Regents in composing and endorsing a prayer for use in the public schools violated the establishment clause of the First Amendment to the United States

Constitution." The Court held that "neither the fact that the prayer may be denominationally neutral, nor the fact that its observance on the part of the students is voluntary can serve to free it from the limitations of the establishment clause."[60]

In debates over federal aid to private schools, release time programs, and prayer in schools, almost all American Jews stood together. Maintaining a strict interpretation of the Constitution furthered postwar Jewish efforts to protect public schools and guarded against anti-Jewish activities. Yet a heroic defense of constitutional principles did not always serve Jewish interests and, in the debate over joint holiday observance, split Jews at both the local and national levels. Conflicting Jewish reactions to the practice of celebrating both Christian and Jewish holidays in schools—of adding Hanukkah songs to the Christmas show or lighting a menorah next to the class Christmas tree—revealed the limits of Jewish support for the establishment clause and overriding importance of social inclusion in American Jewish life.

While the American Jewish Congress and ADL opposed joint holiday observances in public schools, the ADL gave conditional support. Instead of opposing religious activities outright, the ADL distinguished between religious programs, which were not acceptable, and sectarian ones, which were encouraged as a means of promoting interfaith understanding. Many Jews agreed with the ADL position. In Chelsea, Massachusetts, Jewish parents who objected to singing Christmas carols in school faced resistance from some other Jewish parents who wanted their children to participate. In Cleveland, the local JCRC opposed a plan to celebrate both Christmas and Hanukkah in the public schools. When Jewish parents expressed their support of the dual celebration, the JCRC reconsidered and reversed its stance.[61]

The internal dissension over joint holiday observance highlighted competing Jewish interpretations of the church-state question. If the issue focused solely on keeping religion out of the schools, then there would be no debate over joint holiday observance. American Jews would oppose observances with the same vigor as they countered federal aid to private schools, release time programs, and prayer in schools. The fact that many Jewish Americans, and one national organization, were willing to accept a looser interpretation of the establishment clause demonstrates that competing interests were at stake. The joint holiday observance controversy revealed that the underlying rationale for the Jewish community's constitutional argument rested more with the desire for inclusion and acceptance from the larger society than it did from a principled defense of American law.

IMMIGRATION REFORM

The church-state controversy, the campaign for FEPC, and the civil libertarian fights over anti-Communism highlighted the many ways American Jews incorporated larger domestic political issues into their vision of consensus America. In the years after World War II, though, international concerns took on renewed importance as well. The creation of the United Nations gave the United States a new arena to influence world opinion. The Marshall Plan invested American capital in European economic recovery. Creation of the CIA and expansion of worldwide American intelligence activities foreshadowed a reemerging and redefined internationalism.

The Jewish community, still shaken by stories of Nazi atrocities, faced an added burden. For the first time in Jewish history, the United States emerged as the most populous and prosperous Jewish center in the world. The annihilation of six million European Jews and the growing needs of an emerging national home in Palestine gave American Jews an added investment in world affairs. While the Jewish community stepped up its appeals on behalf of European, and later Israeli, Jews, it also turned its attention to another area of vital concern: reform of United States immigration and naturalization laws.

The immigration question touched the soul of American Jewry. In addition to the urgent need for immediate Jewish immigration from Europe, postwar American Jews recalled with fondness the massive turn-of-the-century Jewish migration to the United States that offered their parents and grandparents a safe haven from religious persecution. The American Jewish community measured its upward mobility with a generational yardstick. Grandparents worked in their businesses so they could afford to send their children to university. These children, in turn, rose in the business and professional ranks, affording their offspring all that middle-class America had to offer. A 1950 survey, for example, revealed that 16.3 percent of American Jews worked in professional occupations as compared to 9.6 percent in the rest of the population. Almost one-third of the Jewish community labored as "managers, officials, and proprietors" compared with only 8.4 percent of Americans at large. For Jews, the symbolic power of America rested in its mythical affection for the downtrodden, the outsider, the foreigner, the immigrant. By waging a campaign to liberalize immigration reform, the Jewish community hoped to protect that myth both for themselves and for their desperate European brethren.[62]

The American Jewish Congress linked immigration reform to the same universal principles it used to advance other liberal causes. "The immigration laws of any society both reflect and shape its fundamental character," the organization declared in a statement. "Freedom of movement, both of emigration and immigration, have long been recognized as among the most fundamental of human freedoms." In testimony before the President's Commission on Immigration and Naturalization, one AJCongress official reiterated the symbolic importance of a just immigration system when he held that "immigration laws crystallize and express a society's basic human values." He reminded Americans that their nation's immigration "laws affirm the degree of our acceptance or rejection of the essential quality of all human beings. They codify our prejudice or our freedom from prejudice. They reveal the measure of correspondence between our professed ideals and our practices."[63]

The American Jewish Committee, in a joint statement with the Hebrew Immigrant Aid Society (HIAS), the Jewish Labor Committee, the Synagogue Council of America, and the United Service for New Americans, wove immigration policies into its own vision of American pluralism. "Americanism," these groups argued, "is a tolerant way of life that was devised by men who differed from one another vastly in religion, race, background, education, and lineage, and agreed to forget all these things and ask of a new neighbor not where he comes from but only what he can do and what is his spirit towards his fellowmen. . . . Americanism is, above all, a spirit of tolerance for the other fellow, of respect for his individuality, of live-and-let live." With this lesson in democracy, the five organizations urged "a refashioning of our immigration laws so that they will more adequately reflect the true ideals of America."[64]

The AJC-led coalition considered the absorption of immigrants central to the American character: "It is a matter of prime importance that the immigration legislation of the United States represents in all its aspects the heritage of freedom, equality, and opportunity which has made America great." A country's immigration laws reflected its national conscience. In their first few years in America, the organizations explained, immigrants discovered "the meaning of American individualism. They had been treated in foreign countries, perhaps, as part of statistical totals, as numbers, as hands, as names on lists. When they came to these organizations for help in making their various adjustments to American life, they found themselves treated as human beings, possessed of the infinite potentialities that inhere in every human soul. That, we think, is the highest meaning of American individualism, which has roots in the ancient teachings of the Hebrew prophets."[65]

Just as they had in the debate over FEPC, Jewish leaders drew strength from the foreign policy concerns of the nation that led the free world. "We cannot press for international acceptance of these principles," argued Rabbi Abba Hillel Silver, "and at the same time offend nations and races by discriminating against them in our own immigration laws." In a letter to President Truman, the chair of the NCRAC wrote, "We believe that the maintenance of a liberal immigration policy is necessary in the best interests of the foreign and domestic policies of our country. In the struggle to preserve peace and security in a world free from communist totalitarian domination, we are rendering military and economic assistance to the democratic nations abroad." The NCRAC urged its regional representatives to find experts qualified to discuss "the implications and effect of the U.S. immigration policy and law on the foreign policy of the U.S. and its international relationships."[66]

Immigration laws sought to insulate Americans from political subversion but they also erected barriers to humanitarian aid. In its battle to prevent the Congress from reaffirming a racist quota-based immigration system, the Jewish community idealized American democratic values, arguing that American immigration laws embarrassed a nation purported to be the leader of the free world. Yet in congressional debate over immigration reform, legislators employed the same anti-Communist rhetoric used by Jewish leaders to secure passage of their own restrictionist policies.

The Jewish community enjoyed early success in its immigration reform efforts. In 1948, Congress passed the Displaced Persons Act, increasing the number of European refugees permitted on American soil. Later amendments eased restrictions and made deportation more difficult as worldwide sympathy for the European refugees aided immigration. By 1952, however, expanded fears of Communist aggression sparked a movement to further restrict immigration policies. Senator McCarran, the author of the Internal Security Act, co-authored the McCarran-Walter Immigration and Naturalization Act, a bill that reaffirmed the national origins quota system developed in the 1920s and extended a racially biased criterion for determining absorption eligibility. Provisions of the bill, which, like the McCarran Act, passed over President Truman's veto, eased the procedure for deporting unwanted immigrants and permitted the forced return of even those who were not deportable prior to passage of the act. It gave the chief executive discretionary power to limit immigration if it could be shown to threaten the national interest, and it kept intact many of the anti-Asian provisions of the 1921 and 1924 laws. Reports that the new law would not restrict immigration of former Nazis and Fascists concerned Jewish leaders.[67]

Passage of the McCarran-Walter Act embarrassed the Jewish community. Its support by a majority of Americans uncovered deep-seated prejudices in American society, attitudes that conflicted with popular myths of consensus and mutual understanding. When the bill passed, the UAHC of Judaism's Reform movement condemned "those provisions of the McCarran-Walter Act that contain national origins quotas, threats to the security of foreign-born citizens, and those other violations of the essentials of democracy." The NCRAC passed a resolution against McCarran-Walter, labeling the act "arbitrary, restrictive, and discriminatory." It demanded changes in the law, "if American immigration policy is to be brought into harmony with traditional American concepts of justice."[68]

The Jewish community opposed the McCarran-Walter Act for several reasons: because it threatened to undo the humane advances achieved with the Displaced Persons Act of 1948, because it challenged the United States' status as moral leader of the free world, but most of all because it threatened to redefine the very nature of America as home to the oppressed. Simon H. Rifkind, a judge representing both the NCRAC and SCA, testified before a Senate subcommittee that "our concern with pending legislation, then, is not a concern based upon the plight of our coreligionists abroad. It is rather based upon the impact which immigration and naturalization laws may have upon the temper and the quality of American life, here in our own land. We think it is important to the welfare of our country that no trace of intolerance mark our immigration laws. We think this would still be important for the soul of America even if not a single immigrant actually wanted to come to the United States." The NCRAC committed itself "to an educational program in support of an American immigration policy free from discrimination based on religion, race, or nationality, mindful of the foreign policy and domestic needs of the United States, and in keeping with the tradition of America as a place of refuge for the oppressed of all lands."[69]

Of all the provisions in the McCarran-Walter Act, retention of race-based immigration quotas most alarmed the Jewish community. "I believe it is morally wrong to differentiate between individuals on the basis of race or national origin," Rabbi Silver testified before the President's Commission on Immigration and Naturalization. "Such discrimination is clearly not based upon the inherent worth of the individual, nor upon equal justice to all men." Silver pointed to thirty years of sociological research, much of it funded by Jewish organizations, to prove that the justification for the national origins system "has absolutely no scientific basis. There are no superior races. There are no races endowed by nature with superior qualities of mind and character. There are races more favored than others by circumstances, by environment, by geographic position, by the fertility of the soil, or by unusual wealth underneath the soil. There are differences between the races, but no biological gradation."[70]

The president of the SCA reminded a Senate subcommittee that "even a cursory review of legislative debate in 1924 discloses that the authors of the quota plan deliberately, carefully, and consciously contrived to encourage immigration of the English, French, Irish, Germans, and other Western Europeans and to discourage all other immigration. Resting upon a discredited racist theory, they argued that persons of other national origins represented inferior biological stocks and possessed ethnic qualities making them unassimilable." The NCRAC affirmed its belief that "the national origins quota system should be abolished as a basis for the admission of immigrants."[71]

Will Maslow of the American Jewish Congress worried that the McCarran-Walter Act "would leave untouched in our law a racial anachronism that blemishes our national record. [It] would, in effect, reaffirm the 1924 repudiation of our fundamental democratic concept." In Senate testimony before the bill became law, Maslow urged "the rejection of the omnibus bills under consideration because they retain the national origins system of 1924, based then on prejudice and ignorance and based today, in defiance of all scientific knowledge, on prejudice alone."[72]

The act's deportation statutes alarmed Jewish leaders who believed that forced repatriation constituted unnecessarily cruel punishment. In the wake of the World War II refugee crisis, American Jews could not fathom a policy that sullied the nation's reputation as a haven for the oppressed. "Deportation as a penalty should be eliminated in the case of aliens who have entered on visas for permanent residence," the NCRAC argued, "with the exception of those aliens whose visas were procured through fraud." It further called for a statute of limitations on all deportations and an end to expulsion based on subversive activities that had since been repudiated. The national umbrella organization lobbied to give the attorney general "discretion to admit any alien who had shown good moral character for five years before his admission in spite of his having committed a crime involving moral turpitude." The American Jewish Congress called deportation "a medieval form of punishment" and petitioned for "repeal of all laws providing for deportation of immigrants legally admitted to this country." In congressional testimony and position papers, Jewish organizations took strong stands against provisions that afforded naturalized citizens fewer legal protections than native-born citizens. "The distinction between native-born and naturalized citizens in our immigration laws," the NCRAC held, "should be eliminated as being contrary to the spirit of democracy and the Constitution. Distinctions between native-born and naturalized citizens have no moral, practical, or constitutional justification."[73]

Beyond the moral and ethical implications of the national origins system, Jewish organizations registered their opposition to its administrative procedures. The NCRAC and the United Service for New Americans criticized Congress for basing quota information on the 1920 census, when more accurate censuses from 1940 and 1950 were available. They objected to Congress's decision not to pool unused quotas while the NCRAC argued that "unused quotas in one year should be applied to the next as a short-term step before trying to abolish quotas altogether." Jewish leaders expressed concern for possible abridgment of due process rights. "Our immigration laws must provide for adequate judicial review of administrative decisions," the NCRAC stated. "The Congress should establish a system of fair hearing and appeals respecting the issuance of visas and deportation proceedings. Safeguards to protect the national security must and should be maintained. But national security can be safeguarded without measures which violate the American conception of justice as do many of the provisions of our existing immigration code."[74]

The Jewish community continued its efforts to change immigration laws. In 1953, when Congress considered Senate Bill 2585, an attempt to eliminate the quota sections of the 1952 law, the NCRAC endorsed the proposal, praising it for translating "into legislative terms the humane principles that should be incorporated into American immigration law." Three years later, the national president of B'nai B'rith wrote to President Dwight Eisenhower, commending him for his support for immigration reform. "Such a proposal greatly heartens all right-thinking Americans," he wrote in regard to Eisenhower's plan to eliminate the national origins system, "since adoption of your recommendations would mark a long step forward in removing inequities from our immigration policy and practices." In April 1956, the American Jewish Congress met in convention and urged that "the national origins quota system and all other provisions making the standard for admission of immigrants turn on race, ancestry, or place of birth should be replaced by a standard based on the needs of our country, individual worth, and humanitarian considerations." While Congress relaxed quotas in August 1957, an end to the national origins system would not come until 1965.[75]

Cold war politics challenged American Jews. While the rest of white America retreated from meaningful social reform, the Jewish community struggled to redefine the nation's political agenda. Continued discrimination, a public climate hostile to voices of protest, threats to the sanctity of public education, and thoughts that America's golden immigration door might remain closed motivated America's Jews to renewed action. By connecting their liberal platforms to larger political trends, Jews protected their own community's interests just as they proposed a vision of American democracy that all citizens could support. Yet by tying their reform measures to Cold War ideals, Jewish leaders erected strict barriers to their success. Jewish postwar politics stood as a testament to both the strengths and weaknesses of liberal anti-Communism. American Jews engineered a reform program that challenged the conservative climate of the time just as it adopted many of its political ideals. Jewish leaders offered an alternative to the restrictive character of postwar politics and utilized anti-Communist sentiment for their community's own good, but also understood that creation of a tolerant nation demanded more than just campaigns against anti-Semitism. To achieve the sort of pluralism necessary for continued prosperity, Jews would have to focus their attention on the greatest social injustice of the period, racial inequality.

CHAPTER SEVEN

"Hamans and Torquemadas": Southern and Northern Jewish Responses to the Civil Rights Movement, 1945–1965

IN 1963, at the height of the civil rights movement, Rabbi Richard Winograd, interim director of the B'nai B'rith Hillel Foundation at the University of Chicago, journeyed to Birmingham, Alabama, to protest racial segregation. While local African-American leaders hailed the rabbi as a man committed to high moral ideals, the Birmingham Jewish community opposed Winograd's effort and criticized him for his much-publicized venture. "I had the feeling," the rabbi explained in reference to two great villains in Jewish history, "that we somehow were the Hamans and Torquemadas" to southern Jews.[1]

While one might expect a spiritual leader to admonish his southern co-religionists for their stand on civil rights, Winograd refused. "I was not fully convinced," he explained, "that we had a right to place the Jewish community of Birmingham in a more dangerous position than we are willing and able to place ourselves." From a moral point of view, the rabbi believed, "The scales were very even." Instead of lamenting southern Jewish recalcitrance, Winograd pained over "the circumstances which had led to pitting Jew against Jew."[2]

Winograd understood that in the South, public support for black equality threatened to undo generations of peaceful coexistence between southern Jews and their white neighbors. Liberalism did not offer southern Jews any hope of civic protection. Jews south of the Mason-Dixon line lived in a climate of fear and intimidation. Synagogue bombings, threats of economic boycott, and violence directed against civil rights workers convinced most southern Jews to follow less confrontational strategies. A 1961 poll, for example, revealed that 40 percent of southern Jews considered the Supreme Court's *Brown v. the Board of Education* ruling "unfortunate." A majority of southern Jews believed that desegregation was moving too quickly and criticized "Yankee agitators" and "northern do-gooders" for interfering. While northern Jews fought to secure a federal anti-lynching bill and end segregation in education, housing, and employment, southern Jews hid themselves from view, challenging their rabbis to keep "politics off the pulpit" and their northern brethren to keep quiet. Southern Jews felt that in order to succeed in their America, they had to remain sensitive to the attitudes of those in the surrounding community.[3]

Winograd's Alabama experience captured the complex and sometimes contradictory Jewish attitudes toward the civil rights movement. On one hand, the rabbi's visit demonstrated northern Jewish commitment to racial equality. Scores of Winograd's rabbinic colleagues and thousands of lay Jews punctuated their support for the civil rights movement by traveling south and participating in rallies, marches, and political protests. In just two generations, northern Jews managed impressive successes in business, exerted political influence in local and state elections, and finally began breaking through the quota barriers at the nation's leading colleges and universities. The image of another ethnic minority denied basic civil rights struck a sensitive chord.

For Winograd and his northern brethren, support of the civil rights movement in the South reached beyond opposition to Jim Crow. It served as a metaphor for their own acculturation to American life. A nation committed to safeguarding the rights of blacks in the South offered constitutional protection to all Americans. While their position proved naive and often times paternalistic, most northern Jews believed that the elimination of racist barriers in the South could offer the African-American community their own version of Jewish-American success, just as it guaranteed a pluralist society amenable to continued Jewish mobility.

Yet by painting over the moral dilemma facing southern Jews, Winograd empathized with more than just his Birmingham co-religionists: he offered an unwitting defense for a northern Jewish community nearing its own debate on the wisdom of civil rights reform. In the years after the landmark *Brown* decision, northern Jews discovered that their own desire for social inclusion compromised their liberal civil rights stand and drew them uncomfortably close to the political views of southern Jews. When the racial equality spotlight moved to the urban centers of New York, Chicago, Philadelphia, and Boston, northern Jews realized that, just as the southern Jews adapted to their local community, so, too, had they. Acceptance into the surrounding non-Jewish society mandated that Jews adopt the prevailing social attitudes.

In the postwar urban North, that meant racial separation. While northern racism lacked the legal backing typical of the Jim Crow states, segregation nonetheless remained the rule. Jewish children attended majority white schools, their parents joined racially segregated social organizations, and Jewish organizations adopted whites-only policies in their community centers, playgrounds, and swimming pools. Unwittingly, northern Jews had become part of the very system they were condemning. While they continued to vote Democratic, their newfound suburban lifestyle tempered their ideals. The confrontation in Birmingham revealed how both southern and northern Jews linked their own successful acculturation to the legal status of the nation's African-American minority. Liberalism proved more a political strategy than utopic ideal.[4]

SOUTHERN JEWS AND THE CIVIL RIGHTS MOVEMENT

The story of southern Jews and the civil rights movement began with their distinctive acculturation to the American South. In the antebellum period, German Jews settled throughout the South, establishing themselves as leaders in merchandising and trade. They adapted to the larger non-Jewish white community, enjoying both material prosperity and social acceptance. As late as the 1940s, the South boasted the lowest rate of anti-Jewish discrimination in the country. While incidents such as the Leo Frank hanging in 1915 kept southern Jews aware of their own vulnerability, they escaped most of the ideological anti-Semitism that swept across the urban North and the agricultural midwest in the late nineteenth and early twentieth centuries.[5]

Maintaining good relations with the surrounding white community proved crucial to the southern Jews' physical as well as economic well-being. While geographic and demographic factors insulated northern Jews from much of the ugliness of racial politics, southern Jews lived a more vulnerable existence. In 1964, Birmingham Jews numbered only 4,000 among an overall population of 630,000. Their rabbi lamented that they were "very, very vulnerable." Montgomery claimed 1,800 Jews among a larger population of 134,000. Other southern towns recorded similarly small Jewish communities.[6]

By the end of World War II, southern Jews faced a critical dilemma: how to respond to the growing African-American calls for racial equality. Established southern Jews counted themselves as sons and daughters of Dixie and remained recalcitrant. In Jackson, Mississippi, for example, they assimilated to such a large degree that their rabbi considered them "indistinguishable in ideology" from the surrounding community and "as racist as any white non-Jew." In Montgomery, Jews advertised their affiliation with the White Citizen's Council "in an attempt to show that they are at one with the majority viewpoint in the Gentile community." They claimed that their actions sought "to inhibit the growth of anti-Semitism." The local Jackson newspaper boasted that "today many a fine Jewish leader is part of the southern resistance. Jackson's citizen's council, outstanding in South and Nation, points to them with pride." Even rabbis from long-established southern families defended the distinctive "southern way of life," took issue with northern Jewish critics, and defended the racial status quo.[7]

Other southern Jews, many of whom had only recently relocated from the North, pressed for change. In the rabbinic community, some championed the civil rights cause at great risk to themselves, their families, and their congregations. Others distinguished between what they called a private commitment to racial equality and their public responsibility to protect their synagogue membership from the considerable wrath of the larger white community. In all cases, southern Jews faced the difficult task of choosing between racial equality for blacks and their own physical, economic, and social well-being.

While incidents of anti-Semitism remained rare through the end of World War II, by the 1950s the association of northern and some southern Jews with the civil rights movement fueled a renewed outburst of violent anti-Semitism. At Temple Beth-El in Charlotte, North Carolina, eleven sticks of dynamite were found in November 1957. Within eight months, similar incidents occurred in Birmingham and Gastonia, North Carolina. On March 16, 1958, Miami's Beth-El Congregation rocked as a bombed exploded; the rabbi received threats not to preach about integration. Rabbi Jacob Rothschild of Atlanta acknowledged that a bombing of his Reform temple in October 1958 occurred in part "because I was so obviously identified with the civil rights movement."[8]

While most non-Jewish white civil rights leaders in the South condemned the bombings, they did little to alleviate fears within the southern Jewish community. Bombings waned in 1959 but resumed during the 1960s. In addition to threats of physical violence, public support for the civil rights struggle opened southern Jews to threats of economic boycott from white customers.

Meanwhile, reluctance to support the movement invited action from African-American customers. When Martin Luther King, Jr., organized a picket line around a store in Birmingham, the community's rabbi, Milton Grafman, appealed to the civil rights leader for understanding. During a meeting between the local clergy and civil rights organizers, Grafman explained that his congregants were "caught in a vise between the Negroes and the Whites—they couldn't win for losing." While northern Jews spent the first fifteen years of the civil rights movement observing from afar, southern Jews struggled in the eye of the storm.[9]

As one writer explained in a local Jewish newspaper, the *Southern Israelite*, "Jews who espouse and defend the cause of civil rights jeopardize the security of isolated Jewish communities in the South, threaten their social integration and economic position, and ultimately even their physical safety." "The Jew in the South," one rabbi noted, "despite his long residence in the area and the high place he has attained in communal life, remains insecure." When pressed on the civil rights question, he added, "The vast majority, however doubtful they may be about the morality of segregation, will neither express integrationist sentiments nor identify themselves with an integrationist movement."[10]

Yet by adopting the racial attitudes of the larger white society, southern Jews invited criticism from the African-American community. When asked about the role of southern Jews in the civil rights movement, Mississippi's NAACP director remarked that "the image of the Jew in national civil rights activity has not rubbed off on the Jewish population of Mississippi. There is little difference, if any between the Gentile White and the Jew in their treatment of the Negro." For the NAACP leader, the indifference of southern Jews to racial equality "was the greatest surprise of my civil rights career." Another civil rights leader condemned southern Jews for refusing to use their considerable economic power to help end segregation. "The Jewish people could have done more, since they had control," he wrote to a young rabbinic student in 1965. "If the Jewish people actually were . . . actively committed to crusading and would apply their economic power to it, you would do it overnight." In a letter to Birmingham clergy, Martin Luther King specifically criticized the southern Jewish community for feigning support for racial equality by supporting slow measured change: "I have almost reached the regrettable conclusion that the Negro's greatest stumbling block in the stride toward freedom is not the White Citizen's Councilor or the Ku Klux Klanner, but the white moderate who . . . constantly says, 'I agree with you on the goal you seek, but I can't agree with your methods.' "[11]

The overriding security concerns of southern Jews prevented even those who considered themselves liberals, especially rabbis, from acting publicly. "The whole Jewish community might become a target for antagonism," one such Jew declared. "Other Jews would fear that one was risking the status of the entire ethnic group, and many local Jews felt that no one had any right to upset the delicate balance whereby Jews had been treated well and accepted generally as fellow southerners." Rabbis occupied a difficult and precarious position in southern Jewish life. Their self-selection as guardians of ethics and morality demanded understanding for black inequality, while the congregants they were hired to serve often insisted on keeping politics off the pulpit. Rabbinic attitudes about the civil rights movement tested the relative strength of traditional Jewish values against the realities of southern living.[12]

A few rabbis, transplanted by and large from the North and filling posts in the urban South, managed a vigil in defense of racial equality. Rabbi Rothschild of Atlanta criticized the delaying tactics of those who believed that "you can't legislate the hearts of men." That argument, employed by self-described civil rights moderates, amounted in Rothschild's estimation to "as specious a statement as ever beguiled the soul." "Laws do not wait for general acceptance," he implored. "They stimulate and coerce a way of life that is better." Arthur Levin, the ADL regional director in the South from 1948–1962, hailed another religious leader, Charles Mantinband, as an "example of a rabbi who was outspoken and who made no compromises with his conscience and his congregation," while Malcolm Stern, a colleague of Mantinband, called him "a quiet, self-effacing individual whose fervent belief in the equality of mankind led him, as the rabbi of Hattiesburg, Mississippi, to take the presidency of that state's Council on Human Relations."[13]

Most southern rabbis, however, feared retribution from both the white community and their own congregants and refused to take public stands on civil rights. William Malev, a Houston rabbi in one of the South's largest synagogues, explained that in communities where congregants opposed integration, "the rabbis have not spoken out, and to have done so would have been to invite resentment and anti-Semitism, if not, indeed, violence towards the Jewish community." Rabbi Moses Landau of Cleveland, Mississippi, explained that if he decided to support the civil rights movement, "it would have been limited to twenty-four hours." After that single day, he stated, "I wouldn't be there in the state anymore." With the prevailing segregationist mentality, Landau argued, "The Jewish community could not exist, could not exist, if they were in any way involved in the civil [rights] movement. . . . If you are going to take sides and agitate, you accomplish nothing, except the hostility of the people."[14]

In 1957, Montgomery's rabbi, Eugene Blachschleger, explained that he "made no public pronouncements on [desegregation] either from my pulpit or in the columns of our daily press." The rabbi of Alexandria, Louisiana, Martin Hinchin, refused to discuss civil rights from the pulpit. "I have my own ideas," he acknowledged, but "I don't foist [them] upon my own congregation . . . because I don't want to harm the Jewish community in any way, shape, or form." In a 1965 interview, he said that he "would like to see, of course, the Negro to have fair treatment, in all respects." Yet Hinchin added, "He's going to have to earn it to a certain degree himself." Hinchin adopted the prevailing belief that "you can't legislate sociology" and advocated a measured response to racial inequality. The African American, Hinchin affirmed, "is going to have to prove himself—through education, through his own morals (which he will do, but it's going to take time)."[15]

Some southern rabbis adopted the prevailing regional belief in racial separation. Yet only a few were willing to articulate their attitudes publicly. One who did, Malev of Houston, challenged the validity of the northern Jews' morality-based defense of racial equality. Malev employed segregationist language to redefine traditional notions of Jewish social action and advance a southern interpretation of Jewish ethical responsibility. He showed how spiritual leaders could fashion ethical and moral principles to their own particular needs. While Malev did not say so explicitly, his opposition to desegregation demonstrated that the expression of Jewish political behavior owed more to conditions in the surrounding community than it did to any traditional imperative for Jewish social action.

Rabbi Malev took aim at one of the northern Jewish community's most progressive organizations, the American Jewish Congress, which at the time had announced an integration plan to build new schools in fringe areas between white and black populated areas. "The purpose" of such a plan, Malev insisted, "would be *to make sure* that white and colored children attend the same schools." In an argument that echoed those made by southern segregationists, Malev objected to the fact that desegregation was "not to take place naturally and normally in the community in which white and colored children live, but they are actually to be compelled by city ordinance to go to the same schools, even where the natural centers of population do not indicate it." The rabbi reminded his co-religionists that there existed "no constitutional principle which decrees that integration must be compulsory for white and colored people." Pointing to the letter of the law, Malev noted that the Supreme Court "only stipulates that there can be no compulsory segregation, but certainly no one can argue that we must, by law, compel white and colored children who live in different neighborhoods and who could ordinarily attend their own schools to go to integrated schools, despite the fact that they do not live in the neighborhood and are not interested in attending such integrated schools." For Malev, attempts such as the one by the American Jewish Congress had "not helped the cause of desegregation, and certainly has not made the Jew more popular among his neighbors."[16]

Malev expanded his opposition to civil rights reform by claiming that desegregation orders violated ethical law. "The reason why the Supreme Court decision on desegregation confronts such difficulties in the South," Malev held, "is because the law is not acceptable to many thousands of southerners." The rabbi forwarded the argument that because the white masses opposed federal orders, they bore no responsibility to adhere to them. This argument, a mistaken reinterpretation of Rev. King's contention that God's law superseded the immorality of Jim Crow, ignored the injustices of segregated education and conflicted with what northern Jews considered the very meaning of prophetic Judaism.[17]

Few scenes evoked as much fear and hostility in southern Jews as the sight of northern Jews proclaiming their support for the civil rights movement. Even those southern Jews who offered private support for racial equality objected to the high-profile tactics of their northern co-religionists, especially when they were planned without thought to the precarious position of the local Jewish community. "The participation of our 'defense' organizations," Malev explained in reference to the American Jewish Congress, the ADL, and the American Jewish Committee, "is not an advantage but a liability to the Jewish communities in the South." Malev complained that these Jewish bodies represented only northern interests and failed to understand the unique position of southern Jews. The rabbi criticized the apparent ignorance of the offending Jews, whom he claimed "speak with arrogance, looking down their noses at the backward and timid southern Jews and sometimes commit blunders because of their incomplete knowledge of the situation."[18]

In a few cases, southern Jewish attacks on their northern co-religionists bordered on the personal. When the Reform rabbinate's governing body, the Central Conference of American Rabbis, went on record in support of equal employment opportunities for blacks, conference member Milton Grafman bolted. "My colleagues who have shouted the loudest," he insisted, "have not been willing to take southern pulpits—period." Grafman continued to argue that northern rabbis spoke from high morals but lived for material success. "They like their 15 and 20,000 dollar pulpits," he explained. Grafman finished his condemnation with a rhetorical challenge to the CCAR: "If you are truly sincere about your prophetic Judaism, then you would not hesitate to take a pulpit in Gadsden, Alabama, for $9,000 a year. This is what a prophet does. But he has no right to tell somebody else to commit economic suicide unless he's willing to make a sacrifice himself."[19]

Tensions between the two communities peaked in the summer of 1961, as dozens of northern Jewish volunteers traveled to Mississippi as part of the freedom rides. "The Jews of this Mississippi town are not happy that I am here," one Jewish activist wrote. "Too many of us civil rights workers are Jews, it seems." In Birmingham, Rabbi Grafman condemned the freedom riders for upsetting the balance between Jews and their white neighbors. "He doesn't have to live with these people," Grafman explained in reference to a northern activist, "but we do, and our people have got to live with them." When Martin Hinchin was asked whether freedom riders visited his town of Alexandria, Louisiana, he responded, "No, thank goodness," explaining that the volunteers were adding "salt to the wounds" and "not helping the situation one bit."[20]

Northern Jewish participation in the freedom rides threatened southern Jews who trembled at the thought of white reprisal. In many places, freedom riders faced physical assault from angry whites, and in the worst scenes, segregationists set fire to freedom buses, forcing protesters to flee for their lives. While the buses would continue rolling from town to town, many argued, the local citizenry remained to face the ire of segregationist whites.

After southern law enforcement officials arrested scores of freedom ride protesters, dozens of northern Jews sat in southern jails awaiting trial. Their families and friends back home contacted a local rabbi, Perry Nussbaum of Jackson, Mississippi, to enlist his support. Rabbi Roland Gittelsohn of Boston as well as Henry Schwartzchild, the executive director of a congregation in Glencoe, Illinois, asked Nussbaum to visit congregants jailed at the prison in nearby Parchman. Schwartzchild wrote: "I wish I could be sure that a rabbi in Israel would not need my reminder or urging to do this act of simple compassion and sympathy with an obviously just cause." Invoking his own southern experience, Schwartzchild explained that he "came to Jackson expressly and pointedly as a Jew" and hoped "that the local rabbi, if not his community, would have the courage to *visit* the jail."[21]

Rabbi Nussbaum responded by visiting Parchman and several other local prisons to assist the Jews detained there. Correspondence followed between the rabbi and the families of those arrested. In late July, Nussbaum solicited the help of his colleagues by penning a confidential letter inviting them to a meeting to coordinate jail visitation. "Since my return last Saturday," he wrote in reference to his most recent visit, "I have been involved in getting permission to bring spiritual guidance to the Jews involved (averaging about 20 so far). As you will expect, it took a lot of talking with the authorities concerned, but I insisted on our rights as Jews, regardless of the nature of the 'crime' and as rabbis, regardless of our position on the subject of segregation."[22]

Nussbaum enjoyed little support from his southern colleagues. Rabbi Landau of Cleveland, Mississippi, condemned Nussbaum for his violation of the South's unwritten rules on issues of race. Landau saw no reason for a meeting of rabbis and opposed any jail visitations by uninvited rabbis: "I well understand why the authorities were surprised and indignant and that you had to do 'a lot of talking and insisting on our rights as Jews' when you injected yourself into a situation without being called upon to do so. It is clear from your letter that neither the authorities nor the prisoners have asked for any spiritual help." Landau appealed to Nussbaum to consider the welfare of his congregants. "It is your privilege to be a martyr," he insisted. "There are dozens of vacant pulpits. You can pick yourself up within 24 hours and leave. Can you say the same of the about 1000 Jewish families in the state? I am paid by my Congregation, and as long as I eat their bread, I shall not do anything that might harm any member of my Congregation without their consent."[23]

Rabbi Allen Schwartzman of Greenville, Mississippi, echoed Landau's sentiments. He could not agree with "the unilateral action" taken by Nussbaum, noting that most of the freedom riders "have the wherewithal to pay their fines and be on their way back home, were it not for the cause they seemingly espouse." He questioned the wisdom of such involvement in the race issue: "I am wondering whether we as local rabbis would not be harming our people, our positions as rabbis in our communities, and the good work that we are doing in the racial problems of Mississippi by 'going to bat' for these temporary inmates."[24]

Although some rabbis did volunteer to visit the jails, Nussbaum canceled his proposed meeting for lack of interest. At his own congregation, the board of directors "uneasily" consented to the visits—though with the stipulation that it be done, according to Nussbaum, "without identification of my congregation." Several congregants threatened to resign their temple memberships, while others registered their disapproval with the local sheriff. The freedom rides continued, but without the support of most southern rabbis.[25]

NORTHERN JEWS AND THE CIVIL RIGHTS MOVEMENT

Northern Jews chronicled impressive feats in the struggle for civil rights. Leaders of northern Jewish organizations waged legislative battles on Capitol Hill while their constituents around the country supported the Student Non-Violent Coordinating Committee (SNCC), the Congress of Racial Equality (CORE), and the National Association for the Advancement of Colored People (NAACP). Jewish students comprised roughly two-thirds of all the white freedom riders in the summer of 1961, and over a third of the volunteers for the 1964 Mississippi voter registration campaign. When freedom riders traveled through the South to test complicity with federal desegregation laws, 62 percent of the northern Jewish community approved, and an astonishing 96 percent backed President Kennedy's decision to send U.S. marshals to Montgomery. Northern Jewish representation in the struggle grew so strong that one historian referred to the postwar period as the "Jewish phase of the civil rights revolution."[26]

Yet despite their overwhelming support for the civil rights struggle in the South, northern Jews struggled with the same political forces that limited southern Jewish activism. Between 1945 and 1954, when the national spotlight shone away from the civil rights issue, northern Jews often sacrificed their defense of racial equality in favor of political programs that would speed the Jews' social and economic mobility. Even in the years of rapid political change between the *Brown* decision and passage of the landmark Civil Rights Act of 1964, northern Jews, striving

Figure 8. Rabbi Abraham Joshua Heschel presents Dr. Martin Luther King, Jr., with the Synagogue Council of America's 1965 Synagogue Statesman Award. (Synagogue Council of America records, 1935–1974, I-68, box 45 of 56, folder "Annual Synagogue Statesman Dinner," American Jewish Historical Society, Waltham, Mass.)

for inclusion in their new middle-class suburbs, emulated the race-based policies of their larger communities.

When the civil rights movement focused on northern urban racial inequality in the years after 1965, all but the most ardent Jews faced the uncomfortable realization that they had journeyed much closer to the southern Jewish position on civil rights than they ever anticipated. As Rabbi Winograd's experiences implied, the public divisions between these two groups of American Jews grew more from a common desire for security and success in American life than they did from any basic moral difference between North and South.

Figure 9. The American Jewish Congress joins the 1963 March on Washington. (American Jewish Congress records, 1916–present, I-77, box 197 of 201, folder "Promotional Materials," American Jewish Historical Society, Waltham, Mass.)

The tough moral choices confronting southern Jews from the very beginning of the civil rights movement came to northern Jews at a much slower, measured pace. They enjoyed the privilege of waging a principled campaign against racial injustice at a time when the specter of Jim Crow remained a thousand miles away. Yet despite their geographic isolation, northern Jews still refused to tackle the most pressing problems: some of their efforts, including a campaign to secure a federal anti-lynching law, proved anachronistic, while others, including support of President Truman's Committee on Civil Rights and plans to end segregation in education, restaurants, and places of business, focused on Jewish as well as African-American imperatives.[27]

The northern Jewish campaign in the late 1940s against lynching targeted what had been one of the worst violations of civil rights in the American South. Typified by trumped-up charges of sexual aggression by black men against white women, incidents of lynching had historically been used to scare the southern black community into compliance with the Jim Crow system. Northern Jews were prominent among those who considered the practice of lynching southern blacks an ugly form of racist brutality, a flagrant violation of human rights, and looked to a federal anti-lynching law as an important and obvious first step to preserve the constitutional rights of the nation's black citizens.

Yet the Jewish communal campaign came years too late. Jewish efforts to provide legal protection against lynching proved symbolic at best: they did not effect meaningful change. By the early 1950s, lynching as a means to intimidate African Americans had all but disappeared in the South. Still, the campaign offered important clues to understanding Jewish liberalism in the postwar years. Anti-lynching legislation reaffirmed two beliefs fundamental to Jewish politics: confidence that an expanding federal government could be harnessed to ameliorate injustices perpetrated on the state and local level, and optimism that the Jewish-American experience could be replicated for other minorities. By viewing their own acculturation through the lens of southern blacks, Jews understood both the potential for social mobility and its serious limitations. The absence of a federal law banning lynching reminded the Jewish community of its enviable position in American life. Securing at least basic legal protections for African Americans reaffirmed the Jewish community's optimistic appraisal of American life.

The American Jewish Congress took the lead in the anti-lynching campaign and pressed for immediate federal action to address an issue once considered a state matter. It held that the selective nature of lynching violated African-American rights under both Article 4 of the Constitution, which provided for a republican form of government, and the Fourteenth Amendment, which guaranteed legal equality to all citizens. Under those circumstances, federal intervention was not only permitted but required. In testimony before Congress, Albert E. Arent, the chairman of the American Jewish Congress's executive committee, stated that lynchings "occur where the local community is unwilling to accord to underprivileged groups the equal rights which our federal Constitution guarantees." According to Arent, the purpose of lynching was "to keep the weaker group 'in its place' by the imposition of special punishments and penalties applicable only against that group." He demanded congressional action to counter "private arbitrary mob rule" and guarantee African-American citizens their constitutionally protected "republican form of government, with its safeguards of due process and equal treatment."[28]

American Jews maintained great faith in the national government's ability to insure civil protection. When southern lawmakers pointed out that lynching remained a constitutionally mandated state issue, Jewish leaders balked. Joseph B. Robison, an attorney and lobbyist for the American Jewish Congress, explained that "neither kidnapping nor theft raises a problem of immediate Federal concern. The crimes covered by the [anti-lynching] case bill do." Robison delineated the difference between lynching and other criminal acts. He explained in his congressional testimony that the proposed law would limit federal intervention "to two types of illegal conduct. The first is violence prompted by the race, religion, or ethnic origin of the victim. The second is violence aimed at preventing fair trial and punishment of persons charged with a crime." From a legal point of view, Robison concluded, "both of these offenses undermine constitutional provisions which the federal government is required to enforce."[29]

Northern Jews enjoyed some support at the federal level when President Truman assembled the President's Committee on Civil Rights. The Jewish community, which was represented on the committee by Rabbi Gittelsohn, welcomed the administration's action as an important step in realizing full civil equality. The American Jewish Congress called for the body to enact "basic legislation to protect and extend democratic rights for all minorities." It repeated its demand for a federal anti-poll tax law, a federal anti-lynching law, and fair employment practices reform while including appeals for an end to education and housing discrimination.[30]

In the winter of 1947, the President's Committee on Civil Rights released its findings to the public. It called for strengthening the civil rights section of the justice department, the creation of a special FBI unit trained in civil rights work, and a permanent commission on civil rights in the executive branch. The committee asked Congress to pass laws to increase penalties for civil rights violations, eliminate poll taxes as a requirement for voting, and end segregation in the U.S. military. It petitioned states to create permanent civil rights commissions analogous to those in the federal government and asked the American people to participate in "a long term campaign of public education to inform the people of the civil rights to which they are entitled and which they owe to one another." It attacked the Jim Crow system, pointing to segregation as "the cornerstone of [an] elaborate structure of discrimination against some American citizens." The committee rejected the rationale behind the Supreme Court's 1896 *Plessy v. Ferguson* decision, dismissing the argument that a segregated school "simply duplicates educational, recreational, and other public services." Instead, it blasted the "separate but equal" doctrine by calling it "one of the outstanding myths of American history" and concluding that "it is almost always true that while indeed separate, these facilities are far from equal."[31]

With little surprise, the northern Jewish community offered unqualified support for the committee and its findings. The Truman committee embodied the highest ideals of the northern Jewish civil rights community, demonstrating that the president welcomed their vision of a pluralist nation guaranteeing equal rights to one of its most beleaguered minorities. Even though many in the civil rights movement questioned Truman's resolve, his effort and his decision to include a leading rabbi on the committee reaffirmed the Jewish community's optimistic national vision.

Stephen S. Wise announced that the President's Committee on Civil Rights had "performed a great service for the people of America" and that its recommendations would translate into "a more fruitful and more abundant life for all Americans." Wise, speaking on behalf of the American Jewish Congress but representing the views of all the major Jewish organizations, urged the president to "continue the life of the committee" so that it could "press forward for adoption of its recommendations." Aware of the difficult legislative battles awaiting in Congress, Wise focused on Truman himself, asking for "no delay in the adoption of those recommendations which require no more than administrative action by the President and the executive departments of the Government."[32]

Northern Jewish liberal support of anti-lynching and anti–poll tax measures complemented the Jewish community's own goal of social inclusion. Jewish leaders never tired of explaining that a society that protected African Americans from arbitrary violations of civil rights also guaranteed the sanctity of Jewish rights. As Cincinnati's JCRC stated, "The society in which Jews are most secure, is itself secure, only to the extent that citizens of all races and creeds enjoy full equality." Throughout the early postwar period, though, continued anti-Semitic discrimination reminded American Jews that their rights still needed protection. While northern Jews could pride themselves on their commitment to racial equality at a time before the issue rose to national political prominence, they tempered their support when African-American equality conflicted with efforts to halt domestic anti-Semitism. This apparent retreat did not signal an abandonment of black equality. Instead, it reflected the roots and limitations of Jewish liberalism: each time Jewish leaders favored anti-Jewish discrimination efforts over anti-racism campaigns, they reaffirmed the centrality of Jewish acculturation in their postwar liberal politics. Jews wanted African Americans to follow in their footsteps, but they also wanted their own path free of discriminatory obstacles.[33]

A classic case of competing interests arose in the spring of 1947, when Rabbi Wise testified before a Senate subcommittee on education in support of a federal aid-to-education bill. Wise cherished the public school system and credited it for elevating American Jews in just two generations from immigrant status to full-fledged citizens. Public schools symbolized the successes of the American Jewish past and offered hope for future achievement. In the postwar years, the importance of a quality primary and secondary education grew as more and more graduate and professional schools opened their doors to previously excluded groups. In the eyes of the Jewish community, public schools acted as a social leveler, giving less advantaged Americans the linguistic, social, and educational skills necessary for social advancement.

Southern legislators, fearful of opening the doors of their segregated schoolhouses to Washington's influence, voiced their opposition to the proposed laws. They considered federal support for state schools a threat to the racial status quo. Without even raising a specific objection to the Jewish community's goals of stronger public education, southern lawmakers complicated Wise's political strategy. Ideally, Wise would have wanted to argue for stronger public schools as a Jewish leader concerned about his constituents. By introducing race into the equation, the southerners forced Wise to comment on an unrelated topic, namely, Jewish communal attitudes toward segregated schools in the South.

Wise tried to navigate a moderate course through the shoals of American racial politics. If he honored his commitment to racial equality and refused to support the southerners' segregationist position, the bill's chances for success were diminished. If he sidestepped the thorny issue of segregation in southern schools, he would at best help to delay the question of racial equality. Wise and the American Jewish community chose the latter.

While he began his testimony by condemning state-mandated segregation, Wise fell in line behind southerners who demanded that federal aid to education not be used "as a means to attack the segregated school system." Wise assuaged his potential critics by invoking the "separate but equal" doctrine of *Plessy v. Ferguson*. "So long as the law guarantees that States having segregated school systems do not discriminate financially against children in minority schools," Wise affirmed, "we believe that the bill should be supported." Wise, like most liberals of the era, lobbied for the political success of his favored bill instead of waging a more difficult defense of racial equality.[34]

Jewish leaders sometimes downplayed American racism during efforts to dramatize the seriousness of anti-Semitism. In the aid to education bill, southerners forced Jewish leaders to decide between two alternatives. Yet in the years after that debate, representatives of Jewish organizations echoed Wise's argument without an imminent political threat. American Jews articulated their political views on the basis of their own American experience. Most times, the Jewish community could link its liberal reform campaign to the civil rights struggle since they both shared common roots and goals. When Jews confronted anti-Semitic discrimination, though, they employed the most powerful arguments available, even when they compromised the fight for racial equality. While they did not intend to polarize the black and Jewish communities, Jewish leaders illustrated how competing social and economic needs pit two allies against one another.

The National Community Relations Advisory Council, for example, took Wise's argument to its logical conclusion. Since racism enjoyed widespread social acceptance, it held that "employers have frequently been willing to admit to a discriminatory policy and to face frankly the question of a change in such a policy." In relation to their own community, though, the NCRAC argued that "almost without exception, however, employers are unwilling to admit to a discriminatory policy against Jews and can point to some Jewish employment in their firms as evidence of a fair policy." The national umbrella organization concluded that while "the presence or absence of Negro employees in a plant is easily observable, no such visible check of Jewish workers is possible."[35]

Other Jewish organizations employed similar logic in their calls for anti-discrimination reform. Cincinnati's JCRC echoed its national body's position in a letter it sent to the governor of Ohio. It held that "the task of fact-finding with respect to employment discrimination based upon religion is substantially more difficult than discrimination based upon race." Citing information such as "name, place of residence, birth place of parents," on job applications, the JCRC hoped to convince the state's chief executive that potential employers could easily identify and discriminate against Jews "without asking an applicant direct questions as to his religious affiliation." While employers certainly could use biographical information to discriminate against Jews, the JCRC's argument ignored the very powerful and much more effective means employers used to keep African Americans off their payrolls.[36]

When Jews battled for the creation of a fair employment practices commission to check discrimination in hiring, they took overt steps to distance themselves from the race issue as well. In its own publicity, the NCRAC declared that "FEPC does not promote social equality." It wanted detractors to know that their main concern was job opportunity, that "the bill has nothing to do with personal or social relationships." Irving M. Engel of the American Jewish Committee assured Congress that "no proposed law, either state or federal, suggests that any employer is compelled to hire Negroes, Mexicans, Italians, Catholics, Jews, or members of any other racial, religious or national group." Engel, along with most American Jews of the time, opposed hiring quotas of any kind and used that to reassure critics that FEPC would "not confer special privileges on minorities." The Jewish community believed in meritocratic hiring. It based its reform programs on the principle of equal opportunity. As the NCRAC explained, "Pay the Negro good wages for his work, give him the opportunity to demonstrate his own capacity to learn, work and earn, [and] give him his constitutional rights, and you have solved this so-called race problem." While these reform efforts eased discrimination against Jews, they did not translate into similar gains for the African-American community.[37]

Successes with the Truman committee and fair employment practices paled in comparison to the far-reaching impact of the Supreme Court's landmark ruling in the *Brown* case. On the afternoon of May 17, 1954, after more than a year of tense deliberations, the court handed down its decision. Chief Justice Earl Warren, who labored for months to secure a unanimous ruling, distilled the complex legal argument into one question: "Does segregation of children in public schools solely on the basis of race, even though the physical facilities and other 'tangible' factors may be equal, deprive the children of the minority group of equal educational opportunities?" In a moment long awaited by all civil rights activists, Warren responded, "We believe that it does."[38]

The African-American community hailed the decision. "When the Supreme Court came out with the *Brown* decision in '54," Bayard Rustin, African-American civil rights leader and the executive director of the A. Phillip Randolph Institute, remembered, "Things began rapidly to move. Some of us had been sitting down in the front of these buses for years, but nothing had happened. What made '54 so unusual was that the Supreme Court in the *Brown* decision established black people as being citizens with all the rights of all other citizens." "*Brown*," according to one historian of the period, "heightened the aspirations and expectations of Afro-Americans as nothing ever had before."[39]

White southern reaction ranged from passive complicity to outspoken opposition. Polls indicated that only 20 percent of non-Jewish southern whites backed the Court ruling. While segregationists such as Senator James O. Eastland of Mississippi proclaimed that the South "will not abide by nor obey this legislative decision by a political court," most believed that the decision would have little immediate impact. It pointed with hope to the court's ambiguous request that integration occur "with all deliberate speed" and it remained confident that the local school districts and judges trusted with enforcement responsibilities would find creative ways to bypass the desegregation ruling.[40]

In Washington, the executive and legislative branches refused to carry the civil rights banner. Wary of losing white southern voters, President Eisenhower offered neither "approbation nor disapproval" of Brown. In fact, the president disagreed with the whole notion of legislating social change and often reminded his audiences that he did not "believe you can change the hearts of men with laws or decisions." Congress refused to draft meaningful civil rights legislation and many of its members made clear their opposition to integration. Senator Richard Russell of Georgia called the *Brown* decision "a flagrant abuse of judicial power." Senator Harry Byrd of Virginia denounced the desegregation order as "the most serious blow that has ever been struck against the rights of the states." In the legislators' most public act of defiance, a group of 101 southern congressmen drafted a "Declaration of Constitutional Principles" in March 1956 demanding noncompliance with the Court order.[41]

Northern Jews rejoiced after the *Brown* ruling. Court-ordered desegregation dovetailed with their political priorities: African Americans enjoyed civil protections promised them a century earlier, the government acted aggressively to protect its citizens, and Jews could rest in a nation that would adhere to its constitutional promises. At its convention only days after the historic ruling, the Conservative movement's Rabbinical Assembly congratulated "the Supreme Court of the United States on its historic decision." In November 1954, the Conservative movement's National Women's League pledged "its wholehearted cooperation in the effort that lies ahead." The Reform movement's rabbinic organization announced that it "views with satisfaction the historic decision of the United States Supreme Court which outlaws segregation in the field of public education." It hailed the ruling "as a profound victory of our prophetic tradition and as eloquent expression of the faith of all Americans in the basic justice of our democratic system."[42]

Henry E. Schultz, chairman of the ADL, announced that "the court's decision will wipe out the anachronistic 'separate but equal' doctrine that has been nothing more than a legal cover for the imposition of second-class status on millions of Negro citizens. The people of the South, white and black," he declared, "will be better for it." He boasted that at B'nai B'rith's 1953 Supreme Lodge convention, a resolution was passed demanding "equality of opportunity on an integrated and nonsegregated basis for all, regardless of race or religion, everywhere in our country."[43]

The American Jewish Congress, responding to the southern states' opposition to the ruling, "urged the use of full powers and influence of the federal government to obtain prompt and full compliance with the decisions of the United States Supreme Court condemning state-imposed racial segregation." The National Women's League called on "the United States Congress to pass legislation eliminating discrimination because of race, creed, political belief, or national origin in transportation facilities, hotels, restaurants, places of amusement, hospitals and other institutions serving the public." The American Jewish Committee boasted of its close involvement with the Supreme Court decision, noting that "not only were we active, along with our organizations, in the filing of an amicus brief, but we contributed materially to the social theory upon which the desegregation decision was based."[44]

The *Brown* decision inspired American Jews to step up their campaign for racial equality. In the decade prior to the landmark case, American Jews divided their time between several social causes. Efforts to eliminate anti-Jewish discrimination through a federal FEPC topped the Jewish agenda, while concern about civil liberties infractions and immigration reform in the aftermath of the Holocaust commanded its own share of the Jewish community's limited resources. The easing of anti-Jewish discrimination and renewed national attention on American racism turned the tide in favor of race reform and inspired one ADL official to declare that "desegregation in the public schools is 'human relations problem number one.' "[45]

Throughout the South, school officials enacted laws aimed at neutralizing the effects of *Brown*. "As long as we can legislate," one southern white boasted, "we can segregate." The pupil-placement law, for example, permitted southern school officials to consider "the psychological effect upon the pupil of attendance at a particular school." Upheld by the Supreme Court, the ordinance gave white southerners the discretion to limit student transfers and maintain existing racial divisions in their schools.[46]

Desegregation stood at a standstill as the Jewish community readied itself for a long battle. Four years after the *Brown* decision, seven states still held fast to racial segregation. The five worst states could not count a single black alongside whites in the elementary grades, high school, college, or graduate school. As late as the 1963–64 school year, only 1.2 percent of school-aged blacks across the South attended integrated schools. The American Jewish Congress blasted congressional indifference. "Almost four years after the Supreme Court declared that state-imposed segregation in public schools deprives Negro school children of equal protection of the laws," it submitted in testimony before a House judiciary subcommittee in 1958, "the responsible officials of the states in which these children live are continuing to deny them their declared rights. . . . Today, equal protection of the laws is a meaningless formula for millions of Negro school children."[47]

NORTHERN JEWS AND SUBURBANIZATION

Despite their unprecedented and impressive commitment to the civil rights struggle, northern Jews remained vulnerable to the same political forces that checked their earlier efforts. Ironically, just as some northern Jews sacrificed their time, money, and safety fighting for racial equality in the South, their Jewish friends and neighbors back home acquiesced to the prevailing racial status quo in an attempt to enjoy the hard-fought privileges of middle-class American life. By the late 1950s, northern Jews had taken advantage of both the postwar economic boom and the easing of restrictive housing covenants to move from their urban ethnic enclaves to the new American suburbs. Country clubs and vacation resorts lifted their Gentiles-only policy. Political and business leaders welcomed Jews into their civic organizations. The Jewish community responded with religious programs to promote interfaith dialogue and educational activities aimed at bridging the cultural gap between Jew and non-Jew. Northern Jews lived side-by-side with their Christian neighbors, relished their new social status, and shared in the prevailing consensus mentality.[48]

Yet acceptance into the surrounding non-Jewish society mandated that Jews adopt the prevailing social attitudes as well. In the postwar urban North, that meant racial separation. While racism in the North lacked the legal backing characteristic of the Jim Crow states, segregation remained the rule nonetheless. Jewish children attended majority white schools and their parents joined racially segregated social organizations, while Jewish organizations adopted whites-only policies in their community centers, playgrounds, and swimming pools. Unwittingly, northern Jews had become part of the very system they were condemning.

Northern Jews followed the precedents of their larger communities, emulating race-restrictive policies in their own programs and activities. In Cincinnati, the Jewish neighborhood playground association adopted the larger community's policy of excluding blacks from their facilities. When a group of African-American women in Cincinnati confronted the Jewish community on the issue, JCRC leader Richard Bluestein acknowledged that the problem of Jewish exclusion of blacks had become "increasingly acute," and he promised to search for ways to preserve "the good reputation of the entire Jewish community with Negroes and with the liberals of the city." Civil rights supporter Mike Israel, also of the JCRC, himself a staunch supporter of the civil rights movement, acknowledged that in Cincinnati "there was a strong feeling that as Jews we had enough trouble, [and so] we should not get involved in black problems."[49]

Herman Kaplow, the director of the St. Louis Jewish federation, observed a trend away from racial inclusion. "Perhaps as part of the total and gradual process of acculturation," he explained, "the idea developed that it would be in the best interests of the Jewish community for Jewish centers to serve non-Jews." When centers began to accept non-Jews, Kaplow pointed out, "they did so, in most instances, following the precept of the majority community—whites only." The Jewish compulsion to adopt the broader racial status quo plagued communities across the country. In 1951, the ADL released a survey of Jewish Community Centers in forty-two leading cities. Of the thirty-five facilities that allowed non-Jews, twelve refused to admit blacks.[50]

Northern Jews had little trouble identifying racism in the South, especially when opponents of black equality worked segregation into their local codes and defied federal laws. Racial separation in the urban North, home to the vast majority of American Jews, created more difficult and complex problems. Not only did northern segregation lack legal sanction, making it harder to eliminate, but it enjoyed at least tacit approval from the Jewish community. Restrictive housing covenants limited African-American access to most suburbs, creating segregated neighborhoods and reinforcing existing inequalities. With the concept of neighborhood schools entrenched in the American educational system and with white officials assigning black and white pupils to different schools, northerners achieved the same racial separation as their southern counterparts without all the legal complications. "The process of suburbanization," historian Richard Polenberg noted, "was strengthening the de facto basis for racial segregation even as judicial rulings, militant protest, congressional action, and executive intervention were weakening its de jure basis."[51]

Eliminating racism in the urban North proved as difficult for American Jews as efforts to end Jim Crow in places such as Mississippi and Alabama. "When most Negroes lived in the rural areas of a generally impoverished South," two ADL observers remarked at the time, "it was possible to think of discrimination as a parochial problem and so more or less disregard it. But this attitude is no longer possible."[52]

The American Jewish Congress warned that "when the Supreme Court held that racial segregation of children in public schools 'has a tendency to retard the educational development of Negro children,' its finding was not limited to one part of the country." More and more, American Jews understood Charles Silberman's observation that "the racial crisis will not be solved in Selma or Birmingham or St. Petersburg. It will be solved, if it is to be solved, in New York, Chicago, Philadelphia, Detroit, Rochester, Syracuse, Kansas City, Los Angeles—and in the suburbs of those cities."[53]

The northern civil rights movement gained momentum in the wake of wide-scale demographic changes in the African-American community. Between 1950 and 1960, the black population in New York City increased 46 percent, in Chicago 65 percent, and in Philadelphia 41 percent. Washington, D.C., Los Angeles, and Milwaukee all experienced similar increases. By 1960, nine million African Americans—half the nation's black population—resided outside the eleven southern states. New York City counted one million black residents. Chicago and Detroit had greater African-American populations than Atlanta and Birmingham. The majority of American blacks lived in urban centers, while whites outnumbered blacks in the suburbs by a ratio of thirty-five to one.[54]

The recent arrivals tended to crowd into predominantly black public schools. In Chicago, 87 percent of the city's African-American elementary school students attended virtually all-black schools. Thirty-eight elementary schools in Philadelphia listed their African-American student populations at 99 percent. Similar situations existed in Los Angeles and New York. Pupils in these schools did not enjoy the same quality of education as students in white schools. In New York, for example, the Commission on Integration reported that schools in African-American neighborhoods of Greater New York "have tended to be older, less well equipped and more crowded than the schools in the white neighborhoods; the quality of the teaching provided in these predominantly colored schools has also suffered."[55]

Northern Jews faced a dilemma similar to the one confronted by Stephen S. Wise in his 1947 response to the federal aid-to-education bill—only this time, the segregated schools opened for classes in the northern Jews' own communities. Just as Wise balanced Jewish support for public education against the need to end segregation in the southern states, northern Jews faced the impossible task of protecting the quality and integrity of their neighborhood schools without appearing to abandon the cause of racial equality. The complementary goals of supporting a pluralistic society and fostering Jewish mobility evolved into competing aims. Pluralism demanded integration while Jewish mobility demanded the best public schools.

Middle-class suburban Jews opted for a middle road in the northern desegregation crisis. They opposed legal segregation as it was defined in the South, but they held firm in their support for neighborhood schools and against mandatory integration. While their ambivalence was qualified to some degree by the fact that their college-age children participated in numerous grassroots civil rights campaigns, the Jews' position translated to an acceptance of the racial status quo and an unwillingness to attack northern racism with the same zealousness as they did in the South. Once the civil rights movement focused on the North, its meaning to many urban Jews changed. For many northern Jews, the struggle for racial equality in the South fostered a benevolent self-image. The later civil rights movement, on the other hand, threatened public schools and challenged two generations of successful Jewish acculturation to American life.

Working-class Jews objected to northern civil rights reforms with even greater vigor than their wealthier co-religionists. While middle and upper-class suburban Jews did fear the effects of court-ordered integration or the loss of their neighborhood schools, urban-dwelling Jews lived on the civil rights front lines. They resided in older neighborhoods, most often targeted for desegregation, while suburban Jews managed to insulate their communities from government action. What remained a principled debate for middle-class Jews evolved into a nuts and bolts question for urban Jews. Abandoned, many felt, by upwardly mobile, white-collar Jews who moved their homes, synagogues, and Jewish institutions out of the old neighborhoods, the working-class Jewish community fought to retain its traditional communal structure. Its repudiation of northern liberal civil rights reform reaffirmed the connection between Jewish acculturation and political persuasion. Working-class Jews lived within a different American milieu and their rejection of liberalism reflected their divergent American experience.[56]

National Jewish self-defense organizations feared the conflict created by the northern civil rights movement. In St. Louis, a local Federation executive affirmed that the covert discrimination typical of northern communities was "still very much a part of the attitudes and feelings of the white population generally." Nathan Edelstein of the American Jewish Congress worried in 1960 that the increased contact between blacks and Jews "have been largely ignored [by the Jewish community] and its implications are not too well understood." "Today, as the urbanized Negro reaches out for the better things of life—better housing, better schools," John Slawson of the American Jewish Committee noted, "the whites with whom he competes are often Jews. We see this happening in New York and other cities as well, where conflicts over de facto segregation in the schools are creating new tensions."[57]

The continuing exclusionary practices of some Jewish organizations forced the NCRAC to remind their constituents of appropriate racial policy. "The commitment of the Jewish community to racial equality," it impressed, "can be advanced by Jewish organizations, agencies, and institutions through their scrupulous adherence to racially nondiscriminatory practices in their own operations." The American Jewish Congress, frustrated by growing apathy in the North, lamented that their "appeals to moral excellence ... have evoked only indifference, often hostility." Those young Jews who stepped up their civil rights work during this period affiliated with secular organizations such as SNCC and CORE, whose youthful membership, goals, and strategies paralleled their own American experience.[58]

"Jews and Negroes," Slawson admonished, "are coming more and more into contacts for which neither group is properly prepared." The American Jewish Committee leader advised his brethren to proceed with greater caution. "Certainly we must continue to help clear the Negro's path to equal opportunity," he advised in 1959, "but let us not delude ourselves that the special roadblocks standing in our way will thereby automatically be removed." Slawson anticipated a declining role for Jews in the struggle for racial equality. "With newfound strength emerging from the Negro's own ranks, and with powerful community groups aligning themselves on his side," he concluded, "the moment may be at hand for us to deal more closely, but of course not exclusively with our specifically Jewish problems in the field of civil rights."[59]

Jewish middle-class support of civil rights activities started to wane in the mid-1960s. By 1964, the American Jewish Congress, a voice of the most progressive middle-class northern Jews, lamented that "more and more Jewish voices are being heard expressing the white community's prevalent fear of the advent of the Negroes in their schools, their neighborhoods and their society." It pointed to New York City's Parents and Taxpayers Association, which, it explained, "has been formed to fight the (minimal) integration program of the schools proposed by the Board of Education [and] enjoys much local Jewish support." The American Jewish Congress observed an uncomfortable abandonment of traditional Jewish support for civil rights. "Sadly," it concluded, "even liberals are attracted by the proposition that education can be separate and equal, and all that is required is the upgrading of slum schools."[60]

Attempts to inspire widespread Jewish interest in the northern civil rights movement failed. As early as 1961, the American Jewish Congress labored to solve the northern segregation crisis in a way which respected the needs of both blacks and Jews. In their study "School Segregation, Northern Style," Will Maslow and Richard Cohen took chief aim at school officials who manipulated the letter of the law to evade desegregation rulings. They condemned local administrators who "took the easy way out" by remaining "color-blind in the belief that as long as they could not be accused of listing race formally as a school entrance requirement, they had no legal responsibility toward enforcing the desegregation decision of the Supreme Court."[61]

Maslow and Cohen saw little difference between northern and southern segregation. "The fact that school segregation in the South is imposed by racial laws and in the North by school districts," they explained, "makes it nonetheless segregation for Negro children living in the Bedford-Stuyvesant section of Brooklyn or in Philadelphia, Los Angeles, or other metropolitan centers of the North." Yet they also understood that any viable integration plan needed to respect the neighborhood school, which most Jews supported and which Maslow and Cohen called "probably the biggest single obstacle facing any local school board determined to eliminate school segregation."[62]

They proposed a four point-plan that kept neighborhood schools intact and featured permissive busing, open enrollment, the building of new schools, and realignment of school districts to ameliorate segregation. With permissive busing, students in overcrowded black schools were allowed to transfer to underutilized white institutions. Akin to the permissive busing plan, Maslow and Cohen supported the concept of open enrollment which permitted any students, white or black, in overcrowded schools to transfer to schools with space available. Open enrollment fulfilled both the letter and the spirit of integration rulings. White students in overcrowded schools could, if they wish, transfer to underenrolled schools. "Since the program does not rest on a racial or ethnic base—and because it can also be defended as a device to prevent overcrowding," Maslow and Cohen argued, "this approach appears to be impervious to legal attack as discriminatory or unconstitutional." To counteract the natural segregation of racial housing patterns, Maslow and Cohen supported efforts to build new schools in "fringe" areas, midway between black and white residential areas. While this policy threatened to postpone needed improvements in black schools by channeling capital to fringe areas, it emerged as a viable compromise adopted by New York City.[63]

The practice of gerrymandering school district boundaries presented Maslow and Cohen with their final and most difficult strategy. "If racial integration is to be achieved," they held, educators would have to strive for "racial balance, with school district lines drawn to foster rather than hinder integration." In New Rochelle, New York, for example, creative use of school boundaries dating back to 1930 created an almost all-black elementary school. White students residing in black neighborhoods were allowed to transfer to other schools, but black students were refused permission to switch classes, regardless of availability.[64]

The NCRAC offered only qualified support for the American Jewish Congress program. While it supported plans to build fringe schools, it refused to consider any solution that compromised the concept of neighborhood schools: "We regard the neighborhood school as having important educational values," including "accessibility to pupils, encouragement of after-school association among pupils, [and] convenience of parent participation in school activities." "No specific group," it claimed, had "any special right, legal or otherwise, to enrollment in any school."[65]

The efforts of the American Jewish Congress and others to invent acceptable integration plans ended in frustration. Fewer and fewer Jews shared the American Jewish Congress's civil rights conviction. With the rise of Black Power and the systematic purges of whites, most of the younger grassroots Jewish activists turned away from the movement. Their parents, content with the legal changes secured in the movement's southern campaign and frustrated by the complexity of the race problem in the North, responded to the American Jewish Congress plan with indifference. The very tone of the black-Jewish relationship changed. For Herman Kaplow in St. Louis, that meant putting an end to the paternalistic racial attitudes shared by many American Jews. It was time, he believed, to let go of the civil rights movement and leave its future in the hands of the African-American community. In a striking reversal of the Jews' earlier universalist argument, Kaplow reminded his co-religionists, "It is not the responsibility of a Jewish agency to meet Negro needs *unless it also serves the total general community.*"[66]

The American Jewish community grew smaller during its twenty-year involvement with civil rights. The dramatic regional differences between

Jews faded as northern Jews faced the same charges of hypocrisy and callousness usually reserved for their co-religionists to the South. When northern Jews clashed with their southern brethren in Mississippi and Alabama, they did it with an understanding that both longed for the most elusive prize in all Jewish history, inclusion in and acceptance from the greater society. The civil rights movement taught Jews that there were many "Americas," each with its own character and each demanding different and sometimes conflicting attitudes from its citizens.

CHAPTER EIGHT

A Different Kind of Freedom Ride: American Jews and the Struggle for Racial Equality, 1964–1975

IN NOVEMBER 1971, Cincinnati's Jewish community, like dozens of others across the nation, welcomed the long-awaited Freedom Bus. In the midst of a two-month journey to the nation's capital, organizers of this "freedom ride" hoped to bring attention to repeated, flagrant, and abusive violations of human rights at the hands of an unsympathetic government. They staged rallies, gave speeches, and collected petitions for their cause, hoping to spark a grassroots movement for social change.

This bus did not carry black and white Americans risking their personal safety to fight racial segregation. These "freedom riders" lacked training in the nonviolent tactics of Gandhi and King. When they arrived in city after city, they did not protest the conditions of African Americans in a racist United States. They appealed instead for help in a struggle particular to the Jewish community: the rescue of Soviet Jews from the anti-Semitic policies of the Communist superpower.[1]

The Cincinnati protesters, two Soviet Jewish émigrés escorted by several American hosts, resembled the original freedom riders in name only. Their decision to invoke the language of the civil rights movement reflected their newfound enthusiasm for ethnic nationalist approaches to liberal reform. In the 1950s and early 1960s, American Jews joined African-American civil rights workers in accommodationist-based protests of racial segregation in the deep South. They lobbied Congress for a federal law protecting blacks and celebrated Lyndon Johnson's assent to the Civil Rights Act of 1964. When the Voting Rights Act passed the following year, Jews cheered. Legislative victories achieved in the 1960s what constitutional amendments failed to win a century earlier: the end to state-sponsored racial discrimination.[2]

Despite the impressive gains enjoyed by civil rights workers, legal protection did not always translate into an end to racial discrimination. Eliminating segregation in the rural South proved a daunting task. Achieving lasting economic, political, and social parity between the races seemed almost impossible. In the mid-1960s, civil rights leaders pushed for affirmative action programs and backed President Johnson's Great Society, a social reform program that acknowledged the institutional nature of American racism. As the chief executive explained in a 1965 commencement address at Howard University, "You do not take a person who for years has been hobbled by chains and liberate him, bring him up to the starting line of a race and then say, 'you are free to compete with all the others,' and still justly believe that you have been completely fair." For Johnson, the realization of racial equality demanded that "we seek not just freedom but opportunity. We seek not just legal equity but human ability, not just equality as a right and a theory but equality as a fact and equality as a result."[3]

Many African-American civil rights leaders soured on accommodationist approaches to social reform and turned instead to ethnic nationalism. They rejected political compromise with government officials and took their populist appeals to their own community. Known as Black Power, this strident form of ethnic pluralism rejected almost all interracial cooperation. Only a black-led movement, they argued, could achieve racial equality. Ethnic nationalism invigorated a new generation of civil rights leaders and broadened the goals of the movement just as it alienated many whites who founded their liberalism on principles of inclusion, pluralism, and tolerance.[4]

Johnson and American liberals faced a difficult challenge. For northern white ethnic liberals brought into the Democratic party by the promises of the New Deal and sustained by the nonviolent integrationist goals of the civil rights movement, the transformation of American politics during the Great Society marked the end of their support for the party of FDR. Satisfied with the legal protection offered by the civil rights legislation and disillusioned with the systematic purges that forced white liberals out of leading civil rights organizations, they followed a course to political conservatism, voting for Republican candidates in both the 1966 congressional and 1968 presidential elections.[5]

Few in the Jewish community remained in the struggle for racial equality after it turned militant in the late 1960s. White purges by leading civil rights organizations, the rise of black anti-Semitism, and the failure of Jewish activists to appreciate many of the deeper social and economic issues emerging from the movement all but ended the historic interracial effort. The rules of American politics had changed, leaving the Jewish community's traditional goals outdated and timeworn. When militant blacks purged whites from their organizations, they symbolically rejected Jewish liberal values. The rise of Black Power exploded the myth that Jews and blacks shared common histories or destinies. In the minds of the new civil rights activists, Jewish philanthropy translated into nothing more than Jewish paternalism. No longer could Jews use their common history of discrimination and prejudice as a consensus-building tool in American politics.

Yet most American Jews resisted the allure of renascent conservatism. They continued to vote for the Democratic party and supported the creation of affirmative action programs. When President Johnson proposed aggressive race-based reform ideas, almost all Jewish organizations approved. "America owed the Negroes more than opportunity," Earl Raab, a leader of San Francisco's Jewish community and civil rights supporter, stated. "The battle-cry of the Negro Revolution was not opportunity, but parity in the economy as well as in the society, starting with an instant end to poverty. Toward that goal, the demands were not just for equal treatment, but for compensatory treatment on a kind of reparations basis." For Raab, a leader in calls for black-Jewish dialogue, this second stage of the civil rights movement reflected a "shift from the goal of equal opportunity to the goal of equal achievement, from civil rights to the war against poverty, from the Civil Rights Revolution to the Negro Revolution." While legal guarantees paved the way for European American immigrant mobility, they could do little to ameliorate the historic discrimination that placed blacks far behind whites, and even less to end the subtle forms of racism plaguing American society.[6]

As they had in earlier generations, Jewish leaders created a political program that guaranteed their rights as an ethnic minority as it appealed to American society as a whole. During the consensus era of the 1950s, that meant forging alliances with other minorities to achieve common goals. In the 1960s, it demanded that Jewish leaders adopt an ethnic nationalist approach to American liberalism. By emulating the political strategies of militant black activists, Jews enjoyed the opportunity to take aggressive self-defense measures without risking charges of dual loyalty and without swaying far from the contemporary political norm. By attaching their own political goals to the larger trend toward ethnic nationalism, American Jews preserved their thirty-year-old strategy of promoting successful Jewish acculturation through liberal reform appeals.

THE BLACK POWER MOVEMENT

The rise of black militancy did not hasten an immediate breakup of the black-Jewish alliance. Despite tensions between themselves and some blacks, most Jewish leaders adopted a sympathetic attitude toward African-American ethnic nationalism. They empathized with the frustrations articulated by the new generation of black leaders and lobbied the rest of white America for compassion. Many Jews viewed the Black Power movement through their own American Zionist prism: the same pluralist ideals that permitted Jews to advocate a homeland in Palestine for their brethren a generation earlier encouraged blacks to explore their own national roots in the 1960s. American accommodationism, according to arguments advanced by American Jewish leaders, celebrated open ethnic expression. Jews celebrated black consciousness because it validated their own American democratic ideals. Instead of signaling the end of black-Jewish cooperation, ethnic nationalism reaffirmed both communities' commitment to pluralist democracy.[7]

In the late 1960s, though, Jewish support for African-American ethnic nationalism waned when militant blacks abandoned accommodationism in favor of greater ethnic isolation. American Jews, by and large, demanded that blacks base their activism on the same consensus ideals that legitimated their earlier social reform efforts: constitutional protections, activist government, and intergroup support. When several leading civil rights groups took the difficult and highly contested step of limiting the involvement of whites, many Jewish supporters bolted. They charged that the new black leadership sought an unceremonious end to what had seemed a symbiotic relationship. For them, the rise of African-American militancy challenged ideals basic to their understanding of Jewish liberalism: a humanitarian spirit, a sense of community with oppressed peoples, and a symmetry between liberal political programs and Jewish inclusion in American life. These Jewish leaders argued that when black civil rights workers purged whites from their organizations, they rejected the accommodationist values of Jewish America. They pointed out that Jews provided a disproportionate share of their finances and leadership, prompting several black leaders to counter with charges that Jewish philanthropy translated into little more than paternalism. The rise of Black Power exploded the myth that Jews and blacks shared similar American pasts or could look forward to the same hopeful American future. No longer could Jews use their common history of discrimination as a consensus-building tool in American politics. More and more, Jewish leaders understood how much their historic interracial alliance depended on a firm embrace of accommodationist principles.

Jewish leaders worried about the rise of black militancy as early as 1960, five years before the Black Power movement gained national prominence. At a June 1960 meeting of the National Community Relations Advisory Council, Nathan Edelstein, chair of the American Jewish Congress' governing council, observed a "striking growth in the Negro Moslem movement." With a membership estimated at between 60,000 and 150,000, Edelstein identified the new followers of Islam as "a potent source of anti-Semitism" and explained that since "the movement, by its nature, is pro-Arab, [it] tends to make it anti-Jewish, and some of its elements are outspokenly so." Edelstein sounded a warning to American Jews: "The maturing Negro of today is through with his former inferior status and will no longer allow others to speak for or lead him.... The new militant Negro demands his rights; he will not accept patronizing assurance of future action."[8]

Edelstein's speech proved ominous. By 1965, incidents of black anti-Semitism, white purges, and discord between African Americans and Jews in the urban North threatened to drive a wedge between the two liberal-minded communities. The Jewish Community Relations Council noted that after SNCC abandoned its nonviolent posture in 1964, its members accused Jews of " 'imitating their Nazi oppressors' and committing 'some of the same atrocities against the Arabs.' " The American Jewish Committee noted that "while Jews have recognized the bond they have with the concept of black power, our ambivalence stems from those of its attributes which have never characterized our own search for group identity—namely black power's incipient racism, its appeal to violence, its irrationality and, above all, its rejection of white leadership and even of white cooperative effort." A 1964 study revealed that 47 percent of blacks "scored high on antisemitic beliefs" compared to only 35 percent of whites. Six years later, another study noted that among Los Angeles blacks in their twenties, 73 percent held "highly anti-Semitic" attitudes. The power of integrationist nonviolent leaders such as Martin Luther King, Jr., diminished with the arrival of new militant blacks such as Malcolm X, Stokely Carmichael, Eldridge Cleaver, and Bobby Seale. Threatened by the new rhetoric of the black community, Jews faced estrangement from their one-time allies.[9]

Edelstein, while aware of the real possibility for intergroup conflict, remained hopeful that the spirit of cooperation so prevalent in 1960 would continue. "With full recognition of his new and proper status," he proclaimed, "Jews and Negroes can and must forge a partnership of equals in the effort to achieve our common goal: full equality in a free society.... The answer has been and must be that Jews are dedicated to the cause of justice and equality because it is best for all Americans. Jews as well as Negroes are the beneficiaries of a society that assures full equality for all." Edelstein concluded with a familiar refrain, petitioning the Jewish leadership to "reach the Jewish masses and emphasize that Jewish security requires a healthy, democratic climate where everyone enjoys full security."[10]

In his 1965 keynote address to the Conservative movement's Rabbinical Assembly, Charles Silberman chastised American Jews for their complicity in the alliance's breakup. What Jewish leaders hailed as liberal commitment, Silberman believed, African Americans had come to associate with paternalism. "If we were really listening," he said, in reference to the growing strength of black militants, "we would hear how we sound when we talk to Negroes—and how differently we sound when we talk to whites." Silberman admonished his co-religionists who were "so busy talking—congratulating ourselves . . . on our leadership in the fight for civil rights—that we don't have time to listen to what Negro Americans are trying to say." Silberman scolded his audience for listening to blacks only "as objects of our benevolence, or as instruments of our charitable purpose" and not "as people."[11]

Silberman urged a sea change in attitudes toward civil rights and racial equality. Casting a wide net over the American Jewish community, he argued that "the fight for racial justice has radically changed character and direction in the past several years, but we Jews—and by 'we Jews' I mean the leadership of the major Jewish religious and lay organizations, not just our benighted rank and file—have not changed with it." He took special aim at the leaders of American Jewish life whose ideology he criticized as "inadequate and irrelevant" and in some cases even "downright misleading." Silberman targeted one of the central tenets of Jewish liberalism: the often-heard claim that Jews share a common history of discrimination and persecution with other minority groups. Echoing conclusions drawn by historian Stanley Elkins in his 1959 publication, *Slavery: A Problem in American Institutional and Intellectual Life*, Silberman believed that "Negro slavery in the United States was completely unlike slavery in any other part of the globe and in any other period of history, for slavery completely severed the Negro from his past and from his culture. (And make no mistake about it, Negroes did come from societies with cultures of a very high order.) This never happened to the Jews; neither slavery nor persecution destroyed our history, or religion, or our culture."[12]

Silberman ended with a bitter condemnation of his community's traditional political posture: "White philanthropy, white liberalism, white sympathy and support, as well as white bigotry and discrimination, have had a similar effect of preventing Negroes from standing on their feet, from 'exercising their full manhood rights,' to use W.E.B. DuBois' phrase." According to Silberman, the old civil rights objectives recalled a time and place unfamiliar and irrelevant to contemporary concerns: "Power—not desegregated lunch counters, not integrated schools, not even equal (or for that matter preferential) access to jobs is what 'the Negro revolt' is all about. American Jews have not caught up with this new emphasis on power, conflict and direct action."[13]

Silberman echoed conclusions drawn by social action leader and Reform rabbi Maurice Eisendrath, who held that "Jewish liberalism was most impressive when the measure of commitment was verbal." While the Reform leader praised Jewish organizations who "excelled at heroic resolutions" and rabbis who remained "eloquent in their sermons," he realized that liberal commitment grew into more than "a question of words." "Resolutions do not suffice for revolutions," Eisendrath stated, "only resolution to act counts now. Civil rights no longer means what goes on in Mississippi; it means what goes on in one's child's school, in one's apartment house, in one's business, and in one's heart."[14]

Jewish organizations refocused their efforts in the wake of the Black Power movement, laboring to find a liberal program acceptable to African Americans and consistent with long-standing Jewish imperatives. The American Jewish Congress, the most left-leaning of the national Jewish organizations, "deplore[d] any isolation of the Negro community, whether advocated by Negroes or whites" and vowed to "continue to work in alliance with Negroes and whites for full equality in a free society." In a hopeful overstatement, the national Jewish organization affirmed that in the Jewish community, no "hostility to the upward movement of the Negro" existed and believed that "no matter how much we Jews have been affected and influenced by the attitudes of our countrymen, we remain relatively immunized to racial prejudice."[15]

In an acknowledgment of the changing civil rights direction and the Jews diminishing role in it, the American Jewish Congress reaffirmed its commitment to racial equality just as it acknowledged its more limited participation: "Perhaps the most disheartening aspect of the failure to achieve much more rapid progress in integration—particularly in the North—has been a curious seepage of belief in the finding that was pivotal in the 1954 decision, namely, that separate education not only leads to inferior learning but deprives the Negro child of the incentive for educational achievement." It noted with sorrow that American liberals were "attracted by the proposition that education can be separate and equal." Even among Jews, the American Jewish Congress lamented, "appeals to moral excellence . . . have evoked only indifference, often hostility." "We recognize," it concluded, "that the black community will and must, in large measure, direct its own future within the framework of a democratic society. We therefore pledge our cooperation with black groups seeking to accomplish these goals."[16]

The American Jewish Committee, invoking its traditional strategy of dialogue and compromise, did not think the Black Power movement signaled a long-lasting nor permanent end to accommodationist strategies. While it agreed that "there are some who would make the separation permanent," the American Jewish Committee believed that for "most blacks this separation is seen as temporary, a means not of leaving the mainstream, but of securing entry into it." The AJC acknowledged that "the separatist aspirations on the part of blacks today have bothered us white Jewish liberals," but still empathized with the goals of black militants. While the new ethnic politics may have seemed "so contrary to our cherished notions about integration," the AJC believed that "many of these aspirations, particularly those related to group growth goals, are a necessary and inevitable stage which we must be ready to accept, given the circumstances of American life today."[17]

The AJC joined the ADL in discounting the impact of black anti-Semitism. It pointed to a 1964 Anti-Defamation League survey and its own 1967 study to conclude that "there is less Negro anti-Semitism than there is anti-white feeling, and Jews as a group are most frequently named by blacks as being pro-Negro. Negro anti-Semitism would seem to be a function of anti-whiteism—that is, all Negroes who score high on an anti-Semitic index also score high on an anti-white index. There is, at the moment, a direct relationship between economic position and lifestyle and the amount of Negro anti-Semitism. The lower the income the greater the anti-Semitism. Or, put in another way, levels of Negro anti-Semitism decrease as education, income, and life style improved." A five-year ADL study completed in 1967 by Gary T. Marx showed that levels of anti-Semitism among blacks did not prove much higher than those of non-Jewish whites.[18]

The AJC tried to link African-American ethnic nationalism to its own accommodationist perspective: "Black power stresses black initiative, black self-worth, black identity, black pride. Black Power seeks the growth and development of black economic and political power. Black Power seeks black leadership development. Black Power strives for a form of separation which will permit it to achieve the above goals and then to enter into coalition with whites as psychological, social, and political equals." The AJC thought that black anti-Semitism grew from a variety of sources and required different ameliorative strategies. The pro-Arab, anti-Zionist feelings of SNCC, it believed, differed from intellectual anti-Semitism, working-class black anti-Semitism, and prejudice caused by intergroup competition.[19]

Reform movement social action leader Albert Vorspan wondered why his established, professional, middle-class contemporaries feared the anti-Semitism of a few blacks when an earlier generation of American Jews responded to far more serious threats with much less fanfare. Militant African Americans in the 1960s, Vorspan pointed out, would never match the kind of threat to Jewish life posed by the KKK or Gerald Smith. Instead of rejecting claims for social reparations, Vorspan backed Johnson's call to create two million jobs for unemployed blacks. In 1968, the NCRAC promised not to abandon the civil rights movement "just because some Negroes were violent, ungrateful, or anti-Semitic." Civil rights activist Arthur Waskow justified the criminal behavior of black rioters in the urban North by pointing to the children of Israel's rationale for stealing from the Egyptians: both believed that centuries of slavery offered them a moral right to reclaim some of what was taken from them. Henry Schwartzchild, the Chicago-area congregational leader who earlier petitioned Rabbi Perry Nussbaum to visit freedom riders at Parchman prison, drew parallels between his early years in Nazi Germany and the victimization of blacks in America. Given each nation's history of oppression, Schwartzchild believed, contrarian behavior, even criminal acts, should be placed in a larger historical context.[20]

The rise of black militancy hastened unexpected and surprising parallels between the two community's struggles for group recognition. Just as many Jewish leaders offered support for black militancy, black nationalists, in defense of their separatist views, often drew parallels between their philosophy and those of Jews. Harold Cruse, in his controversial 1967 work, *The Crisis of the Negro Intellectual*, argued that black nationalism and Zionism, while "totally dissimilar in most respects, share one essential motivation: a yearning for national redemption through regaining a 'homeland' that was lost." Nathan Edelstein of the American Jewish Congress characterized the black Muslim movement as "essentially a nationalist drive, emphasizing the African background of the Negro," while Rabbi Dov Peretz Elkins noted that "black power is nothing more and nothing less than Negro Zionism."[21]

Other black spokesmen drew this same connection. In 1966–67, SNCC chairman Stokely Carmichael initially praised Jews and urged African Americans to emulate them. He often cited a variation of Hillel's famous admonition: "If I am not for myself, who will be for me? If I am only for myself, what am I? If not now, when?" In an address to the 1968 National Conference of Jewish Communal Service, the executive vice president of the American Jewish Committee also asked his audience to compare Hillel's words to recent civil rights developments. Hillel's admonition, the AJC official pointed out, "summarizes in a real sense what black power is all about." Jewish leaders hoped that similarities between the two ideologies would create new political bonds with the African-American community. If Jews and blacks could embrace the other's version of ethnic nationalism, then perhaps the two groups could reach a new accommodationist understanding.[22]

Jewish sympathy for African-American militancy extended to some acts of violence as well. In the middle and late 1960s, urban unrest destroyed both African-American neighborhoods and Jewish-owned shops and businesses. Between 1964 and 1968, 329 riots wrecked havoc on 257 different American cities. By 1972, at least twenty-two Jewish businessmen were killed in the Philadelphia riots alone, while about 80 percent of the damaged businesses after one North Philadelphia riot belonged to Jews. Estimates of losses ran to several million dollars. The American

Jewish Congress, while critical of the violent episodes, refused to place all blame on the black community. While it could not "accept, out of a sense of compassion for the cause of riots, the resort to violence as a means of political expression or pressure," the AJCongress went on record in support of the National Advisory Commission on Civil Disorders's "basic determination that the urban crisis is the result of the policies and practices of the white majority in our nation and that it is the white majority that has the responsibility of undoing the tragic results of its past practices." The American Jewish Congress National Governing Council acknowledged that "for years, Negroes have faced racism and violence on the part of whites, frequently with the acquiescence or even the participation of the police" and concluded that "it should be no surprise that their reaction sometimes takes the pathological form of blind hate and senseless violence."[23]

While many Jewish leaders backed black militancy even after it turned violent, events unfolding halfway around the world helped usher in the end of the black-Jewish alliance. In May 1967, Egyptian leader Gamal Abdel Nasser, with military support from the Soviet Union, blocked the strategic straits of Tiran on the Sinai peninsula and promised to "push the Jews into the sea." He ordered United Nations forces out of the area and warned Israel of a massive Egyptian counterattack should the Jewish state opt for a preemptive strike. By the end of the month, Syria, Jordan, Iraq, Saudi Arabia, and Kuwait aligned themselves against the government in Jerusalem. Bowing to U.S. pressure, Israel delayed a military offensive until the morning of June 5, when it launched an air attack against Egyptian forces in the Sinai. In just six days of dramatic battlefield victories, Israel took control of the Sinai peninsula, the West Bank of the Jordan river, and the Golan Heights.

In the days and weeks leading up to the war, Jews in both Israel and the United States feared another genocide. Abraham Joshua Heschel, the great philosopher and theologian who escaped from Nazi Europe in 1940, wrote that "terror and dread fell upon Jews everywhere" and asked if there would "be another Auschwitz, another Dachau, another Treblinka." American Jewish fears intensified when the community's traditional liberal allies refused to rally behind the Jewish state. Christian leaders, the most important constituents in American interfaith relations work, rejected what they termed "Israeli aggression." A past president of the Union Theological Seminary dispatched a biting condemnation to the *New York Times*: "All persons who seek to view the Middle East problem with honesty and objectivity stand aghast at Israel's onslaught, the most violent, ruthless (and successful) aggression since Hitler's blitzkrieg across Western Europe in the summer of 1940, aiming not at victory but at annihilation—the very objective proclaimed by Nasser and his allies which had drawn support to Israel."[24]

While Martin Luther King, Jr., signed a sympathetic newspaper advertisement published before the war began, he later admitted under pressure that he had not read the pro-Israel statement before he assented to it. Militant blacks considered Israel an imperialist aggressor and sided with the Arab states. They paralleled the plight of the Palestinians in the Mideast to their own suffering in the United States: both ethnic groups sought national self-determination as a remedy for the oppressive restraints of a capitalist power. American Jewish support for Israel only reaffirmed black nationalist assumptions about their one-time allies. Whether at home or abroad, they held, Jewish political culture revolved around a paternalistic approach to non-Jews, self-interested goals that did not consider the concomitant effects on other groups, a staunch refusal to reallocate power, and an accommodationist interpretation of democratic pluralism.[25]

SNCC, one of the most vocal anti-Israel civil rights organizations, published an article listing thirty-two "documented facts" about Israeli injustices, including the charge that Israel "conquered the Arab homes through terror, force, and massacres." It also ran a particularly offensive sketch by SNCC artist Kofi Bailey, which depicted an Israeli firing squad with the caption, "This is the Gaza Strip, Palestine, not Dachau, Germany." For SNCC chairman Carmichael, who also supported the Palestinian cause, the war offered "a visible indication of his willingness to break with Jewish former allies and to consolidate his position at the center of an increasingly contentious group of Black Power ideologues."[26]

From the perspective of most Jewish leaders, the 1967 war reaffirmed their community's vulnerability in American society. Despite forty years of political activism, Jews could not rely on support from their historic allies. Just as they learned in their earlier social reform movements, political appeals only worked when they were tied to larger trends in American politics. Liberal apathy toward the State of Israel in 1967 taught Jews the limits of accommodationism and pushed them toward a more isolationist approach to American pluralism. Instead of rooting their particular appeals on broad-based values, Jews emulated militant blacks who understand that social change demanded group recognition. "For both African Americans and Jews," historian Clayborne Carson concluded, "the 1967 Arab-Israeli war signaled a shift from the universalistic values that had once prevailed in the civil rights movement toward an emphasis on political action based on more narrowly conceived group identities and interests." Just as blacks purged whites in their attempt to reclaim power, so too did Jews turn inward in an effort to protect their own communal interests.[27]

American Jewish leaders responded with the most successful private fund-raising effort in U.S. history. In a fifteen-minute spurt, wealthy givers at a New York luncheon pledged fifteen million dollars, while the United Jewish Appeal's Israel Emergency Fund raised over 100 million dollars in just eighteen days. The 1967 campaign more than doubled the previous year's effort. Public opinion polls revealed that "ninety-nine out of every hundred Jews expressed their strong sympathy with Israel." Over 7,500 American Jews gathered their passports, boarded planes for Israel, and took over the civilian jobs of Israeli soldiers. The anti-Zionist American Council for Judaism crumbled when many of its leaders supported the Israel Emergency Fund and others simply resigned. Zionism enjoyed a status and prestige unmatched in American Jewish history as synagogues, Jewish day schools, and summer camps added educational curricula on Israeli history, life, and culture.[28]

Tensions between blacks and Jews surfaced again the following year when Jewish teachers in the Ocean Hill–Brownsville neighborhood of New York city fought African Americans over a plan to decentralize the public schools and give more power to local blacks. African-American parents, concerned that the large, bureaucratic public school administration neglected the needs of their children, won approval for an experimental program that gave them more control. Local leaders hoped the new plan would give them the authority to teach African-American history and culture as well as the ability to respond more quickly and directly to the changing needs of their students. The teachers union, the American Federation of Teachers (AFT), composed of a large number of Jews, worried that local control would compromise the quality and integrity of public education as well as threaten the jobs of many white teachers whose job security would rest with local officials indifferent to rules of seniority.[29]

Jewish fears peaked in September 1968 when a radical proponent of local control placed a leaflet on a Jewish teacher's desk that read, "If Afro-American history and culture is to be taught to our black children it must be done by Afro-Americans who identify with and who understand the problem." In words characteristic of much of the anti-Semitic tone of the debate, the flyer noted that "it is impossible for the Middle-East murderers of colored people to possibly bring to this important task the insight, the concern, the expanding of the truth that is a must if the years of brainwashing and self hatred that has been taught to our black children by these bloodsucking exploiters and murderers is to be overcome." When ten teachers were accused of sabotaging the experimental project and were fired by the local board, the AFT staged a thirty-six-day walkout.[30]

Confrontations such as the one in Ocean Hill–Brownsville plagued communities across the country. In September 1964, the American Jewish Congress reported that "more and more Jewish voices are being heard expressing the white community's prevalent fear of the advent of the Negroes in their schools, their neighborhoods and their society." It noted that New York City's Parents and Taxpayers Association, a group organized in opposition to the city's modest integration program, "enjoys much local Jewish support." In Massachusetts, the local board of rabbis went on record in March 1972 against an education bill that had, as an amendment, a prohibition against busing.[31]

AFFIRMATIVE ACTION

As these incidents played out, however, Jewish organizations paused to reconsider their goals, strategies, and level of commitment. In May 1968, the American Jewish Congress underscored its assertion that "the white community as a whole does not yet understand that the urban crisis and the resulting growth in racial tensions, crime and violence will continue until proper housing, schools, training, and jobs are available to all." In a rebuke to civic-minded whites critical of the new militancy in the black community, the American Jewish Congress affirmed "the primary responsibility of white leaders to bring this understanding to the white community rather than to preach to the Negro community on the virtues of peace and friendly relations." Bayard Rustin told an American Jewish Congress audience in 1966 that "if you are going to [stand for social righteousness] only so long as Negroes remain nice, give it up." He admonished the audience that they had "to learn that there has to be mutual forgiveness and humility. When Jewish people run about boasting about how we Jews made it because we were intellectual, and lifted ourselves by our bootstraps, and we have such extraordinarily beautiful family life that obviously we just went up to the top like cream in coffee—well, this is hot air."[32]

Rustin's thinking, shared by an entire generation of civil rights activists, led to a new generation of liberal reform programs founded on the premise that certain ethnic minorities needed extra assistance, some sort of "affirmative action," to ameliorate generations of race-based discrimination. Legislative gains, however useful in eliminating legal discrimination, did not address more fundamental obstacles to racial equality. As George and Eunice Grier, commissioned by the Anti-Defamation League to study Jewish communal involvement in American liberal politics, explained, "Under present conditions, mere nondiscrimination is no longer enough. Today the United States confronts the much larger task of *reversing* the cumulative effects of generation upon generation of enforced disadvantage." Solving the problems associated with African-American residential mobility emerged as the new civil rights priority. "The most comprehensive and best-enforced laws designed to protect the equal rights of citizens in schools, public facilities, and even employment," they wrote, "can only be partly successful so long as geographic barriers continue to impede many of those affected from taking full advantage of their newly guaranteed rights." Legal equality would not bring real equality, the Griers warned, "so long as residential segregation sets differential frameworks under which that equality can be claimed by the two racial groups concerned."[33]

The realization that actual racial equality required more than legal guarantees prompted government officials to develop new programs to grant minorities special protections in business and education. Even before President Johnson signed the Civil Rights Act, government policymakers sought a more effective plan for achieving social justice. Beginning with Kennedy's New Frontier and continuing through Johnson's Great Society, reform-minded liberals attempted to translate their newfound awareness of systemic racial inequality into a workable plan for civil equality. Their efforts, grouped under the rubric of "affirmative action," began as a modest, if ill-defined, campaign for racial parity.

Government officials first employed the term "affirmative action" at the 1955 White House Conference on Equal Job Opportunity. On March 6, 1961, President John F. Kennedy invoked it once again in Executive Order 10925, requiring that government contractors "act affirmatively to recruit workers on a nondiscriminatory basis." Johnson followed his predecessor's lead and included provisions for "affirmative action" in the Civil Rights Act of 1964. As time passed, the meaning and implications of affirmative action changed. In May 1968, the Department of Labor went further in its program by demanding a "written affirmative action compliance program" from most government contractors. By February 1970, it defined affirmative action as "a set of specific and result-oriented procedures to which a contractor commits himself to apply every good faith." In December 1971, the Department of Labor included requirements for "underutilized" classes, mandating that "an acceptable affirmative action program must include an analysis of areas within which the contractor is deficient in the utilization of minority groups and women."[34]

Almost all American Jewish organizations supported the notion of affirmative action. The American Jewish Committee praised the practice of giving "special assistance to special categories of people on whom society has enforced hardship and injustice." "In essence," the Anti-Defamation League stated, "affirmative action connotes adding qualified minority group members to other qualified applicants for college admission, [and] employment." The National Jewish Community Relations Advisory Council (NJCRAC, formerly NCRAC) supported the principles of affirmative action as well. It called for both government and business to provide "special provisions for compensatory education, training, retraining, apprenticeship, job counseling, and placement, financial assistance and other forms of help for the deprived and disadvantaged, to enable them as speedily as possible to realize their potential capabilities for participation in the mainstream of American life." It supported "intensive recruitment of qualified and qualifiable individuals . . . that reach members of disadvantaged groups" as well as "ongoing review of established job and admissions requirements . . . to make certain that they are performance related and free of bias." The JCRC supported affirmative action programs that searched "for qualified applicants among disadvantaged groups," gave them preferential treatment only "when their qualifications were roughly equal to other applicants," eliminated "cultural bias in determining qualifications," and provided "special training and apprenticeships."[35]

A few Orthodox groups dissented from the majority Jewish view. Bound by laws of traditional Jewish life that dictated a separatist lifestyle, some observant Jews did not share their co-religionists' need to mediate between ethnic and secular culture. Their community's emphasis on education as the key to social prestige and economic advancement inspired a fierce campaign against affirmative action. Agudath Israel, an ultra-Orthodox Jewish organization, refused to accept even the most benign form of affirmative action: "We are unalterably opposed to the concept as well as the application of preferential treatment on the basis of race, sex, religion, age or ethnic origin. . . . Even in situations where two or more candidates are equally well qualified, it is unacceptable to give preference to the candidate who will, for example, 'help meet the Affirmative Action goals of the University.' To do so would unfairly penalize another candidate on the same basis." The organization rejected the argument "of certain well meaning groups that minorities must be helped. . . . This notion is based on the entirely false assumption that minority people cannot compete with the remainder of the population on an equal basis. . . . Preferential treatment, unlike mercy, ravages both the selected as well as the rejected."[36]

Despite early support, affirmative action programs lost popularity with many American liberals, including the vast majority of Jews, when they became associated with restrictive race-based quotas. The idea of imposing collectivist definitions of need scared a Jewish community whose liberal philosophy always stressed individual rights and meritocratic advance. Advocacy of quota programs instilled fears that less worthy minority candidates would usurp positions better reserved for more qualified candidates. In typical fashion, Jews employed universalistic and legalistic arguments to demonstrate the unfairness of the new proposals and show how overzealous affirmative action administrators could compromise the cherished American democratic ideal of equal opportunity. Opposition to restrictive quotas demonstrated the Jewish community's continued embrace of accommodationist principles and helped guarantee their own successful acculturation to a constantly changing American society.

As early as the 1920s, American Jews understood that most institutions of higher learning discriminated against religious and racial minorities in their admissions practices. The number of Jews enrolled in medical and law schools consistently followed university-imposed percentage targets more than they adhered to the merits of any individual applicant. After graduation, American Jews rarely earned positions as professors and almost never enjoyed the security of tenure. In 1947, President Truman's Commission on Higher Education issued a report reiterating what American Jews had known for a generation, that "quota systems and policies of exclusion practiced by American institutions of higher learning had prevented young people of many religious and racial groups—but particularly Jews and Negroes—from obtaining higher education and professional training." The following year, after the conclusion of a ten-year study of Jewish acceptances and rejections to American graduate schools, Stephen S. Wise noted that "the enrollment of Jewish students between the years 1935 and 1946 in professional schools throughout the country declined sharply. In law, Jewish enrollment declined by 57 percent; in medicine 20.1 percent, in business administration, 35.9 percent, in dentistry, 33 percent; in optometry, 53.3 percent, in pharmacy, 38.4 percent." The results of a 1948 study commissioned by the state of New York, a 1949 Connecticut report, and a 1949 American Council on Education finding all confirmed anti-Jewish discrimination.[37]

American Jews saw little difference between the earlier quota programs designed to restrict Jewish mobility and the 1960s version intended to benefit historically disadvantaged minorities. Yet they also understood the necessity of instituting more aggressive civil rights measures. In Los Angeles, the chair of the JCRC explained the awkward position of American Jews: "On the one hand, we are unequivocally opposed to quotas. The very word 'quota' evokes memories of the disabilities imposed on Jews for generations." Nevertheless, the JCRC official asked, "how do we prevent an integrated neighborhood or school or housing project from going beyond the tipping point and becoming completely segregated if not by some kind of quota?"[38]

Every major national Jewish organization made opposition to hiring quotas a priority. "We concluded shortly after the nightmare of the Holocaust," a Philadelphia JCRC member said, "that Jewish security and the strength of the American democratic process were inextricably interwoven." Linking quota programs to medieval institutions that strictly limited mobility and cared little about merit, he warned that the "Jewish self-interest in the long run could not tolerate a society that permitted a caste system. . . . The inevitable turbulence and strife resulting from the failure to end the caste system would in the course of time, as history has so painfully taught us, fall upon the Jewish head."[39]

In a 1970 position paper, the American Jewish Committee noted that it "continues to oppose the creation of a system of quotas for any group including the disadvantaged in education, employment or any other area of American life.... Our society is capable of providing ample educational and employment opportunities for all its people, thus eliminating the need for benefiting one group at the expense of another or resorting to shortcut and dangerous solutions like quotas." The Anti-Defamation League countered that restrictive quotas were "undemocratic" and violated "the American tradition that the individual stands on his own merits." The ADL rejected the system that said "a student's rights are governed and limited by the faith of his fathers and not by his talents.... The quota system arbitrarily renders educational opportunity the privilege of the majority, and denies it to the minority—though all have contributed historically to make this country great."[40]

As affirmative action procedures developed, the ADL lamented that programs were "being distorted and turned with increasing rapidity into preferential treatment for some Americans on the basis of their race or sex." While the ADL acknowledged that "the intent is eradication of the all-too-pervasive reality of unequal opportunity for oppressed minorities," it concluded that "the means constitutes discrimination in reverse." The ADL supported a program that required "a company, government agency, or university to add to its recruitment schedules colleges and universities at which substantial numbers of minority group students are to be found"; it opposed plans that advocated an abandonment of "usual recruiting schedules. The aim of affirmative action should be broad social progress in achieving racial equality, not the assignment of historical blame, and then the penalizing of specific individuals who happen to be members of the majority."[41]

The NJCRAC warned that affirmative action programs "often resulted in practices that are inconsistent with the principle of nondiscrimination and the goal of equal opportunity such programs are designed to achieve." It went on record opposed to "such practices, foremost among which is the use of quotas and proportional representation in hiring, upgrading and admission of minority groups," referring to quotas "as inconsistent with principles of equality" and "harmful in the long run to all." While target goals "serve as a yardstick to measure good faith," a NJCRAC leader argued, quotas constitute "a fixed, rigid requirement." He concluded that "making an idol out of meritocracy may blind us to other values" of import to a diverse and equitable society.[42]

Not surprisingly, Agudath Israel presented the most scathing critique of the quota system: "It is highly improper to permit remedial action or compensation for 'historical wrongs' when applied to an arbitrarily defined group.... The people who suffer are almost always young white males who themselves did no discriminating; they find doors shut to them simply because they are white males." The organization criticized both "the distorted manner in which the affirmative action programs have been implemented" and what they termed "the almost mindless use of statistical data and the glib adoption of unsupported a priori assumptions.... Quotas, described by whatever euphemisms and hidden by whatever legal language and structures, have no place in America." Agudath Israel based its opposition to quotas on its contempt for Great Society liberalism and emphasis on communitarianism: "We reject the concept of group rights; even more so do we reject group guilt. We cannot accept a situation in which a white male with no personal involvement in the discrimination of others should be required to suffer discrimination only because of the fact that he is white and is male. We feel it is entirely improper to correct historical wrongs of the past by assigning guilt and penalties to innocent individuals simply because of their race and sex."[43]

Even the American Jewish Congress, known for its progressive political views and willingness to break with the more moderate Jewish organizations, urged its constituents to "unequivocally oppose all quotas, with no exceptions." David Petegorsky, the executive director of the American Jewish Congress, called the practice of restrictive admissions both "indefensible and anti-democratic." Naomi Levine, the executive director–designate in 1972, lamented that "what started out as a vague concept of 'affirmative action' in a presidential executive order limited to federal contractors has now been by administrative rulings defined as a responsibility to overcome 'the under-utilization of minority groups in the workforce through goals, percentage hiring, and timetables' whether prior discrimination has or has not been established and whether the employer is or is not a federal contractor." Levine did not oppose the use of hiring goals unless they degenerated into strict quotas, but she did fear that government policymakers would continue to lead affirmative action programs down the path to quotas, preferential treatment, and reverse discrimination. As an alternative, Levine and the American Jewish Congress developed a detailed affirmative action plan of their own, meant both to protect the needs of discriminated minorities and the rights of the majority.[44]

To safeguard the rights of worthy nonminority candidates, Levine suggested that "only applicants who meet the minimum and reasonable qualifications applicable to all as established by the employer involved be regarded as eligible." She urged employers not to create new employment positions for minority candidates "by discharging any person already employed," and she asked that goals "be established only on the basis of a bona fide finding as to available qualified talent in the disadvantaged group within the relevant job market, and not on the basis of the proportion of disadvantaged group members to the population as a whole." In order to prevent hiring goals from becoming institutionalized, Levine wanted them to be "used only as a criterion for judgment of good faith efforts" and asked that they be "discontinued when past imbalance has been corrected."[45]

Opposition to quotas led to several legal challenges. One of the earliest and most important, *DeFunis v. University of Washington* (1971), centered on the admissions policy of the University of Washington law school and attracted wide attention in American political circles as a case central to establishing the constitutionality of affirmative action. Appearing four years before the more famous *Bakke* case, *DeFunis* has been largely ignored by historians even though the case prompted more friend of the court briefs than any other case in Supreme Court history. As a precursor to *Bakke*, it offers a vital first look into a divided and frustrated Jewish community struggling over which liberal path to take: a universalist approach demanding equal application of American law to all citizens, or a pluralist acknowledgment that certain minorities in 1960s America, like Jews in wartime Europe, required special attention.[46]

Litigation began when Marco DeFunis, a college graduate with a 3.71 grade-point average, learned that he had been rejected from the University of Washington law school. In August 1971, he filed suit against the school, alleging that his constitutional rights had been compromised by minority applicants who had gained admission with lower test scores and GPAs. On September 22, 1971, a Superior Court judge ruled in DeFunis's favor, arguing that "some minority students were admitted whose college grades and aptitude test scores were so low that had they been white, their applications would have been summarily denied." The Washington State Supreme Court heard the case on appeal. On March 8, 1973, it overturned the Superior Court ruling by a 6–2 vote, finding "the minority admissions policy of the law school to be the only feasible plan that promises realistically to work and promises realistically to work now." DeFunis was allowed to matriculate while his case went through appeals; by the time the U.S. Supreme Court heard oral arguments on January 26, 1974, he had reached his third and final year of law school.[47]

The organized Jewish community split on the DeFunis case. Four Jewish organizations—the American Jewish Congress, the American Jewish Committee, the Anti-Defamation League, and the Jewish Rights Council—sided with DeFunis, while the Reform movement's UAHC and the National Council of Jewish Women (NCJW) sided with the University of Washington. In their amicus brief, the UAHC and NCJW argued, "This is not a racial 'quota' case. Nor does it involve 'reverse discrimination.' The facts of this case are a good deal more complex. . . . The risks of discretionary preferences—though real—are not so large as the risks of endangering all necessary affirmative action programs to bring disadvantaged and minority groups into the mainstream of educational life.... You can't do anything socially constructive without risking some pain to someone somewhere, but the need to do something for the disadvantaged is too great to be denied."[48]

The NCJW and the UAHC joined the Children's Defense Fund in a call for "a proper test [that] will be both flexible enough to honor the right of school authorities to adapt a remedial policy to their own perception of a particular problem, yet not so flexible as to allow establishment of 'reverse racism.'" They believed that the courts could apply reasonable criteria to both permit affirmative action and avoid unfair discrimination against nonminorities: "Remedial racial classifications—including that of the University of Washington Law School—should be permitted unless shown to be unreasonable in initiation or scope."[49]

The rest of the organized community agreed in principle with a Connecticut rabbi who wrote, "Affirmative action, however great in theory, turns out to be discrimination against other students in practice. It turns out to be simply another word for racial quotas." The American Jewish Committee, while remaining sympathetic to the principles of affirmative action programs, registered its opposition to the University of Washington's law school admission policy. "When this case was appealed to the [Washington State Supreme] court," one official recalled, "AJC carefully considered whether or not to participate in it and, if so, on which side." While the American Jewish Congress's national legal committee voted to back DeFunis by a vote of 18–3, with five "in favor of staying out of it altogether," their local Seattle branch voted by a slim majority not to take sides. "Our Seattle people," the AJC representative explained, "had mixed feelings about the relative equities of the case, as well as concern over possible adverse community relations consequences in the event of AJC involvement in it.... In the final analysis, individual merit, measured as accurately and objectively as humanly possible, must be the crucial determinant in educational as well as in employment opportunity, rather than artificially imposed proportional representation based on racial or ethnic extraction. As we have already learned through painful experience, a double-standard society will not work for very long."[50]

When the NJCRAC debated the DeFunis case, the Anti-Defamation League, the Jewish Labor Committee, the Union of Orthodox Jewish Congregations, and the Jewish Community Relations Councils of Minnesota, Omaha, Palm Beach County, and South Bend all registered their opposition to the University of Washington's admissions procedures, arguing that DeFunis' claim "undercut the principle of equal opportunity for all Americans." They regarded "quotas as inconsistent with principles of equality and as harmful in the long run to all, including these groups, some individual members of which may benefit from specific quotas under specific circumstances at specific times." The NJCRAC groups went on record opposed to "discrimination and 'reverse' discrimination equally and recommend that Jewish community relations agencies pursue all such cases with equal vigor."[51]

In a separate brief to the United States Supreme Court, the Anti-Defamation League engaged Alexander M. Bickel of Yale University and Philip B. Kurland of the University of Chicago to record their support of DeFunis. "If the Constitution prohibits exclusion of blacks and other minorities on racial grounds," Bickel and Kurland argued, "it cannot permit the exclusion of whites on racial grounds. For it must be the exclusion on racial grounds which offends the Constitution, and not the particular skin color of the person excluded." They reminded the Court that "for at least a generation the lesson of the great decisions of this Court and the lessons of contemporary history have been the same: discrimination on the basis of race is illegal, immoral, unconstitutional, inherently wrong and destructive of democratic society. Now this is to be unlearned and we are told that this is not a matter of fundamental principle but only a matter of whose ox is gored."[52]

Bickel and Kurland held that "a state-imposed racial quota is a per se violation of the equal protection clause because it utilizes a factor for measurement that is necessarily irrelevant to any constitutionally acceptable legislative purpose.... If the constitution prohibits exclusion of blacks and other minorities on racial grounds, it cannot permit the exclusion of whites on racial grounds." For the ADL, the University of Washington's admissions program operated as a racial quota system regardless of the university administration's claims to the contrary. "A quota is no less a quota because it is not labeled as such or because it is subject to annual adjustment.... The use of the quota system—the segregation of two groups of applicants by race with admission for each group limited to its assigned numbers, makes it clear that this is not simply a case where race was used as one among many factors to determine legislation. Instead, the law school used race as the criterion for imposing entirely separate admissions procedures."[53]

The ADL authors drew an all-important connection between Marco DeFunis and the American Jewish experience. "To the Jewish community," they explained, DeFunis symbolizes "all those Jewish sons and daughters who until very recent times were barred from colleges and graduate schools, including and especially some of the most prestigious, because of overt or tacit restrictive quotas and 'gentleman's agreements' on Jewish admission—barriers that finally came tumbling down only after World War II and only after a sustained fight by the Jewish community in behalf of itself and other minorities similarly discriminated against." The American Jewish response to the DeFunis case did not signal, in the ADL's eyes, a sea change in their constituent's political persuasion. "Jews," they claimed, were "not asking for their group share of the 'action.'" Instead, Bickel and Kurland held, American Jews were "demanding what they have always asked: that each American be accepted or rejected on the basis of his or her individual achievement and worth, without regard to race, religion, ethnic origin, or sex.... The right to be free of discrimination based on group identity was an individual right (a position consistently upheld by the United States Supreme Court), a right that may not be denied even by the well-intentioned effort to render justice toward a disadvantaged group."[54]

The ADL considered "the closing of a door in the face of a Marco DeFunis ... no more justifiable, no less wrong, than the closing of a door in the face of a James Meredith," referring to the first black student at the University of Mississippi, who was initially denied admission by the governor. What the Jewish community claimed was "no more or less than was demanded of employers, employment agencies, and labor organizations in the landmark 1964 Civil Rights Act. That is, equal opportunity for all, without regard to race ... The evils attendant upon preferential treatment, the invidious new discrimination imposed on individuals because of the accidents of their birth; the consequent loss to society of those who might serve it best; the demand for proportional quotas and the inevitable group antagonisms that follow, the ethnic census and ethnic reporting, with their invasion of privacy and threat of discrimination (old style and new style)—far outweigh any temporary or even long-range social benefits it might help to achieve."[55]

Many in the black community viewed Jewish support of DeFunis and later Bakke as an abandonment of their stand for racial equality. After Jewish groups challenged the University of Washington's affirmative action program, columnist William Raspberry of the *Washington Post* articulated the disappointment of many African Americans: "The fight against affirmative action programs designed to help blacks and other minorities into the American mainstream is being led by Jews.... Jewish organizations could have offered their people as consultants and maintained a low profile themselves." Instead, he explained, Jews "chose not to do so and filed independent *amicus curiae* briefs," creating "an understandable bitterness in the black community."[56]

On April 23, 1974, the Supreme Court decided that it would not rule on the DeFunis case. Five of the nine justices held that since DeFunis was scheduled to graduate the following month, and since the school promised not to prevent him from finishing his studies should the Court rule against him, the case was moot. The Supreme Court's decision, in effect, nullified the Washington State ruling, though without issuing a mandate on the question of affirmative action.[57]

The debates over *DeFunis*, Black Power, affirmative action, and the future of the civil rights movement reflected an American Jewish embrace of inward-looking ethnic politics. By 1975, strong support for public schools gave way to calls for more Jewish day schools. The Reform movement, once American Judaism's most vocal proponent of public education, joined the growing chorus of voices demanding private Jewish elementary and secondary schools. Many Reform Jews opened their worship service to more tradition, keeping their heads covered during worship and their plates free from non-kosher foods. Orthodox communities grew, reestablishing many ethnic neighborhoods abandoned in the early postwar period. The plight of oppressed Jews in the Communist bloc and elsewhere eclipsed civil rights as the most important social cause of organized Jewry. American rabbis joined the movement to save Ethiopian Jewry, and Jewish college students volunteered to work in impoverished neighborhoods in Israel. And when the plight of Soviet Jewish refuseniks inspired the Jewish community to stage a nationwide Freedom Ride, American Jews responded with an enthusiasm and conviction once reserved for, and reminiscent of, an earlier era in liberal politics.

"Just Another Foreigner":
An Epilogue

Just another foreigner in another foreign land,
But these strangers are my brothers as they take me by the hand...
Welcome my brothers, welcome one and all,
Welcome my sisters, welcome one and all,
B'ruchim ha'ba'im, shalom aleichem.

IN "Just Another Foreigner," the American Jewish folk group Safam describes a young American Jew visiting Kiryat Shmoneh, an immigrant town on Israel's northeastern border. Surrounded by Jews from Arabic-speaking Yemen and Iraq, the new arrival has trouble understanding their words of welcome. "Just another foreigner," the traveler laments, "in another foreign land." Yet within moments, the Israeli hosts greet their guest with the familiar Hebrew welcome, "*b'ruchim ha'ba'im*." Now at ease in the once-uncomfortable surrounding, the American Jew realizes that "these strangers are my brothers as they take me by the hand."[1]

Safam's song captures the essence of American Jewish political culture in the last quarter of the twentieth century. For the young Jewish leaders born into the social protest era of the 1960s but raised in the conservative climate of the 1970s and 1980s, Safam's musical narrative evoked powerful autobiographical memories. Instead of expressing their social reform ideals by practicing civil disobedience and rallying in defense of fellow Americans, the new generation of Jews journeyed to Israel, learned Hebrew, and studied the works of major Zionist thinkers. Bred in the geographic and cultural isolation of middle-class Jewish suburbs, these young Jews knew little of the poverty that led their grandparents to embrace the New Deal and could only recall the Holocaust from lessons learned in religious school. Their knowledge of the rise and fall of the black-Jewish alliance grew from video images and their parents stories, instead of personal experience. When Safam's American Jewish protagonist mentioned brothers taking him by the hand, he referred to Jews from different nations, not Americans of varying ethnic backgrounds.

The younger generation's political maturation testifies to the phenomenal success achieved by the Eastern European American Jewish community after just one hundred years on American shores. They had joined the national elite. In the American political system, the pro-Israel lobby is one of the strongest, while high Jewish voter turnout in America's urban centers often affords the community kingmaker status. American Jews remain generous contributors and strategists within the Democratic and now Republican parties. The door to government that FDR opened in 1933 continues to welcome Jews to cabinet-level positions. In education, Jewish undergraduates represent over 20 percent of the student population at the nation's top Ivy League colleges, and advanced degrees have become the norm. In the entertainment industry, built by Jewish filmmakers in the early part of the century, Jews have remained a powerful force. For the first time in American Jewish history, a younger generation will not top the education, income, or social status enjoyed by its parents.[2]

The meteoric social rise of American Jews since 1975 coincided with a dramatic decline in domestic anti-Semitism. As historian Leonard Dinnerstein noted, "American Jews have never been more prosperous, more secure, and more 'at home in America' than they are today." In 1990, the NCRAC reported that "the long-term downward trend of antisemitism, well-documented since the 1960s, probably did not reverse course during the last two years," and a 1991 AJC report concluded that "on most indicators anti-Jewish attitudes are at historic lows." While Jewish defense organizations such as the ADL noted increases in African-American anti-Semitism, and college campuses have remained a center for anti-Jewish expression, neither poses a serious threat to the American Jewish community. In a dramatic departure from the 1930s, American anti-Semitism today, according to Dinnerstein, "is neither virulent nor growing. It is not a powerful social or political force." American Jews enjoy a political culture where "prejudicial comments are now beyond the bounds of respectable discourse and existing societal restraints prevent any overt anti-semitic conduct except among small groups of disturbed adolescents, extremists, and powerless African Americans."[3]

The Jewish leaders coming of age in the 1970s and 1980s encountered a political world shaken from many of its consensus-based liberal roots. When the rise of black militancy forced most whites out of civil rights organizations, many Jews responded by turning inward and embracing political issues of particular concern to their own community. Once-sacred communal policies endured sustained attack. Jewish support for affirmative action, public education, and social justice wavered on the domestic scene while Jewish leaders scrutinized U.S. humanitarian missions overseas. The idealistic veneer protecting the State of Israel from

American Jewish criticism evaporated under the penetrating heat of the Lebanese invasion, the rise of Jewish fundamentalism, and the assassination of Prime Minister Yitzchak Rabin by an Israeli Jew. Jews appeared ready to end a generations-long commitment to liberal social reform.

American Jewish support for public education has waned in the years since 1975. While Jews traditionally valued government-sponsored schooling as a social leveler and raised a high barrier between church and state, many Jewish parents in the 1990s decried the state of public schools, rejoiced in the dramatic growth of Jewish day schools, and seemed less concerned with church-state issues. Just as public schools had served as agents of acculturation for Jews in the first seventy-five years of the century, Jewish day schools have emerged as the next logical step in the evolution of American Jewish education. They provide a quality curriculum, skilled instructors, and, most important, include Jewish religious and cultural training.

When advocates of school vouchers launched their campaign for government subsidies of private schools, they enjoyed strong backing from some in the Jewish community. Barry Shrage, the president of the Combined Jewish Philanthropies of Boston, acknowledged that the Jewish community needed to reassess its opposition to school vouchers. "Jewish supporters of vouchers," conservative commentator Jonathan S. Tobin noted, "see the knee-jerk opposition of Jewish groups to vouchers as outdated thinking which fails to take into account the Jewish community's own need to nurture its day schools, which are our best tool to advance Jewish continuity." For voucher supporters, concerns over a weakened public school system fell on deaf ears. As Tobin explained, "I think this is resonating less and less with a secure American Jewish community that needs to worry more about its own continuity than fears of a bygone era. The Jewish devotion to the public schools as 'temples of liberty,' as Rabbi Isaac Mayer Wise, a 19th century American rabbi put it, does not answer the problems of the present."[4]

Even Jewish opposition to the voucher initiative revealed dramatic political shifts. Sylvia M. Neil, a member of both the Cook County and the state of Illinois Human Rights Commissions, framed her 1997 antivoucher analysis on pragmatic rather than ideological concerns. Instead of pressing for a strong public education system intent on fostering democracy and social equity, Neil based her argument on evidence that Jewish schools would receive less financial support than their Catholic and Protestant counterparts. For Neil, an unequal distribution of wealth proved a more powerful critique than a principled defense of quality public education.[5]

The Reform movement, which championed social justice causes for over thirty years, has moved away from its earlier emphasis on liberal protest and toward an inner-directed spirituality. In 1998 the president of CCAR, Rabbi Richard Levy, sparked fierce debate when he drafted his "Statement of Principles for Reform Judaism." A far cry from both the classical beginnings of mid-nineteenth century German Jews and the socially conscious civil rights workers of the 1950s and 1960s, Levy's document emphasized a Torah-based spiritual revival. While many, including the UAHC's own president, distanced themselves from his document, it has created a debate over whether the Reform movement will remain committed to its accommodationist roots or return to a more traditional pedagogy centered on ritual and prayer.[6]

In foreign policy, Jews who once advocated liberal internationalism now offer words of caution when the United States extends itself overseas. While most major Jewish organizations backed U.S. intervention in the Balkans in 1999—including Nobel laureate Elie Wiesel, who argued that "we must come to the defense of defenseless victims"—recent humanitarian efforts have faced growing opposition. Rabbi Steven Jacobs, who accompanied Reverend Jesse Jackson on his 1999 mission to free three U.S. serviceman held prisoner by the Serbs in the Kosovo conflict, advised President Clinton that "there are many wonderful Serbs, as well as 3,000 Jews, in Belgrade who are living in constant fear of air raids." He recounted the story of Aca Singer, the seventy-year-old head of the Yugoslav Jewish community, who told the rabbi, "I did not survive Auschwitz in order to be killed by American bombs in Belgrade."[7]

Others feared a Vietnam-style stalemate. The Jewish War Veterans of America supported NATO air strikes in Kosovo but refused to endorse the deployment of ground forces in a "civil war in a sovereign nation," while Bob Zweiman, past national commander and international liaisons officer for the group, admonished U.S. policymakers to "get in and get out as soon as possible" and create "a firm exit strategy." Deborah Dwork, director of the Center for Holocaust studies at Clark University, criticized the administration's belief that military action could solve a humanitarian problem. She rejected the argument, reminiscent of another made to American Jewish leaders in World War II, that the best way to help refugees is win the war: "I don't know whether this military intervention will ameliorate the lot of those individual people." In the final analysis, American Jews occupied a tense and dynamic political place. They understood the need for internationalism but feared its application.[8]

Support of Israel, once a mainstay for American Jews, has wavered in recent years. Israel has shed its image as the needy younger sibling of American Jewry and emerged in the last twenty-five years as a powerful force in international politics and Jewish life. Dovish organizations such as "Peace Now" emerged to challenge the Israeli political establishment's long-time ban against negotiating with Palestinian terrorists, while the San Francisco–based Jewish magazine *Tikkun* articulated its own leftist critique of Israeli and American Jewish life. In the 1990s, groups headed by Reform and Conservative Jews launched a movement to gain religious legitimacy in the Orthodox-controlled Israeli political establishment. They demanded recognition of their clergy's right to perform weddings and conversions, staged protests at Jerusalem's Western Wall, and sought inclusion on local religious councils.[9]

Recent immigration trends to Israel reflect the new relationship. Between 1967 and 1973, almost 60,000 American Jews packed their belongings and moved to the Jewish state. Most hailed from nontraditional religious backgrounds and looked to immigration to Israel—*aliyah*, literally "ascent" in Hebrew—as an opportunity to help create an idealistic Jewish homeland. For some of the new arrivals, Israel replaced the United States as the object of liberal social activism, as American-born Jews filled the ranks of Israel's most progressive political parties.

By the 1990s, though, the number of American immigrants plummeted to fewer than 3,000 a year. The new arrivals constituted a disproportionate share of West Bank settlers, most adhered to Orthodox Judaism, and few affiliated with left-wing Israeli political parties. "The percentage of Orthodox Jews was probably the lowest during [the period between 1967 and 1973]," Steven Cohen of Hebrew University's Melton Center observed, "while conversely the percentage of politically and culturally progressive types was probably at its highest." What was once perceived by American Jews as a progressive nation committed to socialist egalitarian ideals matured into a modern nation-state struggling with issues of religious diversity, conflicting political opinions, and divergent ideas about the nature of Zionism.[10]

Recent historical revisionism even soured American Jews on their onetime national hero, Franklin D. Roosevelt. In 1984, historian David Wyman published his pathbreaking book, *The Abandonment of the Jews: America and the Holocaust, 1941–1945*. Building on his earlier research, Wyman meticulously documented a concerted attempt by the State Department to create "paper walls," layer upon layer of government bureaucracy, to prevent Jewish refugees from immigrating to the United States. Wyman's book unleashed a fierce communal reaction as American Jews took a second look at FDR. Once the surrogate father of a nation reeling from economic depression, the New Deal leader reemerged as the worst incarnation of the pragmatic politician, one willing to compromise the humanitarian needs of European Jews in order to achieve a larger political objective. Younger Jews criticized their parents for maintaining an accommodationist wartime stance, while those old enough to remember Roosevelt turned bitter at the mention of his name.[11]

For most white ethnic immigrant groups, the dramatic political realignments in the years after 1975 hastened a retreat from liberal activism. What started with Richard Nixon in 1968 reached full maturity with Ronald Reagan's election in 1980. The New Deal coalition collapsed, with millions of working-class white ethnics fleeing the Democratic party. In Chicago and Detroit, long-time labor unionists broke with the party of FDR and joined the Republican revolution. Italian Americans in New York's Canarsie neighborhood turned against liberalism, while in Boston, long considered the bastion of urban progressive politics, Irish Americans took to the streets in protest of court-ordered busing. In the South, the Republican party rose from virtual non-entity status to wrest control from the Democrats, who had enjoyed one-party dominance since Reconstruction.[12]

But American Jews did not abandon liberalism after 1975. Most resisted conservatism and redefined their liberal beliefs to mesh with a new political mindset gaining popularity among leftist activists. Cultural nationalism, as it came to be known, celebrated the distinctive contributions of ethnic minorities to American life. Buoyed by Johnson's Great Society programs, the rise of Black Power, and the politicization of new constituencies, ethnic leaders, including Jews, took advantage of a more permissive political culture to broaden the limits of acceptable ethnic expression. The renamed SNCC (Student National Coordinating Committee), for example, labored to reduce economic inequality among the nation's urban African Americans as they moved from the *de jure* discrimination struggle of the Martin Luther King years to the *de facto* racism of contemporary America. The National Organization of Women (NOW) led the call for gender equality after many women criticized the latent sexism permeating even the most liberal civil rights groups. The American Indian Movement (AIM) demanded greater recognition of American Indian rights and claims, while Mecha (*Movimiento Estudiantil Chicano de Aztlan*) organized as a political voice for Mexican-American students. "The desperation of the late 1960s," two observers concluded, "led some to . . . senseless violence. . . . But others found new directions in their effort to build a viable radical community . . . within their own kind—women, Catholics, . . . homosexuals, teachers and Jews."[13]

Jews directed their impressive political potential toward their own communal interests. A leadership which based its New Deal, World War II, and Cold War political platforms on interreligious alliances spearheaded separatist campaigns on behalf of Jews in the Soviet Union, Israel, and around the world. A new generation of Jewish leaders revisited Stuyvesant's seventeenth-century admonition to "take care of one's own" and fashioned a brand of liberal activism on models created by the same militant blacks accused of anti-Semitism just a decade earlier. As one observer noted, "If white society valued straight hair, then blacks made naturally kinky hair a symbol of pride, calling the hairstyle an 'Afro.' In cultural politics, wearing an afro became a political statement. Jews followed suit, naming their naturally kinky hairstyle a 'Hebrew Afro,' or just a 'Hebrew.' "[14]

Jewish communal leaders hoped this new approach to liberal politics would compensate for the end of the New Deal coalition by encouraging cultural pluralism and promoting ethnic activism. The same ideology that many feared would undo generations of Jewish mobility emerged as a powerful force in American Jewish cultural survival, exploding the myth that liberalism had died and ethnic nationalism had been the culprit. What seemed a rapid retreat from liberal politics actually marked an embrace of the era's new self-directed credo.

Two events helped steer the American Jewish community onto its cultural nationalist course: the creation of the Black Power movement described in Chapter 8 and the New Left's anti-Israel pronouncements following the 1967 Six Day War. African-American militancy, capped by successful efforts to purge Jews and other whites from civil rights leadership positions, inspired Jewish activists to focus on their own ethnic rebirth. "When the blacks tried to enter the melting pot," leftist Arthur Waskow argued, "the temperature inside got too high and the pot shattered. Simultaneously, the Vietnam War showed America, not as a defender against a holocaust, but as a perpetrator of one. From both events, many young Jews whose parents had proudly assimilated to the American promise . . . [found] they do not want to be American after all." These representatives of a new generation rejected economic status as a primary communal goal. "The eighty-year upward mobility process was shattered," Waskow concluded. Jewish activists rejected the accommodationist stance of their parent's generation and soured on the classic 1950s version of the American dream.[15]

Despite their strong affinity for New Leftist perspectives, Jews faced a critical test when several of the progressive political organizations criticized Israel's occupation of the West Bank and Gaza Strip. Noted one commentator, "The New Left—at one point, the only hope for morality in this country—sold out [the Jewish activist on campus] by its pointless acceptance of the 'good-guy-bad-guy' dualism in the middle east." When African-American representatives pressed for adoption of an anti-Zionist platform at the 1967 National Conference for New Politics in Chicago, Jewish delegates left the meeting in protest. In 1969, Rabbi M. J. Rosenberg affirmed in a *Village Voice* article, "From this point on, I will support no movement that does not accept my people's struggle.

If I must choose between that Jewish cause and a 'progressive' anti-Israel SDS," he explained, "I shall always choose the Jewish cause, not blindly, not arbitrarily, but always with full knowledge of who I am and where I must be."[16]

Combining the ethnic nationalist component of the Black Power movement with the training and strategy of earlier civil rights efforts, Jewish leftists turned their attention to the most emblematic American Jewish cause of the contemporary era, the Soviet Jewry movement. When African Americans argued that whites should not lead civil rights organizations, Jews replied by focusing on the human rights needs of their own co-religionists. Since most Jews in the United States had already achieved middle-class status, communal leaders looked elsewhere to find a Jewish minority persecuted by an anti-Semitic government. "As the civil rights struggle petered out and the nonviolent era of student activism drew to a close," one historian noted, "the Soviet Jewry movement emerged. With its peaceful tactics, it satisfied the needs of those who could not subscribe to the student militancy of the late sixties."[17]

While Jews in the Soviet Union suffered discrimination for decades, and Jewish organizations, especially those affiliated with labor unions and Zionism, had long worked on their behalf, it was not until the advent of ethnic nationalist politics that the struggle to free Soviet Jews gained national and then international attention. On April 5, 1964, the NJCRAC, the SCA, the AJC, the ADL, and ten other Jewish organizations convened an American Jewish Conference on Soviet Jewry. Weeks later, Jacob Birnbaum founded the Student Struggle for Soviet Jewry (SSSJ) and in a matter of days organized a thousand-person strong anti-Soviet demonstration. By October 1964, SSSJ leaders counted over 2,000 protesters, including notable senators and Johnson administration officials. Within two years, Soviet Jewry organizers cheered protest crowds numbering 15,000.[18]

Jewish activists borrowed a page from the African-American civil rights strategy book, imitating the style, technique, and rhetoric of earlier liberal protests. The 1974 "Freedom Ride" from Washington, D.C., to Seattle recalled a previous action against racial inequality. The Student Struggle for Soviet Jewry estimated that 28 percent of its activists had participated in the civil rights movement. When asked why American Jews should protest the condition of Soviet Jews, Birnbaum responded, "Many young Jews today forget that if injustice cannot be condoned in Selma, USA, neither must it be overlooked in Kiev, USSR." One of the earliest meetings, a Conference on the Status of Soviet Jews held in October 1963, counted civil rights leader Martin Luther King, Jr., Supreme Court Justice William O. Douglas, and labor leader Walter Reuther as sponsors. The Soviet Jewry movement offered American Jews disillusioned with the breakup of the black-Jewish coalition the opportunity to serve their

Figure 10. The 1972 Washington, D.C., Prayer Vigil for Soviet Jewry, Farragut Square. (Synagogue Council of America records, 1935–1974, I-68, box 45 of 56, folder "Promotional Materials," American Jewish Historical Society, Waltham, Mass.)

own ethnic community while returning to the nonviolent tactics they preferred.[19]

By focusing on Soviet human rights abuses, Jewish activists not only helped their Eastern European brethren but also took advantage of American opposition to the Communist state in the Cold War. In 1972, Senator Henry Jackson of Washington rallied seventy-six colleagues to co-sponsor legislation tying U.S. economic incentives to the human rights records of Communist nations. An April 1972 House resolution calling on "the Soviet government to permit the free expression of ideas and the exercise of religion by all its citizens" passed by a 360–0 vote. Once again, Jewish leaders linked the particular goals of their social reform program to larger trends in American politics: even the Jewish community's commitment to Soviet Jewry demonstrated the importance of the acculturation process in American Jewish politics.[20]

American Jews directed some of the era's political energy toward a religious and cultural revival. Just as more and more Americans searched for their spiritual roots in the 1970s, so too did American Jews. In 1973, the Jewish Publication Society released Richard Siegel, Michael Strassfeld, and Sharon Strassfeld's era-defining book, *The Jewish Catalog*, a how-to guide for Jewish religious practice geared toward the Jews of the counterculture. By the early 1980s, 200,000 copies had been sold, second only to the Bible in JPS sales. At the same time, a host of alternative Jewish religious centers have offered once-marginal Jews a path to spiritual redemption. In a more traditional vein, Jewish ethnic neighborhoods have reemerged in urban centers across the country as tens of thousands of well-educated Jewish professionals have chosen to leave their nontraditional upbringings and embrace Orthodoxy. Observance of Jewish rituals, shunned by most non-Orthodox Jews during the 1950s consensus, reemerged in the wake of the civil rights revolution.[21]

Within the Jewish spiritual revival, the *havurah* movement emerged as the most successful expression of inward-directed Judaism. Revolving around small, intimate prayer communities designed as countercultural alternatives to the Protestant-influenced accommodationist style of 1950s American Judaism, participants (known as *haverim*, Hebrew for "friends") borrowed from the New Leftist critique of American culture. As one participant noted, the New Left and *havurah* movements "developed almost identical styles, which encouraged intimacy and virtually outlawed authority. For instance, members of the SDS and the *havurah* movement sat in circles, not in rows. Both organizations insisted on a leadership that rotated frequently, arrived at all their decisions by consensus, not by votes or by the decree of some central committee." *Havurah* members sought to build a spiritual community that moved away from the rigid decorum of mainstream Judaism and toward a new conceptual understanding of Jewish ritual, prayer, and tradition. The *havurah* movement, one historian concluded, "was the first movement in American Judaism to criticize the suburban and monumental urban synagogue as a viable expression of Jewish life."[22]

The *havurah* movement redefined the politics of acculturation. While postwar consensus Jews modified their religious practice in order to conform to the larger society, *havurah* members refused. "Jewish success was bought at a price," two researchers explained. "It destroyed Jewish culture and ethnic solidarity, forced Jews to rely on others' good will and alienated masses of young Jews. It is a price the Jewish Left is unwilling to pay." Americanization, they believed, led to a Judaism that merely imitated the middle-class values of mainstream Protestantism. American Jews in the 1970s and 1980s rejected accommodation and returned to small ethnic-centered communities.[23]

The ethnic nationalism of the 1960s also translated into renewed American Jewish interest in the State of Israel. American Zionism, which lost prominence during the 1950s and early 1960s, gained strength in the last years of the decade. When war broke out between Israel and her Arab neighbors in 1967, American Jews reacted with such an outpouring of support that even their leadership reacted with shock and (pleasant) surprise. After the war, relations between blacks and Jews in the United States soured when many African-American militants sided with the Palestinian cause and linked the Israeli government to imperialist aggression. In a classic reformulation of contemporary ethnic politics, American Jewish leaders employed language typical of the Black Power movement to campaign against militant anti-Zionist rhetoric.

Mixing Zionist ideology with the ethnic politics of 1960s America, Jews paralleled their love of Israel to the spirit of African-American ethnic nationalism. Just as militant civil rights workers argued that their white purges amounted to nothing less than "Black Zionism," more and more American Jews looked to the Jewish state as a source of ethnic pride. One former American noted in 1972 that he chose to immigrate to Israel because "blacks in America have gone too far in their demands." Another explained that "a lot of people were running away from the Vietnam war, from the civil rights battles, from Richard Nixon. At the time people were saying that Richard Nixon should have been awarded the Zionist of the year award for inspiring *aliyah*." American Jews capitalized on their Zionist leanings to test the expanding limits of American ethnic expression. "They were," according to one historian, "very much continuing the American Jewish tradition of political liberalism."[24]

The new activist political approach also extended to Jews who abandoned liberalism and turned to the conservatism of the Republican party. If cultural nationalism encouraged blacks to adopt self-interested positions, Jewish neoconservatives reasoned, then Jews too should be afforded the same opportunity to advance their own social ideals. For them, "turning inward" demanded preservation of the consensus-based liberal ideals that powered Jewish activism in the previous two generations. When the Democratic party backed affirmative action programs and acknowledged group-based social inequality, many one-time liberal Jews bolted, charging that cultural nationalism diverted liberalism away from its consensus-oriented and rights-based values. Individual rights, equal opportunity, and the rule of law dominated their political worldview and forced them into a standoff with their more progressive co-religionists.

Without the Democrats to carry their banner, some disgruntled Jews turned to a Republican party intent on capturing white ethnics by promising a more inclusive platform and trumpeting the political ideals held so dear by American Jews. For this Jewish minority, the values behind Jewish liberalism remained, if reincarnated through a different party affiliation. Their choice was not between liberalism and conservatism. It was between a Democratic party that they believed abandoned liberal idealism and a Republican party making strides to reinvent itself as an advocate of Jewish political values. It was not that they had left the Democratic party, as Ronald Reagan enjoyed saying of himself; the Democratic party had left them. Inertia alone, they concluded, stood between Jews and the Republican party.

Jewish support for conservative causes led some to agree with the biting 1970s aphorism that "a neo-conservative is nothing more than a liberal who got mugged by reality." Conservative Republican Ronald S. Lauder now heads the Conference of Presidents of Major American Jewish Organizations. Jewish voters in Los Angeles's 1997 mayoral election favored incumbent Republican Richard Riordan over Democratic challenger and former SDS leader Tom Hayden. Christine Whitman, a moderate Republican who boasted a good relationship with the Jewish community, earned one-third of the Jewish vote in her 1993 election as governor of New Jersey, a dramatic increase over most Republican candidates. In academic circles, Jewish conservatism enjoyed a burst of new scholarly attention when Murray Friedman, head of the AJC's mid-Atlantic states region and one-time member of Ronald Reagan's Civil Rights Commission, brought together many of the nation's leading American Jewish scholars for a conference billed as the "first major exploration of the history of American Jewish political conservatism in this country."[25]

This conservative interpretation of cultural nationalism advanced Jewish communal interests and reinforced the political importance of the acculturation process. The Republican party, which historically has disregarded Jewish voters, now enjoys the support of a vocal Jewish minority. As the liberal Democratic director of the Reform movement's Religious Action Center argues, Jewish needs are best served by remaining open to both political parties. Vouchers promised a financial boost to fledgling Jewish day schools, and the end of the secular activist Jewish-liberal alliance heralded a renewed emphasis on Jewish education. Jewish neoconservatives, by linking the cultural nationalist's goal of "turning inward" to the Republican party, redefined the politics of acculturation and forced their more progressive co-religionists to consider more fully the implications of their newfound liberalism.[26]

The growth of a neoconservative interpretation of cultural nationalism also highlighted a bitter disagreement over the legacy of accommodationism in American Jewish political culture. When the Democratic party embraced ethnic distinctiveness, many Jews flinched, fearing that a "hyphenated America" would derail this nation's great democratic journey. Individualism would give way to group identity. Rights, as affirmative action cases seemed to imply, would be granted according to one's racial, ethnic, or gender makeup. The promises of the European Enlightenment reinvented on American shores would face grave threats unless the country could agree on a new set of binding principles. In a political culture defined by multilingualism, cultural relativity, and compensatory public policy, consensus seemed an impossibility.[27]

In the final analysis, though, ethnic nationalism in both its liberal and conservative forms failed to produce a worthy successor to FDR's New Deal coalition. While the Soviet Jewry, American Zionist, and spiritual renewal movements helped liberal and neo-conservative Jews stake out new ethnic claims, they also alienated the Jewish community from its one-time allies. Common ground ceased to be a goal of community activists, as each constituent group lobbied for its own narrowly defined self-interest. Accommodationist politics, once the hallmark of Jewish liberal activism, disintegrated when the new militancy proved a greater defender of American Jewish interests. Acculturative forces, more than empathy for the downtrodden, once again inspired American Jewish politics. Despite the tremendous political energy it unleashed, ethnic nationalism doomed any chance of coalition-building by pitting Americans against one another. What Franklin Roosevelt began as an exercise in coalition-building ended with groups distant and self-absorbed.

By employing cultural nationalist thinking to justify a retreat from liberal programs, Jewish neoconservatives distanced themselves from their one-time allies and lent truth to the criticism that opportunism motivated Jewish social action. Their embrace of the Republican party alienated them from co-religionists who could not lend support to a group that has counted Patrick Buchanan, Jerry Falwell, and Pat Robertson among its faithful. While their numbers still remain small, the growth of Jewish Republicanism raises the central question in contemporary American political culture: will Jews look to the federal government as an agent of positive social change or join other white ethnics and turn away from government activism? The answer to this question will speak volumes about the nature and limits of American Jewish liberalism. If liberalism emerges as a natural outgrowth of Judaism's prophetic tradition, then Jews will remain committed to achieving a just society even after they enjoy material success. But if American Jewish political culture remains sensitive to larger social trends, then liberalism will become a footnote in American Jewish history, assigned the temporary role of expediting the community's rise up the social ladder but jettisoned once that goal was reached.

A new liberal coalition will not be created from the fractiousness of ethnic nationalism, nor will it emerge from the naive belief that legal guarantees will remedy historic social discrimination. The ultimate goal of Jewish liberals—social inclusion in the larger society—demands that contemporary Jews return to what their parents and grandparents knew all along: that cultural pluralism must be rooted in accommodationism. But unlike earlier generations, American Jews cannot seek accommodation to middle-class Protestant America. With the political emergence of women, African Americans, and other racial minorities since 1975, mainstream American politics has changed. What was once a Jewish appeal to the power elite has evolved into complex negotiations with a variety of once-marginal groups. For a new liberal coalition to succeed, Jewish leaders will have to reconsider many of their assumptions about American life and acculturate to a more diverse political culture.

Notes

Introduction

1. Irving Howe, *World of Our Fathers* (New York: Simon and Schuster, 1976), 393.

2. A majority of American Jews voted Democratic in every election from 1932 to 1996. In 1948, Harry Truman won 75 percent of the Jewish vote; in 1952 and 1956 Adlai Stevenson won 64 and 60 percent, respectively; in 1960 John F. Kennedy won 82 percent; in 1964 Lyndon Johnson won 90 percent; in 1968 Hubert Humphrey won 81 percent; and in 1972 George McGovern won 65 percent. Since then, American Jews have supported Jimmy Carter, Walter Mondale, Michael Dukakis, and Bill Clinton in numbers greater than any other white ethnic group. Evelyn Lewis, "The Jewish Vote" (Ph.D. dissertation, Ball State University, 1976).

3. See Beverly and Wesley Allinsmith, "Religious Affiliation and Politico-Economic Attitude," *Public Opinion Quarterly* 7 (September 1948), 377–389.

4. See David Biale, Michael Galchinsky, and Susannah Heschel, eds., *Insider/Outsider: American Jews and Multi-Culturalism* (Berkeley: University of California Press, 1998); Arthur M. Schlesinger, Jr., *The Disuniting of America: Reflections on a Multi-Cultural Society* (New York: W. W. Norton, 1998); John A. Hall and Charles Lindholm, *Is America Breaking Apart?* (Princeton: Princeton University Press, 1999); David A. Hollinger, *Beyond Multiculturalism: Postethnic America* (New York: Basic Books, 1995); and Nathan Glazer, *We Are All Multiculturalists Now* (Cambridge: Harvard University Press, 1997).

5. See Werner Cohn, *Sources of American Jewish Liberalism—A Study of the Political Alignments of American Jews* (Ph.D. dissertation, New School For Social Research, 1956). In 1976, the *American Jewish Historical Quarterly* devoted its December issue to "Jews and American Liberalism: Studies in Political Behavior," while that same year William Berlin offered a related dissertation, *The Roots of Jewish Political Thought in America*, at Rutgers University, New Brunswick, New Jersey. Numerous journals and magazines have featured discussions of American Jewish liberalism, including *Commentary*, "Liberalism and the Jews: A Symposium" (January 1980), and Lucy S. Dawidowicz and Leon J. Goldstein, "The American Jewish Liberal Tradition," appearing in Marshall Sklare, ed., *The Jew in American Society* (New York: Behrman House, 1974). See also Steven M. Cohen, *The Dimensions of American Jewish Liberalism* (New York: American Jewish Committee, 1989); Daniel J. Elazar, *The New Jewish Politics* (Lanham, Md.: University Press of America, 1988); and part 3 of Henry L. Feingold, *Lest Memory Cease: Finding Meaning in the American Jewish Past* (Syracuse: Syracuse University Press, 1996).

6. Moses Rischin, *The Promised City: New York's Jews, 1870–1914* (Cambridge: Harvard University Press, 1962); Lawrence Fuchs, *The Political Behavior of American Jews* (New York: Free Press, 1956); Henry Feingold, "A Midrash on

American Jewish History," in Murray Friedman, *Utopian Dilemma: New Political Directions for American Jews* (Bryn Mawr: Ethics and Public Policy Center, 1985), 7. See also Howe, *World of Our Fathers*. While only 39 percent of American Jews voted for Ronald Reagan in his reelection campaign in 1984, 85 percent of the ultra-Orthodox Jewish vote favored the Republican incumbent. Herbert L. Solomon, "The Republican Party and the Jews," *Judaism* 37 (June 1988), 279.

7. See Gary Gerstle, "The Protean Character of American Liberalism," *American Historical Review* 99 (October 1994), 1043–1073.

8. See Jacob Katz, *Out of the Ghetto: The Social Background of Jewish Emancipation, 1770–1870* (Cambridge: Harvard University Press, 1973).

9. See Henry L. Feingold, *Zion in America: The Jewish Experience from Colonial Times to the Present* (New York: Hippocrene, 1974); Jacob R. Marcus, *Colonial American Jew* (Detroit: Wayne State University Press, 1970); Eli Farber, *A Time for Planting: The First Migration* (Baltimore: Johns Hopkins University Press, 1992); Jonathan Sarna, *Jacksonian Jew: The Two Worlds of Mordechai Noah* (New York: Holmes and Meier, 1981); Stanley Chyet, "The Political Rights of the Jews in the United States: 1776–1840," in Abraham Karp, ed., *Critical Studies in American Jewish History: Selected Articles From American Jewish Archives* 2 (Cincinnati: American Jewish Archives, 1971), 27–88.

10. See Howe, *World of Our Fathers*, and Lucy S. Dawidowicz, *On Equal Terms: Jews in America, 1881–1981* (New York: Holt, 1982).

11. For more on liberalism in the Progressive era, see John D. Buenker, *Urban Liberalism and Progressive Reform* (New York: Scribners, 1973).

12. See Albert I. Gordon, *Jews in Suburbia* (Boston: Beacon Press, 1959).

13. See Naomi Cohen, *Not Free to Desist: History of the American Jewish Committee, 1906–1966* (Philadelphia: Jewish Publication Society, 1972); Stuart Svonkin, *Jews Against Prejudice: American Jews and the Fight for Civil Liberties* (New York: Columbia University Press, 1997), 12; and Leonard Dinnerstein, *Anti-Semitism in America* (New York: Oxford University Press, 1994), 73. The Reform movement of Judaism originated in enlightenment Germany and sought to combine the benefits of legal equality with the morality of Jewish law. For a complete history of the movement, see Michael A. Meyer, *Response to Modernity: A History of the Reform Movement in Judaism* (New York: Oxford University Press, 1988).

14. For more on the Galveston project, see Bernard Marinbach, *Galveston: Ellis Island of the West* (Albany: State University of New York Press, 1984), and Menahem Kaufman, *An Ambiguous Partnership: Non Zionists and Zionists in America, 1939–1948* (Detroit: Wayne State University Press, 1991), 16. For an excellent analysis of the relations between German and Eastern European Jews in America, see Naomi Cohen, *Encounter with Emancipation: The German Jews in the United States, 1830–1914* (Philadelphia: Jewish Publication Society, 1984); Arthur Goren, *New York Jews and the Quest for Community: The Kehillah Experiment 1908–1922* (New York: Columbia University Press, 1970); and Deborah Dash Moore, *At Home in America: Second Generation New York Jews* (New York: Columbia University Press, 1981).

15. "Draft of Proposed Report to Be Submitted by a Sub-Committee of the Committee of Seven to the Administrative Committee of the American Jewish

Congress," 1934, 2–3, American Jewish Historical Society (AJHS). See Morris Frommer, *The American Jewish Congress: A History 1914–1950* (Ph.D. dissertation, The Ohio State University, 1978).

16. *Five Who Led* (New York: Jewish Labor Committee, 1976–77), 1; "Jewish Labor Committee Aims and Objectives," Papers of the General Jewish Council, box 2, p. 4, AJHS. See also Henry L. Feingold, *A Time for Searching: Entering the Mainstream, 1920–1945* (Baltimore: Johns Hopkins University Press, 1992).

17. See Deborah Dash Moore, *B'nai B'rith and the Challenge of Ethnic Leadership* (Albany: State University of New York Press, 1981).

18. Ninety-seven percent of all American Jews lived in a community bound by a local federation (Feingold, *A Time for Searching*, 161–162, 164). See also Marc Lee Raphael, *A History of the United Jewish Appeal* (Providence: Scholars Press, 1982), and *Understanding American Jewish Philanthropy* (New York: Ktav, 1979); Philip Bernstein, *To Dwell in Unity: The Jewish Federation Movement in America Since 1960* (Philadelphia: Jewish Publication Society, 1983); Harry L. Lurie, *A Heritage Affirmed: The Jewish Federation Movement in America* (Philadelphia: Jewish Publication Society, 1961); and Milton Goldin, *Why They Give: American Jews and Their Philanthropies* (New York: Macmillan, 1976).

19. See Meyer, *Response to Modernity*; Marshall Sklare, *Conservative Judaism: An American Religious Movement* (New York: Schocken, 1972); and Jenna Weissman Joselit, *New York's Jewish Jews: The Orthodox Community in the Interwar Years* (Bloomington: Indiana University Press, 1990). *American Jewish History* 69 (December 1979) is devoted to Orthodox Judaism as well.

20. See Moore, *At Home in America*.

21. Their experience echoed historian Bruce Stave's findings on city politics in Pittsburgh just as it cast an even wider net: Jewish social workers showed how FDR's co-option strategy also enveloped private and religious groups. See Bruce Stave, *The New Deal and the Last Hurrah: Pittsburgh Machine Politics* (Pittsburgh: University of Pittsburgh Press, 1970).

Chapter One

1. *Proceedings, National Conference of Jewish Social Service, 1933*, 7. The National Conference of Jewish Social Service (NCJSS), later renamed the National Conference of Jewish Social Welfare (NCJSW), brought together leaders in every field of Jewish social service to present and discuss papers of topical interest. The conference served as the major forum for presenting ideas and opinions on the state of Jewish social welfare in America. For more on Isaac Rubinow, see J. Lee Kreader, *America's Prophet for Social Security: A Biography of Isaac Max Rubinow* (Ph.D. diss., University of Chicago, 1988).

2. See Michael B. Katz, *In the Shadow of the Poorhouse: A Social History of Welfare in America* (New York: Basic Books, 1986), and Shelly Tenenbaum, *A Credit to Their Community: Jewish Loan Societies in the United States* (Detroit: Wayne State University Press, 1993). Naomi W. Cohen, "Responsibilities of Jewish Kinship: Jewish Defense and Philanthropy," in Gladys Rosen, ed., *Jewish Life in America: Historical Perspectives* (New York: Institute of Human Relations Press of the American Jewish Committee, 1978), 126. Quoted in Beth Wenger,

Uncertain Promise: New York Jews and the Great Depression (New Haven: Yale University Press, 1996), 140. A small minority of Jewish communal leaders simply rejected the avalanche of reform in an attempt to preserve the Stuyvesant Pledge. "What kind of Jewish heart have we now, that we can't take care of our own? Haven't we always taken care of our own?" one social worker admonished in 1938. *Proceedings, National Conference of Jewish Social Welfare, 1938,* 23–24. "The Jewish case-working organization cannot turn over its load, or even a part of it [to the government]," another argued. "A group which has held high the banner of justice in its dealings with the underprivileged cannot shrug its shoulders and say 'under present conditions we cannot help ourselves." *Jewish Social Work, 1933,* 20.

3. William E. Leuchtenburg, *Franklin D. Roosevelt and the New Deal, 1932–1940* (New York: Harper Torchbooks, 1963), 347; Laura Kalman, *Abe Fortas: A Biography* (New Haven: Yale University Press, 1990), 28. See Abraham Cronbach, "Jewish Pioneering in American Social Welfare," *American Jewish Archives* 3 (June 1951), 51–78.

4. In his history of Woonsocket, Rhode Island, Gerstle contended that "New Deal icons like the Blue Eagle . . . offered individual Americans security and a sense of belonging to a greater whole in a time of deep distress. These symbols and terms," he concluded, "thus encouraged adjustment rather than rebellion, conformity rather than dissent." Lizabeth Cohen, in her study of Depression-era Chicago, asserted that local ethnic networks collapsed under the weight of federal intervention. It was a time, Cohen concluded, "when the nation moved . . . from diverse social worlds circumscribed by race, ethnicity, class, and geography to more homogeneous cultural experiences." Gary Gerstle, *Working-Class Americanism: The Politics of Labor in a Textile City, 1914–1960* (New York: Cambridge University Press, 1989), 7; Lizabeth Cohen, *Making a New Deal: Industrial Workers in Chicago, 1919–1939* (New York: Cambridge University Press, 1990), 8, 362.

5. *American Jewish Year Book* 32 (1930–1931), 299–306; *Jewish Social Work, 1931,* 31. *Jewish Social Work*, published by the Bureau of Jewish Social Research, served as the main statistics-gathering publication of the Jewish community, *Jewish Social Work, 1930,* 45, 46. Lurie, *A Heritage Affirmed,* 112. *American Jewish Year Book* 36 (1934–1935), 65, and *Proceedings, National Conference of Jewish Social Service, 1932,* 77. *American Jewish Year Book* 39 (1937–38), 90–91.

6. *American Jewish Year Book* 33 (1931–1932), 381, 39. *Jewish Social Work, 1931,* 5. A third more Jewish Americans sought relief in 1933 than in the previous year. In thirteen large cities, Federations reported a decline in contributions from $8.8 million in 1930 to $5.9 million in 1933. Robert Morris and Michael Freund, eds., *Trends and Issues in Jewish Social Welfare, 1899–1952; The History of American Jewish Social Welfare, Seen Through the Proceedings and Reports of the National Conference of Jewish Communal Service* (Philadelphia: Jewish Publication Society of America, 1966), 280; *American Jewish Year Book* 36 (1934–1935), 67–68. See also *American Jewish Year Book* 34 (1932–1933), speech by Benjamin Selekman on the fund-raising abilities of the Jewish federations. From *Notes and News* 25 (December 20, 1934), 10, in Lurie, *A Heritage Affirmed,* 423. The U.S. government's February 1934 *Monthly Labor Review* reported a decline

of 21.2 percent in the cost of living between December 1929 and December 1933; *Jewish Social Work,* 1933, 12. By 1933, about "ninety-four percent of relief money came from public funds as compared to eighty-two percent in 1931, and seventy-five percent in 1929 and 1930." *Jewish Social Work, 1933,* 3.

7. Josephine Chapin Brown, *Public Relief: 1929–1939* (New York: Henry Holt, 1940), 3, 39.

8. Brown, *Public Relief,* 112, 110. See also Walter I. Trattner, *From Poor Law to Welfare State: A History of Social Welfare in America* (New York: Free Press, 1989), especially chapter 5.

9. Brown, *Public Relief,* 110; Frances Fox Piven and Richard A. Cloward, *Regulating The Poor: The Functions of Public Welfare* (New York: Vintage, 1972), 54.

10. Sydney Ahlstrom, *A Religious History of the American People* (New Haven: Yale University Press, 1972), 923–924.

11. In 1931, northern Baptists used their national meeting to voice support for activist government while the Episcopalians and Methodists offered their own defense of a liberal welfare state. The following year, the Federal Council of Churches reversed its laissez-faire platform and advocated more aggressive public intervention while the *Christian Century* feared that FDR would not take decisive action. The 1934 National Council of Methodist Youth marked its national convention by demanding that its membership affirm the pledge: "I surrender my life to Christ. I renounce the capitalist system." Ahlstrom, *A Religious History of the American People,* 921–924.

12. Katz, *In the Shadow of the Poorhouse,* 61, in Jay P. Dolan, *Immigrant Church: New York's Irish and German Catholics, 1815–1865* (South Bend: University of Notre Dame Press, 1983), 122–128; Cohen, *Making a New Deal,* 269.

13. Max I. Dimont, *The Jews in America: The Roots, History, and Destiny of American Jews* (New York: Simon and Schuster, 1978); Cohen, *Making a New Deal,* 223–227. See Roy Lubove, *The Professional Altruist: The Emergence of Social Work as a Career, 1880–1930* (Cambridge: Harvard University Press, 1965); Clarke A. Chambers, *Seedtime of Reform: American Social Service and Social Action, 1918–1933* (Minneapolis: University of Minnesota Press, 1963); and Marc Lee Raphael, "The Origins of Organized National Jewish Philanthropy in the United States, 1914–1939," in Moses Rischin, ed., *The Jews of North America* (Detroit: Wayne State University Press, 1987), 213–223.

14. These conclusions were issued by Hoover's "Organization on Unemployment Relief."

15. Brown, *Public Relief,* 15; *American Jewish Year Book* 39 (1937–38), 128; Marc Grossman, president, Cleveland Jewish Social Service Bureau, *Proceedings, National Conference of Jewish Social Service, 1931,* 25. From a lecture delivered at the International Conference on Jewish Social Work, London, England, July 8–10, 1936, reprinted in the *American Jewish Year Book* 39 (1937–38), 128.

16. *American Jewish Year Book* 34 (1932–1933), 68–69. In 1934, the Reform movement's Central Conference of American Rabbis (CCAR) called for a forty-hour work week, the elimination of child labor, old age pensions, unemployment insurance, public works projects, and collective bargaining. The same year, both the Reform and Conservative movements in Judaism called for a tax system that

was based on income redistribution. See *Proceedings, National Conference of Jewish Social Welfare, 1938*, 37. In 1935, the CCAR supported Roosevelt's social security program. See *Proceedings, National Conference of Jewish Social Welfare, 1938*, 38. In June 1931, the National Conference of Jewish Social Service passed a resolution calling on "the President of the United States to take such steps in the form of federal emergency relief on a large enough scale to alleviate existing and future suffering, construction of public works to stimulate and revive industry; the formulation of a comprehensive program of social insurance; and the creation of such commissions as will assure wise social administration of these and other necessary measures." *Proceedings, National Conference of Jewish Social Service, 1931*, 8; *Proceedings, National Conference of Jewish Social Service, 1932*, 99; *Proceedings, National Conference of Jewish Social Service, 1931*, 54–55.

17. *Proceedings, National Conference of Jewish Social Service, 1931*, 25; *Proceedings, National Conference of Jewish Social Service, 1934*, 28; *Proceedings, National Conference of Jewish Social Service, 1932*, 29; *Proceedings, National Conference of Jewish Social Service, 1930*, 101–102.

18. Between 1930–1931, Jewish social welfare organizations reported a 12.7 percent rise in total volume. The number of active care cases fell 17.6 percent while the total amount of money spent on relief jumped 33.7 percent. *Jewish Social Work, 1931*, 7. In 1933, Jewish agencies reported an 18.4 percent drop in private contributions. *Jewish Social Work, 1933*, 12. Milton Meltzer, *The Jewish Americans: A History in Their Own Words, 1650–1950* (New York: Crowell, 1982), 136–137.

19. Letter from Franklin Roosevelt to Bishop Francis J. McConnell, April 16, 1929, appearing in Wilbur J. Cohen, ed., *The Roosevelt New Deal: A Program Assessment Fifty Years After* (Richmond: Virginia Commonwealth University, 1986), xiv. Brown, *Public Relief*, 90, 94–97 and Stave, *The New Deal and the Last Hurrah*, 110. See also Trattner, *From Poor Law to Welfare State*, chapter 13.

20. *Jewish Social Work, 1933*, 15–16. The Bureau of Jewish Social Research reported that "the volume of need among Jewish agencies would have been vastly increased were it not for the rapid development of new public resources for unemployment relief and the continuance of public welfare service." *Jewish Social Work, 1931*, 5, 8. See also Trattner, *From Poor Law to Welfare State*, 260.

21. *Proceedings, National Conference of Jewish Social Service, 1933*, 39, 40–42.

22. *Proceedings of the National Council of Jewish Social Service, 1932*, 217; *Jewish Social Science Quarterly* 8 (September 1931), 2. From Herman D. Stein, "Jewish Social Work In The United States, 1920–1955," appearing in Marshall Sklare, ed., *The Jews: Social Patterns of an American Group* (Glencoe: Free Press, 1958), 176. See Brown, *Public Relief: 1929–1939*, chapter 1, and Piven and Cloward, *Regulating the Poor*, 51–52. From Herman D. Stein, "Jewish Social Work in the United States, 1920–1955," appearing in Sklare, *The Jews*, 176.

23. In the electorate as a whole, FDR won the support from a broad coalition of Americans. Election returns gave Roosevelt a commanding 57.4 percent majority over rival Herbert Hoover's 39.6 percent. Roosevelt had successfully forged an alliance of farmers and businessmen, southerners and westerners, African Americans and working-class ethnic whites. Jewish support for Roosevelt rose to

85 percent in the 1936 election and increased again to 90 percent in both the 1940 and 1944 campaigns. From Lewis, *The Jewish Vote*, 45. In 1936, even Jewish socialists joined the liberal mainstream and voted for Roosevelt. See Werner Cohn, *Sources of American Jewish Liberalism: A Study of the Political Alignment of American Jews* (Ph.D. dissertation, New School For Social Research, 1956), 87. For more on the New Deal and American Jews, see Leonard Dinnerstein, "Jews and the New Deal," *American Jewish History* 72 (June 1983), as well as his "Franklin D. Roosevelt, American Jewry, and the New Deal," appearing in Cohen, *The Roosevelt New Deal*. James MacGregor Burns, *Roosevelt: The Lion and the Fox* (New York: Harcourt, Brace, Jovanovich, 1984), 164.

24. From Isador Lubin, Commissioner, Bureau of Labor Statistics, United States Department of Labor, "Recent Economic Trends in Relation to Jewish life," *Proceedings, National Conference of Jewish Social Service, 1934*, 8. In 1935, 44 Jewish agencies took 7,035 cases, 11.9 percent fewer than 1934. *1935 Yearbook of Jewish Social Work: Part One: Service Trends in Family Welfare, Child Care, Care of the Aged, Hospitals, Clinics*, 2; "Recent Economic Trends," *Proceedings, National Conference of Jewish Social Service, 1934*, 7–8; *Proceedings, National Conference of Jewish Social Welfare, 1935*, 26.

25. *B'nai B'rith Messenger* 47 (April 1933), 201. *Proceedings, National Council of Jewish Social Service, 1933*, 8. Presidential address by Isaac M. Rubinow, "The Credo of a Jewish Social Worker," *Proceedings, National Conference of Jewish Social Service, 1933*, 7. Just days after Rubinow's speech, the social policy committee of the NCJSS presented a detailed report outlining its position on increased government aid. See *Proceedings, National Council of Jewish Social Service, 1933*, 104–111. Delivered on January 7, 1934, before the Free Synagogue at Carnegie Hall; Papers of Stephen S. Wise, box 21, AJHS. See Melvin Urofsky, *A Voice That Spoke for Justice: The Life and Times of Stephen S. Wise* (Albany: State University of New York Press, 1982), and Stephen Wise, *Challenging Years: The Autobiography of Stephen Wise* (New York: Putnam, 1949).

26. *Jewish Social Work, 1933*, 17, 26. See Oscar Leonard's comment in *Proceedings, National Conference of Jewish Social Service, 1930*, 112–113. See, for example, responses by southern planters to the Agricultural Adjustment Act, big business to the National Recovery Administration, and state governments to federal control of relief administration. *American Jewish Year Book* 34 (1932–1933), 69–70; *Jewish Social Work, 1933*, 19–20.

27. James Patterson, *America's Struggle Against Poverty, 1900–1980* (Cambridge: Harvard University Press, 1986), 58.

28. Brown, *Public Relief*, 113.

29. *Jewish Social Service Quarterly* 7 (December 1930), 13; *Proceedings, National Conference of Jewish Social Service, 1930*, 105; *Jewish Social Work, 1933*, 20.

30. *Jewish Social Work, 1933*, 16; *American Jewish Year Book* 36 (1934–1935), 72.

31. Just as the president signed FERA into law, he advised delegates to a Human Needs Conference in early September 1933 that government aid would only be an emergency measure and ultimately the responsibility for relief would

return to "individual citizens, to individual responsibility, and to private organizations." See Stave, *The New Deal and the Last Hurrah*, 114.

32. *1935 Yearbook of Jewish Social Work*, Part I, 22, 20. Harry L. Lurie, former president of both the Jewish Social Service Association and the National Social Service Association, estimated that by 1934, between 70 and 90 percent of Jewish dependent families were receiving public relief. Jewish social service agencies reduced their relief budgets for the first time since the onset of the Depression. *Proceedings, National Conference of Jewish Social Service, 1934*, 7–8; *Proceedings, National Conference of Jewish Social Welfare, 1935*, 26.

33. *Jewish Social Work, 1933*, 4, 1, 15. The findings reflected the conditions of Jews in the twenty cities with the highest Jewish population. For the few Jews who lived in rural areas, the reported stated, "The Jewish agency still retains its traditional responsibility for dependency in its own community." From "The Minneapolis Jewish Communal Survey," *Proceedings, National Conference of Jewish Social Welfare, 1937*, 93.

34. *Jewish Social Work, 1933*, 17; *Proceedings, National Conference of Jewish Social Service, 1933*, 39–42, 43; *Jewish Social Work, 1933*, 21; *Jewish Social Work, 1933*, 17.

35. Solomon Lowenstein, *Proceedings, National Conference of Jewish Social Service, 1935*, 15.

36. *Proceedings, National Conference of Jewish Social Welfare, 1938*, 23. Dr. Solomon Lowenstein of New York's Federation of Jewish Philanthropies wrote that "it is easier to raise money today than it was two or three years ago." From *Proceedings, National Conference of Jewish Social Welfare, 1936*, 19; *Proceedings, National Conference of Jewish Social Welfare, 1934*, 7; *Proceedings, National Conference of Jewish Social Welfare, 1938*, 23; *American Jewish Year Book* 39 (1937–38), 90; *1939 Year Book of Jewish Social Welfare*, section 1, n.p. In Allegheny County, Pennsylvania, for example, private funds comprised 54 percent of all direct relief aid in 1922 while it totaled less than 1 percent in 1935. From Stave, *The New Deal and the Last Hurrah*, 109.

37. Speech by Benjamin Selekman, meeting of the National Conference of Jewish Federations and Welfare Funds, *American Jewish Year Book* 36 (1934–1935), 65. "Federal Emergency Relief Administration Monthly Report," May 22 to June 30, 1933, 1–2, quoted in Brown, *Public Relief, 1929–1939*, 146. At that time, four million families, or eighteen million people, claimed some form of support from the public dole. As a proportion of the total population, one in every six families was dependent. These estimates were made by the Reconstruction Finance Corporation and were quoted in the "FERA Monthly Report," May 22 to June 30, 1933, 1, quoted in Brown, *Public Relief: 1929–1939*, 145–146.

38. *Proceedings, National Conference of Jewish Social Service, 1936*, 11–12; *American Jewish Year Book* 34 (1932–1933), 76.

39. *Jewish Social Service Quarterly* 7 (September 1930), 1. *Proceedings, National Conference of Jewish Social Service, 1928*, 87–89.

40. See Charles I. Schottland, "Federation and Community Building," *Proceedings, National Conference of Jewish Social Welfare, 1938*, 142.

41. See Joselit, *New York's Jewish Jews*, chapter 5; *Proceedings, National Conference of Jewish Social Service, 1932*, 90; *Proceedings, National Conference of*

Jewish Social Service, 1931, 41–46, 50; Kurt Peiser, executive secretary of the United Jewish Social Agencies in Cincinnati, *Proceedings, National Conference of Jewish Social Service, 1932*, 92–93.

42. Harry J. Sapper, *Proceedings, National Conference of Jewish Social Service, 1932*, 86; Kurt Peiser, executive secretary of the United Jewish Social Agencies in Cincinnati, *Proceedings, National Conference of Jewish Social Service, 1932*, 92–93; *Proceedings, National Conference of Jewish Social Service, 1931*, 37.

43. Jacob Golub, *Proceedings, National Council of Jewish Social Service, 1936*, 12.

44. *Proceedings, National Conference of Jewish Social Service, 1932*, 40. For more on the origins of the Central Jewish Institute, see Mel Scult, *Judaism Faces the Twentieth Century: A Biography of Mordecai M. Kaplan* (Detroit: Wayne State University Press, 1993), 199–202.

45. *Proceedings, National Conference of Jewish Social Service, 1932*, 40–41.

46. *Proceedings, National Conference On Jewish Welfare, 1935*, 1, *Jewish Social Work, 1935*, 20; *Proceedings, National Conference Of Jewish Social Service, 1935*, 104; *Proceedings, National Conference Of Jewish Social Welfare, 1937*, 53, 12, 60. In 1939, that figure rose to almost 75 percent. *American Jewish Year Book* 38 (1936–1937), 235; *United Jewish Welfare Fund Yearbook, 1938*, 32–33; *United Jewish Welfare Fund Yearbook, 1939*, 48–49.

47. Wenger, *Uncertain Promise*, 59, 162.

48. *Proceedings, National Council of Jewish Social Service, 1931*, 27.

49. Maurice Taylor, "The Functional Agency and the Federation in Community Planning: Discussion," *Jewish Social Science Quarterly* 9 (December 1932), 62, as quoted in Wenger, *Uncertain Promise*, 142.

Chapter Two

1. Philip Gleason, *Speaking of Diversity: Language and Ethnicity in Twentieth-Century America* (Baltimore: Johns Hopkins University Press, 1992), 19; Horace Kallen, "Democracy versus the Melting Pot," *Culture and Democracy in the United States* (New York: Boni and Liveright, 1924), 144–55, quoted in Feingold, *A Time for Searching*, 122. For more on Kallen, see Sarah Schmidt, *Horace M. Kallen: Prophet of American Zionism* (Brooklyn: Carlson Publishing, 1995), and William Toll, "Horace M. Kallen: Pluralism and American Jewish Identity," *American Jewish History* 85, 57–74.

2. See Madison Grant, *The Passing of the Great Race, or the Racial Basis of European History* (New York: Scribner, 1916); William Z. Ripley, *The Races of Europe: A Sociological Study* (New York: D. Appleton, 1899). For more on the KKK of the 1920s, see Leonard Moore, *Citizen Klansmen: The Ku Klux Klan in Indiana, 1921–1928* (Chapel Hill: University of North Carolina Press, 1997).

3. Gleason, *Speaking of Diversity*, 52.

4. Ibid., 56; Alexander M. Dushkin, "Proceedings of the National Conference of Jewish Social Welfare," in *Jewish Social Service Quarterly* 17 (September 1940), 49. Dushkin was born in Poland in 1890 and immigrated to the United States in 1911. His 1917 doctoral dissertation, "Jewish Education in New York

City," was the first to focus on a Jewish educational theme. In 1919, he journeyed to Palestine for a two-year teaching stint before he returned to Jewish communal work in Chicago. In 1934, he headed once again to Palestine to organize the Department of Education of the Hebrew University of Jerusalem. In 1939, he moved to New York to run the Jewish Education Committee, a position he held for ten years.

5. *American Jewish Year Book* 32 (1930–31), 59.

6. Cohen, *Making a New Deal*, 363; Gerstle, *Working-Class Americanism*, 195.

7. Richard Breitman and Alan M. Kraut, *American Refugee Policy and European Jewry, 1933–1945* (Bloomington: Indiana University Press, 1987), 12. Paul Baerwald, "The Overseas Scene," *Proceedings, National Conference on Jewish Welfare, 1935*, 66. Hicem represented the combined efforts of HIAS, the Hebrew Immigrant Sheltering and Aid Society, and the International Cooperation Administration of the Jewish Colonization Association. Gleason, *Speaking of Diversity*, 245. See also Moshe Gottlieb, *American Anti-Nazi Resistance: An Historical Analysis, 1933–1941* (New York: Ktav, 1982).

8. Breitman and Kraut, *American Refugee Policy*, 90.

9. Quote from Jay Pierrepont Moffat, appearing in Breitman and Kraut, *American Refugee Policy*, 88–89; Breitman and Kraut, *American Refugee Policy*, 90. See Louis M. Hacker and Mark D. Hirsch, *Proskauer: His Life and Times* (Tuscaloosa: The University of Alabama Press, 1978); Joseph Prauskauer, *A Segment of My Time* (New York: Farrar, Straus, 1950).

10. Aaron Berman, *Nazism, the Jews, and American Zionism, 1933–1948* (Detroit: Wayne State University Press, 1990), 38. In December 1933, the league adopted the name "Non-Sectarian Anti-Nazi League to Champion Human Rights." See Marc L. Raphael, *Abba Hillel Silver: A Profile In American Judaism* (New York: Holmes and Meier, 1989); Mark A. Raider, Jonathan D. Sarna, and Ronald W. Zweig, eds., *Abba Hillel Silver and American Zionism* (London: Cass, 1997); Moshe Gottlieb, *The Anti-Nazi Boycott Movement in the American Jewish Community, 1933–1941* (Ph.D. diss., Brandeis University, 1967); Gottlieb, "The Anti-Nazi Boycott Movement in the United States: An Ideological and Sociological Appreciation," *Jewish Social Studies* 35 (July 1973), 198.

11. Breitman and Kraut, *American Refugee Policy*, 90; Feingold, *A Time for Searching*, 236; Papers of the Joint Boycott Council, box 6, Manuscript Room, New York Public Library. See Gottlieb, *American Anti-Nazi Resistance*, xi–xii. The league and council never could unite, and they remained two separate boycott organizations. The Jewish communities of Great Britain and Poland also engaged in boycotts of German goods, though the American boycott proved to be the most effective. See Gottlieb, *American Anti-Nazi Resistance*, xi.

12. Feingold, *A Time for Searching*, 235; Kaufman, *An Ambiguous Partnership*, 47.

13. Charles Shulman, "Boycott of Germany—What Course Shall the Jews Follow," Manuscript Collection 124, box 3, folder 4, p. 3, American Jewish Archives, Cincinnati. Shulman also opposed the proposed boycott of the Berlin Olympics: "This can make the majority of Americans bitter against our own Jews here because we were instruments or the bone of contention over which America did not participate in Olympics" (pp. 4–5).

14. Letter to Abraham Gottinger and Simon Gansl from Emanuel H. Licht, June 1934, Papers of the Joint Boycott Council, box 6, Manuscript Room, New York Public Library. Confidential Report of the Chairman of the Boycott Committee of the American Jewish Congress to Members of the Administrative Committee, February 28, 1935, Papers of the Joint Boycott Council, box 6, Manuscript Room, New York Public Library.

15. Letter from Jacob Chaitkin to Dr. Joseph Tenenbaum, July 24, 1934, Papers of the Joint Boycott Council, box 6, Manuscript Room, New York Public Library.

16. *New York Times*, December 28, 1938, p. 5, quoted in David Brody, "American Jewry, the Refugees, and Immigration Restriction, 1932–1942," *American Jewish Historical Society Quarterly* 45 (June 1956), 219; *Proceedings, 1937 Council of Jewish Federations and Welfare Funds, General Assembly*, 3, AJHS.

17. Gottlieb, *American Anti-Nazi Resistance*, 262. A May 1939 Gallup poll revealed that 66 percent of Americans would also be willing to join a movement to stop buying goods made in Japan. See Gallup, *The Gallup Poll*, v. 1, 160. This comes from a November 1938 Gallup Poll which revealed that 61 percent of American Protestants and 64 percent of American Catholics would join in a movement to stop buying German-made goods. Among American Jews, an overwhelming 96 percent responded in the affirmative. Gallup, v. 1, 130. See also *American Jewish Year Book* 41 (1939–40), 194, 291, 105. A November 1938 Gallup poll revealed that 97 percent of American Catholics disapproved of the Nazi treatment of the Jewish and Catholic religious minorities in Germany. Gallup, v. 1, 128. The poll observed "a marked reduction in anti-Jewish activities during the first few months of the war." *American Jewish Year Book* 42 (1940–41), 286.

18. See Zosa Szajkowski, "Budgeting American Jewish Overseas Relief," *American Jewish Historical Quarterly* 59 (September 1969), 91; *Notes and News* 62 (June 1940), 19, quoted in Lurie, *A Heritage Affirmed*, 426; *Notes and News* 1 (March 20, 1931), quoted in Lurie, *A Heritage Affirmed*, 423, and *Proceedings, National Conference on Jewish Welfare, 1935*, 16; *American Jewish Year Book* 36 (1934–35), 135. After enjoying a yearly income of $1.6 million following Arab riots in Palestine in 1929, JDC fund-raising dropped to just over $385,000 by 1932. Following Hitler's rise to power, JDC income skyrocketed to $1.1 million in just a single year. By 1936, its yield more than doubled to $2.3 million. In the three years to follow, JDC's fund-raising figures increased exponentially. By 1939, income stood at an unprecedented $8.1 million. The NRS task of securing American visas was complicated by the U.S. government's decision to suspend all immigration activities in Europe until Americans could be evacuated. National Refugee Service, Inc., *Information Bulletin #2*, September 22, 1939, 1, Papers of the National Refugee Service, I-92, box 7, AJHS. Refugee Immigration to the United States totaled a mere 4,134 in 1933. Strict quotas limited the number of refugees to 6,972 in 1934, 7,772 in 1935, and 10,564 in 1936. Efforts to expand quota limits allowed 17,051 to arrive in 1937 and 42,424 in 1940. *Refugee Immigration to the United States, July 1933–June 1940*, Table 1, 25, *Refugees, 1940, the Annual Report of the National Refugee Service, Inc.* NRSA, I-92, box 7, AJHS. See also David Wyman, *The Abandonment of the Jews: America and the Holocaust*,

1941–1945 (New York: Pantheon Books, 1984). In 1935 and 1936, twelve American Jewish welfare funds devoted 47.8 percent of their total fund-raising for overseas work. In 1937, thirty-eight welfare funds raised $2.5 million, or 49.9 percent of their total philanthropic budget, for relief efforts in Europe. The following year, an additional thirty welfare funds joined the overseas campaign and raised over $9.4 million for overseas assistance. Just over half the overseas aid, $5.1 million, was spent in Europe and other countries, while $4.3 million went to Palestine. By 1939, Jewish welfare funds were spending 71.4 percent of their expenditures on overseas aid. See Zosa Szajkowski, "Budgeting American Jewish Overseas Relief," *American Jewish Historical Quarterly* 59 (September 1969), 91; *Notes and News* 62 (June 1940), 19, quoted in Lurie, *A Heritage Affirmed*, 426; *Notes and News* 1 (March 20, 1931), quoted in Lurie, *A Heritage Affirmed*, 423, and *Proceedings, National Conference on Jewish Welfare, 1935*, 16.

19. *Proceedings, National Conference on Jewish Welfare, 1938*, 136. See Alan Brinkley, *Voices of Protest: Huey Long, Father Coughlin, and the Great Depression* (New York: Vintage, 1983).

20. George Backer, *Proceedings, The 1937 General Assembly, Council of Jewish Federations and Welfare Funds*, 7–8. Backer ran as an unsuccessful labor candidate for U.S. Congress in 1937 and 1938. In 1939, he bought and became the editor of the *New York Post*, guiding it toward a liberal editorial policy. While Backer did not share the political conservatism typical of many in his organization, his desire to help Jewish people on a grassroots level led him to the JDC, and his leftist orientation led him to his assimilationist position. See Joseph Hyman, *Twenty-Five Years of American Aid to Jews Overseas* (New York: Joint Distribution Committee, 1939), and Yehuda Bauer, *My Brother's Keeper: A History of the American Jewish Joint Distribution Committee, 1929–1939* (Philadelphia: Jewish Publication Society, 1974).

21. *Proceedings, The 1937 General Assembly, Council of Jewish Federations and Welfare Funds*, 8.

22. Administration–U.S. State Dept. 1933–45, J. N. Rosenberg–J. C. Hyman, Sept. 9, 1939, Archives of JDC, New York, as quoted in Bauer, *American Jewry and the Holocaust* (Detroit: Wayne State Press, 1981), 35.

23. Already seventy years old by the time of the European crisis, Rabbi Samuel Schulman immigrated to the United States in 1868 at the age of four, received his rabbinic training in Berlin, and returned to the United States in 1889, where he served in New York City, Helena, Montana, and Kansas City. Rev. Dr. Samuel Schulman, Rabbi Emeritus, Congregation Emanu-el, New York City, "Religion in a World at War," address at the Tri-faith meeting, Hunter College, May 28, 1941, 5–6, 8, Manuscript Collection 90, box 43, folder 1, AJA. Not surprisingly, the American Jewish community condemned Hitler's aggression. The Reform movement's UAHC passed a resolution expressing profound sympathy "with the victims both Jewish and non-Jewish of the ravages of war and with all who are denied their elemental human rights by aggressor nations." It affirmed an "unalterable devotion to democratic principles, and with all faith and confidence look forward to the day when such democratic ideals will surely triumph over the totalitarian forces of darkness." Convention Proceedings, 1941, UAHC Resolutions Adopted by the Thirty-Seventh Council, April 27, 1941, Manuscript Collection

72, box 68, folder 2, 154, AJA. The AJC noted that "wherever we find antidemocratic forces arrayed against liberal civilization and against its conception of human freedom and of the rights of every individual, we find anti-Jewish measures a major part of their program." Report of the Committee on Peace Studies, AJC, *American Jewish Year Book* 43 (1941–42), 737.

24. *American Jewish Year Book* 39 (1937–38), 285. "Report of the American Jewish Committee, Annual Report of the Executive Committee," *American Jewish Year Book* 41 (1939–40), 636.

25. Papers of the Joint Boycott Council, box 17, Manuscript Room, New York Public Library. Review of the Year 5700 (July 1, 1939, to June 30, 1940), *American Jewish Year Book* 42 (1940–41), 286.

26. Samuel Dinin, "Conflicting Issues in Jewish Education," "Proceedings of the National Conference of Jewish Social Welfare," appearing in *The Jewish Social Service Quarterly* 18 (September 1941), 80.

27. Joseph C. Hyman, Observations on Problems of Jewish Readjustment Overseas, May 1940, "Proceedings of the National Conference of Jewish Social Welfare," appearing in *Jewish Social Service Quarterly* 17 (September 1940), 23. Dushkin, "Proceedings of the National Conference of Jewish Social Welfare," 49. S. C. Kohs, "Proceedings of the National Conference of Jewish Social Welfare," appearing in *Jewish Social Service Quarterly* 17 (September 1940), 52.

28. See Mordechai Kaplan, *Judaism as a Civilization: Towards Reconstruction of American Jewish Life* (New York: Macmillan, 1934); Mel Scult, *Judaism Faces the Twentieth Century: A Biography of Mordechai Kaplan* (Detroit: Wayne State University Press, 1993); Jacob Agus, "The Conservative Movement: Reconstructionism," appearing in Jacob Neusner, *Understanding American Judaism*, v. 2, p. 213.

29. Mordechai Kaplan, "World Situation and Jewish Cultural Life, May 1940," "Proceedings of the National Conference of Jewish Social Welfare," appearing in *Jewish Social Service Quarterly* 17 (September 1940), 36.

30. See Morton Rosenstock, *Louis Marshall, Defender of Jewish Rights* (Detroit: Wayne State University Press), 1965.

31. "Minutes of the Meeting Held Tuesday, August 2," Papers of the General Jewish Council (GJC), box 1, AJHS.

32. Ibid.

33. Telegram from leaders of B'nai B'rith, American Jewish Committee, American Jewish Congress, and the Jewish Labor Committee, June 13, 1938, Papers of the GJC, box 1, AJHS. Telegram from Henry Monsky to Edgar Kaufmann, June 18, 1938, Papers of the GJC, box 1, AJHS. Confidential Resolutions Submitted to the GJC, September 16–17, 1939, p. 2, to be voted on at special meeting called for October 1, September 18, 1939, Papers of the GJC, box 2, AJHS. Minutes of the meeting held Tuesday, August 2, Papers of the GJC, box 1, AJHS.

34. Papers of the GJC, box 2, AJHS, unsigned, undated but probably late 1938.

35. Ibid.

36. Memorandum A, Letter to the GJC, January 28, 1939, from Jerome Michael, chair, Papers of the GJC, AJHS. Report of Executive Committee, Arthur S. Meyer, chairman, January 18, 1940, p. 2, Papers of the GJC, AJHS.

37. The bills in question were SJ Resolution 216 and 207, and HJ Resolution 430, 449, 412, 473, 436, 478, and 471. Letter from Stephen S. Wise, April 12, 1940, Papers of the GJC, box 2, AJHS. The GJC noted in April 1940 that "several resolutions have been introduced in both houses of Congress under which money would be appropriated to enable the President to purchase in the United States and transport and distribute food and clothing for the relief of the suffering people of Poland." It noted that HJ Resolution 473 would appropriate $15,000 and had already been received the support of the House Foreign Affairs Committee. That bill would have expanded the area of support from Poland to include "other similarly afflicted areas." Letter from the Committee on Public Relations to the General Jewish Council, April 28, 1940, p. 2, Papers of the GJC, AJHS. Mordechai Kaplan, "The World Situation and Jewish Cultural Life," *Proceedings of the National Conference on Jewish Social Welfare, 1940*, 34. "Refugees, 1940, the Annual Report of the National Refugee Service, Inc." N.R.S.A., I-92, box 7, p. 10, AJHS.

38. *American Jewish Year Book* 28 (1926–27), 471. Melvin I. Urofsky, "Zionism: An American Experience," appearing in Jonathan D. Sarna, ed., *The American Jewish Experience* (New York: Holmes and Meier, 1997), 251. See Melvin I. Urofsky, "The Brandeis Era," appearing in Jack Fischel and Sanford Pinsker, eds., *Jewish-American History and Culture: An Encyclopedia* (New York: Garland Publishing, 1992), 661. See also Melvin I. Urofsky, *American Zionism from Herzl to the Holocaust* (New York: Doubleday), 1975.

39. Kaufman, *An Ambiguous Partnership*, 13, 11.

Chapter Three

1. Breitman and Kraut, *American Refugee Policy*, 88. In addition, 18 percent favored business restriction of Jews. Twenty-four percent sought Jewish exclusion from government, 31.9 percent thought that Jews possessed too much business power, and 10.1 percent believed that Jewish immigrants should face deportation. Nearly a third of the respondents to a July 1939 Gallup poll thought that Jews possessed too much business power and recommended action to curtail Jewish influence. As German-Jewish refugees labored to secure one of the coveted quota spaces, more than 10 percent of Americans indicated that these Jewish immigrants should be deported from U.S. shores. Stephen S. Wise, "Can It Happen Here? Is Democracy Safe?," sermon delivered on March 8, 1936, Stephen S. Wise Papers, box 22, "Publications, Sermons, Speeches, Tributes," AJHS. Bauer, *American Jewry and the Holocaust*, 40. In *Antisemitism in America*, Leonard Dinnerstein concludes that "the deepening economic crisis contributed to an explosion of unprecedented antisemitic fervor" (105). See also Sander E. Diamond, *The Nazi Movement in the United States, 1924–1941* (New York: Cornell University Press, 1974).

2. Gleason, *Speaking of Diversity*, 59.

3. Richard Weiss, "Ethnicity and Reform: Minorities and the Ambience of the Depression Years," *Journal of American History* 66 (December 1979), 566; Gleason, *Speaking of Diversity*, 59. For more on American Jewish participation in the intergroup dialogue movement, see Svonkin, *Jews against Prejudice*.

4. Papers of the Joint Boycott Council, box 17, Manuscript Room, New York Public Library (delivered on radio station WMCA).

5. Review of the Year 5700 (July 1, 1939, to June 30, 1940), *American Jewish Year Book* 42 (1940–41), 293; Hanna Fried, "Movements For Better Understanding," *American Jewish Year Book* 43 (1941–42), 124, 30, 117, 124. See also Howard Singer, "The Rise and Fall of Interfaith Dialogue," *Commentary* 83 (May 1987), 50–55.

6. Review of the Year 5700 (July 1, 1939, to June 30, 1940), *American Jewish Year Book* 42 (1940–1941), 293, 306; Hanna Fried, "Movements For Better Understanding," *American Jewish Year Book* 43 (1941–42), 124, 30, 117, 31, 33.

7. See Will Herberg, *Protestant, Catholic, Jew: An Essay in American Religious Sociology* (Chicago: University of Chicago Press, 1955).

8. For more on Orthodox Jewish life in this period, see Joselit, *New York's Jewish Jews*.

9. *American Jewish Year Book* 41 (1939–40), 217; Report of the American Jewish Committee, Annual Report of the Executive Committee, *American Jewish Year Book* 41 (1939–40), 641.

10. Review of the Year 5700 (July 1, 1939, to June 30, 1940), *American Jewish Year Book* 42 (1940–41), 293; Hanna Fried, "Movements For Better Understanding," *American Jewish Year Book* 43 (1941–42), 124, 30, 117, 124. The Jewish community's intense desire to foster goodwill between American religious groups was not limited to the United States. Months before the Americans entered the European conflict, Jewish organizations proposed that European nations adopt pluralistic attitudes similar to those backed by Jews in the United States. Dr. Everett R. Clincy, Review of the Year 5700 (July 1, 1939, to June 30, 1940), *American Jewish Year Book* 42 (1940–41), 296; Hanna Fried, "Movements For Better Understanding," *American Jewish Year Book* 43 (1941–42), 112; Richard W. Steele, "The War On Intolerance," *Journal of American Ethnic History* 9 (Fall 1989), 19.

11. Hanna Fried, "Movements For Better Understanding," *American Jewish Year Book* 43 (1941–42), 124, 30, 117, 31, 33; *American Jewish Year Book* 44 (1942–43), 162; Review of the Year 5700 (July 1, 1939, to June 30, 1940), *American Jewish Year Book* 42 (1940–41), 294–295; Steele, "The War On Intolerance," 17.

12. Dinnerstein, *Anti-Semitism in America*, 116. See also Alan Brinkley, *Voices of Protest: Huey Long, Father Coughlin, and the Great Depression* (New York: Vintage Books, 1983).

13. Dinnerstein, *Anti-Semitism in America*, 118; Kaufman, *An Ambiguous Partnership*, 46; Breitman and Kraut, *American Refugee Policy and European Jewry*, 87; Dinnerstein, *Anti-Semitism in America*, 126. Thirty-five percent of those Americans surveyed agreed with Coughlin's ideas.

14. Weiss, "Ethnicity and Reform," 569; Cohen, *Making a New Deal*, 325–327.

15. Cohen, *Making a New Deal*, 325–327; Robert S. Lynd and Helen Merrell Lynd, *Middletown in Transition: A Study in Cultural Conflicts* (New York: Harcourt, Brace and Company, 1937), 264, as quoted in Cohen, *Making a New Deal*,

330–331. For an excellent discussion of radio and its effects on the Chicago working class, see Cohen, *Making a New Deal*, chapter 8.

16. See Papers of the GJC, box 2, Reports of the Four Constituent Organizations, January 1, 1939, to September 30, 1939, AJHS.

17. From Enclosure No. 1, Explanation of Various Items in Radio Kit for Use by Local Communities, pp. 1–3, Papers of the GJC, box 2, AJHS.

18. Sidney Wallach, December 26, 1939, The American Jewish Committee, Letter from Sidney Wallach to Ilse Schrier, January 24, 1940, Papers of the GJC, box 2, AJHS.

19. Letter to GJC from Committee on Public Relations, January 18, 1940, p. 1, Papers of the GJC, AJHS.

20. Ibid.

21. It also raised constitutional objections, asserting that "the provision making the condemned publications non-mailable imposes a prior restraint upon expression of which the Committee cannot approve." Letter to GJC from Committee on Public Relations, January 18, 1940, p. 3, Papers of the GJC, AJHS.

22. Letter to GJC from Committee on Public Relations, January 18, 1940, p. 3, Papers of the GJC, AJHS.

23. Ibid.

24. Ibid.

25. Letter from the Committee on Public Relations to the GJC, April 28, 1940, p. 1, Papers of the GJC, AJHS. On April 28, 1940, the bill had passed the House and was before the Senate Post Office Committee.

26. Report of Committee on Public Relations, October 14, 1940, pp. 4–5, General Jewish Council, Papers of the GJC, AJHS.

27. Ibid., 1–3.

28. Ibid., 4–6.

29. Ibid., 7.

30. Kaufman, *An Ambiguous Partnership*, 50; *American Jewish Year Book* 42 (1940–41), 269, 286–287; *American Jewish Year Book* 44 (1942–43), 151.

31. Bauer, *American Jewry and the Holocaust*, 40; "American Jewish Committee," File of the Council of Jewish Federations and Welfare Funds (CJFWF), box 7, p. 1, AJHS; Stephen S. Wise, "Can It Happen Here? Is Democracy Safe?," sermon delivered on March 8, 1936, Stephen S. Wise Papers, box 22, "Publications, Sermons, Speeches, Tributes," AJHS; Bauer, *American Jewry and the Holocaust*, 40.

32. Lilian Greenwald, *American Jewish Year Book* 44 (1942–43), 151–152. See Edward S. Shapiro, "The Approach of War: Isolationism and Anti-Semitism," *American Jewish Historical Quarterly* 74 (September 1984).

33. Dinnerstein, *Antisemitism in America*, 129; Greenwald, *American Jewish Year Book* 44 (1942–43), 151–152.

34. Greenwald, *American Jewish Year Book* 44 (1942–43), 151–152.

35. Address by Isaiah Minkoff, October 31, 1941, p. 2, Papers of the GJC, Collection I-17, box 2, AJHS.

36. Ibid. Lindbergh and America First failed in their bid to turn the American public against isolationism and the Jewish community. A Gallup Poll conducted in October 1941 revealed that Americans considered Jews the least active group agitating for war. In order of frequency, respondents' answers were as follows: the

Roosevelt Administration and the Democratic party, Big business and profiteers, British organizations and agents, American groups with pro-British sympathies, and Jews (from Gallup, v. 1, 302–303). Even as war appeared imminent, American Jews held firm in their belief that the safety of both European and American Jews hinged on continued loyalty to the policies of the U.S. government.

37. Breitman and Kraut, *American Refugee Policy and European Jewry*, 108; "America—Not Isolationist, but Internationalist, Address to be delivered by Rabbi F. M. Isserman over Station KXOK on Sunday afternoon, October 8th, 1939 from 4:30 to 5:00 p.m.," p. 2, Manuscript Collection 6, box 22, folder 5, AJA. Statement by GJC, Papers of the GJC, box 2, pp. 1–2, AJHS; Israel Knox, editor, *The Call* (October 1939), 4, quoted in Laura Rappaport, "The Workman's Circle through the Second World War" (AJA, June 1986), 2; Review of the Year 5700 (July 1, 1939, to June 30, 1940), *American Jewish Year Book* 42 (1940–41), 307; *American Jewish Year Book* 43 (1941–42), 34.

38. Convention Proceedings, 1941, UAHC Resolutions Adopted by the Thirty-Seventh Council, April 27, 1941, Manuscript Collection 72, box 68, folder 2, p. 154, AJA; Proceedings, Jewish War Veterans of the United States, 1941 convention, Small Collection, AJA, 59; Israel Knox, editor, *The Call* (July 1941), 12, quoted in Laura Rappaport, "The Workman's Circle through the Second World War" (AJA, June 1986), 3. At its 1941 convention, the National Conference of Jewish Social Welfare pledged "their full and unremitting support to the effort to develop and sustain the national unity upon which the future of our free institutions and way of life depends." The UAHC called for "maximum support of the democracies in their war against totalitarianism" as well as "full support of the United States defense program, coupled with a denunciation of Nazism, Fascism, and Communism," while the CCAR extended "whole-hearted loyalty and cooperation" to any plan aimed at aiding European democracies." Resolution considered by 1941 Proceedings of the National Conference of Jewish Social Welfare, in *Jewish Social Science Quarterly* 18 (September 1941), 197–198. While conference delegates supported the resolution, they refused to bring it to a vote since its topic was deemed "inconsistent with the scope of the conference as defined in the Constitution." *American Jewish Year Book* 43 (1941–42), 36, 37.

39. Kaufman, *An Ambiguous Partnership*, 72.

40. *American Jewish Year Book* 43 (1941–42), 28.

Chapter Four

1. Richard W. Steele, "The War on Intolerance: The Reformulation of American Nationalism, 1939–1941," *Journal of American Ethnic History* 9 (Fall 1989), 30; Dinnerstein, *Antisemitism in America*, 150, 130; Stephen S. Wise, "United States of America, Before a Sub-Committee of the Senate Committee on Labor and Public Welfare, Holding Hearings on S. 984, a Bill to Prohibit Discrimination in Employment Because of Race, Religion, Color, National Origin, or Ancestry," *CLSA Reports* (New York: American Jewish Congress, June 12, 1947), 4; Steele, "War on Intolerance," 23; Weiss, "Ethnicity and Reform," 566; Gleason, *Speaking of Diversity*, 59. See also Gleason, "Americans All: World War II and the Shaping of American Liberalism," *Review of Politics* 43 (October 1981), 483–518. The AJC looked forward to continuing its prewar community relations

efforts: "The present war situation furnishes us an unusual chance to discredit, once and for all, not only the whole gang of anti-Semitic leaders, but anti-Semitism itself as un-American and dangerous." The AJC believed that the American alliance against Hitler altered the fabric of anti-Semitism from an "un-American, immoral and intolerant" vice to "a Nazi trick to weaken our country in the face of danger by confusing issues, by getting Americans to fight each other instead of the common enemy, and by hamstringing national action through setting group against group, religion against religion." In 1943, the AJC Public Relations Committee hoped that the Allied effort might "blunt the edge of the more violent type of anti-Semitic agitation," hypothesizing "that Pearl Harbor will somewhat offset the misconception that the Jews were the 'war mongers,' "; nevertheless the AJC warned that the Jewish community "must be constantly aware of the new emotional tensions of war, which can easily arouse dormant animosities into acute antagonisms." Report of the Public Relations Committee to the Members of the American Jewish Committee, Thirty-fifth annual report, *American Jewish Year Book* 44 (1942–43), 488, 486.

2. These included the Institute for Propaganda Analysis, Friends of Democracy, and the Council for Democracy. See Steele, "The War on Intolerance," 29. Report of the Public Relations Committee to the Members of the American Jewish Committee, Thirty-fifth annual report, *American Jewish Year Book* 44 (1942–43), 488. Lillian Greenwald of the AJC reported the growth of "new fields of interfaith cooperation" including the creation of "committees of Catholic, Protestant, and Jewish community leaders to assist with the local civilian defense programs." She noted the successful effort of Connecticut's governor to enlist the aid of the state's clergy in civilian defense activities. In the Northeast, the New England Regional Defense Office mobilized to create its own chaplain committees. The National Conference of Christians and Jews expanded its activities by establishing a Department of Camps to work on military bases, while the National Council of Catholic Women recommended that its membership "study the bases of Catholic teachings on race, and combat all evidences and manifestations of discrimination and hatred, particularly among those of our own Faith, who have been misled by demagogues." *American Jewish Year Book* 44 (1942–43), 161, 162, 165; Rabbi Charles Shulman, "America's Fateful Hour," December 14, 1941, pp. 1, 3, Manuscript Collection 124, box 2, folder 15, AJA; *American Jewish Year Book* 44 (1942–43), 140; Gleason, *Speaking of Diversity*, 164.

3. In the 1940 poll, 46 percent responded positively to the question, "Have you heard any criticism or talk against the Jews in the last six months?" In 1942, the number rose to 52 percent. A 1945 poll asking whether Jews had too much power yielded a 58 percent "yes" response. Seventy-eight percent of respondents to a 1942 poll asking high school students to list their least favorite roommate listed "Negroes," while 45 percent responded "Jews." None of the other ethnicities surpassed a 9 percent rating. Dinnerstein, *Antisemitism in America*, 131–132. When asked "what nationality, religious, or racial groups in this country are a menace to Americans," survey respondents first expressed more aversion to Japanese than Jews but later switched. In February 1942, 24 percent labeled the Japanese a menace compared to 15 percent who cited the Jews. In June 1944, however, nearly a quarter listed the Jews while only 9 percent answered the Japanese. A

1945 poll of American high school students about "their last choice as a roommate" ranked Jews second only to blacks. Dinnerstein, *Antisemitism in America*, 131–132.

4. See Alan Brinkley, *The End of Reform: New Deal Liberalism in Recession and War* (New York: Knopf, 1995).

5. For a history of American Jews during World War II, see Feingold, *A Time for Searching*. See also Isidore Kaufman, *American Jews in World War II: The Story of 550,000 Fighters For Freedom* (New York: Dial, 1947).

6. Alexander S. Kohanski, ed., *The American Jewish Conference: Its Organization and Proceedings of the First Session: August 29 to September 2, 1943* (New York: American Jewish Conference, 1944), 70.

7. From Nathan Perlmutter, director of the ADL, quoted in Cheryl Greenberg, "Black and Jewish Responses to Japanese Internment," *Journal of American Ethnic History* 14 (Winter 1995), 5. For more on the history of Japanese immigration to the United States, see Roger Daniels, *The Politics of Prejudice* (Berkeley: University of California Press, 1962).

8. Of all the episodes in post–New Deal American Jewish political life, none has received more scholarly attention than the American Jewish response to Hitler's "Final Solution." See Arthur D. Morse, *While Six Million Died: A Chronicle of American Apathy* (New York: Random House, 1967); Wyman, *Abandonment of the Jews*; Henry L. Feingold, *The Politics of Rescue: The Roosevelt Administration and the Holocaust, 1938–1945* (New York: Holocaust Library, 1980); Haskel Lookstein, *Were We Our Brother's Keepers? The Response of American Jews to the Holocaust, 1938–1945* (New York: Hartmore, 1986).

9. Maurice Wertheim, President of the Executive Committee, *The AJC Thirty-fifth Annual Report* (New York, 1942), 42.

10. See Michael R. Marrus, *The Unwanted: European Refugees in the Twentieth Century* (New York: Oxford University Press, 1985); David H. Shpiro, *From Philanthropy to Activism: The Political Transformation of American Zionism in the Holocaust Years, 1933–1945* (Oxford: Pergamon Press, 1994); Kaufman, *Ambiguous Partnership*.

11. See Samuel Halperin, *The Political World of American Zionism* (New York: Information Dynamics, 1985).

12. *American Jewish Year Book* 44 (1942–43), 96, 137, 97. See Nathan C. Belth, ed., *Fighting for America: An Account of Jewish Men in the Armed Forces from Pearl Harbor to the Italian Campaign* (New York: National Jewish Welfare Board, 1944). Dr. Louis I. Dublin estimated the number of Jewish enlisted men at about 400,000, though his figure was preliminary. *Notes and News* (June–July 1944), quoted in Samuel C. Kohs, *Jews in the United States Armed Forces* (New York: YIVO, 1945), 15, 16. Demographers estimate the American Jewish population at between 3 and 5 percent of the overall population. See *American Jewish Year Book* 44 (1942–43), 43–47. Not even the heavy burdens placed on Jewish philanthropic and social service organizations slowed American Jewish optimism. The Joint Distribution Committee, for example, suffered the loss of many of its employees to recruitment or enlistment in the armed forces. Given the new military and political situation in Europe, Jewish relief organizations faced the awesome task of restructuring their operations. "The entrance of the United

States into active belligerency on December 7, 1941," Eli Ginzberg reported in 1942, "had a marked effect upon the present scope and future prospects of the constituent organizations of the United Jewish Appeal." Ginzberg noted that "new work had to be undertaken, other work had to be redirected, and some work had to be dropped." Eli Ginzberg, *Report to American Jews on Overseas Relief, Palestine, and Refugees in the United States* (New York: Harper and Brothers, 1942), 74; Bauer, *American Jewry and the Holocaust*, 178.

13. "Proceedings of the National Conference of Jewish Social Welfare," June 4–9, 1942, appearing in *Jewish Social Service Quarterly* 19 (September 1942), 168. Similar resolutions were offered by the UAHC at its 1943 convention: "In the name of the Jews of America, the Conference respectfully addresses a most earnest appeal to the President of the United States not to suffer democracy to go down in defeat on the first front opened by Hitler in his war on civilization. The Conference affirms its faith that democracy has it in its power to deny victory on this front to Hitler and take the fate of the Jewish people in Europe out of his hands." See Convention Proceedings, UAHC, 1943, Resolution on Rescue adopted by the American Jewish Conference and approved by UAHC, 122, Manuscript Collection 72, box 68, folder 3, AJA. *American Jewish Year Book* 44 (1942–43), 96; *The Jewish Spectator* 7 (January 1942), 4.

14. Louis Kraft, Jewish Social Services in a Nation at War, "Proceedings of the National Conference of Jewish Social Welfare," June 4–9, 1942, appearing in *Jewish Social Service Quarterly* 19 (September 1942), 44.

15. Ahlstrom, *Religious History of the American People*, 949.

16. Albert Abrahamson, Report of the Executive Director to the Members and Board of Director, "The National Refugee Service in 1942," National Refugee Service Archives, Collection I-92, box 7, p. 1–2, AJHS. According to a National Refugee Service bulletin updating the status of enemy alien laws and practices issued a week after Pearl Harbor, "no plan for a general round-up of alien enemies is in prospect." As of December 12, 1941, only 2,541 German, Japanese and Italians living in United States faced government arrest<M->this out of a total enemy alien population estimated at 1.1 million.

17. Abrahamson, Report of the Executive Director, 1–2, 3. This situation was especially true for the large number of German Jewish refugee physicians.

18. Select Committee Investigating National Defense Migration, *Hearings Before the Select Committee Investigating National Defense Migration, House of Representatives, Seventy-seventh Congress, Second Session, Part 29, San Francisco Hearings, February 21 and 23, 1942* (Washington, D.C.: Government Printing Office, 1942), 11271–11272.

19. Dr. Felix Guggenheim, Select Committee Investigating National Defense Migration, *Hearings Before the Select Committee Investigating National Defense Migration, House of Representatives, Seventy-seventh Congress, Second Session, Part 31, Los Angeles and San Francisco Hearings, March 6, 7, and 12, 1942* (Washington, D.C.: Government Printing Office, 1942), 11736, 11796–11797. See also Select Committee Investigating National Defense Migration, *Hearings Before the Select Committee Investigating National Defense Migration, House of Representatives, Seventy-seventh Congress, Second Session, Part 30, Portland and Seattle Hearings, February 26 and 28, and March 2, 1942* (Washington, D.C.:

Government Printing Office, 1942), 11518–11520. Select Committee Investigating National Defense Migration, *Hearings Before the Select Committee Investigating National Defense Migration, House of Representatives, Seventy-seventh Congress, Second Session, Part 29, San Francisco Hearings, February 21 and 23, 1942* (Washington, D.C.: Government Printing Office, 1942), 11272–11273, 11277–11279.

20. Abrahamson, Report of the Executive Director, 4.

21. For more on the Japanese and Japanese-American internment, see Peter Irons, *Justice at War* (New York: Oxford University Press, 1983); Jacobus Ten Broek, Edward N. Barnhart, and Floyd W. Matson, *Prejudice, War, and the Constitution* (Berkeley: University of California Press, 1954); Roger Daniels, *Concentration Camps USA* (New York: Holt, Rinehart, and Winston, 1972); Michi Weglyn, *Years of Infamy: The Untold Story of America's Concentration Camps* (New York, William Morrow, 1976); John W. Dower, *War without Mercy: Race and Power in the Pacific War* (New York: Pantheon Books, 1986).

22. *Los Angeles B'nai B'rith Messenger* 45 (December 26, 1941), 20. See also the *National Jewish Monthly* 1941–45. Werner Rosenberg, "Aliens-Friends or Enemies," *Contemporary Jewish Record* 5 (June 1942), 289.

23. Select Committee Investigating National Defense Migration, *Hearings Before the Select Committee Investigating National Defense Migration, House of Representatives, Seventy-seventh Congress, Second Session, Part 31, Los Angeles and San Francisco Hearings, March 6, 7, and 12, 1942* (Washington, D.C.: Government Printing Office, 1942), 11624.

24. Ibid. Tokie Slocum, a Japanese American and U.S. veteran, offered the only evidence of popular American Jewish concern. In his testimony to the Toland subcommittee, he recounted how local Jews feared that they might be targeted next. "I have heard Jews say to me, 'Well, you know there are a lot of Ku Klux Klan members in San Fernando Valley where I live so we may get it next.' " Ibid., 11720, 11624.

25. Ibid., 11624–11625; Greenberg, "Black and Jewish Responses to Japanese Internment," 11–12.

26. Ellen Eisenberg, "Looking the Other Way: Portland Jewry's Non-Response to Japanese Internment," paper delivered at the Western Jewish Studies Association Conference, Los Angeles, 1998, 3–5, 13.

27. Ibid., 3–5.

28. "Statement of Views on the Present Situation in Jewish Life," adopted at the annual meeting of the American Jewish Conference, January 31, 1943, *Thirty-Seventh Annual Report* (New York: American Jewish Committee, 1943), 7. See *American Jewish Year Book*'s Year in Review as well as the report of the Public Relations Committee, 1941–45. *Los Angeles B'nai B'rith Messenger* 45 (December 26, 1941), 20. See also the *National Jewish Monthly*, 1941–45; Werner Rosenberg, "Aliens-Friends or Enemies," *Contemporary Jewish Record* 5 (June 1942), 289; Greenberg, "Black and Jewish Responses to Japanese Internment," 12, 13, 14.

29. Select Committee Investigating National Defense Migration, *Hearings Before the Select Committee Investigating National Defense Migration, House of Representatives, Seventy-seventh Congress, Second Session, Part 29, San Francisco*

Hearings, February 21 and 23, 1942 (Washington, D.C.: Government Printing Office, 1942, 11201–11202).

30. Ibid. Nisei refers to second-generation Japanese Americans.

31. Weglyn, *Years of Infamy*, 112, 114, 298.

32. Hirabayashi and Yasui's convictions for curfew violations were upheld by the Court in June 1943. A December 1944 ruling affirmed the conviction of Korematsu for residing in a prohibited area (his hometown), while on the same day, the justices refused to rule on Endo's claim that the internment violated constitutional protections. See Irons, *Justice at War*, vii. For a fascinating and inspiring story of how attorneys employed an obscure legal code to launch a successful modern-day appeal of the World War II rulings, see Peter Irons, ed., *Justice Delayed: The Record of the Japanese American Internment Cases* (Middletown, Conn.: Wesleyan University Press, 1989). TenBroek et al., *Prejudice, War, and the Constitution*, 2.

33. Daniels, *Concentration Camps USA*, 78, 79.

34. Weglyn, *Years of Infamy*, 111–112. The San Francisco leadership did enjoy support from A. L. Wirin, the attorney for the southern California branch of the ACLU. During the Toland hearings, Wirin joined Louis Goldblatt, the secretary of state of the CIO, in protest of Executive Order 9066. "There must be a point," they stated, "beyond which there may be no abridgment of civil liberties and we feel that whatever the emergency, that persons must be judged, so long as we have a Bill of Rights, because of what they do as persons. . . . We feel that treating persons, because they are members of a race, constitutes illegal discrimination, which is forbidden by the Fourteenth Amendment whether we are at war or peace." Select Committee Investigating National Defense Migration, Hearings Before the Select Committee Investigating National Defense Migration, House of Representatives, Seventy-seventh Congress, Second Session, Part 31, Los Angeles and San Francisco Hearings, March 6, 7, and 12, 1942 (Washington, D.C.: Government Printing Office, 1942), 11798. See also Daniels, *Concentration Camps USA*, 78.

35. Weglyn, *Years of Infamy*, 111, 112.

36. Kaufman, *Ambiguous Partnership*, 72; Berman, *Nazism, the Jews, and American Zionism*, 97, 100. For more on how and when news of Hitler's "Final Solution" reached the United States, see Walter Laqueur, *The Terrible Secret: Suppression of the Truth about Hitler's "Final Solution"* (Boston: Little, Brown, 1980).

37. Morris D. Waldman served as secretary of the AJC while Cyrus Adler chaired the JDC's cultural committee and led the AJC until 1940. Bauer, *American Jewry and the Holocaust*, 181–182.

38. Kohanski, *American Jewish Conference, First Session*, 15. For detailed discussions on the American Jewish Conference, see Kaufman, *An Ambiguous Partnership*, chapter 3, and Berman, *Nazism, the Jews, and American Zionism*, chapter 4.

39. For more on the history of B'nai B'rith, see Moore, *B'nai B'rith and the Challenge of Ethnic Leadership*.

40. Kohanski, *American Jewish Conference, First Session*, 15–16, 41–42; Moore, *B'nai B'rith*, 186–187.

41. Kohanski, *American Jewish Conference, First Session*, 15.

42. Ibid., 229–230; Moore, *B'nai B'rith*, 187.
43. Kohanski, *American Jewish Conference, First Session*, 40.
44. Kaufman, *Ambiguous Partnership*, 111, 112.
45. Even in his later years, Proskauer remained an unrepentant non-Zionist. As he was completing his autobiography, *Reminiscences*, the one-time head of the American Jewish Committee still criticized the Zionist attempts to "create a Jewish enclave either in America or in the world." Hacker and Hirsch, *Proskauer*, 132–133.
46. Kaufman, *Ambiguous Partnership*, 109–115.
47. Kohanski, *American Jewish Conference, First Session*, 40–41.
48. Ibid., 280–281. The White Paper, issued by the British government in 1939, limited Jewish immigration to Palestine.
49. Ibid., 41.
50. Both Agudath Israel of America and the New Zionist Organization of America (the Revisionists) withdrew their support from the American Jewish Conference after the Pittsburgh meeting but before its first convention. "Their dissatisfaction was predicated upon the number of delegates allocated to them by the executive committee." Ibid., 41–42, 75.
51. Ibid., 55, 49. The primary work of the conference was conducted in one of three commissions: Palestine, Jewish Rescue, and Post-War Reconstruction. The Palestine commission worked to "implement the resolution on Palestine adopted by the conference," while the commission on rescue aimed to "devise and present plans to our government for the use of governmental funds in connection with the feeding and rescue of European Jews." See "Memorandum on the Functions of the American Jewish Conference," Collection I-67, box 3, p. 1–3, AJHS. The General Zionists boasted the largest contingent with 116 delegates. The American Jewish Congress followed with 111 and B'nai B'rith with 63. Moore, *B'nai B'rith*, 189.
52. Kohanski, *American Jewish Conference, First Session*, 67.
53. Moore, *B'nai B'rith*, 191. For more on the life of Abba Hillel Silver, see Raphael, *Abba Hillel Silver*.
54. Walter Laqueur, *A History of Zionism* (New York: Schocken Books, 1972), 342, 346–353; Feingold, *Time for Searching*, 100–102; Kaufman, *Ambiguous Partnership*, 95, 97, 73.
55. For a collection of essays on Roosevelt's wartime position, see Verne W. Newton, ed., *FDR and the Holocaust* (New York: St. Martins Press, 1996).
56. Berman, *Nazism, the Jews, and American Zionism*, 117.
57. Ibid., 124–125, 134. When the State Department refused to offer its support, Silver demanded that the AZEC condemn the administration. Wise, fearful that such action would backfire, rejected Silver's request, leading the Cleveland rabbi to resign his chairmanship in December 1944.
58. Kohanski, *American Jewish Conference, First Session*, 280–281.
59. Kaufman, *Ambiguous Partnership*, 21; Kohanski, *American Jewish Conference, First Session*, 280–281. The JDC also elected not to participate in a 1945 attempt by Nahum Goldmann of the WJC to coordinate Jewish agencies for European relief and reconstruction duties. Bauer, *American Jewry and the Holocaust*, 184–185.

60. For more on Hyman and Morissey, see Bauer, *American Jewry and the Holocaust*, 183.

61. They also offered support for abrogation of the White Paper and large-scale immigration to Palestine. Alexander S. Kohanski, ed., *The American Jewish Conference: Proceedings of the Second Session* (New York: American Jewish Conference, 1945), 221. The conference was held from December 3–5, 1944, in Pittsburgh. Kohanski, *American Jewish Conference, First Session*, 280–281. The JDC also elected not to participate in a 1945 attempt by Nahum Goldmann of the WJC to coordinate Jewish agencies for European relief and reconstruction duties. Bauer, *American Jewry and the Holocaust*, 184–185.

62. Kohanski, *American Jewish Conference, First Session*, 286, 287–288. Still, by the time of the First American Jewish Conference, not even the most liberal U.S. immigration policy could have addressed the needs of all the oppressed Jews in Europe. See Rabbi Elmer Berger, *American Jewish World* 33 (June 8, 1945), in the pamphlet "Something Must Be Done," Manuscript Collection 46, box 1, folder 15, AJA.

63. Kohanski, *American Jewish Conference, First Session*, 286, 287–288.

64. Ibid., 178–181. Zionists demanded that Britain honor the Balfour Declaration, a pledge made by the Crown after World War I to settle Palestine as a Jewish state, and at the same time called for the "immediate withdrawal in its entirety of the Palestine White Paper of May 1939."

65. Ibid. At its 1943 biennial, the UAHC passed a similar resolution: "We call upon our Government, and through it on the United Nations, to see that in the postwar settlement adequate provision shall be made to safeguard their rights, as well as the rights of all people who have been persecuted because of race or religion. . . . We ask that our Government use its good offices to see that Palestine is opened as quickly as possible for settlement of as many Jews as desire to go there and who can be taken care of." Jewish Post-War problems, Convention Proceedings, 1943, adopted by the thirty-eighth Biennial Council of the UAHC, Manuscript Collection 72, box 68, folder 3, p. 268, AJA. The American Jewish Conference statement made reference to a 1790 letter by George Washington to the Hebrew Congregation in Newport, Rhode Island, in which he declared, "The government of the United States . . . gives to bigotry no sanction, to persecution no assistance."

66. Berman, *Nazism, the Jews, and American Zionism*, 126–127.

67. Kohanski, *American Jewish Conference, First Session*, 282–284.

68. Ibid.

69. Ibid.

70. "Resolution on Gratitude to the United States," adopted by the American Jewish Conference and approved by the UAHC, "UAHC 1943 Convention Proceedings," Manuscript Collection 72, box 68, folder 3, p. 123, AJA. At its thirty-eighth Biennial Convention in 1943, it also passed a resolution, "Maximum Effort for Victory," which commended "the high level of patriotism manifested by our congregations in furthering the war effort in every possible way in upholding the hands of our President in the present crisis" and urged "them to further increase such efforts and sacrifices to the limit of their ability so that an early victory may be achieved." "Maximum Effort for Victory," Convention Proceedings, 1943,

adopted by the thirty-eighth Biennial Council of the UAHC, Manuscript Collection 72, box 68, folder 3, p. 266. For a detailed discussion of the Reform movement's debate on Zionism, see Howard R. Greenstein, *Turning Point: Zionism and Reform Judaism* (Chico, Calif.: Scholars Press, 1981).

71. Kohanski, *American Jewish Conference, First Session*, 229–230.

72. Ibid., 79–80.

73. Ibid., 80. A rabbi from Detroit suggested that American Jews follow the example of the British, who sent representatives to the United States to curry public favor. "If the British government wants to influence American public opinion," he argued, "I do not see why the representatives of the largest Jewish community in the world should in any way be reluctant to influence the nation at this time." Patriotism, once used by Jewish leaders to justify political bashfulness, evolved into a justification for even more forceful public policy stands. For the local religious leader, American Jews had "perhaps erred in the direction of not informing American public opinion as well as we might have done." Rabbi Benedict Glazer, Verbatim Transcript of the 1943 American Jewish Conference, Palestine Committee, Collection *I-67, box 5, p. 253, AJHS. The vice-chair of the Jewish Labor Committee shared a similar attitude. When he rose to address the delegates, he "berated the so-called 'far-sighted' statesmen who believe that Jews should remain quiet about the sufferings of their people lest it be construed that they are trying to save only their own, or that they were the cause of this war." The JLC official concluded that the leaders "who believe that we should remain silent about the slaughter of millions of innocent men, women, and children, could neither win the war nor establish peace in this world." Joseph Weinberg, vice-chair of the Jewish Labor Committee, quoted in Kohanski, *American Jewish Conference, First Session*, 77.

74. Judge Morris Rothenberg, Verbatim Transcript of the 1943 American Jewish Conference, Palestine Committee, Collection *I-67, box 5, AJHS, 129, 163; Kohanski, *American Jewish Conference, Second Session*, 129, 163.

75. Collection *I-67, box 6, Rescue Committee, August 31–September 2, 1943, 163–166, AJHS.

Chapter Five

1. Martin Gilbert, *Atlas of the Holocaust* (London: Michael Joseph Limited, 1982), 142, 149, 150, 156. For more on how and when the Allies learned of Hitler's "Final Solution," see Walter Laqueur, *The Terrible Secret: Suppression of the Truth about Hitler's "Final Solution"* (Boston: Little, Brown, 1980) and Walter Laqueur and Richard Breitman, *Breaking the Silence* (New York: Simon and Schuster, 1986). For a study detailing how the American press reported the Holocaust, see Deborah E. Lipstadt, *Beyond Belief: The American Press and the Coming of the Holocaust, 1933–1945* (New York: The Free Press, 1986).

2. Kohanski, *American Jewish Conference, Second Session*, 54; Papers of the American Jewish Conference, Second Session, First Plenary, Collection *I-67, box 6, 22–23, AJHS. When Americans were asked in November 1944, "Do you believe the stories that the Germans have murdered many people in concentration camps?" 76 percent answered "yes," 12 percent answered "no," while another

12 percent expressed no opinion. To those who answered "yes," the following question was asked: "Nobody knows, of course, how many may have been murdered, but what would be your best guess?" Twenty-seven percent answered 100,000 or less, 5 percent answered 100,000 to 500,000, 1 percent believed the numbers totaled between 500,000 and one million, 6 percent responded between one and two million, 8 percent answered between two and six million, while only 4 percent believed the number was six million or more. Twenty-five percent were unwilling to guess. Gallup, v. 1, 472, 555.

3. Jewish leaders pressed Washington for assurances that Jewish refugees would receive adequate aid once allied forces liberated them from Nazi occupation. Their efforts paid off when President Roosevelt issued an executive order in January 1944 creating a War Refugee Board, whose mandate stipulated that it "include without limitation the development of plans and programs . . . for the rescue, transportation, maintenance and relief of the victims of enemy oppression and the establishment of havens of temporary refuge of such victims." The AJC, despite its discomfort with the tone of the demonstration, offered its support. Kohanski, *American Jewish Conference, Second Session*, 54; Papers of the American Jewish Conference, Second Session, First Plenary, Collection *I-67, box 6, 22–23, AJHS. In one such action, American Jewish Congress president Stephen S. Wise organized a July 1944 open air meeting at Madison Square Park where 60,000 people attended and called for the rescue of Jews from Axis-dominated Europe.

4. Kaufman, *Ambiguous Partnership*, 73; Louis Brandeis, quoted in Melvin I. Urofsky, "Zionism: An American Experience," appearing in Sarna, *American Jewish Experience*, 250.

5. Interview with Joseph Proskauer by Joseph Orbach, Oral History Collection, Columbia University, 1962, N447, p. 56, as quoted in Kaufman, *Ambiguous Partnership*, 146; Kohanski, *American Jewish Conference, Second Session*, 58.

6. Kohanski, *American Jewish Conference, Second Session*, 58–59.

7. Ibid.

8. Ibid.

9. They demanded that Allied leaders "make it clear that the instigators of crimes against the Jews, as well as the accomplices and agents of the criminals, will be brought to justice; that all who prevent the release of Jews from Axis captivity and their departure to havens of refuge, will be punished for their complicity in the policy of extermination; and that resistance to the policy of extermination and aid given to victims of Nazi policy will be taken into consideration on the day of reckoning." Verbatim Transcript of the First American Jewish Conference, Collection *I-67, box 6, Rescue Committee, August 31–September 2, 1943, 163–166, AJHS.

10. Kohanski, *American Jewish Conference, Second Session*, 42.

11. Ibid.

12. American Jewish Committee, *Toward Peace and Equity: Recommendations of the American Jewish Committee* (New York: American Jewish Committee, February, 1946), 15, 1–2.

13. Kohanski, *American Jewish Conference, Second Session*, 45–46.

14. Ibid., 229, 46, 49, 50. The American Jewish Conference passed a multifaceted plan calling for the indictment of war criminals, trials in national courts (except in Germany where trials would be heard in international courts), extradition rights, amici curiae rights of Jewish representatives, and locus standi authority to be a representative of the Jewish people.

15. Ibid., 232, 236, 229.

16. Ibid., 49–50, 46, 47.

17. Hacker and Hirsch, *Proskauer*, 135, 137–138.

18. Ibid.; Ruth Hershman, ed., *The American Jewish Conference: Proceedings of the Third Session* (New York: American Jewish Conference, 1946), 42. The conference was held from February 17–19, 1946, in Cleveland. See Louis Lipsky, *Memoirs In Profile* (Philadelphia: Jewish Publication Society, 1975).

19. Hacker and Hirsch, *Proskauer*, 135, 137–138. Proskauer's appeal worked. Secretary of State Stettinius submitted the proposal to the American delegation that evening and subsequently forwarded it on to the conference at large, where it was ultimately incorporated into the UN charter. For more on the failures of the international bill of rights, see Jerold S. Auerbach, "Human Rights At San Francisco," *American Jewish Archives* 16 (April 1964). American Jewish Committee, *Toward Peace and Equity*, 15, 1.

20. Hacker and Hirsch, *Proskauer*, 136; American Jewish Committee, *Toward Peace and Equity*, 15.

21. American Jewish Committee, *Toward Peace and Equity*, 17–18. Similar provisions were included in the constitution of the Ecosoc Committee, including "recommendations for the purpose of promoting respect for, and observance of, human rights and fundamental freedoms for all" (Article 62, section 2). Article 76 required the General Assembly's Trusteeship council "to promote the rights and liberties of the individual in 'trust territories.'" The trusteeship system, according to the UN, should "encourage respect for human rights and for fundamental freedoms for all without distinction as to race, sex, language, or religion" (Article 76, section C).

22. Ibid., 9.

23. Hershman, *American Jewish Conference, Third Session*, 3, 33–34. The American Jewish Conference considered the question of indemnification as well. Louis Lipsky expressed frustration over the difficulties encountered by Jewish organizations trying to secure economic restitution for Europe's Jews: "Jewish survivors emerging from the underground and from concentration camps have encountered great difficulties in securing a restoration of their property. There are no claimants for much of the property, for its owners and heirs have been killed." The conference leader criticized the European governments who opted to use the confiscated Jewish property for their own purposes. "The hope that some of the property would be held in trust for the Jewish people," he lamented, "has not been encouraged by the national governments concerned, which are disposed to have this property transferred to the state to be used for state purposes." When Allied leaders established a modest restitution fund for European war refugees, Lipsky objected. "In view of the enormous losses suffered by the Jewish people and the need for large sums to assure the rehabilitation of the survivors," he argued, "it is clear that the amount of reparations provided by the Paris Agreement

is wholly inadequate." Instead, the conference proposed that the United States, France, Britain, and Russia stipulate in the peace treaties "that all property looted or confiscated from Jews by Nazi action, directly or indirectly, shall be considered the property of Jewish individuals or of the Jewish people." The conference also repeated calls for punishment of war criminals and denazification of Europe. Lipsky called on the victorious nations "to create the necessary legal apparatus and to formulate a definite policy for the punishment of war criminals" and to acknowledge "the fact of a Nazi conspiracy to destroy the Jewish people, which began in 1933." In its resolution on safeguarding the peace, the conference called "upon our own government, and upon the governments allied with it, to pursue relentlessly the process of denazification as agreed upon in the Potsdam Declaration." Hershman, *American Jewish Conference, Third Session*, 43, 242, 43–44, 239–240.

24. Ibid., 6.
25. Ibid., 7.
26. Ibid., 27, 39.
27. Ibid., 5, 38.
28. Kaufman, *Ambiguous Partnership*, 160.
29. Ibid., 177, 149–150.
30. Hershman, *American Jewish Conference, Third Session*, 13.
31. Ibid., 38, 47. Figures for the Jewish population of Soviet Russia dropped from 3.02 million to 2.25 million. Of those in western Germany, 850,000 lived in the British, 675,000 in the American, and 150,000 in the French zone of occupation. American Jewish Committee, *Toward Peace and Equity*, 54–55.
32. Fifteen percent expressed no opinion. Gallup, v. 1, 501, 504–505. The median guess of the number of dead increased from 100,000 to 1,000,000.
33. Berman, *Nazism, the Jews, and American Zionism*, 156, 158.
34. Kohanski, *American Jewish Conference, Second Session*, 54; Papers of the American Jewish Conference, Second Session, First Plenary, Collection *I-67, box 6, 22–23, AJHS; and Hershman, *American Jewish Conference, Third Session*, 51, 14. For more on American indifference to Jewish refugees in Europe, see Leonard Dinnerstein, *America and the Survivors of the Holocaust* (New York: Columbia University Press, 1982). Also see David S. Wyman, *Paper Walls: America and the Refugee Crisis, 1938–1941* (Amherst: University of Massachusetts Press, 1968).
35. Hershman, *American Jewish Conference, Third Session*, 51, 14; Dinnerstein, *America and the Survivors of the Holocaust*, ix.
36. Hershman, *American Jewish Conference, Third Session*, 22, 21. Just months after Allied victory, Professor Hayim Fineman reiterated Monsky's plea, explaining that "American Jews constitute the largest Jewish community in the world" and "as such, they cannot and dare not shirk their responsibilities.... The present generation of American Jews is charged with a sacred trust: to care for the safety, the dignity and the very survival of the Jewish people." Hershman, *American Jewish Conference, Third Session*, 49.
37. Hershman, *American Jewish Conference, Third Session*, 38–39.
38. Kaufman, *Ambiguous Partnership*, 204–205, 213; Berman, *Nazism, the Jews, and American Zionism*, 166–168.

39. Berman, *Nazism, the Jews, and American Zionism*, 167–168. Nahum Goldmann considered the AACI recommendations "at best a very poor statement of non-Zionism" but still called for their support. Goldmann, joined by Silver, Wise, David Ben-Gurion, and most other Zionist leaders, focused their appeals on securing the 100,000 immigration quota and ignored the AACI's refusal to endorse a Jewish state. Kaufman, *Ambiguous Partnership*, 186, 195–197. In the year prior to the AACI report, non-Zionists had inched their way toward a call for Jewish settlement of Palestine. As late as January 1945, the AJC called on DPs to return to their native lands. Kaufman, *Ambiguous Partnership*, 105. Only after more than 200,000 Jewish DPs refused to return home in August 1945 did the non-Zionist group acknowledge the necessity of Palestinian immigration. "The immigration gates of all countries of the world," reported John Slawson, the executive director of the AJC, "are practically closed to the Jews." Letter from John Slawson to Ira M. Younker, September 14, 1945, AJC Archives, box II/5, quoted in Kaufman, *Ambiguous Partnership*, 195. The next month, AJC leaders announced a major policy shift: they would support the Balfour Declaration, call for wide-scale immigration to Palestine, pressure the Truman administration to use its diplomatic muscle to gain immediate entry for some 100,000 DPs in Europe, and demand Jewish self-rule in Palestine as the only viable means of realizing mass migration. Kaufman, *Ambiguous Partnership*, 197.

40. Verbatim Transcript of the Third American Jewish Conference, 1, Collection *I-67, box 8, AJHS; American Jewish Committee, *Toward Peace and Equity*, 8. When asked if Jews constituted a religious group or a national group, only 10.5 percent of those American Jews surveyed in a 1945 poll refused to recognize a national component to Jewish identity. Hershman, *American Jewish Conference, Proceedings of the Third Session*, 30; Gallup, v. 1, 554. After some initial wavering, the U.S. government offered its support of a Jewish nation in Palestine. President Truman, who had helped author a pro-Zionist platform at the 1944 Democratic party convention in Chicago, changed his mind in December 1945 when fears that Palestine would become a "racial state" caused him to withdraw his support of congressional resolutions sympathetic to Jewish claims for statehood. Verbatim Transcript of the Third American Jewish Conference, 234, Collection *I-67, box 8, AJHS. That same month, Congress approved a compromise resolution supporting a Jewish homeland, calling on the United States to "use its good offices with the Mandatory Power to the end that Palestine shall be opened for free entry of Jews into that country to the maximum of its agricultural and economic potentialities, and that there shall be full opportunity for colonization and development, so that they may freely proceed with the upbuilding of Palestine as the Jewish National Home and in association with all elements of the population, establish Palestine as a democratic commonwealth in which all men, regardless of race or creed, shall have equal rights." American Jewish Committee, *Toward Peace and Equity*, 128–129. A December 1945 Gallup Poll revealed that 76 percent of those who followed the debate over Palestine supported Jews' right to establish a state. Gallup, v. 1, 554. A May 1946 poll showed that only 50 percent of the American public followed the Palestine debates. Of those, 78 percent supported the Jewish right to a national homeland in Palestine, 14 percent did not, and 8 percent expressed no opinion. Gallup, v. 1, 584. An October 1947 Gallup

poll revealed that 65 percent of the American public favored the UN partition plan while only 10 percent were opposed. Gallup, v. 1, 686; Hershman, *American Jewish Conference, Third Session*, 30. Verbatim Transcript of the Third American Jewish Conference, 1, Collection *I-67, box 8, AJHS.

41. Kaufman, *Ambiguous Partnership*, 201, 14.

42. Kaufman, *Ambiguous Partnership*, 251 (see also chapter 5); Berman, *Nazism, the Jews, and American Zionism*, 171–172 (see also chapter 6). In addition, see Zvi Ganin, "The Limits of American Jewish Political Power: America's Retreat from Partition, November 1947–March 1948," *Jewish Social Studies* 39 (March 1977), 1.

43. Kaufman, *Ambiguous Partnership*, 253–254; Central Conference of American Rabbis, *Year Book* (1947), 23, 146, 224, 237, as quoted in Kaufman, *Ambiguous Partnership*, 252–253.

44. Berman, *Nazism, the Jews, and American Zionism*, 178; Raphael, *Abba Hillel Silver*, 160; Hershman, *American Jewish Conference, Third Session*, 30; Gallup, v. 1, 554; and Verbatim Transcript of the Third American Jewish Conference, 1, Collection *I-67, box 8, AJHS.

45. Berman, *Nazism, the Jews, and American Zionism*, 179.

46. Kaufman, *Ambiguous Partnership*, 278–279, 292, 294, 295.

47. Hacker and Hirsch, *Proskauer*, 147.

48. Ibid., 151.

49. Ibid., 154–155.

50. Hershman, *American Jewish Conference, Third Session*, 21.

Chapter Six

1. Arthur Schlesinger, Jr., *The Vital Center: The Politics of Freedom* (Boston: Houghton Mifflin, 1949). For more on liberal anti-Communism, see Steven M. Gillon, *Politics and Vision: The ADA and American Liberalism, 1947–1985* (New York: Oxford University Press, 1987). Between 1948 and 1958, some twelve million Americans packed their belongings and moved from urban areas to new neighborhoods on the outskirts of town. Americans, comprising a mere 6 percent of the world's population, consumed over five times their share of the world's economic output. Economic productivity, one historian reflected, stood as "the single most impressive development of the postwar years." The national thirst for new and better products sparked a 500 percent increase in demand for short-term credit. See William H. Chafe, *The Unfinished Journey* (New York: Oxford University Press, 1991), 84, 112, 115; Gordon, *Jews in Suburbia*, 1. Suburbs grew seven times as fast as cities between 1950 and 1955. Not all shared in the tremendous postwar boom. Organized labor, which enjoyed unprecedented growth due to wartime regulations, suffered in the years after 1945. Anti-Communism and the changing nature of the workforce made unionizing more difficult. Women, while recovering many of the jobs lost in the initial transition to a peacetime economy, still earned less than men employed in the same or comparable vocations. Substantial moves toward greater racial equality would have to wait until the civil rights movement mobilized blacks for change in the late 1950s and early 1960s. See Chafe, *The Unfinished Journey*, chapter 5.

2. See Robert Griffith, *The Politics of Fear: Joseph R. McCarthy and the Senate* (Amherst: University of Massachusetts Press, 1987). The emerging Cold War, according to the chairman of the National Community Relations Advisory Council, had moved American discrimination "around from a backyard domestic issue to a front-porch exposure for all the world to see." Stephen Whitfield, *The Culture of the Cold War* (Baltimore: Johns Hopkins University Press, 1991), 5–6; Henry Epstein, *FEPC Reference Manual* (National Community Relations Advisory Council, 1948 edition), 18.

3. In medicine, the last quotas were not lifted until the mid-1950s. Other professional positions that opened to Jews in this period included partnerships in major law firms, CPAs in large corporations, and academic positions at major universities. The government's 1957 religious census revealed that over 55 percent of American Jews listed their vocations as "professionals and technical" or "managers, officials, and proprietors," compared to only 23 percent for the American public at large. As an example of Jewish flight from urban to suburban areas, the west side of Chicago, which boasted 131,000 Jewish residents in 1931, saw that population dwindle to 12,000 by 1958. The more suburban north side of Chicago counted 127,000 Jews in 1958 as compared to only 56,000 persons in 1931. Howe, *World of Our Fathers*, 609. See Gordon, *Jews in Suburbia*; Marshall Sklare and Joseph Greenblum, *Jewish Identity on the Suburban Frontier* (Chicago: University of Chicago Press, 1979); Judith R. Kramer and Seymour Leventman, *Children of the Gilded Ghetto: Conflict Resolutions of Three Generations of American Jews* (New Haven: Yale University Press, 1961); Arthur Hertzberg, *The Jews in America: Four Centuries of an Uneasy Encounter* (New York: Simon and Schuster, 1989), 321, 311; Lurie, *Heritage Affirmed*; and David Sidorksy, ed., *The Future of the Jewish Community in America* (Philadelphia: Jewish Publication Society, 1973), 94–95. Studies on postwar suburban American Jews include Benjamin B. Ringer, *The Edge of Friendliness: A Study of Jewish-Gentile Relations* (New York: Basic Books, 1967); and Nathan Glazer, "The American Jew and the Attainment of Middle-Class Rank: Some Trends and Explanations," appearing in Sklare, *The Jews: Social Patterns of an American Group*. See Lurie, *Heritage Affirmed*, especially chapter 8. For more on the growth in synagogue memberships, see C. Bezazel Sherman, *The Jew Within American Society* (Detroit: Wayne State University Press, 1965), 208–210.

4. "A Statement by the Jewish Community Council of Cincinnati," Manuscript Collection 202, box 57, folder 6, AJA. See Alexander Bittelman, *Program for Survival: The Communist Position on the Jewish Question* (New York: New Century Publishers, 1947). On this point, American Jews stood in agreement with J. Edgar Hoover, who commissioned a confidential study, "Communism versus the Jewish People," to determine the Jewish community's disposition toward Communism. The study concluded, among other things, that "the Jewish religion, accepting God as the Creator of all things and recognizing the supremacy of divine law over human law, can never be reconciled with the atheism and the material basis for law found in Marxism-Leninism." "Communism Versus the Jewish People" (Washington: Federal Bureau of Investigation, United States Department of Justice, 1957), iii, located at the AJHS. For information on an AJC study linking Communism with anti-Semitism, see "Protection of Civil Liberties: Role of Jewish

Community Relations Agencies," in NCRAC, "Report of the Eighth Plenary Session, May 25–28, 1950," Manuscript Collection 202, box 51, folder 3, AJA, 9. For a theological argument against Communism, see Homer A. Jack, ed., *Religion and Peace: Papers from the National Inter-Religious Conference on Peace* (Indianapolis: Bobbs-Merrill Company, 1966), 8–20. Svonkin, *Jews Against Prejudice*, 113. See Melech Epstein, *The Jew and Communism: The Story of Early Communist Victories and Ultimate Defeats in the Jewish Community, USA, 1919–1941* (New York: Trade Union Sponsoring Committee, 1959); Arthur Liebman, "The Ties That Bind: The Jewish Support of the Left in the U.S.," *American Jewish Historical Quarterly* 74 (September 1984), 45–65. For more information on the importance of Communism and socialism in American Jewish history, see Howe, *World of Our Fathers*.

5. While anti-Semitism began to decline after 1945, American Jews still faced strict barriers to social advancement, especially during the early postwar years. Until the late 1950s, Jewish high school students confronted restrictive admission quotas when they applied to the nation's leading colleges and universities. Many middle-class suburbs and most country clubs still excluded Jews. Dinnerstein, *Anti-Semitism in America*, 150. See Stephen Steinberg, *The Academic Melting Pot: Catholics and Jews in American Higher Education* (New York: McGraw-Hill, 1974); and Dan Oren, *Joining the Club: A History of Jews at Yale* (New Haven: Yale University Press, 1987).

6. Lurie, *Heritage Affirmed*, 168, from Ben Seligman, "The American Jew—Some Demographic Features," *American Jewish Year Book* 51 (1950), 3–52; Ben Seligman, "Changes in Jewish Population in the United States, 1949–50," *American Jewish Year Book* 52 (1951), 3–16. Even the American Jewish Committee, long the non-democratic voice of America's elite Jews, realized that "one cannot do things for the Jewish people, one must do it with the Jewish people." Friedman, *Utopian Dilemma*, 9; "Point with Pride: 1956 Accomplishments of the American Jewish Committee and Anti-Defamation League of B'nai B'rith," 1, File of the CJFWF, box 7, AJHS; Howe, *World of Our Fathers*, 609.

7. Friedman, *Utopian Dilemma*, 8.

8. Fourteen local agencies joined the NCRAC as charter members. By 1960, some fifty-two agencies claimed membership status. See Lurie, *Heritage Affirmed*, 201–203; Dinnerstein, *Anti-Semitism in America*, 148–149.

9. See for example Irwin Ross, *The Communists: Friends or Foes of Civil Liberties* (New York: American Jewish Committee, 1950). Even the NCRAC warned of Communist infiltration of civil rights organizations. At its 1953 annual meeting, it passed a resolution warning "against the continuous attempts by communists and their front organizations to subvert civil rights movements to their own use and to inject a false note of anti-Semitism into issues and private and public forums where it is non-existent." "Resolution on Communism," NCRAC, Eleventh Plenary Session, October 10–12, 1953, Manuscript Collection 202, box 51, folder 3, AJA. *The American Jewish Committee Background and Emphases for AJC's 1955 Domestic Program*, January 1955, p. 2–4, CJFWF, box 7, AJHS; "Protection of Civil Liberties," 8.

10. Svonkin, *Jews Against Prejudice*, 158.

NOTES TO CHAPTER SIX 261

11. Ibid., 151; Rabbi S. Anhil Fineberg, AJC memorandum, "Public Comment on the Atom Spies," May 1951, pp. 1–2, in AJC records, box 249, "Atom Spies," as quoted in ibid.; AJC memorandum, S. Anhil Fineberg to John Slawson, "AJC Activities Re Communism Since January 21, 1953," August 25, 1953, p. 4, in AJC Records, box 248, "Communism Program 53–57," as quoted in ibid.

12. Svonkin, *Jews Against Prejudice*, 151–152; NCRAC Statement, May 13, 1952, as quoted in ibid., 154.

13. From Lucy S. Dawidowicz, " 'Anti-Semitism' and the Rosenberg Case: The Latest Communist Propaganda Trap," *Commentary* 14 (July 1952), 43, as quoted in ibid., 155.

14. Svonkin, *Jews Against Prejudice*, 162. See Jeffrey Martin Marker, "Communism and Liberalism in the Jewish Community: The Struggle for Control of the American Jewish Congress, 1949," master's thesis, University of Maryland, 1976.

15. Rabbi S. Anhil Fineberg and Edwin Lukas, as quoted in Svonkin, *Jews Against Prejudice*, 163, 164. Samuel H. Flowerman, "Portrait of the Authoritarian Man," *New York Times Magazine*, April 23, 1950, p. 28, as quoted in Svonkin, *Jews Against Prejudice*, 115.

16. Svonkin, *Jews Against Prejudice*, 165–168. The union in question was the Social Service Employees Union, and the other groups which objected to their leftism were the American Zionist Council, the Jewish National Fund, the Joint Defense Appeal, the Joint Distribution Committee, the Mizrachi Women's Organization, the National Jewish Welfare Board, the New York Association for New Americans, the Organization for Rehabilitation and Training, the United Jewish Appeal, the Zionist Organization of America, and the 92nd Street YM/YWHA.

17. Ibid., 170–171.

18. Ibid., 169; Resolution of the AJCongress National Administrative Committee, November 19, 1950, quoted in David Petegorsky, "Progress and Prospect-A Report on the American Jewish Congress," submitted by the Executive Director to the Biennial National Convention, November 17–19, 1951 (dated November 14, 1951), p. 24–26, in AJCongress records, box 20, as quoted in ibid., 170; Rabbi Irving Miller in Lucy S. Dawidowicz, "The American Jewish Congress Against Communism," February 2, 1951, p. 3, in AJC records, box 251, "Polit Phil Communism Other Organizations-Jewish," as quoted in ibid., 170.

19. John T. McGreevy, *Parish Boundaries: The Catholic Encounter with Race in the Twentieth Century Urban North* (Chicago: University of Chicago Press, 64). See also Donald F. Crosby, "The Politics of Religion: American Catholics and the Anti-Communist Impulse," in Robert Griffith and Athan Theoharis, eds., *The Specter: Original Essays on the Cold War and the Origins of McCarthyism* (New York: New Viewpoints, 1974).

20. The bill included provisions from the failed Mundt-Ferguson-Johnston bill, the Nixon bill, and the Hobbs bill. "The Internal Security Act of 1950 (The McCarran Act), An Evaluation and Analysis," CLSA, New York, p. 1, Manuscript Collection 202, box 51, folder 6, AJA; Merle Miller, *Plain Speaking: An Oral Biography of Harry S Truman* (New York: Berkley Medallion, 1974), 444. See also Whitfield, *The Culture of the Cold War*, 49; and Chafe, *The Unfinished Journey*, 105.

21. "Resolution on Civil liberties, May 28, 1950," p. 1, Manuscript Collection 202, box 51, folder 3, AJA. In November 1950, the United Synagogue of America, a constituent of Judaism's Conservative movement, called on "the Congress of the United States of America to repeal the McCarran Act (known as the 'Internal Security Act of 1950') recently enacted which, in many of its provisions, flagrantly departs from American democratic principles and long-established practices." The National Women's League of United Synagogue of America urged "the repeal of the omnibus subversive control measure (McCarran law) and the abolition of the House Un-American Activities Committee." *Justice, Justice Shalt Thou Pursue: Resolutions on Social Action Adopted by the Constituent Bodies of the Conservative Movement in Judaism* (New York: Joint Commission on Social Action, The United Synagogue of America, n.d.), 1, 2.

22. "Resolution on Civil Liberties," May 28, 1950, p. 1, Manuscript Collection 202, box 51, folder 3, AJA; "Joint Statement on the Mundt-Ferguson-Johnston and Nixon Bills (S. 2311 and HR 7595)," March 24, 1950, Manuscript Collection 202, Box 51, Folder 3, AJA, p. 2.

23. "Joint Statement on the Mundt-Ferguson-Johnston and Nixon Bills," p. 2.

24. Israel Goldstein, "An American Immigration Policy," reprinted from *Congress Weekly*, November 3, 1952, Manuscript Collection 202, box 51, folder 6, AJA; Civil Liberties Union of Massachusetts, "The McCarran Act: A Return to the Infamous Alien and Sedition Laws," October 1951, p. 2, Manuscript Collection 202, box 51, folder 6, AJA; Shad Polier, *The Internal Security Act of 1950, Evaluation and Analysis*, II, III, Manuscript Collection 202, box 51, folder 6, AJA; For a full treatment of the internal dynamics of anti-Communism in the American Jewish Congress, see Marker, "Communism and Liberalism in the Jewish Community."

25. Ross, *Communists*, 23–25.

26. Richard Polenberg, *One Nation Divisible: Class, Race, and Ethnicity in the United States since 1938* (New York: Viking Press, 1980), 126; "Protection of Civil Liberties," 9, 7–8.

27. *American Jewish Committee Background and Emphases*, 5. See also Friedman, *Utopian Dilemma*, 21. For a biography of Senator McCarthy, see David M. Oshinsky, *A Conspiracy So Immense: The World of Joe McCarthy* (New York: Free Press, 1983), and Donald F. Crosby, *God, Church, and Flag: Senator Joseph R. McCarthy and the Catholic Church* (Chapel Hill: University of North Carolina Press, 1978). Svonkin, *Jews Against Prejudice*, 172.

28. *Justice, Justice*, November 9–13, 1952, pp. 2–3, June 22–27, 1953, p. 4.

29. "Resolutions on Civil Liberties," NCRAC, Eleventh Plenary Session, October 10–12, 1953, p. 1, Manuscript Collection 202, box 51, folder 3, AJA.

30. *National Jewish Monthly* 68 (March 1954), 5; "Resolutions on Civil Liberties," 1–2; "Re: Censure of Senator McCarthy, Text of Resolution Adopted by the National Administrative Committee of the American Jewish Congress, November 28, 1954," CLSA, Manuscript Collection 202, box 46, folder 7, AJA.

31. Surveys in the cities of New York, Cincinnati, Los Angeles, and Chicago as well as the states of Illinois and Maryland revealed discrimination in employment and higher education. For a survey on American Jewish attitudes about the presence of anti-Semitism, see *The Bayville Survey*, Miscellaneous file, S.C.-8132,

AJA. "Jewish Employment Problems, Report of a Conference, December 15–16, 1953, New York City," 32, 26, Manuscript Collection 202, box 54, folder 2, AJA. In 1948, Jewish Vocational Service conducted a survey of opportunities for Jews in public accounting. It found that "out of a total of 286 accountants, only three Jewish accountants were employed in the fifteen largest public accounting firms." "One third of all professional and managerial openings were discriminatory," its report stated; "more than half of these included anti-Jewish specifications. Slightly over three-fourths of all clerical openings bore discriminatory specifications, approximately 27% of which were anti-Jewish." "Jewish Employment Problems," Report of a Conference, 26. In Chicago, the Bureau of Jewish employment found that "2,000 of the 8,000 orders [job orders at an employment agency], or 25 percent, barred Jews, and that one-third of the 1500 employers were guilty of discrimination." *Congress Weekly* 21 (January 4, 1954), 4. "Visits to 134 Employment agencies in 10 cities indicated that 89% of the agencies included questions about religion on their registration forms, and two-thirds of the same agencies reported greater difficulty in placing Jewish workers." In 1945 and 1946, the JCRAC conducted a survey of "help wanted" ads in eight cities comprising 80 percent of the Jewish population in the United States and found an increase of 195 percent in discriminatory ads for 1946 over 1945, despite "a marked decline in the total volume of help-wanted advertising."Epstein, *FEPC Reference Manual* (1948 edition), 6–7. See also "Report on 1947 Investigations under Section 40 of the Civil Rights Law," AJC and ADL, Joint Memo, CJFWF, box 19, AJHS.

32. See also Marcia Graham Synnott, *The Half-Opened Door: Discrimination and Admissions at Harvard, Yale, and Princeton, 1900–1970* (Westport, Conn.: Greenwood Press, 1979); Steinberg, *Academic Melting Pot*, 100–101; and Sherman, *The Jew Within American Society*, 174–178.

33. Executive Order 8802, issued June 25, 1941, also affirmed the "belief that the democratic way of life within the Nation can be defended successfully only with the help and support of all groups within its borders." See "Employment Barriers in Wartime, Report of Activity, May 1, 1942," Bureau of Jewish Employment Problems, Chicago, 5; Epstein, *FEPC Reference Manual* (1948 edition), NCRAC, Committee on Employment Discrimination, New York, 37, 50–51. For a general history of FEPC, see Merle E. Reed, *Seedtime for the Modern Civil Rights Movement: The President's Committee on Fair Employment Practice, 1941–1946* (Baton Rouge: Louisiana State University Press, 1991); Louis Ruchames, *Race, Jobs, and Politics: The Story of FEPC* (New York: Columbia University Press, 1953); and Louis Kesselman, *The Social Politics of FEPC: A Study in Reform Pressure Movements* (Chapel Hill: University of North Carolina Press, 1948). For a biography of A. Philip Randolph, see Paula F. Pfeffer, *A. Philip Randolph: Pioneer of the Civil Rights Movement* (Baton Rouge: Louisiana State University Press, 1990).

34. Truman signed the order on December 20, 1945. Epstein, *FEPC Reference Manual* (1948 edition), 36–39, 41, 48, 49. "The FEPC," wrote historian Denton Watson, "throughout its short life, from 1941–1946, reflected the tumultuous circumstances that had led to its creation. It was besieged by attacks from its enemies. The first committee was composed of a chairman and six members, who were unpaid, and a paid executive secretary." The FEPC "had no independent

authority and could not enforce its orders. It was merely an investigatory agency." See Denton Watson, *Lion in the Lobby: Clarence Mitchell Jr.'s Struggle for the Passage of Civil Rights Laws* (New York: Morrow, 1990), 132, 149.

35. "American Jewish Congress," 5, General Jewish Council Files, box 2, AJHS; "Memorandum of Law, Submitted by the American Jewish Congress and the Cincinnati Jewish Community Council before the City Council of Cincinnati, Ohio, in the Matter of the Proposed Municipal Fair Employment Practice Ordinance, December 6, 1946," 2, Manuscript Collection 202, box 14, folder 9, AJA. As one Cincinnati Jewish leader explained, "The society in which Jews are most secure, is itself secure, only to the extent that citizens of all races and creeds enjoy full equality." "JCRC, Program of Action for the Cincinnati Jewish Community in the Present Race Relations Emergency," appendix A, p. 3, Manuscript Collection 202, box 16, folder 4, AJA. By 1947, Maslow and his colleague Joseph Robison went so far as to warn their fellow Americans that "our democracy is insecure so long as second-class citizenship endures." Will Maslow and Joseph B. Robison, "A Civil Rights Program For America," in *CLSA Reports*, 12, American Jewish Congress, New York, reprinted from *Lawyers Guild Review* 7 (May-June 1947). The American Jewish Committee supported FEPC, as well, employing many of the same arguments as the American Jewish Congress. Nathaniel H. Goodrich, AJC's Washington representative, affirmed "that the welfare of Jews is inextricably bound up with equality of treatment for all." He sought to inspire his co-religionists to political action by arguing that "the infringement of the rights of one minority is a threat to the security of all minorities." "Statement of Nathaniel H. Goodrich," p. 1, Manuscript Collection 202, box 14, folder 10, AJA.

36. "Statement of June 12, 1947," *CLSA Reports* (New York: American Jewish Congress, n.d.).

37. Stephen S. Wise, "United States of America, Before a Sub-Committee of the Senate Committee on Labor and Public Welfare, Holding Hearings on S. 984, a Bill to Prohibit Discrimination in Employment Because of Race, Religion, Color, National Origin, or Ancestry, June 12, 1947," 9, 11, *CLSA Reports*. Opponents of S. 984 managed to stall its progress in committee. It was never debated on the Senate floor and never came up for a vote. Epstein, *FEPC Reference Manual* (1948 edition), 66–67.

38. "Statement of Irving M. Engel on Behalf of the American Jewish Committee to the House Committee on Labor and Education Sub-Committee on Discrimination in Employment, May 25, 1949," 5, Manuscript Collection 202, box 14, folder 10, AJA; News Clipping, James Heller, March 1, 1948, Manuscript Collection 202, box 14, folder 11, AJA. The Anti-Defamation League of B'nai B'rith, trying to discover if professional sports were void of prejudice and discrimination, went so far as to title its study, "Survey of Democracy in Sports," playing on the Cold War dialectic between democracy and Communism. See Arnold Forster, *A Measure of Freedom: An Anti-Defamation League Report* (Garden City, N.Y.: Doubleday, 1950), 166. For a discussion of the African-American community's relationship to Cold War politics, see Penny M. Von Eschen, *Race Against Empire: Black Americans and Anticolonialism* (Ithaca, N.Y.: Cornell University Press, 1997), and Brenda Gayle Plummer, *Rising Wind: Black Americans and U.S. Foreign Affairs, 1935–1960* (Chapel Hill: University of North Carolina Press, 1996).

39. "Statement on Behalf of the American Jewish Committee Before the Subcommittee on Labor and Public Welfare, May 25, 1949," 2, 3, Manuscript Collection 202, box 14, folder 10, AJA.

40. Ibid.

41. Epstein, *FEPC Reference Manual* (1948 edition), 66–67; "Statement on Behalf of the American Jewish Committee Submitted by Irving M. Engel, Before the Subcommittee on Labor and Public Welfare," 6, Manuscript Collection 202, box 14, folder 10, AJA; *American Jewish Year Book* 51 (1950), 101; NCRAC, "Recommendations for Program in 1953," Committee on Discrimination in Employment, 1–2, Manuscript Collection 202, box 51, folder 2, AJA; Presidents Eisenhower and Kennedy followed Roosevelt and Truman when they issued executive orders to maintain bans on discrimination in government agencies and in private firms with government contracts. Eisenhower issued Executive Order 10590 in January 1955; Kennedy issued Executive Order 10925 in March 1961. See *The People Take the Lead: A Record of Progress in Civil Rights, 1954–1962* (New York: American Jewish Committee, 1962).

42. Shad Polier, *The Work of CLSA: A Bibliography of Representative Publications of the Commission on Law and Social Action, August 1945–June 1957* (New York: American Jewish Congress, 1957), v; "Model Fair Employment Practice Ordinance for Municipalities," section 3 (b), September 1947, *CLSA Reports* (New York: American Jewish Congress, 1947), 3.

43. *American Jewish Year Book* 49 (1948–49), 197; *Civil Rights in the United States in 1949: A Balance Sheet of Group Relations* (New York: American Jewish Congress and NAACP, 1949), 7; Epstein, *FEPC Reference Manual* (1948 edition), 43–44.

44. See Gregg Ivers, *To Build a Wall: American Jews and the Separation of Church and State* (Charlottesville: University Press of Virginia, 1995).

45. See, for example, Gleason, *Speaking of Diversity*, chapters 8, 10, and 11.

46. See Meyer, *Response to Modernity*. The Jewish experience in Eastern Europe taught American Jews not to trust state-controlled churches. See Robert T. Gan, "The Jews and the Problem of Separation of Church and State, 1960–1965," box 2654, AJA. As early as 1925, the United Synagogue of America opposed "any effort to introduce religious instruction into the public schools, and reiterate[d] strongly its absolute disapproval of any effort to introduce religious instruction of any nature into the public school system." *Justice, Justice*, 55. See also Friedman, *Utopian Dilemma*, 28–31; Jonathan D. Sarna and David G. Dalin, *Religion and State in the American Jewish Experience: A Documentary History* (South Bend, Ind.: University of Notre Dame Press, 1997); and Naomi Cohen, *Jews in Christian America: The Pursuit of Religious Equality* (New York: Oxford University Press, 1992).

47. Gleason, *Speaking of Diversity*, 64–65.

48. At its November 1950 meeting, the National Women's League of the United Synagogue urged the government "to enact legislation designed to correct the inequality of standards in education throughout the country without jeopardizing the principle of separation of Church and State, and that Federal aid be limited to public schools only." See *Justice, Justice*, 19. Press Release, JCRC, Cincinnati, January 28, 1964, pp. 3–4, Miscellaneous file, Church and State, AJA;

Judge Stanley Mosk, "Highlights," 1959 CJF General Assembly, quoted in Philip Bernstein, *To Dwell in Unity: The Jewish Federation Movement in America Since 1960* (Philadelphia: Jewish Publication Society of America, 1983), 215.

49. "Statement of Stephen S. Wise, President of the American Jewish Congress, in Respect to Legislation for Federal Aid to Education, Before the Subcommittee on Education of the Senate Committee on Labor and Public Welfare (S. 80, 170, 199, 472)," April 25, 1947, Papers of Stephen S. Wise, box 64, AJHS.

50. Press Release, JCRC, Cincinnati, January 28, 1964, p. 2, 8, Miscellaneous File, "Church and State," AJA. The original resolution was adopted on April 24, 1961. Minutes of the Church-State Committee, March 27, 1961, p. 2, Manuscript Collection 202, box 7, folder 8, AJA. The AJC, American Jewish Congress, Hadassah, National Council of Jewish Women, the ADL, and the American Association of Jewish Education all opposed further incursion of religion in the public schools. See Robert T. Gan, "The Jews and the Problem of Separation of Church and State, 1960–1965," 20. For details on the American Jewish Congress position, see Richard Lehrman, "The American Jewish Congress Weekly: A Study of Its Editorials, 1955–1959," Box 2389, AJA.

51. *CCAR Resolutions*, 1890–1962, Microfilm 894, AJA. Rabbi Morris Sherer served as executive vice-president of Agudath Israel of America. By supporting government aid to parochial schools, the Orthodox joined the Catholic community, whose large network of private religious schools stood as a model for how a religious minority could perpetuate its own traditions in the face of a secular and free public school system. The National Society for Hebrew Day Schools reaffirmed that Catholic-Orthodox alliance when it condemned the "other Jewish organizations" for "creating a 'false image' of the Jewish community as engaged 'in a bitter struggle with the Catholic church.' " *American Jewish Year Book* 63 (1962), quoted in Gan, "The Jews and the Problem of Separation of Church and State, 1960–1965," 20.

52. See William W. Brickman, *Chronology and Bibliography of Church-State-School Relations* (New York: National Society of Hebrew Day Schools, 1970), as well as the yearly summary of *The Civil Rights and Civil Liberties Decisions of the United States Supreme Court: A Summary And Analysis* (New York: Commission on Law and Social Action).

53. Of the thirty-five classes cited in the McCollum case, thirty-one were Protestant and one was Catholic. Jewish students either attended the Protestant class or a study hall. The first recorded use of a release-time plan occurred in 1913 in Gary, Indiana. The superintendent of schools ordered the students out of regular classes one hour early so that they could participate in classes in religion, music, or art. Clergy from the local churches soon began conducting religious classes during this hour and urged parents to send their children along. Eventually, other communities adopted Gary's plan, sometimes making attendance mandatory, sometimes conducting classes on school property, and in some cases moving the release period to the middle of the day. See Henry Epstein, "Supreme Court of the United States, October Term, 1947, Illinois v. McCollum, Brief of *Amici Curiae* and Motion," p. 8, Special Collections box A-89 379, Klau Library, Hebrew Union College, Cincinnati. See also *Congress Weekly* 21, number 15. "Brief of *Amici Curiae*, People of the State of Illinois ex rel. Vashti McCollum, in the

Supreme Court of the United States, October Term, 1947, number 90," 7–11, Special Collections box A-89 379, Klau Library.

54. The Synagogue Council of America (SCA), which signed the brief, listed its constituents as follows: the Orthodox Rabbinical Council of America, Union of Orthodox Jewish Congregations of America, the Conservative Rabbinical Assembly of America and United Synagogue of America, and the Reform Central Conference of American Rabbis and Union of American Hebrew Congregations. The NCRAC listed its constituents as the AJC, American Jewish Congress, ADL, Jewish Labor Committee, Jewish War Veterans of the United States, UAHC, Jewish Community Councils from Akron, Alameda and Contra Costa Counties, Baltimore, Boston, Bridgeport, Brooklyn, Cincinnati, Cleveland, Detroit, Essex County, Indiana, Indianapolis, Kansas City, Los Angeles, Milwaukee, Minnesota, New Haven, Philadelphia, Pittsburgh, Rochester, St. Louis, San Francisco, Southwestern region, and Springfield. "Brief of *Amici Curiae*, People of the State of Illinois ex rel. Vashti McCollum," 1–2.

55. Ibid., 4.

56. *Justice, Justice*, 57–58. See Gan, "The Jews and the Problem of Separation of Church and State, 1960–1965," 6.

57. See Brickman, *Chronology and Bibliography of Church-State-School Relations*, 13.

58. The prayer said, "Almighty God, we acknowledge our dependence upon thee, and we beg Thy blessings upon us, our parents, our teachers and our country." See "Supreme Court of the United States, number 468, October Term, 1961, Steven I. Engel, et al., Petitioners, v. William J. Vitale, Jr., et al.," 1, 2; Brickman, *Chronology and Bibliography of Church-State-School Relations*, 15.

59. News Release, June 26, 1962, Cincinnati JCRC, pp. 1–2, Manuscript Collection 202, "News Releases," 1957–1964, AJA.

60. "Church and State, U.S. Supreme Court Decision in the Engel v. Vitale Case, June 25, 1962," Miscellaneous File, AJA. "Supreme Court of the United States, number 468, October Term, 1961, Steven I. Engel, et al., Petitioners, v. William J. Vitale, Jr., et al.," 9. For a discussion of the Catholic church's opposition to the ruling, see chapter 16 of Arthur Hertzberg, *Being Jewish in America: The Modern Experience* (New York: Schocken Books, 1979).

61. "Religious Holiday Observances in the Public Schools, NCRAC, Report of the Eighth Plenary Session," 25–28 May 1950, 24, 32–33, 35. Manuscript Collection 202, box 51, folder 3, AJA. Despite the protests from some parents over the holiday observance issue, postwar American Jews still resisted the fundamental agent of assimilation—intermarriage. The 1957 U.S. census, which included questions on religion, revealed that only 7.2 percent of couples with at least one Jewish partner also had a non-Jewish partner. See U.S. Bureau of the Census, "Religion Reported by the Civilian Population of the United States: March 1957," *Current Population Reports*, Series P-20, No. 29 (2 February 1958), quoted in Sklare, *The Jew in American Society*, 310–311. See also Sherman, *The Jew Within American Society*, 183–189.

62. See U.S. Bureau of the Census, *Seventeenth Census of the United States: 1950*, volume 2, Population, tables 73 and 75. Figures for Jewish occupations

derived from Council of Jewish Federations and Welfare Funds surveys in sixteen different areas, as quoted in Sherman, *The Jew Within American Society*, 100.

63. "Statement of the American Jewish Congress on the McCarran-Walter Omnibus Immigration Bills (S. 716 and H.R. 2379) submitted to Joint House-Senate Committee on the Judiciary, Presented by Will Maslow, General Counsel, Washington D.C., March 15, 1951," p. 1, Manuscript Collection 202, box 52, folder 1, AJA; "Statement of Rabbi Simon G. Kramer Before the President's Commission on Immigration and Naturalization Regarding Basic Concepts of U.S. Immigration and Naturalization Policy and Deficiencies in U.S. Immigration and Naturalization Law," New York City, September 30, 1952, p. 3, Manuscript Collection 202, box 51, folder 6, AJA.

64. "Americanizing Our Immigration Laws," the American Jewish Committee, New York, March 1949, pp. 55, 57, presented before Senate Immigration Subcommittee on September 23, 1948, by Irving M. Engel, chairman of the American Jewish Committee's Administrative Committee. Statement written by Felix S. Cohen, lecturer at Yale Law School.

65. Ibid., 1, 2.

66. For more on the relationship between immigration reform and anti-Communism, see Polenberg, *One Nation Divisible*, 116. "Statement by Rabbi Abba Hillel Silver of The Temple, Cleveland, Before the President's Commission on Immigration and Naturalization, October 6, 1952," p. 2, Manuscript Collection 202, box 51, folder 6, AJA; Irving Kane, "Letter from Irving Kane to Harry S Truman, June 23, 1952," p. 1, Manuscript Collection 202, box 51, folder 6, AJA; "Guide for Testimony at Regional Hearings of President's Commission on Immigration and Naturalization," NCRAC, 1952, p. 11, Manuscript Collection 202, box 51, folder 6, AJA.

67. A Gallup poll on the McCarran-Walter Act revealed that 53 percent of Americans wanted change in immigration laws. Of those, 26 percent wanted laws to be more strict while 68 percent wanted them more liberal. See George Gallup, "Majority Willing to Let in More Aliens," appearing in *Public Opinion* (June 15, 1955), from "Memo from Jule Cohen to JCRC executives, June 21, 1955," Manuscript Collection 202, box 52, folder 2, AJA. See Ann S. Petluck, "Immigration and Nationality Act of 1952," United Service for New Americans, July 31, 1952, Collection I-69, box 266, CJFWF Papers, AJHS; "Memo from Ann S. Petluck to Cooperating Committees, August 1, 1952," p. 1, Collection I-69, box 266, CJFWF papers, AJHS. After reading a November 12, 1952, report in the *New York Times* that former Nazis would be admitted to the United States under the McCarran-Walter Immigration law, Henry Edward Schultz, the national chairman of the ADL, penned a letter to Secretary of State Dean Acheson expressing his alarm "that the U.S. State Department had interpreted article 101(a)(37) of the McCarran-Walter Immigration law as not being applicable to members of the Nazi or Fascist political parties or organizations." Letter from Henry Edward Schultz to Dean Acheson, November 24, 1952, Manuscript Collection 202, box 51, folder 6, AJA. In fact, Schultz's concerns were well-founded. With the nation's attention focused away from Nazism and toward Communism, many war criminals managed to immigrate to the United States with the tacit acquiescence of the State Department. See Dinnerstein, *America and the Survivors of the Holocaust*.

68. Memo From Albert Vorspan to NCRAC Agencies, April 20, 1954, p. 1, Manuscript Collection 202, box 52, folder 2, AJA. See also Manuscript Collection 72, box 69, folder 1, AJA. "Resolution on Immigration, NCRAC, Eighth Plenary Session, May 26, 1950," p. 1, Manuscript Collection 202, box 51, folder 3, AJA. See also "NCRAC, Eleventh Plenary Session, October 10–12, 1953," Manuscript Collection 202, box 51, folder 3, AJA.

69. "Statement of Hon. Simon H. Rifkind before Joint Subcommittee of Senate and House Judiciary Committees Concerning Omnibus Immigration Bills Submitted in Behalf of SCA, NCRAC," March 21, 1951, p. 3, Manuscript Collection 202, box 52, folder 1, AJA; "Resolution on Immigration, NCRAC, Eleventh Plenary Session, October 10–12, 1953," Manuscript Collection 202, box 51, folder 3, AJA.

70. In September 1952, the president appointed a commission to review and assess immigration policy and called for a revision of the McCarran-Walter Immigration bill. Phil Baum, "For A New Immigration Policy, The Commission Points The Way," *Congress Weekly* (January 12, 1953), Manuscript Collection 202, box 51, folder 6, AJA. Truman issued Executive Order 10392, which "established in the executive office of the president a commission to be known as the President's Commission on Immigration and Naturalization." See Executive Order 10392, September 4, 1952, Manuscript Collection 202, box 51, folder 6, AJA. The NCRAC prepared a guide for testimony at regional hearing of the President's Commission on Immigration and Naturalization, held September 26, 1952. It suggested a four-pronged attack on the immigration question. Constituents were instructed to focus on the injustices of the national origins quota system, deportation, distinctions between naturalized and native-born citizens, and lack of judicial review. See "Guide for Testimony at Regional Hearings of President's Commission on Immigration and Naturalization," 1. "Statement by Rabbi Abba Hillel Silver of The Temple, Cleveland, Before the President's Commission on Immigration and Naturalization, October 6, 1952," p. 1, Manuscript Collection 202, box 51, folder 6, AJA.

71. Rabbi Abraham J. Feldman, "Summary of Testimony Before Senate Judiciary Subcommittee on Immigration and Naturalization (Kilgore Committee) November 21, 22, 30, and December 1, 1955, American Immigration Conference, New York," Manuscript Collection 202, box 52, folder 2, AJA; "Guide for Testimony at Regional Hearings of President's Commission on Immigration and Naturalization," 2.

72. "Statement of the American Jewish Congress on the McCarran-Walter Omnibus Immigration Bills (S. 716 and H.R. 2379) submitted to Joint House-Senate Committee on the Judiciary, Presented by Will Maslow, General Counsel, Washington, D.C., March 15, 1951," pp. 6, 11, Manuscript Collection 202, box 52, folder 1, AJA.

73. *The Quota System* (New York: NCRAC, n.d.), 23, 25, 12, Manuscript Collection 202, box 52, folder 2, AJA; *Congress Weekly* (January 17, 1955), 3–4, quoted in Lehrman, "The American Jewish Congress Weekly: A Study of Its Editorials, 1955–1959," 11. "Guide for Testimony at Regional Hearings," 7.

74. "The Quota System," 6, 7, Manuscript Collection 202, box 52, folder 2, AJA; Ann S. Petluck, "Immigration and Nationality Act of 1952," United Service

for New Americans, July 31, 1952, p. 2, Collection I-69, box 266, CJFWF Papers, AJHS; "Guide for Testimony at Regional Hearings of President's Commission on Immigration and Naturalization," 7.

75. Philip M. Klutznik, "Resolution on Immigration, NCRAC, Eleventh Plenary Session, October 10–12, 1953," Manuscript Collection 202, box 51, folder 3, AJA; *National Jewish Monthly* 70 (March 1956), 31; *Congress Weekly* (January 17, 1955), 3–4, quoted in Lehrman, "The American Jewish Congress Weekly: A Study of Its Editorials, 1955–1959," 11.

Chapter Seven

1. Richard Winograd, "Birmingham: A Personal Statement," 1963, p. 1, Miscellaneous File, Desegregation, AJA. For a similar account, see Rabbi Andre Ungar of Westwood, New Jersey's Temple Emanuel, "To Birmingham and Back," in *Conservative Judaism* 18 (Fall 1963), 1–17.

2. Winograd, "Birmingham: A Personal Statement," 1.

3. Ninety-seven percent of the northern Jewish population registered its approval for the landmark *Brown* decision. Alfred O. Hero, Jr., "Southern Jews, Race Relations, and Foreign Policy," *Jewish Social Studies* 27 (October 1965), 216. See also Seth Forman, "The Unbearable Whiteness of Being Jewish: Desegregation in the South and the Crisis of Jewish Liberalism," *American Jewish History* 85 (June 1997), 121, and Forman, *Blacks in the Jewish Mind: A Crisis of Liberalism* (New York: New York University Press, 1998). Two issues of *American Jewish History* were devoted to southern Jewry: Mark K. Bauman and Bobbie Malone, guest editors, *American Jewish History* 85 (September, December 1997).

4. For an overview of the African-American struggle for racial equality, see Harvard Sitkoff, *The Struggle for Black Equality: 1954–1980* (New York: Hill and Wang, 1981). For a discussion of non-Jewish white liberals, see William H. Chafe, *Civilities and Civil Rights: Greensboro, North Carolina, and the Black Struggle for Freedom* (New York: Oxford University Press, 1981). For an oral history of the period, see Howell Raines, *My Soul Is Rested: The Story of the Civil Rights Movement in the Deep South* (Harrisonburg: Penguin Books, 1981), or Henry Hampton and Steven Fayer, *Voices of Freedom: An Oral History of the Civil Rights Movement from the 1950s through the 1980s* (New York: Bantam, 1990). For a history of SNCC, see Clayborne Carson, *In Struggle: SNCC and the Black Awakening of the 1960s* (Cambridge: Harvard University Press, 1981). The legacy of the 1965 Voting Rights Act is covered in David J. Garrow, *Protest at Selma: Martin Luther King, Jr., and the Voting Rights Act of 1965* (New Haven: Yale University Press, 1978). One of the few works on the early movement is Sitkoff, *A New Deal for Blacks* (New York: Oxford University Press, 1978). For information on the political behavior of non-Jewish liberals, see Morton Sosna, *In Search of the Silent South: Southern Liberals and the Race Issue* (New York: Columbia University Press, 1977); John T. Kneebone, *Southern Liberal Journalists and the Issue of Race, 1920–1944* (Chapel Hill: University of North Carolina Press, 1985); Thomas Krueger, *And Promises to Keep: The Southern Conference for Human Welfare, 1938–1948* (Nashville: Vanderbilt University Press, 1967); John A. Salmond, *The Conscience of a Lawyer: Clifford A. Durr and American*

Civil Liberties, 1899–1975 (Tuscaloosa: University of Alabama Press, 1990); Anne C. Loveland, *Lillian Smith, A Southerner Confronting the South: A Biography* (Baton Rouge: Louisiana State University Press, 1986); Ralph McGill, *No Place to Hide: The South and Human Rights* (Macon: Mercer University Press, 1984). For a different interpretation of Black-Jewish relations, see Murray Friedman, *What Went Wrong? The Creation and Collapse of the Black-Jewish Alliance* (New York: Free Press, 1995).

5. See John Higham, *Send These to Me: Immigrants in Urban America* (Baltimore: Johns Hopkins University Press, 1984), especially chapters 5–7. See also Leonard Dinnerstein, *The Leo Frank Case* (New York: Columbia University Press, 1968), and part 2 of Leonard Dinnerstein, *Uneasy at Home: Antisemitism and the American Experience* (New York: Columbia University Press, 1987).

6. Much of the material on southern rabbis has been gleaned from the rabbinic thesis notes of Allan Krause. Krause, a student at Hebrew Union College–Jewish Institute of Religion, Cincinnati, researched and interviewed scores of Reform rabbis in the South for his thesis, "The Southern Rabbi and Civil Rights" (1967). The timeliness of his interviews provides scholars with one of the few contemporary oral histories available on the subject of southern rabbis and civil rights. In order to protect his subjects from possible reprisals and to guarantee the highest possible level of candor, Krause agreed to restrict all scholarly access to his notes until the political climate changed. With the permission of Rabbi Krause and the director of the American Jewish Archives, Krause's confidential notes were released, for the first time, to the present author. Citations to Krause's notes, rather than to the thesis itself, are indicated by Krause, Thesis notes, box number 1747, AJA. Allen Krause, "The Southern Rabbi and Civil Rights," 26, 20. Norfolk had 8,500 Jews out of 305,000 residents in 1964, while Jackson claimed 150 Jewish families in a total population of 147,000. In 1962 New Orleans counted 10,000 Jews among an overall population of 627,000. See Krause, "The Southern Rabbi and Civil Rights," 18, 16–17, and Leonard Reissman, "The New Orleans Jewish Community," *Jewish Journal of Sociology* 4 (June 1962), 112.

7. While a sizable number of northern Jews migrated south in the years after World War II, they settled almost exclusively in more urban centers and remained far more liberal on race issues. A mail survey of Jews in Roanoke, Virginia, revealed that more than 70 percent favored the *Brown* decision. While these Jewish families enjoyed the protection of stronger communal organizations in the South's major cities, they nevertheless remained susceptible to the overbearing power of the segregationists around them. Fuchs, *Political Behavior of American Jews*, 108; Theodore Lowi, "Southern Jews: The Two Communities," *Jewish Journal of Sociology* 6 (July 1964). Even so, the postwar migration did little to change the character even of the South's larger centers. As late as 1958, a survey revealed that in New Orleans, only 11 percent of the Jewish population had lived in the city for less than ten years. See Reissman, "The New Orleans Jewish Community," 113. Krause, "The Southern Rabbi and Civil Rights," 16–17, 23, 24, 17. See also Mark K. Bauman and Berkley Kalin, eds., *The Quiet Voices: Southern Rabbis and Black Civil Rights, 1880s to 1990s* (Tuscaloosa: University of Alabama Press, 1997).

8. In a survey conducted between 1939 and 1946, Charles Herbert Stember reported, "Southerners ranked lowest in anti-Semitic responses to six of nine

questions." Charles Herbert Stember, *Jews in the Mind of America* (New York: Basic Books, 1966), 390. Most radical hate groups in the South included anti-Semitism in their rhetoric but rarely translated their words into action. See Arnold Shankman, "A Temple Is Bombed—Atlanta, 1958," *American Jewish Archives* 23 (November 1971); Leonard Dinnerstein and Mary Dale Palsson, eds., *Jews in the South* (Baton Rouge: Louisiana State University Press, 1973), 374; Melissa Greene, *The Temple Bombing* (Reading, Mass.: Addison, 1996); Dinnerstein, *Anti-Semitism in America*. Abraham Levitan served as rabbi of Miami's Beth-el Congregation.

9. Shankman, "A Temple Is Bombed"; Gordon Gladstone, "Anti-Jewish Bombing Outrages in the United States, 1959–1970" (1971), box number 518, p. 1–7, AJA. For Grafman, King's critique of store owners implied deeper meaning. Grafman recalled, "I told him that in the city of Birmingham, when you talked about 'merchants' you might as well use the word 'Jew' and that there was certainly implied anti-Semitism here." Krause, "The Southern Rabbi and Civil Rights," 85.

10. Isaac Toubin, "Recklessness or Responsibility," *Southern Israelite*, February 27, 1959, 13–15, cited in Arnold Shankman, "A Temple is Bombed"; James A. Wax, "The Attitude of the Jews in the South Toward Integration," *CCAR Journal* 26 (June 1959), 18, cited in Krause, "The Southern Rabbi and Civil Rights."

11. Letter from Aaron Henry to Allen Krause, July 22, 1966, letter from Fred Shuttlesworth to Allen Krause, 1965, both cited in Krause, "The Southern Rabbi and Civil Rights," 47, 45–46. Krause, Thesis notes, 309.

12. Krause, "The Southern Rabbi and Civil Rights," 17, 23, 24.

13. Ibid., 145; Krause, Thesis notes, 317; Malcolm Stern, "Role of the Rabbi in the South," appearing in Nathan M. Kaganoff and Melvin I. Urofsky, eds., *Turn to the South: Essays on Southern Jewry* (Charlottesville: University Press of Virginia, 1979), 31.

14. William S. Malev, "The Jew of the South in the Conflict of Segregation," *Conservative Judaism* 13 (Fall 1958), 36; Krause, "The Southern Rabbi and Civil Rights," 69–70, 78.

15. Krause, "The Southern Rabbi and Civil Rights," 63, 62, 69–70, 78.

16. Malev, "The Jew of the South in the Conflict of Segregation," 39. In Birmingham, Rabbi Grafman acknowledged the need for desegregation but held firm to his conviction that integration should not be forced. See Krause, "The Southern Rabbi and Civil Rights," 82.

17. Malev, "The Jew of the South in the Conflict of Segregation," 39.

18. Ibid., 36–37.

19. Krause, "The Southern Rabbi and Civil Rights," 79.

20. Krause, "The Southern Rabbi and Civil Rights," 238, 82, 77.

21. Krause, Thesis notes, 285; emphasis in the original.

22. Ibid., 285, 287–288.

23. Ibid., 292.

24. Ibid., 291.

25. Ibid., 294. Rabbi Sidney Goldstein of Meridian, Mississippi, exclaimed, "Blessings on you! You make me feel very proud that the rabbinate comes up with

people like you!" Rabbi Charles Mantinband signaled his support by accepting the invitation to meet. In the end, only Mantinband, Goldstein, and Rabbi Irwin Schor of Clarksdale would have attended the proposed meeting. Ibid., 293, 292.

26. American Jews looked with pride on their historic commitment to racial equality. In 1909, they helped form the NAACP, and Joel E. Springarn served as its chairman for most of the years between 1914 and 1939. Wealthy German-American Jews sponsored numerous philanthropies that benefited the country's black community. William and Julius Rosenwald, Herbert Lehman, and Felix Warburg all made generous donations to the NAACP. Julius Rosenwald established 5,357 black elementary schools in the South that by 1932 were credited with educating over 650,000 students, an estimated 25 to 40 percent of the black school-age population. See Jonathan Kaufman, *Broken Alliance: The Turbulent Times Between Blacks and Jews in America* (New York: Scribners, 1988), 2, 30–31, 91; *Justice, Justice*, 7; and *American Jewish Year Book* 60 (1959), 18. Martin Luther King's Southern Christian Leadership Conference (SCLC), as well as SNCC and CORE, received most of their financial support from the Jewish community. See Kaufman, *Broken Alliances*, 19, 286. While Jews were heavily represented in the civil rights movement, they represented 3.04 percent of the total 1958 U.S. population (5,261,550 Jews lived among a total population of 173,260,000). See Friedman, *Utopian Dilemma*, 24; Hero, "Southern Jews, Race Relations, and Foreign Policy," 216; Gary Gerstle, "Race and the Myth of the Liberal Consensus," *Journal of American History* 82 (September 1995), 579. For more on the history of black-Jewish relations, see William M. Phillips, Jr., *An Unillustrious Alliance: The African American and Jewish American Communities* (New York: Greenwood Press, 1991); Hasia Diner, *In the Almost Promised Land: American Jews and Blacks, 1915–1935* (Baltimore: Johns Hopkins University Press, 1995); and Jack Salzman and Cornel West, eds., *Struggles in the Promised Land: Toward a History of Black-Jewish Relations in the United States* (New York: Oxford University Press, 1997).

27. The American Jewish Congress led the Jewish community with a strategy combining grassroots activism with pressure on local, state, and federal government agencies. The American Jewish Committee and Anti-Defamation League opted for a more conciliatory approach, focusing instead on education and dialogue. See Friedman, *Utopian Dilemma*, 23. For examples of the American Jewish Congress's strategies, see "Statement of Dr. Stephen S. Wise, President of the American Jewish Congress, On the Report of the President's Committee on Civil Rights," *CLSA Reports*, 1, and Maslow and Robison, 7. For background on the American Jewish Committee and ADL's strategy, see "Point with Pride," 5.

28. Since state governments maintained jurisdiction in murder cases, federal law enforcement officials cited the civil rights protection guaranteed in the Constitution to justify their intervention. Will Maslow and Joseph B. Robison, "American Jewish Congress Before Subcommittee of the Senate Committee on Judiciary, re: S. 42, S. 1352, and S. 1465, Bills To Protect Citizens and Other Persons From Mob Violence and Lynching, February 2, 1948," *CLSA Reports*, 2; Albert E. Arent, "Statement Before the Senate Judiciary Sub-Committee Holding Hearings on S. 42, S. 1352, and S. 1465, Bills to Protect Citizens and Other Persons from Mob Violence and Lynching," 1–3.

29. Joseph B. Robison, "Before the House Sub-Committee on the Judiciary considering H.R. 3488, An Anti-Lynching Bill," February 4, 1948, *CLSA Reports*, 6–7.

30. Maslow and Robison, "A Civil Rights Program for America," 8. The National Women's League of United Synagogue called on the Eighty-third Congress to pass an anti–poll tax law, an anti-lynching bill, approve an FEPC, eliminate discrimination in the military, and end discrimination in places of public accommodation. See *Justice Justice*, 9. For more information on the committee's recommendations, read *NCRAC Legislative Information Bulletin* 6 (December 15, 1947), Special Collections box A-83, 1019, Klau Library.

31. "Recommendations of the President's Committee on Civil Rights, October 29, 1947," CLSA *Reports*. *NCRAC Legislative Information Bulletin* 6, 7.

32. "Statement of Stephen S. Wise, President of American Jewish Congress, on Report of the President's Committee on Civil Rights," 1–2, *CLSA Reports*. On June 23–26, 1952, the Conservative movement's Rabbinical Assembly called for laws "to implement the program of the President's [1947] Committee on Civil Rights." See *Justice Justice*, 10.

33. "Program of Action for the Cincinnati Jewish Community in the Present Race Relations Emergency," Appendix A, p. 3, Manuscript Collection 202, box 16, folder 4, AJA. "Program of Action for the Cincinnati Jewish Community in the Present Race Relations Emergency," July 15, 1963, p. 3.

34. "Statement of Stephen S. Wise, in Respect to Legislation for Federal Aid to Education, Before the Subcommittee on Education of the Senate Committee on Labor and Public Welfare (S. 80, 170, 199, 472), April 25, 1947," Papers of Stephen S. Wise, box 64, AJHS. For a state-by-state breakdown of desegregation progress in elementary schools, high schools, and universities between 1954 and 1961, see *Statistical Summary of School Segregation-Desegregation in the Southern and Border States* (Nashville: Southern Education Reporting Service, 1961).

35. "Statement of Dr. Stephen S. Wise, President, American Jewish Congress, United States of America, Before a Subcommittee of the Senate Committee on Labor and Public Welfare, Holding Hearings on S. 984, a Bill to Prohibit Discrimination in Employment Because of Race, Religion, Color, National Origin, or Ancestry, June 12, 1947," *CLSA Reports* (New York: American Jewish Congress, n.d.); "Recommendations on Scope, Methods, and Procedures Respectfully Presented to the President's Committee on Government Contracts by the Constituent National Agencies and Community Organizations of the National Community Relations Advisory Council," Manuscript Collection 202, box 15, folder 3, p. 2, AJA.

36. "Statement to the Governor's Commission on Civil Rights on Behalf of the Jewish Community Relations Committee, August 7, 1958," Manuscript Collection 202, box 15, folder 8, AJA. Similar strategies were employed by Irving Kane, chairman of the NCRAC, in testimony before the Eighty-first Congress in May 1949 and by a 1954 conference of public anti-discrimination agencies and private Jewish organizations. See "Statement Submitted by Irving Kane Before the Eighty-first Congress: First Session, in the Matter of H.R. 4453 Entitled 'A Bill To Prohibit Discrimination in Employment Because of Race, Color, Religion, or

National Origin, May 19, 1949,' " Manuscript Collection 202, box 14, folder 10, AJA, and *JTA News* (November 18, 1954), Manuscript Collection 202, box 15, folder 3, p. 5, AJA.

37. *FEPC Reference Manual* (1948 edition), 64; "Statement of Irving M. Engel on Behalf of the American Jewish Committee to the House Committee on Labor and Education Subcommittee on Discrimination in Employment," May 25, 1949, Manuscript Collection 202, box 14, folder 10, p. 10, AJA; *Colliers* (July 28, 1945) cited in *FEPC Reference Manual* (1948 edition), 23.

38. Sitkoff, *Struggle for Black Equality*, 21–22. See also Richard Kluger, *Simple Justice* (New York: Alfred A. Knopf, 1976).

39. Hampton and Fayer, *Voices of Freedom*, xxvii; Sitkoff, *Struggle for Black Equality*, 23.

40. Only 8 percent believed that "every measure should be used to bring it [integration] about in the near future." Hero, Jr., "Southern Jews, Race Relations, and Foreign Policy," 216; Sitkoff, *Struggle for Black Equality*, 23.

41. Sitkoff, *Struggle for Black Equality*, 25, 26. After Congress refused to take serious steps to achieve racial equality, Henry Edward Schultz, national chairman of the ADL, complained that the 1959 congressional record was "highly disappointing." *National Jewish Monthly* 74 (March 1960), 30. Though Eisenhower did, on September 9, 1957, sign the first civil rights bill to be approved by Congress since Reconstruction, it offered only nominal changes in the status quo. See Sitkoff, *Struggle for Black Equality*, 33, and *Not the Work of a Day: The Story of the Anti-Defamation League of B'nai B'rith* (New York: Anti-Defamation League), 49.

42. *Justice, Justice*, 12, 13; *CCAR Resolutions*, 1954, Microfilm 893, AJA.

43. *National Jewish Monthly* 68 (June 1954), 3.

44. *Congress Weekly* (April 30, 1956), 4, cited in Lehrman, "The American Jewish Congress Weekly: A Study of Its Editorials, 1955–1959," box number 2389, AJA; *Justice, Justice*, 13; Statement of Dr. John Slawson, Executive Vice-President, American Jewish Committee, *American Jewish Year Book* 56 (1955), 631.

45. The *Brown* decision also brought attention to injustices against other non-white minority groups. By 1957, the Central Conference of American Rabbis acknowledged the plight of non-black minorities when it announced that "in calling for fuller justice and freedom for the Negro section of our population, our attention should at the same time be directed to all tragically neglected minority groups, such as the American Indians, Mexicans, Puerto-Ricans, and others who have been the victims of shameless expropriation and neglect, and who continue to be subjected to indignity and economic oppression." "CCAR Resolution," 1957, Microfilm 893, AJA. See the *American Jewish Year Book* 57 (1956), 511; *American Jewish Year Book* 60 (1959), 27; *American Jewish Year Book* 61 (1960), 13; *American Jewish Year Book* 62 (1961), 67; *American Jewish Year Book* 65 (1964), 15, 20; Alexander F. Miller, the National Community Service Director of the ADL, *National Jewish Monthly* 69 (February 1955), 19.

46. Sitkoff, *Struggle for Black Equality*, 27.

47. Sanford H. Bolz, Washington Counsel, American Jewish Congress, "Statement of the American Jewish Congress Submitted to Subcommittee #5 of the

House of Representatives Committee on the Judiciary Holding Hearings on H.R. 10672, H.R. 12896, H.R. 13189, relating to Civil Rights," New York, July 9, 1958.

48. For information on interfaith dialogue, see Gordon, *Jews in Suburbia*; Howard Singer, "The Rise and Fall of Interfaith Dialogue," *Commentary* 83 (May 1987), 50–55; Rodney Stark and Stephen Steinberg, "Jews and Christians in Suburbia," *Harper's* 235 (August 1967), 73–78; Lanie Sussman, " 'Toward Better Understanding': The Rise of the Interfaith Movement in America and the Role of Rabbi Isaac Landman," *American Jewish Archives* 34 (April 1982), 35–51. For evidence of educational activities, see "Point With Pride." For more on synagogue worship during this era, see Gordon, *Jews in Suburbia*. For more on the Jewish intergroup relations campaign, see Svonkin, *Jews Against Prejudice*.

49. Letter to Charles Posner from Richard Bluestein, June 13, 1950, Manuscript Collection 202, box 14, folder 16, AJA. *Oral History of Clarence E. Israel*, volume 27, Biographies File, AJA.

50. Herman Kaplow, "Jewish Federations, Their Agencies and the Integration Struggle," 3, Special Collections box A-89 247, Klau Library. The report concluded that "in 23 [JCCs], the facilities were open to all regardless of race or creed, in 12 the facilities were open to non-Jews exclusive of Negroes; and in 7 the facilities were closed to all non-Jewish including Negroes." *Civil Rights in the United States in 1951: A Balance Sheet of Group Relations* (New York: American Jewish Congress and the NAACP, 1951), 111.

51. Polenberg, *One Nation Divisible*, 153. The rationale for neighborhood schools was best articulated by the Public Education Association, which listed five reasons for maintaining the system: "1. minimizing the distance from home to school, 2. avoiding traffic hazards and topographical barriers (ditches, steep hills, etc.), 3. taking advantage of convenient and accessible public transportation when necessary to use it, 4. utilizing school space and facilities to the maximum, 5. avoiding shifting pupils, thus ensuring continuity of instruction." See Will Maslow and Richard Cohen, *School Segregation, Northern Style* (New York: Public Affairs Committee, American Jewish Congress, 1961), 10. For a 1959 study detailing the attitudes of Americans, including Jews, toward integration, see table 115, p. 200, in Stember, *Jews in the Mind of America*.

52. George and Eunice Grier, *Equality and Beyond: Housing Segregation and the Goals of the Great Society* (Chicago: Quadrangle Books, 1966), 8. This book was commissioned by the Anti-Defamation League.

53. Maslow and Cohen, *School Segregation, Northern Style*, 1; Charles Silberman, "A Jewish View of the Racial Crisis," *Conservative Judaism* 19 (Summer 1965), delivered in slightly different form to the 1965 Rabbinical Assembly Convention.

54. The black population in Washington, D.C., increased by 47 percent, in Los Angeles by 96 percent, and in Milwaukee by 187 percent. Grier and Grier, *Equality and Beyond*, 6–7; Nathan L. Edelstein, "The Jewish Relationship with the Emerging Negro Community in the North," presented to the National Community Relations Advisory Council, June 23, 1960, p. 1, Special Collections box A-89 310, Klau Library; Polenberg, *One Nation Divisible*, 150.

55. "In Los Angeles, 43 elementary schools have at least 85 percent Negro attendance. More than one-third of New York's one million public school pupils are Negro or Puerto Rican, and there are 95 public elementary schools with Negro or Puerto Rican enrollments above ninety percent." Maslow and Cohen, *School Segregation, Northern Style*, 3, 5.

56. For more on working-class Jews, see Jonathan Rieder, *Canarsie: The Jews and Italians of Brooklyn Against Liberalism* (Cambridge: Harvard University Press, 1985); Yona Ginsberg, *Jews in a Changing Neighborhood: The Story of Mattapan* (New York: Free Press, 1975); J. Anthony Lukas, *Common Ground: A Turbulent Decade in the Lives of Three American Families* (New York: Random House, 1985); and Hillel Levine and Lawrence Harmon, *A Tragedy of Good Intentions: The Death of an American Jewish Community* (New York: Free Press, 1992).

57. Kaplow, "Jewish Federations, Their Agencies and the Integration Struggle," 1; Nathan L. Edelstein, "The Jewish Relationship with the Emerging Negro Community in the North," presented to the National Community Relations Advisory Council, June 23, 1960, p. 1, Special Collections box A-89 310, Klau Library; John Slawson, "Basic Assumptions Underlying Jewish Community Relations Programs," 544, presented at the annual meeting of the National Conference of Jewish Communal Service, Pittsburgh, May 29, 1959, reprinted from *Journal of Jewish Communal Service* 36 (Winter 1959), 111–119, cited in Graenum Berger, ed., *The Turbulent Decades: Jewish Communal Services in America, 1958–1978* (New York: Conference of Jewish Communal Service, 1980).

58. Herman Kaplow, "Jewish Federations, Their Agencies and the Integration Struggle," *Congress Bi-Weekly* 31 (September 14, 1964), 3.

59. Slawson, "Basic Assumptions Underlying Jewish Community Relations Programs," 111–119.

60. *Congress Bi-Weekly* 31 (September 14, 1964), 3; *Congress Bi-Weekly* 31 (May 25, 1964), 3.

61. Public schools in the North, according to the American Jewish Congress lobbyists, justified their stall tactics by relying "on lower court decisions that the equal protection clause of the Fourteenth Amendment does not 'affirmatively command' integration but merely forbids the use of official or governmental powers to enforce segregation," In the 1896 *Plessy* case, Maslow and Cohen explained, Justice John Harlan "first used the phrase 'colorblind' to describe the classic legal concept which held that government must disregard a man's color in its relations with him. But in terms of the choice confronting Northern school boards, being color-blind meant refusing to assume any responsibility for school segregation so long as it did not result from any school board policy or action." Maslow and Cohen, *School Segregation, Northern Style*, 4.

62. Ibid., 1, 10.

63. Ibid., 15. In New York City, permissive busing was used to reassign 919 students from overcrowded classrooms in Bedford-Stuyvesant to available space in white schools in Queens. When a similar plan was instituted in Detroit, 1,200 students boycotted classes for three days to protest the new students' arrival. A plan to move 794 students from East Harlem to Yorkville provoked little white opposition. Maslow and Cohen remained confident that "the initial tension that often accompanies such transfers can be reduced sharply or even

eliminated." New York instituted such a plan in the fall of 1960. "Under this program," Maslow and Cohen wrote, "all pupils from twenty-one junior high schools with heavy concentrations of Negro and Puerto Rican students were given the opportunity to transfer to twenty-eight other schools that were being used at less than ninety percent of capacity." Maslow and Cohen, *School Segregation, Northern Style*, 14, 15.

64. Ibid., 16. Between 1957 and 1959, New York City built fifty-four new elementary and intermediate schools. They put thirteen in predominantly black and Puerto Rican areas, seventeen in white neighborhoods, and twenty-four in fringe areas. Ibid., 10. The New Rochelle case ended up in federal court, where Judge Irving R. Kaufman ruled against the school district and demanded a viable plan for desegregation. See ibid., 7–8. The AJC, ADL, and American Jewish Congress filed briefs against the New Rochelle Board of Education. See "Joint Memo of American Jewish Committee and Anti-Defamation League from Sol Rabkin and Theodore Leskes," September 14, 1961, Papers of the Council of Jewish Federations and Welfare Funds, box 19, AJHS, as well as "De Facto Segregation in Public Schools: A Position Paper for the Guidance of Jewish Communities and Agencies," National Community Relations Advisory Council, New York, 1964.

65. "De Facto Segregation in Public Schools," 3.

66. Herman L. Kaplow, Executive Director, St. Louis Federation, "Jewish Federations, Their Agencies and the Integration Struggle," 5 (emphasis in the original).

Chapter Eight

1. See Manuscript Collection 202, "Freedom Bus, 1970," box 63, folder 5, AJA. For more on the history of the Soviet Jewry movement, see William Orbach, *The American Movement to Aid Soviet Jewry* (Amherst: University of Massachusetts Press, 1979), and Paul S. Appelbaum, "The Soviet Jewry Movement in the United States," in Michael N. Dobkowski, ed., *Jewish American Voluntary Organizations* (Westport, Conn.: Greenwood, 1986).

2. In a wide-ranging assault on racial inequality, the Civil Rights Act promised equal access to electoral politics and places of public accommodation, desegregation of public facilities and public education, a more powerful federal commission on civil rights, and an end to discrimination in federally assisted programs and employment. Nathan Glazer, *Affirmative Discrimination: Ethnic Inequality and Public Policy* (Cambridge: Harvard University Press, 1987), 44. The Voting Rights Act, signed in the wake of protests throughout the South, mandated the placement of federal officials in all precincts with low African-American voter turnout and brought almost immediate redress to a century-old civil inequality. See David J. Garrow, *Protest at Selma: Martin Luther King and the Voting Rights Act of 1965* (New Haven: Yale University Press, 1978).

3. Commencement address at Howard University, "To Fulfill These Rights," June 4, 1965, *Public Papers of the Presidents of the United States: Lyndon B. Johnson, 1965*, vol. 1 (Washington, D.C.: Government Printing Office, 1965). For more on President Johnson, see Robert Dallek, *Lone Star Rising: Lyndon Johnson and His Times, 1908–1960* (New York: Oxford University Press, 1992),

and Dallek, *Flawed Giant: Lyndon Johnson and His Times, 1961–1973* (New York: Oxford University Press, 1998).

4. For more on SNCC and the Jewish Community, see Jerome Bakst, "Negro Radicalism Turns Anti-Semitic: SNCC's Volte Face," *The Wiener Library Bulletin*, New Series no. 10, v. 22, no. 1 (Winter 1967–68); and *The Black Panther Party: The Anti-Semitic and Anti-Israel Component* (New York: American Jewish Committee, January 23, 1970), Special Collections box A-90 140, Klau Library. See also Clayborne Carson, *In Struggle: SNCC and the Black Awakening of the 1960s* (Cambridge: Harvard University Press, 1981).

5. Earl Raab, "The Black Revolution and the Jewish Question," *Commentary* 49 (May 1969), 3. On the breakup of the New Deal coalition, see Gary Gerstle and Steven Fraser, *The Rise and Fall of the New Deal Order* (Princeton: Princeton University Press, 1989).

6. Raab, "Black Revolution," 2–3. See also George and Eunice Grier, *Equality and Beyond*, 15. In 1968, polls showed that 86 percent of Jews supported Humphrey for president, compared to 46.2 percent of Catholics and 28.5 percent of white Protestants. Nixon enjoyed support from 64.5 percent of white Protestants and only 11.8 percent of the Jewish population. Similarly, 35.4 percent of Jews polled considered civil rights progress "too slow" compared to 23.4 percent of white Protestants. Almost twice as many Jews as white Protestants considered racial inequality the "most important major issue." Conversely, 24 percent of white Protestants listed "law and order" as the "most important major issue" compared to only 8.3 percent of Jews. See Allen S. Maller, "Notes on California Jews' Political Attitudes—1968," *Jewish Social Studies* 33, no. 2 (1971), 161–163.

7. Friedman, *What Went Wrong?*, 273.

8. Nathan L. Edelstein, chairman, governing council, American Jewish Congress, presented to National Community Relations Advisory Council, June 23, 1960, pp. 2, 3, 11, 6, Special Collection box A-89 310, Klau Library.

9. Jewish Community Relations Council, "Members of the JCRC, SNCC Criticized for Israel Stand," August 16, 1967, p. 2, Manuscript Collection 202, box 18, folder 5, AJA; Bertram H. Gold, *Jews and the Urban Crisis, 1968*, from his address at the National Conference of Jewish Communal Service, June 10, 1968, Detroit, 5; Dinnerstein, *Antisemitism in America*, 209, cited in Friedman, *What Went Wrong?*, 319.

10. Edelstein, presented to National Community Relations Advisory Council, 9, 11. For more on black Muslims, see Manuscript Collection 202, "Black Muslims 1961–1965," box 16, folder 7 and 10, AJA.

11. Charles E. Silberman, address to the American Jewish Congress 1966 convention, appearing in *Congress Bi-Weekly* 33 (May 23, 1966), 6; Charles E. Silberman, "A Jewish View of the Racial Crisis," *Conservative Judaism* 19 (Summer 1965), 1. Silberman was an editor of *Fortune* magazine; this article was delivered in a slightly different form to the 1965 Rabbinical Assembly convention. See also Charles Silberman, *Crisis in Black and White* (New York: Random House, 1964).

12. Silberman, "A Jewish View of the Racial Crisis," 1–3. See Stanley Elkins, *Slavery; A Problem in American Institutional and Intellectual Life* (Chicago: University of Chicago Press, 1959, 1976).

13. Ibid.

14. Ibid.

15. "Statement Adopted by the National Governing Council of the American Jewish Congress on January 14, 1968," American Jewish Congress resolution on the urban crisis adopted at its biennial convention, Miami, Florida, May 14–19, 1968, p. 4 of Appendix, Klau Library; Shad Polier, news release, "The Jews and the Racial Crisis," Office of Jewish Information, American Jewish Congress, July 15, 1964, p. 3, Papers of Shad Polier, Collection *P-572, box 14, AJHS, Waltham, Massachusetts; Shad Polier, *Congress Bi-Weekly* 31 (September 14, 1964), 6.

16. *Congress Bi-Weekly* 31 (May 25, 1964), 3; *Congress Bi-Weekly* 31 (September 14, 1964), 3; "American Jewish Congress Resolution on the Urban Crisis Adopted at Its Biennial Convention Miami, Florida, May 14–19, 1968," p. 1, Klau Library; *Jewish Currents* 24 (February 1970), 3.

17. Gold, *Jews and the Urban Crisis, 1968*, 6, 7–8.

18. Ibid.; Friedman, *What Went Wrong?*, 272–273.

19. Gold, *Jews and the Urban Crisis, 1968*, 5–6, 10.

20. Friedman, *What Went Wrong?*, 273, 270, 271.

21. Harold Cruse, *The Crisis of the Negro Intellectual* (New York: Quill, 1984), 490. See Shlomo Avineri, "The New Left and Israel," Klau Library. Not all in the African-American community supported the anti-Israel stance. After the Arab oil boycott in 1974, a group of blacks organized the Black Americans to Support Israel Committee (BASIC). BASIC was headed by A. Philip Randolph, with Bayard Rustin, director, and Lionel Hampton, treasurer. Members included Hank Aaron, Ralph Abernathy, Tom Bradley, Ralph Ellison, Vernon Jordan, Coretta Scott King, Martin Luther King, Sr., Rosa Parks, Roy Wilkins, Andrew Young, and Myrlie Evers. "Resolution of Jewish Community of Cincinnati, June 8, 1967," p. 2, Manuscript Collection 202, box 40, folder 10, AJA. Edelstein, Presented to National Community Relations Advisory Council, June 23, 1960, p. 3, Special Collections box A-89 310, Klau Library.

22. Clayborne Carson, "Black-Jewish Universalism in the Era of Identity Politics," 187, in Saltzman and West, eds., *Struggles in the Promised Land*; Bertram H. Gold, *Reconstructionist* (May 17, 1968), quoted in Gold, *Jews and the Urban Crisis, 1968*, 5, 4.

23. Friedman, *What Went Wrong?*, 213, 214; *Congress Bi-Weekly* 31 (September 14, 1964), 2; "Statement Adopted by the National Governing Council of the American Jewish Congress on January 14, 1968," from p. 1 and p. 3 of the appendix to the American Jewish Congress Resolution on the Urban Crisis, Adopted at Its Biennial Convention, Miami, Florida, May 14–19, 1968, Klau Library. See Fred R. Harris and Tom Wicker, *The Kerner Report: The 1968 Report of the National Advisory Commission on Civil Disorders* (New York: Pantheon Books, 1988).

24. Quoted in Wertheimer, "The Turbulent Sixties," in Sarna, ed., *The American Jewish Experience*, 340. The U.S. government flinched as well. While the State Department condemned Nasser's aggression, it refused to force the Egyptians from the Sinai, violating an agreement reached with Israel after the 1956 Sinai war. Henry P. Van Dusen, past president, Union Theological Seminary, quoted in Wertheimer, "The Turbulent Sixties," 341. See also Lawrence Grossman, "Trans-

forming Through Crisis: The American Jewish Committee and the Six-Day War," *American Jewish History* 86 (March 1998), 27–54.

25. Friedman, *What Went Wrong?*, 250–251.

26. Carson, "Black-Jewish Universalism," 188, in Saltzman and West, eds., *Struggles in the Promised Land*; Friedman, *What Went Wrong?*, 230.

27. Carson, "Black-Jewish Universalism," in Saltzman and West, eds., *Strangers in the Promised Land*, 192.

28. Gerald Sorin, *Tradition Transformed: The Jewish Experience in America* (Baltimore: Johns Hopkins University Press), 215; Wertheimer, "The Turbulent Sixties," 340; Edward S. Shapiro, *A Time for Healing* (Baltimore: Johns Hopkins University Press, 1992), 208; Wertheimer, "The Turbulent Sixties," 340.

29. For a summary of events detailing the late civil rights movement, black anti-Semitism, and the New York teachers controversy, see Fred V. Davidow, "Black Anti-Semitism, American Jewry and Israel," unpublished paper, AJA. For information on the 1968 teachers' strike in New York, see Melvin Urofsky, *Why Teachers Strike: Teachers Rights and Community Control* (New York: Anchor Books, 1970).

30. "Jewish Teachers Association Bulletin," (September 1969), 1; Jackofsky, "Negro-Jewish Relations on the Contemporary American Scene," 57.

31. *Congress Bi-Weekly* 31 (September 14, 1964), 3. See "Massachusetts Board of Rabbis, Correspondence," box number 828, AJA.

32. Sharyn Henry, "Cleveland Jewry in 1968: A Year of Conflict and Crisis Through the Eyes of the Cleveland Jewish News," Small Collections, AJA, May 27, 1986; Frank Stern, "The Jews and the Presidential Campaign of 1964 as it is Reflected in Various Jewish News Sources Between December 1, 1963, and February 15, 1964," Small Collections, AJA, February 1964; "Statement Adopted by the National Governing Council of the American Jewish Congress on January 14, 1968," from p. 3 of the appendix to the American Jewish Congress Resolution on the Urban Crisis Adopted at Its Biennial Convention, Miami, Florida, May 14–19, 1968, Klau Library. Bayard Rustin, Address to the American Jewish Congress 1966 Convention, *Congress Bi-Weekly* 33 (May 23, 1966), 11.

33. Grier, *Equality and Beyond*, 6, 8.

34. See Naomi Levine, Executive Director Designate, American Jewish Congress, "Affirmative Action, Preferential Treatments and Quotas: Papers from the Plenary Session, NJCRAC, June 28–July 2, 1972, Los Angeles," 13, New York, Klau Library. See also Glazer, *Affirmative Discrimination*, ix, 46, 44. Businesses employing fewer than fifty employees or engaged for contracts valued at less than $50,000 remained exempt from the policy. Glazer, *Affirmative Discrimination*, 46, 47–48, quoted from Labor Department code CFR, 60-2.10.

35. Policy statement of the American Jewish Committee, *Jewish Currents* 24 (March 1970), 4; Benjamin R. Epstein, National Director of the ADL quoted in Levine, "Affirmative Action, Preferential Treatments and Quotas," 6; "Joint Program Plan for Jewish Community Relations, 1980–81" (New York: NJCRAC, 1980), 47, 52, quoted in Bernstein, *To Dwell in Unity*, 212. Eight years later, they reaffirmed their support of affirmative action programs "including, (a) intensive recruitment of qualified and qualifiable individuals, utilizing not only traditional referral sources, but all those public and private resources that reach members of

disadvantaged groups, (b) an ongoing review of established job and admission requirements, including examinations and other selection methods, to make certain that they are performance-related and free of bias." They agreed that "in order to overcome unequal history and move more rapidly towards the goal of equal opportunity, . . . special consideration should be given to individuals who have been disadvantaged by such factors as poverty, cultural deprivation, inadequate schooling, discrimination or other deprivation; but no individual performing satisfactorily should be dismissed to afford opportunity for such special consideration." Adopted by the NJCRAC Plenary Session, NJCRAC, "Papers From The 1974 Plenary Session, Affirmative Action—After the DeFunis Decision, A Panel Discussion," 19–20, June 23–26, 1974, Nearprint File–DeFunis, AJA. Albert D. Chernin, Executive Director, JCRC of Philadelphia, quoted in Levine, "Affirmative Action, Preferential Treatments and Quotas," 19.

36. Bernard Fryshman, chairman, Commission on Legislation and Civil Action, Agudath Israel of America, *Affirmative Action and Equal Opportunity, An Overview*, June 1976, 12–13.

37. For information on college admissions see *Congress Weekly* 21, no. 20. President's Commission on Higher Education, *Higher Education for American Democracy*, vol. 2, 1947, quoted on p. 121 of Arnold Forster, *A Measure of Freedom: An Anti-Defamation League Report* (New York: Doubleday, 1950). The greatest opposition to ending the quota system, as one might imagine, came from those already in power in the nation's colleges and universities. They argued that since graduate programs needed to reflect the relative percentage of Jews in the overall population, limitations were justified. By keeping student populations relative to the overall American populations, colleges and universities would be maintaining their social obligation of educating the entire society. This defense, of course, ignores the Jewish community's cherished system of meritocracy just as it ignores the fact that intelligent blacks were routinely denied admissions, even though their college numbers remained well below national population averages. Wise noted as well that the declines "occurred at a time when general enrollments were increasing and when there was no reduction in the number of applications from Jewish students." Letter from Stephen S. Wise to Mildred McAfee Horton, January 11, 1948, *CLSA Reports* (New York: American Jewish Congress), 2. The 1948 New York report concluded that Jewish applicants from New York high schools faced unfair admissions quotas that made it more difficult for them to earn college acceptances. The Connecticut Interracial Commission study concluded that Jewish applicants applied to a greater number of schools but still had fewer acceptances. A 1949 American Council on Education study showed that Catholic and Protestant students had a greater chance of college acceptance than an academically comparable Jewish student. See "Factors Affecting the Admission of High School Seniors to College," A Report by Elmo Roper for the Committee on a Study of Discriminations in College Admissions, American Council on Education, 1949, quoted in Forster, *A Measure of Freedom*, 121.

38. Robert Weil, chair, Community Relations Committee of the Los Angeles Jewish Federation Council, quoted in Levine, "Affirmative Action, Preferential Treatments and Quotas," 4; Glazer, *Affirmative Discrimination*, xi. By the mid-1950s, most major colleges and universities had lifted their quota policies. With

an expanding economy and the GI bill making tuition payments more affordable, the number and size of colleges and universities grew at an unprecedented rate. As the American Jewish Committee reported in 1955, competition for coveted places in freshman classes decreased while discrimination against Jews eased. Within a generation, Jews would rank among the leaders in academia, law, and medicine. "At Cornell Medical School, a stubborn example," the AJC noted, "the present (1954–1955) freshman class is 35% Jewish as compared with the senior class with eighteen percent Jewish students." "The American Jewish Committee Background and Emphases for AJC's 1955 Domestic Program," January 1955, Files of the CJFWF, box 7, AJHS.

39. Albert D. Chernin, quoted in Levine, "Affirmative Action, Preferential Treatments and Quotas," 18.

40. "Policy Statement of the American Jewish Committee," *Jewish Currents* 24 (March 1970), 5; Forster, *A Measure of Freedom*, 119. Jewish organizations uncharacteristically avoided any direct attacks on the prejudicial nature of admissions quotas. The American Jewish Congress, usually outspoken in its defense of Jewish rights, opted to explain the apparent rise in Jewish applicants to the common practice among minority students of making multiple applications. From Theodore Leskes and Nathan Goldberg, "Survey of Filings of Applications for Admission to American Medical Schools," November 24, 1947, *CLSA Reports*. Instead of defending the rights of qualified Jews to enroll in undergraduate and professional programs, the ADL took a more apologetic stand. Reticent to challenge the prevailing consensus mentality of the time, they acknowledged that the best way to alleviate the anticipated influx of new students was to secure cooperation from a large number of universities so that "minority group students would disappear into the national collegiate body [and] no school would have to contend with a disproportionate number." See Forster, *A Measure of Freedom*, 119.

41. Epstein, quoted in Levine, "Affirmative Action, Preferential Treatments and Quotas," 5, 7, 8.

42. "Joint Program Plan for Jewish Community Relations, 1980–81" (New York: NJCRAC, 1980), 52, quoted in Bernstein, *To Dwell in Unity*, 212; Albert Chernin, quoted in Levine, "Affirmative Action, Prefential Treatments and Quotas," 21, 24.

43. Fryshman, *Affirmative Action and Equal Opportunity*, 6, 9, 14, 26.

44. David Petegorsky, *CLSA Reports*, American Jewish Congress, New York. Their plan included employment directives encouraging "(a) massive government manpower training programs; (b) intensified efforts to open unions and union training programs; (c) career ladders for training in skills and technical occupations; (d) vigorous enforcement of anti-discrimination laws; (e) the use of examination and other selection processes which are free of cultural bias, and which are job-related and of predictive validity; (f) intensive recruitment of qualified members of minority groups; and (g) the use of sensitivity and attitudinal tests and criteria for those jobs dealing largely with minority groups." Education directives "urged the expansion of (a) college open enrollment programs, with full funding, which broaden educational opportunities for all persons, including racial minorities; (b) remedial programs such as SEEK and college discovery; (c) vigorous recruitment efforts to find qualified minority group members, including

special efforts to recruit in colleges and high schools attended predominantly by minority group members; (d) flexible admission criteria (not including quotas or percentage goals) that would include—in addition to objective standards—relevant factors such as community service and qualifications that would help identify potentially successful students from disadvantaged backgrounds; and (e) conditional admission programs that accept students with lower grades on the condition that they complete special appropriate preparatory work programs which the university must make available." Levine, "Affirmative Action, Preferential Treatments and Quotas," 14, 16.

45. Levine, "Affirmative Action, Preferential Treatments and Quotas," 15–16.

46. The case inspired twenty-six separate friend of the court briefs. NJCRAC, "Papers from the 1974 Plenary Session, Affirmative Action—After the DeFunis Decision, A Panel Discussion, June 23–26, 1974," Nearprint File–DeFunis, AJA. The Bakke case centered on the unsuccessful application of a white student, Alan Bakke, to the University of California, Davis, medical school. When Bakke sued, claiming that his rejection amounted to reverse discrimination, the California Supreme Court ruled 6–1 "that the special admissions program at the Davis Medical School of the University of California violated the Equal Protection Clause of the United States Constitution because it granted preferential treatment to minorities at the expense of 'better qualified whites." Bakke, like DeFunis, twice applied and was twice rejected from the graduate program. Unlike DeFunis, he was not admitted to any other schools. Davis held sixteen of one hundred slots for special minority admissions programs and used a double application system, where special action went to one group and regular admissions to another. See Commission on Law and Social Action, *Discrimination, Segregation and Affirmative Action— 20 Recent Civil Rights Decisions Affecting the Jewish Community* (New York: American Jewish Congress, May 19, 1977), 42–44. For more on the *Bakke* case, see J. Harvie Wilkinson III, *From "Brown" to "Bakke": The Supreme Court and School Integration, 1954–1978* (New York: Oxford University Press, 1979).

47. Benjamin R. Epstein and Arnold Forster, *Preferential Treatment and Quotas* (New York: Anti-Defamation League, 1974), 3–4, Nearprint File–DeFunis, AJA. Epstein was the national director of the ADL while Forster was the ADL's associate director.

48. "Fact Sheet on UAHC Position in the Case of Marco De DeFunis v. University of Washington," 1, Manuscript Collection 26, box 19, folder 2, AJA. A compelling exchange of letters between various Reform leaders, lay and professional, over UAHC's support of the University of Washington is found in the Nearprint File–DeFunis, AJA. Rabbi Howard Singer, Emanuel Synagogue, West Hartford, Connecticut, "The DeFunis Case and the Jewish Organizations," 1, Nearprint File–DeFunis, AJA.

49. Albert E. Arent, Chairman, Commission on Social Action of Reform Judaism, *A Civil Rights Crunch for Jewish Groups*, 2, AJA.

50. Rabbi Howard Singer, "The DeFunis Case and the Jewish Organizations," 1, 6; "Memo to Area Directors from Samuel Rabinove, May 1, 1973," American Jewish Committee, Nearprint File–DeFunis, AJA; Brief of *Amicus Curiae*, American Jewish Committee, quoted in Washington Letter of American Jewish Committee, March 15, 1974, issue 74, number 2, p. 6, Nearprint File–DeFunis, AJA.

51. NJCRAC, "Papers from the 1974 Plenary Session, Affirmative Action—After the DeFunis Decision," 20.
52. Epstein and Forster, *Preferential Treatment and Quotas*, 5, Nearprint File–DeFunis, AJA.
53. "DeFunis, et al. v. Odegaard, et al.: Establishment of Racial Quotas For Preferential Admission to a State Law School," Anti-Defamation League Brief, 2, 3, January 1974, Manuscript Collection 26, box 19, folder 2, AJA.
54. Epstein and Forster, *Preferential Treatment and Quotas*, 6, 7.
55. Ibid., 31, 7, 28. For a long listing of discriminatory practices and reverse discrimination, see ibid., 8–13.
56. Singer, "The DeFunis Case and the Jewish Organizations," 6.
57. Epstein and Forster, "Preferential Treatment and Quotas," 5.

Epilogue

1. J. Sussman and R. Solomon (words), J. Sussman (music), "Just Another Foreigner," from *Safam: The Soul of Jewish America* (RTV Communications Group, 1983).
2. See Neal Gabler, *An Empire of Their Own: How the Jews Invented Hollywood* (New York: Crown, 1988).
3. Dinnerstein, *Anti-Semitism in America*, 228, 230, 236, 243.
4. Jonathan S. Tobin, "Will Jews Change Their Minds About School Choices?" *The Connecticut Jewish Ledger* (May 30, 1997).
5. Sylvia M. Neil, "Both Sides: Two Views on Vouchers," *Chicago Jewish News* (October 31, 1997).
6. The draft of Rabbi Richard Levy's statement of principles approved by the CCAR at its May 1999 meeting can be found at http://ccarnet.org/platforms/principles.html.
7. Daniel Kurtzman, "Lessons of Holocaust Demand Action in Kosovo, Many Jews Say," Jewish Telegraphic Agency (March 28, 1999); Tom Tugend, "Conservation with Rabbi Steven Jacobs," Jewish Telegraphic Agency (May 4, 1999).
8. Kurtzman, "Lessons of Holocaust."
9. See Thomas L. Friedman, *From Beirut to Jerusalem* (New York: Doubleday, 1990); Michael I. Karpin and Ina Friedman, *Murder in the Name of God: The Plot to Kill Yitzhak Rabin* (New York: Holt, 1998); Robert Owen Freedman, *The Intifada: Its Impact on Israel, the Arab World, and the Superpowers* (Miami: Florida International University Press, 1991); and Yaron Ezrahi, *Rubber Bullets: Power and Conscience in Modern Israel* (Berkeley: University of California Press, 1988). For a Palestinian perspective, see Edward W. Said and Christopher Hitchens, *Peace and Its Discontents: Essays on Palestine in the Middle East Peace Process* (New York: Vintage Books, 1995).
10. Quoted in Michele Chabin, "North American Olim Who Came After 1967 War Maintain Idealism" (Jewish Telegraphic Agency, n.d.), and Chaim I. Waxman, *American Aliya: Portrait of an Innovative Migration Movement* (Detroit: Wayne State University Press, 1989), 169.
11. See the books by David Wyman, *The Abandonment of the Jews* and *Paper Walls*. For other interpretations, see Newton, ed., *FDR and the Holocaust*.

12. See Rieder, *Canarsie*, and Lukas, *Common Ground*. Most historians share the view that Nixon dismantled the New Deal coalition and ended liberalism as a powerful force in American politics. Democratic losses in the 1966 congressional elections and the 1968 presidential contest, they argued, signaled an ideological realignment. Allen Matusow's history of liberalism in the 1960s, for example, is titled *The Unraveling of America*, while political scientist Theodore Lowi called his seminal work *The End of Liberalism*. These and other studies echo the prevailing belief that by the time Richard Nixon recited the oath of office in January 1969, the New Deal liberal coalition had dissolved into a conservative "silent majority." See Allen Matusow, *The Unraveling of America: A History of Liberalism in the 1960s* (New York: Harper and Row, 1985); Theodore Lowi, *The End of Liberalism: The Second Republic in the United States* (New York: Norton, 1979). Ample evidence exists to support such a conclusion. By the time Lyndon Johnson signed the landmark Civil Rights Act of 1964 and Voting Rights Act of 1965, American liberalism had already suffered severe blows from both sides of the political spectrum. From the left, militant African Americans, dissatisfied with the ideology and tactics of Martin Luther King, Jr., rejected nonviolent integrationist protest in favor of Black Power and the politics of ethnic nationalism. New Left activists on college campuses across the nation dissented from the liberalism of their parents and condemned U.S. policies governed, in their minds, by imperialist objectives. From the right, urban northern white ethnics, once the backbone of the New Deal coalition, opposed the war on poverty, abandoned the Democratic party, and worried especially about maintaining law and order.

13. Jack Nusan Porter and Peter Dreier, eds., *Jewish Radicalism: A Selected Anthology* (New York: Grove Press, 1973), quoted in Riv-Ellen Prell, *Prayer and Community: The Havurah in American Judaism* (Detroit: Wayne State University Press, 1989), 76. For a history of SNCC, see Carson, *In Struggle*.

14. Prell, *Prayer and Community*, 88. See Rieder, *Canarsie*, and Alan J. Steinberg, *American Jewry and Conservative Politics: A New Direction* (New York: Shapolsky, 1988).

15. Arthur Waskow, quoted in Prell, *Prayer and Community*, 79.

16. Ibid., 86–87.

17. Orbach, *The American Movement to Aid Soviet Jewry*, 4.

18. Ibid., 20, 24, 29. See also Paul S. Appelbaum, "The Soviet Jewry Movement in the United States," in Dobkowski, ed., *Jewish American Voluntary Organizations*.

19. Orbach, *The American Movement to Aid Soviet Jewry*, 4, 5, 20.

20. Ibid., vii, 129.

21. Prell, *Prayer and Community*, 16. See Phyllis Deutsch, "Theater of Mating: Jewish Summer Camps and Cultural Transformations," *American Jewish Historical Quarterly* 75 (September 1985), 307–321; Gerald Showstack, *Suburban Communities: The Jewishness of American Reform Jews* (Ithaca: Cornell University Press, 1988); Paul F. Bradshaw and Lawrence A. Hoffman, *The Changing Face of Jewish And Christian Worship in North America* (South Bend: University of Notre Dame Press, 1991); Rebecca Alpert and Jacob J. Staub, *Exploring Judaism: A Reconstructionist Approach* (New York: Reconstructionist Press, 1985); James A. Sleeper and Alan Minz, eds., *The New Jews* (New York: Random House,

1971); M. Herbert Danzinger, *Returning to Tradition: The Contemporary Revival of Orthodox Judaism* (New Haven: Yale University Press, 1989); and Lynn Davidman, *Tradition in a Rootless World: Women Turn to Orthodox Judaism* (Berkeley: University of California Press, 1991).

22. Prell, *Prayer and Community*, 15, 16, 90.

23. Jack Nusan Porter and Peter Dreier, quoted in ibid., 78.

24. Zvi Gitleman and Steven Cohen, quoted in Michele Chabin, "North American Olim Who Came After 1967 War Maintain Idealism," Jewish Telegraphic Agency (n.d.). See Waxman, *American Aliya*, 159; Naomi Cohen, *American Jews and the Zionist Idea* (New York: Ktav, 1975); and Melvin Urofsky, *American Zionism: From Herzl to the Holocaust* (New York: Doubleday, 1975).

25. Lawrence Cohler-Esses, "Choosing American Jewry's leader," *New York Jewish Week* (February 7, 1997); Robert Eshman, "Year of the Grudge 5757," *Los Angeles Jewish Journal* (October 3, 1997); David Twersky, *New Jersey Jewish News* (July 18, 1997). Information on the April 1999 Washington, D.C., conference of American Jewish conservatism can be found at http://www.temple.edu/feinsteinctr/fc-conf.html. See also Mark Gerson, ed., *The Essential Neo-Conservative Reader* (Reading: Addison Wesley, 1996), and Irving Kristol, *Neo-Conservatism: The Autobiography of an Idea. Selected Essays, 1949–1995* (New York: Free Press, 1995).

26. Rabbi David Saperstein heads the Washington, D.C.–based Religious Action Center.

27. See David Biale, Michael Galchinsky, and Susannah Heschel, eds., *Insider/Outsider: American Jews and Multi-Culturalism* (Berkeley: University of California Press, 1998); David A. Hollinger, *Post-Ethnic America: Beyond Multiculturalism* (New York: Basic Books, 1995); and Nathan Glazer, *We Are All Multi-Culturalists Now* (Cambridge: Harvard University Press, 1997).

Index

affirmative action, 10, 18, 192–93, 203–13, 215, 224

Agudath Israel, 14, 82, 153, 205, 207–208, 251n.50, 266n.51

America First, 61, 73–75, 244n.36, 245n.36

American Civil Liberties Union, 71, 90–91, 250n.34

American Council for Judaism, 100–101, 119, 124, 202

American Emergency Committee for Zionist Affairs, 99. *See also* American Zionist Emergency Council

AFL (American Federation of Labor), 99, 102

American Jewish Assembly, 94–97. *See also* American Jewish Conference

American Jewish Committee, The; and affirmative action, 204, 207, 209–10; and the American Jewish Assembly, 93–97; and the American Jewish Conference, 96–97, 99–101, 109–10; and the Anglo-American Committee of Inquiry, 122–23; and anti-Communism, 132–36, 142; and the anti-German boycott, 47–49; on anti-Semitism 72–73 ; and the Black Power movement, 195, 197–99; and church/state separation, 150–51, 154–55, 267n.54; and the civil rights movement, 171, 182, 187, 278n.64; and conservatism, 225; and fair employment practices, 144, 146, 180, 264n.35; and the General Jewish Council, 55–57; and the Great Depression, 22; history of, 11–12, 25, 44; on the Holocaust, 120, 123; and immigration reform, 158; on the International Bill of Rights, 112, 115; and the internment of Japanese Americans, 86–88; and interfaith dialogue, 61–62, 64–65, 246n.2; and isolationism, 73, 75; and the Jewish Federation, 14; and the McCarran Act, 139–40; and radio, 67–68; and the rise of Hitler, 45–46, 49, 50, 52–54, 241n.23; on Soviet Jews, 220; on the United Nations, 112, 114–18, 255n.21; and U.S. entry into World War II, 76, 79; and World War II, 77–78, 80–82, 245n.1, 246n.1; on Zionism, 58–59, 92–97, 108, 118–20, 123–24, 126–27

American Jewish Conference, The: The First American Jewish Conference; 96–97, 111, 251n.51, 254n.9; The Second American Jewish Conference, 109–14, 255n.14, The Third American Jewish Conference, 109, 118, 122, 125, 255n.23, 256n.23; *See also* American Jewish Assembly

American Jewish Conference on Soviet Jewry, 221

American Jewish Congress, The, and affirmative action, 203, 208–10, 283n.40, 283n.44, 284n.44; and the American Jewish Conference, 97, 109; and anti-Communism, 130, 136–37, 142; on the anti-German boycott, 47–48; and anti-lynching legislation, 176; and the Black Power movement, 194–95, 197, 199–200; and church/state separation, 149–50, 152, 155–56, 267n.54; and the civil rights movement, 170–71, 175, 177–78, 182–83, 185–89, 277n.61, 278n.64; and the Cold War, 132; Commission on Law and Social Action, 132–33; and fair employment practices, 143–47; and the General Jewish Council, 55, 57; history of, 11, 13; and the Holocaust, 91; and immigration reform, 157–58, 161–62; on the internment of Japanese-Americans, 87; on interfaith dialogue, 61–62; and the Jewish Federation, 14; and the McCarran Act, 139; and McCarthy, 141; and Ocean Hill-Brownsville, 202–203; and radio, 67–68; and the rise of Hitler in Europe, 44–46, 53–54; and the Rosenberg case, 135; on U.S. entry into World War II, 79; during World War II, 81; on Zionism, 58, 92

American Jewish Labor Council, 137

American Jewish War Veterans, 46

American Palestine Committee, 102
American Zionist Emergency Council, 98–99, 251n.57. *See also* American Emergency Committee for Zionist Affairs
Anglo-American Committee of Inquiry, 122–24
anti-Communism, 10, 17, 129–44
Anti-Defamation League, The, on affirmative action, 203–204, 207, 209–12, 283n.40; and Black Power, 198; and church/state separation, 156, 267n.54, 268n.67; and the civil rights movement, 169, 171, 182–85, 275n.41, 278n.64; history of, 11; on the internment of Japanese Americans, 89; and interfaith dialogue, 65; on Ocean Hill-Brownsville, 202; and radio, 68; and the Rosenberg case, 134–36; and Soviet Jews, 221; *See also* B'nai B'rith
anti-Semitism, in the African-American community, 192, 195, 198; during the Cold War, 130–31, 137, 142, 150, 178, 262n.31, 263n.31; and fair employment practices, 143; during the 1920s, 41; during the 1930s, 48–49, 62, 66, 72–74; during the 1970s, 215; in the post-war era, 119, 167; and the Rosenberg case, 134; in the South, 166, 271n.8, 272n.8; during World War II, 77–78, 84, 246n.3, 247n.3
Arent, Albert E., 176

Bailey, Kofi, 201
Bakke case, 209, 212, 284n.46
Balfour Declaration, The, 95, 98, 123, 125, 252n.64, 257n.39
Bauman, Morton A., 87
Ben-Gurion, David, 92, 127
Bernstein, Philip, 120–21
Birnbaum, Jacob, 221
Blachschleger, Eugene, 169
Black Americans to Support Israel Committee, 280n.21
Black, Hugo, 90, 154
Black Muslim, 199
Black Power, 189, 192–203, 213, 219–21, 224
Blaustein, Jacob, 115, 127
B'nai B'rith, 26, and the American Jewish Assembly, 93; and the American Jewish Congress, 97, 128; and the anti-German boycott, 47–48; and civil rights, 164, 182;

and the General Jewish Council, 55–57; history of 13; and immigration reform, 162; and interfaith dialogue, 65; and the internment of Japanese Americans, 88–89; and radio, 67; and the rise of Hitler, 46; on U.S. entry into World War II, 53; on Zionism, 13, 58–59, 108, 119, 124. *See also* Anti-Defamation League
Board of Rabbis (New York), 155
boycott (anti-German), 45–49, 238nn.11 and 13
Brandeis, Louis, 13, 58–59, 102, 109
Brickner, Barnett, 98
Brown, Josephine, 24, 28, 31–32
Brown v. Board of Education, Topeka, Kansas, 164–65, 173, 181–83, 275n.45
busing, 188–189
Byrd, Harry, 181

Carmichael, Stokely, 195, 199, 201
Carson, Clayborne, 201
Catholic Church, The, 25, 66, 83–84, 137, 148–49, 216, 219, 266n.51
Central Conference of American Rabbis, 14, 52, 75, 98, 101, 119, 125, 152, 171, 182, 217, 233n.16, 245n.38, 267n.54, 275n.45. *See also* Reform movement
Central Jewish Institute, 38
church-state separation. *See* separation of church and state
civil libertarianism, 68–73, 78, 80, 131, 140, 142
Civil Rights Act of 1964, The, 10, 147, 173, 191, 204, 212, 278n.2
civil rights movement, 10, 17, 164–90
Cleaver, Eldridge, 195
Cohen, Lizabeth, 21, 67
Cohen, Richard, 188–189
Columbus Platform, 98
Combined Jewish Philanthropies of Boston, 216
Commission on Higher Education (Truman), 206
Commission on Law and Social Action, 147. *See also* American Jewish Congress
Committee on Civil Rights. *See* President's Committee on Civil Rights (Truman)
Committee on National Security and Fair Play, 89
Committee for Service to Émigrés, 85
communism, 7, 130, 134–43, 259n.4
community chests, 82–83

Conference of Presidents of Major American Jewish Organizations, 225
Conference on the Status of Soviet Jews, 221
CIO (Congress of Industrial Organizations), 99, 102, 250n.34
CORE (Congress of Racial Equality), 173, 187, 273n.26
Conservative movement, The, and the Black Power movement, 195–96; and church/state separation, 152–54; and the civil rights movement, 182; and the First American Jewish Conference, 97; history of, 11; and interfaith dialogue, 64; and the New Deal, 233n.16, 234n.16; and Zionism, 218
Coughlin, Father Charles, 50, 61, 66–67, 73
Crisis of the Negro Intellectual, The, 199
Cruse, Harold, 199
cultural nationalism, 193–94, 219–21, 223–26
cultural pluralism, 41, 43–44, 49, 77, 80–82, 92, 97, 101, 110, 186, 201

DeFunis v. University of Washington, 209–13
Democratic party, 9–10, 42, 99, 146, 165, 193, 215, 219, 224–25
Dewey, Thomas, 147
DeWitt, John L., 90
displaced persons, 17, 108, 117, 121–24, 126, 257n.39
Displaced Persons Act of 1948, 159–60
Douglas, William O., 155, 221
DuBois, W.E.B., 196
Dushkin, Alexander, 43, 237n.4, 238n.4

Eastern-European American Jews, 8, 12, 22, 35–38, 42–44, 97, 132, 149; 215
Edelstein, Nathan, 187, 194–95, 199
Eisendrath, Maurice N., 111–14, 119, 121, 196–97
Eisenhower, Dwight D., 120, 162, 181, 265n.41, 275n.41
elections, of 1928, 25; of 1932, 9, 14, 29, 234n.23; of 1936, 25, 234n.23, 235n.23; of 1940, 235n.23; of 1944, 235n.23; of 1948, 1952, 1956, 1960, 1964, 229n.2, of 1966, 192; of 1968, 192, 229n.2, 279n.6; of 1972, 229n.2; of 1984, 7

Elkins, Dov Peretz, 199
Emergency Committee for European Jewish Affairs, 94, 97
enemy aliens, 84–86
Engel v. Vitale (New York Regents Case), 155
Engel, Irving, 146, 180
enlightenment (European), 8, 52, 58
Epstein, Henry, 154
ethnic nationalism. *See* cultural nationalism
Executive Order 8802, 144, 263n.33
Executive Order 9066, 10, 16, 79, 90
Executive Order 9664, 144
Executive Order 10925, 204

Fair Employment Practices Commission, 142–47, 152, 180–82, 263n.34, 264n.34
Federal Emergency Relief Act, 33–35, 235n.31, 236n.31
Feingold, Henry, 7
Fineberg, S. Anhil, 135–36
Flaherty Bill (HR 5454), 68–70
Ford, Henry, 73–74
Forster, Arnold, 89
Fortas, Abe, 90
Frank, Leo, 166
freedom bus, 191, 213, 221
freedom rides, 171–173, 191, 221
Friedman, Murray, 225
Fuchs, Lawrence, 7

Galveston Project, 12
Gansl, Simon, 48
General Jewish Council, 55–59, 69–72, 74–75, 242n.37
German-American Jews, 8, 12, 14, 43–44, 97, 110, 132, 166
Gerstle, Gary, 21
GI Bill of Rights, 129
Gillie Bill (HR 5757), 70–71
Gittelsohn, Roland, 172, 177
Glazer, Nathan, 132
Gold, Wolf, 103
Goldmann, Nahum, 113, 122, 124, 257n.39
Goldstein, Israel, 105–106
Goldstein, Jonah J., 3
Gordis, Robert, 101
Gore, Thomas, 24
Gottinger, Abraham, 48

Grafman, Milton, 167, 171, 272nn.9 and 16
Great Depression, The, 9, 15, 20, 22–27, 50
Great Society, The, 10, 18, 192, 204, 208, 219. See also Johnson, Lyndon
Grier, George and Eunice, 203
Guiding Principles of Reform Judaism, 98. See also Columbus Platform

Hadassah, 136
Haganah, 98
Harrison, Earl G., 120
havurah movement, the, 54, 223
Hayden, Tom, 225
Hebrew Immigrant Aid Society, 158
Hebrew Union College, 14, 82, 124. See also Reform Movement
Hebrew University of Jerusalem, 92
Heller, James, 98, 101
Herberg, Will, 64
Hershman, Ruth, 118
Herzl, Theodore, 59
Heschel, Abraham Joshua, 174, 200
Hillel foundation, See B'nai B'rith
Hinchin, Martin, 169, 171
Hirabayashi case, 90
Hitler, Adolf, 42–44, 52, 78, 80
Holocaust, 116–17, 183, 214
Hoover, Herbert, 9, 23–25, 29–30
Hopkins, Harry, 24, 33
House Committee on Un-American Activities, 140–41
"House I Live In, The," 77
Howe, Irving, 7
Hull, Cordell, 113
Hyman, Joseph, 100

Illinois v. McCollum, 153–55, 266n.53, 267n.54
Immigration Act of 1924, The, 59, 159
Immigration and Naturalization Service, The, 71, 86
immigration reform, 17, 157–63
Interfaith Committee for Aid to the Democracies, 66
Interfaith Dialogue Movement, The, 62–66, 77, 108, 184
Internal Security Act, The, 159
International Bill of Rights, The, 112, 114–15

internment, 10, 16, 78–80, 86–91, 248n.16, 249n.24, 250nn.32 and 34
isolationism, 73–76
Israel Emergency Fund, 202
Israel, Mike, 184
Israel, State of, 92, 127, 200–202, 214–19, 223–24. See also Palestine

Jabotinksy, Vladimir (Zeev), 98
Jackson, Henry, 222
Jackson, Jesse, 217
Jackson, Mississippi, 166–67, 172
Japanese American Citizens League, 86
Japanese-American internment. See internment
Jewish Agency, The, 113
Jewish Catalog, The, 222–23
Jewish Club of 1933, The, 85
Jewish Community Center, The, 13, 35–36, 39, 54, 184, 276n.50
Jewish Community Relations Council, The, 11, 149, 152, 155–56, 178, 180, 184, 195, 205–207, 210–11; 264n.35
Jewish Daily Forward, The, 130
Jewish Federation Council, 11, 13–14,19, 22, 37,
Jewish Labor Committee, 47, 55–58, 67–68, 93, 97, 119, 158, 210, 253n.73, 267n.54
Jewish People's Fraternal Order, 137
Jewish Rights Council, 209
Jewish Social Research, Bureau of, 22, 26
Jewish Theological Seminary, 14, 53. See also Conservative movement
Jewish War Veterans, 75–76, 135, 217, 267n.54
Jim Crow laws, 115, 165, 170, 175, 177, 184–85
Johnson, Lyndon B., 10, 18, 147, 191–93, 204, 198, 219. See also Great Society
Joint Boycott Council, 47
Joint Distribution Committee, 44, 46, 50, 52, 57, 100, 120, 124
Joint Emergency Committee for European Jewish Affairs, The, 97. See also Emergency Committee for European Jewish Affairs

Kallen, Horace, 41–43
Kaplan, Mordechai, 54
Kaplow, Herman, 184, 189

Karpf, Maurice, 26–27, 30
Kaufman, Menaham, 124
Kaufmann, Edgar J., 55–56
Kennedy, John F., 10, 173, 204, 265n.41
King, Martin Luther, Jr., 167–68, 170, 174, 191, 195, 201, 219, 221, 273n.26, 280n.21
Korematsu case, 90
Kraft, Louis, 83
Krause, Allan, 271n.6
Kristallnacht, 49, 66
Ku Klux Klan, 41, 168, 198

LaFollette Industrial Espionage Act, 72
Landau, Moses, 169, 172–73
Landon, Alf, 25
League of Nations, 84
Levin, Arthur, 169
Levine, Naomi, 208–209
Levinthal, Louis, 95
Levy, Felix, 98
Levy, Richard, 217
liberalism, 3, 7–9, 20, and affirmative action, 209; and the American Jewish Assembly, 93, 95; and the American Jewish Conference, 98,110–11; and church/state separation, 149–50; and the civil rights movement 164–66, 168, 176, 178, 186–88; during the cold war, 130–31, 142; and the creation of the United Nations, 114; and cultural nationalism, 193, 196–97, 220; and the Great Society, 192, 208; and the internment of Japanese-Americans, 90; and the McCarran Act, 137–143; and neo-Conservatism, 219, 224, 226; during the 1930s, 20–22, 42, 45–46, 52; during the 1970s, 213, 215; and the Rosenberg case, 135; during World War II, 79, 108; and Zionism, 81, 109, 201
Lindbergh, Charles, 73–74
Lippmann, Walter, 90
Lipsky, Louis, 115, 118, 121–22, 125
Lookstein, Joseph H., 101
Lubin, Isadore, 30
Lurie, Harry, 26, 38, 50
lynching, 175–177

Magnes, Judah, 98
Magnin, Edgar F., 87
Malev, William, 169–71
Mantinband, Charles, 169, 273n.25

Manzanar internment camp, 89
March on Washington (1941), 144
March on Washington (1963), 175
Marshall, Louis, 54, 92
Marshall Plan, 121
Maslow, Will, 145–46, 161, 188–89
McCarran Act, The, 137–43, 159, 262n.21
McCarran, Patrick, 137, 159
McCarran-Walter Immigration and Naturalization Act, 159–61, 268n.67, 269n.70
McCarthy, Joseph, 129, 140–42
McCollum decision. See *Illinois v. McCollum*
Mead, James, 53
melting pot, 41, 43
Meltzer, Milton, 26
Minkoff, Isaiah, 74–75
Mizrachi. *See* Religious National Orthodox Bloc
Monsky, Henry, 13, 26, 56, 93–94, 97, 121, 128
Morgenstern, Julian, 124
Morissey, Evelyn, 100
Morning Freiheit, 134
Mundt-Ferguson-Johnston bill, 138
Murphy, Frank, 90
Murray, Philip, 102

Nasser, Gamal Abdel, 200
National Advisory Commission on Civil Disorders, The, 200
National Association for the Advancement of Colored People (NAACP), The, 168, 173, 273n.26
National Brotherhood Week, 66
National Committee to Secure Justice in the Rosenberg Case, The, 135
National Community Relations Advisory Committee, The, 14, 130, 135, 138–139, 141, 147, 154, 159–162, 180, 187, 189, 194–95, 198, 260n.9, 267n.54, 269n.70
National Conference for New Politics, The, 220
National Conference of Christians and Jews, The, 65–66, 77
National Conference of Jewish Communal Service, The, 199
National Conference of Jewish Social Welfare, The, 19, 25, 29–30, 37–38, 76, 231n.1, 245n.38

National Council of Jewish Education, The, 37
National Council of Jewish Women, The, 87, 89, 136, 209–210
National Council on Jewish Social Welfare, The, 82
National Jewish Community Relations Advisory Council, 204–205, 207, 210–11, 221, 281n.35, 282n.35. *See also* National Community Relations Advisory Committee
National Refugee Service, The, 50, 57, 84–85
National Women's League of United Synagogue (Conservative movement), 140–41, 154, 182, 265n.48, 274n.30
neo-conservatism, 18, 224–26
New Deal, The, 9–10, 14, 20–21, 30–31, 33–40, 192, 214
New Left, 220, 223
New York Regents Case. See *Engel v. Vitale*
1967 War. *See* Six Day War
Nixon, Richard, 138, 219, 224
Nussbaum, Perry, 172–73, 199
Nye, Gerald, 73–74

Ocean Hill-Brownsville controversy, 202–203
Orthodox movement, The, 11, and affirmative action, 205; and the American Zionist Emergency Council, 99; and electoral voting, 230n.6; and ethnic neighborhoods, 213; and the First American Jewish Conference, 97; and interfaith dialogue, 64, 102; and neo-Orthodoxy, 223; and separation of Church and state, 131–32, 149, 151–53, 266n.51; and Zionism, 102–103, 218
Orthodox Rabbinical Council of America, 153, 267n.54

Palestine, 92, 96, 98–106, 108, 114, 122, 258n.40. *See also* Israel
Peace Now, 218
Pearl Harbor, 76–78, 80, 82–84
Petegorsky, David, 136, 208
Pittsburgh Platform, 59, 98
Plessy v. Ferguson, 177, 179, 277n.61
President's Commission on Immigration and Naturalization, 160

President's Committee on Civil Rights (Truman), 175, 177–78, 181.
Proskauer, Joseph, 46–47, 92, 94–97, 99–100, 109, 112, 114–15,118–19, 123, 126–27, 251n.45, 255n.19
Protestant church, 83–84
Protocols of the Elders of Zion, 74

quotas, 207–208, 211, 259n.3, 282nn.37 and 38, 283nn.38 and 40

Rabbinical Assembly, 14, 101, 141, 152–54, 182, 195–96, 267n.54, 274n.32. *See also* Conservative movement
Rabbinical Council of America, 101. *See also* Orthodox movement
Rabin, Yitzchak, 218
radio, 66–68
Randolph, A. Philip, 144, 280n.21
Reagan, Ronald, 10–11, 219, 224–25
Reconstruction Finance Corporation, 9, 29
Reform movement, The, 11, and affirmative action, 209–10; and the American Council For Judaism, 100; and the American Jewish Conference, 97–98, 100, 110–11; and Black Power, 196–98; and church/state separation, 148, 152–53; and the civil rights movement, 167, 171, 182; and conservatism, 225; and immigration reform, 159; and the International Bill of Rights, 112; and Jewish day schools, 213, 216; and liberalism, 14; and the New Deal, 25, 233n.16, 234n.16; and the rise of Hitler, 46, 240n.23; and interfaith dialogue, 63–64; on ritual observance, 216–17; on U.S. entry into World War II, 50, 52–53; during World War II, 80; on Zionism, 58–59, 103–104, 108, 124–25, 218
refugee, 13, 88. *See also* displaced persons; enemy aliens
Registration Act of 1940, The, 71–72
Reichert, Irving F., 89
Reigner, Gerhart, 91
relief, federal government, 25–32
Religious National Orthodox Bloc, 101, 103. *See also* Orthodox movement
Republican party, 99, 146; 192, 215, 219, 224–25
Reuther, Walter, 221
Reynolds, Senator Robert, 72
Rifkind, Simon H., 121, 160

Rischin, Moses, 7
Robison, Joseph B., 176–77
Roman Catholic Church. *See* Catholic Church
Roosevelt, Eleanor, 120
Roosevelt, Franklin D., and the anti-German boycott, 47; and civil liberties, 71; on civil rights, 143–44; death of, 119; and the election of 1932, 9; on enemy aliens, 84, 86; on fair employment practices, 265n.41; and historical revision, 218–19; on the internment of Japanese Americans, 91; and isolationism, 75–76; legacy of, 226; during the New Deal years, 19–20, 29–32, 39, 42; as New York governor. 27, 29; in the 1970s, 215; and radio, 67; and the rise of Hitler, 46; and Stephen S. Wise, 99; on the United Nations, 115; during World War II, 78, 82; and Zionism, 103, 108. *See also* New Deal
Roosevelt, Theodore, 9, 24, 31
Rosenberg, Julius and Ethel, 133–37
Rosenberg, M. J., 220–21
Rosenberg, Werner, 86
Rosenwald, Lessing, 124
Rosenwald-Levy, Adele, 124
Rothenberg, Morris, 105
Rothschild, Jacob, 167–69
Rubinow, Isaac, 19, 25, 27, 30
Rustin, Bayard, 181, 203, 280n.21

Safam, 214
Samuel, Herbert, 98
Schiff, Jacob, 12, 19
Schlesinger, Arthur Jr., 129
Schoolman, Albert P., 38
Schultz, Henry E., 182, 268n.67, 275n.41
Schwartzchild, Henry, 172, 199
Schwartzman, Allen, 173
Seale, Bobby, 195
segregation, 115, 170, 186. *See also* Jim Crow laws
Select Committee Investigating National Defense Migration, 85. *See also* internment
Selekman, Benjamin, 26, 30–32, 35
separation of church and state, 17, 131, 148–56, 216
Shotwell, James T., 114
Shrage, Barry, 216
Siegel, Richard, 222

Silberman, Charles, 185, 195–96
Silver, Abba Hillel, and the American Zionist Emergency Council, 99; and the Anglo-American Committee of Inquiry, 122–23; on the anti-German boycott, 46–47; on church/state separation, 158–59; on displaced persons, 123; and the First American Jewish Conference, 98–99, 110–11, 122; and immigration reform, 160; on the partition plan, 125–26; and the United Nations Special Commission on Palestine, 124; on U.S. entry in World War II, 81; on Zionism, 92, 108, 125
Sinatra, Frank, 77–78
Six Day War, The, 200–202, 220, 223–24, 280n.24
Slawson, John, 36, 187
Smith, Al, 25
Smith, Gerald, 198
social Darwinism, 8–9, 20, 24
Social Justice, 66
Social Security Act of 1935, The, 33
Socialist party, 7, 76, 91, 130, 139
Southern Baptist Convention, 25
Soviet Jews, 191, 213, 219, 221–22, 226
Stern, Malcolm, 169
Stettinius, Edward R., Jr., 115
Stimson, Henry L., 90
Strassfeld, Michael and Sharon, 222
Student National Coordinating Committee, 219. *See also* Student Non-Violent Coordinating Committee
Student Non-Violent Coordinating Committee, 173, 187, 195, 198–99, 201, 273n.26. *See also* Student National Coordinating Committee
Student Struggle for Soviet Jewry, 221
Students For A Democratic Society, 223, 225
Stuyvesant Pledge, 19, 40, 219, 232n.2
suburbanization, 183–90, 214, 223, 258n.1
Supreme Court of the United States. 90
Synagogue Council of America, 63, 75, 82, 105, 154–55, 158, 160, 174, 221, 267n.54

Taft, Robert, 99
Tenenbaum, Joseph, 48
Thomas, Norman, 91
Thorkelson, Jacob, 49

Tikkun, 218
Tobin, Jonathan, 216
Tolan, John H., 85, 89
Truman, Harry S., 92, 120, 126–27, 129, 138–39, 144–45, 159, 175, 178, 206, 257nn.39 and 40, 265n.41

Union of American Hebrew Congregations, and affirmative action, 209–10; and the American Jewish Conference, 100, 111, 252nn. 65 and 70; and church/state relations, 267n.54; and immigration reform, 159–60; and interfaith dialogue, 63; and liberalism, 14; and neutrality, 75; and the rise of Hitler, 240n.23, 245n.38; and ritual observance, 217; and Zionism, 103–104, 119. *See also* Reform movement
Union of Orthodox Jewish Congregations, 210, 267n.54
unions (labor),13
United Jewish Appeal, 124, 202, 247n.12, 248n.12
United Jewish Welfare Fund, 39
United Nations, 17, 92, 107–108, 112, 114–18, 121–27, 145, 200
United Service for New Americans, 158, 161
United Synagogue, 64, 262n.21, 265n.46, 267n.54. *See also* Conservative movement

Vietnam war, 220
Voorhis registration bill, 72
Vorspan, Albert, 198
Voting Rights Act of 1965, The, 10, 191, 278n.2
vouchers, 216, 225

Waldman, Morris, 47
Wallace, Henry, 103, 120
War Refugee Board, 254n.3
Warren, Earl, 90, 181
Wagner, Robert, 102
Waskow, Arthur, 198–99, 220
Wiesel, Elie, 217

Weizmann, Chaim, 94, 98–99
White Citizen's Council, 166, 168
Wilkie, Wendell, 146
Wilson, Edwin C., 113–14
Winograd, Richard, 164–65, 174
Wise, Isaac Mayer, 216
Wise, Stephen S., and affirmative action, 206; and the American Jewish Conference, 97–99, 110, 122; and the American Jewish Congress, 13; and the American Zionist Emergency Council, 99; and the Anglo-American Committee of Inquiry, 122; on the anti-German boycott, 47; on anti-Semitism, 73, 282n.37; and church/state separation, 152; and the civil rights movement, 178–80, 186; and fair employment practices, 145–46; on Franklin D. Roosevelt, 30; on the Holocaust, 91; on neutrality, 75; on partition, 126; on the rise of Hitler, 46; on World War II, 77, 79, 81; on Zionism, 92, 108
Workman's Circle, 75–76
Works Progress Administration, 34
World Jewish Congress, 55, 91–92, 113
World Zionist Organization, 105
Wyman, David, 121, 218

Young Men's Hebrew Associations, 36, 39

Zangwill, Israel, 43
Zionism, and the American Jewish Assembly, 94–97; and the American Jewish Conference, 97–106; and the Black Power movement, 194, 199; and B'nai B'rith, 13; growth in the United States, 17, 58–60; in the immediate post-war period, 118–28, 257n.40; in the 1930s, 44, 53; in the 1970s, 214; in the 1980s, 217–18, 223–24, 226; and the Six Day War, 202; and the United Nations, 114, 117; during World War II, 81, 91–97
Zionist Organization of America, 95, 120–21
Zorach v. Clauson, 154–55
Zwieman, Bob, 217